CORPORATE SENIOR SECURITIES

Analysis and Evaluation of Bonds, Convertibles and Preferreds

RICHARD S. WILSON

Probus Publishing Company
Chicago, Illinois

Library of Congress Cataloging in Publication Data
Wilson, Richard S.
    Corporate senior securities.

    Includes index.
    1. Bonds—United States.   2. Convertible bonds—United
States.   3. Preferred stocks—United States.
4. Convertible preferred stocks—United States.   I. Title.
HG4963.W56   1987   332.63′2   87-6980

ISBN 0-917253-79-5

Library of Congress Catalog Card No.

Printed in the United States of America

1   2   3   4   5   6   7   8   9   0

TO:

Barbara
Jennifer
Kristina

PREFACE

Much of the corporate bond work being done at the current time involves portfolio management techniques, the analysis of interest rates and other market related activities, as well as the quantitative aspects of bonds, such as duration, discounted cash flow, present value, future value, total returns, and option valuation, among other things. These matters are very important for the proper evaluation of debt securities. But also of great importance to successful debt investing is the basic knowledge of the issuer's ability to meet its obligations or bond contracts on a timely basis, and the analysis of the details of that contract or obligation.

Corporate Senior Securities: Analysis and Evaluation of Bonds, Convertibles and Preferreds addresses itself to what I view as the basic needs of many bond investors, analysts, salesmen, and traders. The idea for this book originated nearly fifteen years ago when I began to give lectures to salesmen and traders about corporate bonds. If it were written then, the book would probably have amounted to about half of the current size; the bond market was much less complex, much less active, and much smaller. Today, the bond market is much more involved and volatile, making the analysis more difficult and time consuming. Several years ago an article appeared in a publication of the Federal Home Loan Bank Board which stated: "The optimal corporate debt security, as far as the investor is concerned, is one having a relatively high after-tax yield, excellent marketability, no default risk, is non-callable, is convertible into a common stock with an outstanding appreciation potential, and sells at no premium over conversion or investment values. Unfortunately, the optimal corporate bond does not exist. The investor has to be ready to compare a variety of packages of call, sinking fund, default risk, marketability, and taxability of return characteristics. The time frame for making these analyses and arriving at investment decisions is extremely short due to the dynamic nature of the financial markets."

I hope that *Corporate Senior Securities* answers many of the questions about corporate bonds and preferred stocks which readers may have. One must be able to put the quantitative, market, and fundamental elements together in order to evaluate the value of the securities in question. Corporate finance courses of a generation ago used the texts of such people as Dewing, Bellmore, Grodinsky, Graham and Dodd, and Guthman and Dougall. What was in their books on corporate senior securities covered several chapters. Modern day finance texts relegate this topic to only a chapter or two. Discussions of the "old" corporate finance and debt topics, according to recent discussions with a number of finance professors, now are often found in courses given in the law schools, not in modern day finance courses. Years ago too little time was allotted to the quantitative properties of debt instruments and to such concepts as yield and total returns. It is my feeling that today too little time is spent on the introductory elements of corporate senior securities.

Innovations in the corporate securities market are quite rapid nowadays and, out of necessity, a book such as this has to have a cutoff date after which new developments cannot be covered. Depending on the chapter, the cutoff date varies between June and December 1986. The preferred chapters (5, 6, and 7) were finished prior to the enactment of the Tax Reform Act of 1986. Fortunately, changes affecting preferred stocks are relatively minor. The dividends received deduction dropped from 85 percent to 80 percent but income tax rates also declined. Thus the effective tax rate for eligible corporate dividends at the marginal tax rate went from 6.9 percent in 1986 to 8 percent in 1987 and 6.8 percent for 1988 and beyond (assuming Congress leaves things as they now stand). Thus, in 1986

93.1 percent of the dividends were tax free compared with 92 percent in 1987 and 93.2 percent in 1988.

ACKNOWLEDGMENTS

Several people have been important to this book. First, I wish to thank Mr. William Richard Gordon, former treasurer of the Univerity of Pennsylvania and lecturer in the introductory course in corporate finance (1b) at the Wharton School of Finance and Commerce. I was fortunate to have Mr. Gordon as my class instructor in the spring of 1955. He made finance a living and exciting subject and brought Wall Street to the classroom. Then there is Professor Frank J. Fabozzi, a well-known and prolific author and editor of financial books and articles. As I had written chapters for several of Frank's books, he encouraged me to take on this project for Probus Publishing.

Of course, a number of my colleagues should also be acknowledged. Periodic discussions with James Grant of *Grant's Interest Rate Observer* kept me on top of many of the developments in the corporate bond world, especially with regard to junk bonds. Eunice T. Reich of Merrill Lynch Capital Markets long ago suggested that I put my thoughts on corporate bonds into a book. I thank her for her support through the years. Loretta J. Neuhaus, also of Merrill Lynch Capital Markets, provided valuable assistance and encouragement throughout the writing of the book. She listened to its problems and progress as we commuted to work or had breakfast at "Fast Eddies." I must also acknowledge Nancy Maybloom, my manuscript editor, without whom this book would not have gotten this far. Finally, thanks to Harry Poulakakos, proprietor of the Restaurant on the Square, better known as "Harry's," for providing a haven for many "bondinis" after a hard day's work.

I am also grateful to my employer, Merrill Lynch, Pierce, Fenner & Smith, Inc., Merrill Lynch Capital Markets, and the Securities Research and Economics Division, for supporting my effort. Miss Rita Hughes, chief librarian, her capable assistants, and the staff of the securities research library were quite helpful to my research ef-

forts. It should be emphasized, however, that the views expressed
are entirely my own and do not necessarily reflect those of Merrill
Lynch.

Richard S. Wilson

CONTENTS

EPIGRAPHY

A loan is the only true investment.
Chamberlain, *The Principles of Bond Investment,*
1st. edition, 1911

A simon pure investment is always a loan.
Chamberlain, *The Principles of Bond Investment,*
2nd. edition, 1927

Superior management, so far as is possible, avoids debt, especially short-term obligations which may mature at an inconvenient time.

Debts are considered to be not only objectionable but potentially dangerous.

The ideal is a financial structure represented by common stock, with no bank loans or long-term obligations. This is a financial goal which every well-managed corporation desires to attain.

One of the exploded fallacies among the former rules of financial practice is that trading on the equity is both profitable and prudent. It is sometimes profitable. It is not often prudent.
Edward Sherwood Mead and Julius Grodinsky
The Ebb and Flow of Investment Value, 1939

Ours is a day of debt—of the systematic substitution of debt for equity on corporate balance sheets, of record consumer borrowing and of the belief that our grandfathers' fear of borrowing is an anachronism. Our conviction is that the world is gripped by a kind of debt fever.

James Grant, *Grant's Interest Rate Observer,* 1986

CHAPTER 1

OVERVIEW
OF U.S. CORPORATE BONDS

This chapter introduces nonconvertible, publicly issued corporate bonds. It discusses the size of the market as well as the general terms of the instruments, including secured and unsecured debt. Maturity features, interest rate characteristics, and redemption provisions are reviewed in chapters 2, 3, and 4. Throughout these chapters we will use the term bond(s) in the general sense of corporate debt instruments; when required, we will use more specific terminology, such as notes and debentures.

WHAT IS A CORPORATE BOND?

A corporate bond used to be defined as a promise to pay a specified sum of money at a fixed future date along with periodic interest payments. However, the bond instrument has undergone so many changes over the past decade that some may view the "plain vanilla" type of paper, so dear to the hearts of many old-timers, as an anachronism. Bonds with gimmicks, often difficult for the investor to understand, the salesman to sell, and the trader to price, have become increasingly accepted in the 1980s.[1] In many cases, the interest rate (if any) changes weekly; the maturity date is not always fixed, as issuers can redeem the bonds prior to maturity and holders may demand prepayment; and the specified sum or principal payment may fluctuate. Nevertheless, a bond is a debt instrument denoting the issuer's obligation to satisfy the claim holder's; it is essentially an I.O.U., although somewhat more complex than the run-of-the-mill variety.

The issuer's rights and duties are spelled out in a loan agreement, also known as an *indenture*. The indenture may be fairly simple and straightforward, although for most laymen it is complex and often runs to many pages—after all, it is a legal contract between two parties, debtor and trustee. The bond, or evidence of the debt obligation, is printed on a single sheet of paper that summarizes the more important sections of the loan agreement. Technically this certificate is the agreement between the issuer and the lender.

The term *bond* actually refers to a debt instrument that customarily is secured by collateral, such as land and buildings or financial instruments. The indenture for secured debt contains a section describing the mortgaged (pledged) collateral. A *debenture* is an unsecured loan, but its indenture sets forth the rights and duties of the borrower. A *note* used to be characterized as a less formal debt obligation than a debenture or a bond. According to *Commentaries*:

> There is no basic or historically established distinction between "debentures" and "notes." There has emerged, however, a clear and useful distinction in modern usage. According to this usage, in the area of long-term debt securities, a security is properly termed a "note" when it is not issued pursuant to an indenture and there is no indenture trustee. However, it may be, and usually is, issued to one or a few purchasers pursuant to a purchase or loan agreement which, in addition to provisions dealing with the terms of purchase, includes many of the contractual rights found in an indenture. In today's nomenclature the security is properly termed a "debenture" when it is issued pursuant to an indenture and there is an indenture trustee.[2]

Thus, the popular "medium-term notes" are more properly called "medium-term debentures," as most have been issued under an indenture.[3] Today, however, "notes" has a slightly different meaning. To many, a note has more to do with the time remaining to the security's maturity than with the formality of the documentation; thus, notes are short- to intermediate-term maturity paper, while bonds and debentures are long-term issues. However, there can also be short-term bonds and long-term notes. Thus, while we disagree with this usage in describing a corporate bond's time to maturity, we can understand why many have adopted it: It is a fallout from the securities markets for U.S. Treasury issues—government bonds are long-term, unsecured obligations, and government notes are obligations issued in the one- to ten-year maturity range.

The bond used to be quite an attractive piece of paper, and some were fairly large in size. Attached to or printed on the same page were interest coupons that holders would clip and send in for collection through normal banking channels. In this age of registered bonds, however, they are more uniform, typically the size of normal letter paper or of stock certificates. Coupons are no longer required, as interest payments to the registered holder are made by check. The form of the security is covered by the indenture. The front of the certificate contains the company name and items such as maturity date, interest rate, certificate number, and principal amount. It also bears the corporate seal and the signature(s) of the appropriate corporate officer(s) and of the trustee attesting to the certificate's authenticity. Most important, it gives the name of the registered holder. The reverse of the certificate contains a summary of the important indenture terms, including call and redemption provisions, as well as a printed bond power or a form of assignment and certain other forms, if needed. In order to reduce the risk of counterfeiting, the New York Stock Exchange has prescribed minimum standards for the bond certificate. Certain portions of the bond's face must be engraved and include a vignette.

SIZE OF THE CORPORATE BOND MARKET

Total corporate debt outstanding at the end of 1985, according to the Board of Governors of the Federal Reserve System, was $714.1 billion (see Table 1-1); to this is added another $68.3 billion of foreign bonds for a grand total of $782.4 billion. Since the end of 1970, total debt securities outstanding has increased at a rate of 9.43 percent. the biggest growth rate was posted by commercial banks (22.77 percent annually), while nonfinancial business corporate debt increased at an average rate of 8.17 percent. Outstanding bonds of

Table 1-1
Corporate Bonds Outstanding, by Issuer, 1970-1985
($ Billions)

	Total	Nonfinancial Corporate Business	Foreign	Commercial Banking	Finance Companies	Other
1985	$782.4	$543.6	$68.3	$69.4	$91.1	$10.0
1984	667.3	469.7	64.3	52.5	75.2	5.7
1983	596.6	423.6	63.0	39.6	66.1	4.3
1982	565.1	407.5	59.9	31.2	62.4	4.1
1981	527.3	388.9	53.3	25.2	56.0	3.9
1980	494.7	366.1	47.8	23.2	52.4	5.1
1979	464.6	338.5	47.0	21.9	52.3	5.0
1978	438.0	321.2	43.1	22.1	48.0	3.6
1977	404.8	300.0	38.9	21.1	41.6	3.1
1976	364.9	277.2	33.9	18.0	33.8	2.0
1975	327.0	254.3	25.3	14.5	30.7	2.2
1974	286.7	227.1	19.1	10.4	28.0	2.1
1973	261.9	207.5	17.0	9.2	26.2	1.9
1972	247.3	198.3	16.0	8.3	23.3	1.4
1971	227.0	186.1	15.0	5.2	19.7	1.0
1970	202.4	167.3	14.1	3.2	17.2	0.6

Source: Flow of Funds Accounts Financial Assets and Liabilities, Year-End, 1961-85, Board of Governors of the Federal Reserve System.

finance companies increased 11.75 percent annually, while foreign debt sold in this country rose by 11.09 percent.

While the total amount of corporate debt is quite large, much of it does not directly concern us since it has been privately placed with, or issued directly to, banks, insurance companies and other financial intermediaries. We are concerned mostly with publicly issued debt—bonds, debentures, and notes—that can be traded either on the established securities exchanges or in the over-the-counter markets. At the end of 1985, outstanding publicly issued corporate bonds were estimated at about $475 billion, including high grades as well as low grades, straight bonds, and convertibles. Who owns this debt? Again, let us go to the flow of funds accounts (see Table 1-2). Life insurance companies are the largest holders of corporate bonds, with about $274 billion at the end of 1985. In a distant second are the

Table 1-2
Ownership of Outstanding Corporate Bonds, 1970-1985
($ Billions)

	1985	1984	1983	1982	1981	1980	1979	1978
Households	$54.1	$38.5	$41.9	$54.8	$52.3	$56.2	$67.9	$72.2
Foreign	101.7	60.4	45.5	41.0	30.4	22.2	13.8	11.2
Commercial banks	23.7	17.8	13.5	8.8	7.7	7.7	7.1	7.4
Savings banks	18.0	20.4	21.9	19.0	20.3	21.2	20.5	21.6
Life Insurance	274.2	242.8	219.1	202.3	186.1	178.8	170.1	158.5
Private pensions	119.4	113.7	103.3	91.6	85.1	79.7	67.6	54.0
Public pensions	123.3	118.1	106.6	107.3	103.8	94.5	85.0	81.9
Other insurance	33.9	25.7	21.6	25.8	26.3	23.6	23.6	21.6
Mutual funds	20.1	16.5	13.0	10.2	10.1	8.5	7.2	6.4
Brokers/dealers	14.0	13.4	10.1	4.4	5.3	2.6	1.9	3.3
	1977	1976	1975	1974	1973	1972	1971	1970
Households	$76.4	$76.4	$65.9	$59.1	$51.5	$51.2	$46.5	$36.2
Foreign	9.3	5.5	4.6	4.0	3.1	3.1	3.0	2.7
Commercial banks	7.7	7.8	8.4	6.6	5.6	5.2	3.9	3.0
Savings banks	21.5	20.3	17.5	14.0	13.1	14.2	12.0	8.1
Life insurance	141.2	122.4	105.5	96.4	92.5	86.6	79.6	74.1
Private pensions	45.4	40.1	42.4	35.0	32.9	29.4	28.6	29.4
Public pensions	72.9	66.9	61.8	54.9	48.4	43.2	39.0	35.1
Other insurance	19.8	16.1	12.2	10.0	8.0	8.1	8.9	8.6
Mutual funds	7.0	6.0	5.6	4.9	4.3	4.2	3.7	3.5
Brokers/dealers	3.7	3.4	3.0	1.8	2.4	2.0	1.8	1.7

Source: Flow of Funds Accounts Financial Assets and Liabilities, Year-End, 1961–1985, Board of Governors of the Federal Reserve System.

public pension funds, with about $123 billion, closely followed by private pension funds, with $119 billion. Foreign holders of domestic debt have increased their ownership considerably since the mid-seventies, from under $5 billion to more than $100 billion. On the other hand, households have decreased their direct ownership from $76 billion in 1977 to $54 billion in 1985, which is, however, up sharply from 1984's $38.5 billion. While the direct U.S. savings rate is less than that of some other countries, indirect holdings of corporate bonds through mutual funds, pensions plans, and the like somewhat counteract this discrepancy.

Volume of New Corporate Bond Issues

As interest rates declined in 1984 and 1985, corporations issued an increasing amount of nonconvertible debt in the public markets. In 1985 a record-setting $80.118 billion of corporate new-issue debt was offered, compared with $48.89 billion in 1984 and only $35.697 billion in 1983. Table 1-3a shows the public volume for 1973 through 1985. Excluded from these figures are best-efforts offerings, debt issued in exchanges, and structured transactions such as certain asset-based financings that are based on the asset and the offering's structure rather than on the corporation's credit. The composition of the new-issue market by type of issuer has changed since 1980. In that year, utilities (communications, electric, gas, and water) accounted for 36.5 percent of the total volume, followed by industrial names (33.4 percent) and financial institutions (19.99 percent). In 1985, utilities declined both absolutely and relatively, selling somewhat more than $11 billion of debt, or 13.89 percent of the $80.118 billion volume. Over the 13-year period industrial companies raised the largest amount of public debt—$145.025 billion—followed by utilities, with $126.16 billion, and financial institutions, with $125.223 billion.

Another way of looking at new-issue volume is by rating category (see Table 1-3b). According to Moody's Investors Service rating categories (see Chapter 9 for more information about debt ratings), there has been a considerable decline in new issues of prime-rated ("Aaa") credits, from a high of 42.6 percent of 1977's volume to only 11.25 percent in 1985. The rating sector with the greatest growth has been the below-investment-grade category— "Ba" and lower, including nonrated issues (see Chapter 11 for a discussion of debt in this classification)—rising from 9.71 percent of 1977's volume to 21.02 percent in 1985. An increasing share of the market has also been captured by medium-grade credits ("A" and "Baa"). Of course, there are fewer "Aaa" issuers, as many have been knocked down to lower debt-rating categories.

Table 1-4 shows that since the early 1970s, the average size of a new corporate bond issue has increased. In 1973, the average for the 238 issues that came to market was slightly under $56 million. It passed the $100 million mark in 1981, and, in 1985, was just over

Table 1-3a
Public Financing in the Taxable Bond Markets by Issuer Classification, 1973–1985
(Nonconvertible Bond Offerings—Par Value [$ Millions])

	Total	Communications	Electrics	Gas and Water	Industrials	Finance	Banks and Thrifts	Transportation	International
1985	$80,118	$3,210	$6,354	$1,566	$32,161	$19,817	$9,638	$1,427	$5,945
1984	48,890	830	5,000	825	19,510	10,223	8,255	1,247	3,000
1983	35,697	1,965	5,400	1,470	9,391	5,927	6,758	896	3,890
1982	44,168	720	7,170	1,665	14,281	8,373	5,217	1,062	5,680
1981	40,655	3,820	6,425	1,640	12,729	7,175	1,975	1,316	5,575
1980	36,695	5,975	6,418	1,000	12,257	5,310	2,025	1,445	2,265
1979	24,941	3,700	4,760	555	6,114	3,236	2,200	991	3,385
1978	20,779	2,880	4,708	170	3,287	4,140	630	734	4,250
1977	25,929	2,625	5,306	302	4,472	5,723	1,520	873	5,108
1976	30,165	2,200	5,012	1,058	7,635	5,510	1,185	1,270	6,295
1975	34,918	3,035	6,932	1,319	14,100	2,538	920	967	5,107
1974	26,663	3,396	7,642	752	7,853	2,125	2,325	920	1,650
1973	13,315	3,149	4,757	449	1,235	1,923	555	522	725
Total	$462,953	$37,505	$75,884	$12,771	$145,025	$82,020	$43,203	$13,670	$52,875

Table 1-3b
Public Financing in the Taxable Bond Markets by Moody's Classification, 1973–1985
(Nonconvertible Bond Offerings—Par Value [$ Millions])

	Total	Aaa	Percent of Total	Aa	Percent of Total	A	Percent of Total	Baa	Percent of Total	Ba and Lower*	Percent of Total
1985	$80,118	$9,016	11.25%	$16,539	20.64%	$27,953	34.99%	$9,772	12.20%	$16,838	21.02%
1984	48,890	2,350	4.81	13,730	28.08	15,117	30.92	4,145	8.48	13,548	27.71
1983	35,697	3,920	10.98	11,110	31.12	9,030	25.30	5,125	14.36	6,512	18.24
1982	44,168	6,072	13.75	14,659	33.19	15,340	34.73	4,274	9.68	3,823	8.65
1981	40,655	11,835	29.11	9,980	24.55	12,662	31.15	4,085	10.05	2,093	5.14
1980	36,695	10,109	27.55	10,721	29.22	11,900	32.43	2,540	6.92	1,425	3.88
1979	24,941	10,400	41.70	5,712	22.90	5,780	23.17	1,744	6.99	1,305	5.24
1978	20,799	7,967	38.30	5,646	27.15	4,415	21.23	1,618	7.78	1,153	5.54
1977	25,929	11,046	42.60	5,239	20.21	5,033	19.41	2,093	8.07	2,518	9.71
1976	30,165	9,907	32.84	8,786	29.13	8,039	26.65	3,023	10.02	410	1.36
1975	34,918	11,348	32.50	8,932	25.58	12,011	34.40	2,482	7.11	145	0.41
1974	26,663	7,420	27.83	8,510	31.92	7,500	28.13	1,933	7.25	1,300	4.87
1973	13,315	4,046	30.39	3,225	24.22	4,052	30.43	519	3.90	1,473	11.06
Total	$462,953	$105,436	22.77%	$122,789	26.52%	$127,432	27.53%	$43,353	9.36%	$63,943	13.81%

*"Ba and lower" category includes nonrated issues.

Table 1-4
Average Size of Issue, 1973-1985
Public Financing in the Taxable Bond Markets:
(Nonconvertible Bond Offerings—Par Value [$ Millions])

	Total Financing	Number of Issues	Average Size of Issue
1985	$ 80,118	655	$122.32
1984	48,890	403	121.32
1983	35,697	379	94.19
1982	44,168	467	94.58
1981	40,655	333	122.09
1980	36,695	378	97.08
1979	24,941	250	99.76
1978	20,799	244	85.24
1977	25,929	328	79.05
1976	30,165	395	76.37
1975	34,918	471	74.14
1974	26,663	350	76.18
1973	13,315	238	55.95
Total	$462,953	4,891	$94.65

$122 million. It would have taken only about 109 issues of 1985's average size to fill up the 1973 calendar of $13.315 billion; in 1985, there were 229 issues of at last $125 million.

CORPORATE BOND TRADING

Many believe that individuals should confine their corporate bond investments to issues listed on the New York or American Stock Exchange and avoid unlisted issues in the over-the-counter market. Professional investors find that the over-the-counter market best serves their needs. The reason is very simple: Listed trading activity consists primarily of small orders for "retail" or individual investors, in lots of as little as $1,000 par value. An institution wanting to sell a block of $5 million par value of an issue would find the listed auction market would be unable to handle it; such trade has to be done in the negotiated unlisted market. Individuals like to see their bonds quoted in the newspaper; unlisted corporate bonds are not quoted unless, perhaps, they are recent issues. Also, many retail stockbrokers can easily obtain the last sale, current quotation, and size of the bid/offering from their quotation machines. Unlisted quotations and bids/offers are less readily obtained by brokers handling small investors. Of course, brokers can easily get investors lists of offerings from the firm's own inventory, but not always offerings of the investors' choosing.

None of this means that the listed market will always provide individual investors with higher bids and lower offerings than the unlisted market. The two markets often behave independently of each other. The listed market and its quotes can easily be affected by small trades. It is not uncommon to see the price of a bond fall five points or so on one trade and rise four or five points on a succeeding trade. This often happens because the broker carelessly placed the order; more than likely, the order was to sell (buy) "at the market" without regard for the size of the current bid or offering. It is often better to place limits on orders, especially for issues that are not actively traded. It is amusing how many investors place limit orders when trading in stocks that have very active and liquid markets but ignore limit orders for thinly traded bonds. As one writer said in Forbes, "The listed market is so small and thin, it is easy to manipulate."[4] While this might sound a little extreme, it has more than a grain of truth. However, despite some of the drawbacks for individuals, the listed market for bonds, by publishing trades for all to see, provides many investors with much needed peace of mind.

The New York Stock Exchange has what is called the "nine bond rule." This is Rule 396, which requires that all orders for nine bonds or fewer be sent to the floor of the Exchange for execution. If the order can be executed at a better price after the floor market has been diligently sought and ascertained, it may then be executed "upstairs." Some of the larger stockbrokerage firms may extend this rule to 25 or 50 bonds—that is, they will normally send all orders up to those sizes to the floor.

There are no minimum requirements for listing bonds on the New York Stock Exchange. However, the public distribution and aggregate size of the issue must be large enough to warrant listing. Appropriate distribution might mean a minimum of 250 to 300 bondholders or an issue size of about $20 million. If the aggregate market or principal value falls to less than $1 million, the Exchange may delist the bonds, as it might if the company defaults and files for bankruptcy (but not in all cases). When a company is in bankruptcy, many holders of its bonds probably need the listed market for solace.

Currently there is a one-time listing fee for bonds on the New York Stock Exchange. From 1981 through 1984, there were annual fees. Several companies did not pay this former annual fee, including New York Telephone, Southern Bell Telephone, and Southwestern Bell Telephone. In 1985, the New York Stock Exchange delisted 58 issues of the three telephone companies after negotiations failed to move the squabblers from their respective positions. Subsequently, Southwestern Bell Telephone listed 12 of its debenture issues on the American Stock Exchange. *The Wall Street Journal* reported, "Since the vast majority of the holders . . . affected by the dispute are institutions, the companies said they don't believe trading in the bonds will be affected."[5]

The average daily bond volume (including convertibles and a small number of listed foreign issues) on the New York Stock Exchange reached a record $35.9 million in 1985. The lowest average daily volume of $1.8 million was posted in 1913. The lowest daily volume on record in this century was $500,000 on August 13, 1900; the highest single day's activity was on September 6, 1939, when $83.1 million was traded. Investors probably thought that the U.S. exchanges would close temporarily while most European countries were declaring war on one another; they remembered August, 1914, when the lamps were "going out all over Europe" and the exchanges closed for several months.

The Securities Industry Association began keeping figures on over-the-counter corporate bond trading in May 1985. From May through December 1985, the average daily corporate bond volume was a whopping $10.208 billion! Thus, the New York Stock Exchange volume is less that 0.5 percent of the unlisted market. In the first seven months of 1986, the daily average amounted to $14,332 billion. These numbers show that listed trading is very insignificant compared with total corporate bond trading volume. It is safe to guess that a decade ago the average trading volume was considerably less. The increase has been due to a number of factors, including more participants in a much larger market and portfolio managers taking shorter-term views which encourages turnover. Bonds are not for buying and holding to maturity (if they ever were) for they can readily be traded as they get under- and overvalued against one another. Sound bond investment requires constant assessment of relative values of issues in a market that is not always "efficient." The increasing internationalization of the debt markets and new trading techniques, including the use of options and futures in portfolio hedging strategies, are two other factors contributing to today's great trading volume.

The listing of a company's debt on a stock exchange is not without cost. It involves paying fees to the exchange and the opportunity cost of the time management spends on listing documentation. How valuable is a listing? The over-the-counter market is much bigger and works extremely well, especially for the more important buyers and sellers, namely institutions. Do corporations really care for odd-lot bond buyers and worry whether or not investors can quote their bonds in the daily financial pages? Do they have the interests of the small investor at heart? There has been no real evidence that listing reduces an issuer's interest costs or flotation expenses. Except for some small odd-lot trading activity, it is questionable whether marketability is even improved. Thus, while individuals with small investments in corporate bonds may find the exchange market more suitable for their needs, issuers will obtain little except, perhaps, some prestige factor. After all, the market for municipal and U.S. Treasury bonds is the unlisted market.

MORE ABOUT INDENTURES[6]

Since indentures spell out the issuer's rights and duties, a few words about them are in order. The buyer of a bond in a secondary market transaction becomes a party to the contract even though he or she wasn't, so to speak, present at its creation. Yet many investors are not too familiar with the terms and features of the obligations they purchase. They know the coupon rate and maturity but often are unaware of many of the issue's other terms, especially those that can affect the value of their investment. In most cases—and as long as the company stays out of trouble—much of this additional information may be unnecessary and thus considered superfluous by some. But this knowledge can become valuable, such as during times of financial stress; when the company is involved in merger or takeover activity; or when interest rates have dropped, making the issue vulnerable to some type of premature or unexpected redemption. Knowledge is power, and the informed bond investor has a better chance of avoiding costly mistakes.

Let us briefly look at what indentures contain (some indenture provisions and articles will be discussed more fully in later chapters). In order for corporate debt securities to be publicly sold, they must (with some permitted exceptions) be issued in conformity with the Trust Indenture Act of 1939 (TIA). The TIA requires that a debt issue subject to regulation by the Securities and Exchange Commission have a trustee. Also, the trustee's duties and powers must be spelled out in the indenture. Some corporations' debt issues are issued under a blanket or open-ended indenture; for others, a new indenture must be written each time a new series of debt is sold. A blanket indenture is often used by electric utility companies and other issuers of general mortgage bonds, but it is also found in unsecured debt, especially since the shelf registration procedure became effective several years ago. The basic indenture may have been entered into 30 or more years ago, but as each new series of debt is created, a supplemental indenture is written. For instance, the original indenture for Baltimore Gas and Electric Company is dated February 1, 1919, but it has been supplemented many times since then due to new financings. A more recent example of an industrial debenture issue is found in the Dayton Hudson Corporation debt prospectus dated October 16, 1986, which says that "the Indenture does not limit the amount of Debt Securities that may be issued thereunder and provides that Debt Securities may be issued thereunder from time to time in one or more series." The indenture of Fruehauf Finance Company, according to its prospectus dated December 11, 1985, gives the company the ability to "reopen" a previous issue of securities and to issue additional securities having terms and provisions identical to any such previous issues of debt.

The model indenture described in *Commentaries* has 15 articles and a preamble, or preliminary statement, called *parties and recitals*. The model mortgage bond indenture form has 16 articles and a preliminary statement.[7] Of course, the number of articles depends on the terms of debt being issued. The consolidated mortgage bonds of Illinois Central Gulf Railroad Company, as supplemented, has 23 articles. The preliminary statements note that the bonds or debentures have been authorized by the corporation's board of directors, which has the authority to execute the indenture. The introductory statements contain granting clauses describing the mortgage property, which is important for secured debt.

Definitions, Form of Securities, and Denominations

The first article of an indenture usually includes the definitions of special words and phrases used therein and certain general provisions covering acts of bondholders, notices to the trustee, the company, and debtholder, the governing law, among other things. The second article covers the form of the bond or debenture and spells out what is to appear on the actual security certificate. The third article is called "The Bonds" or "The Debentures," as the case may be. Here the securities' title or series is stated, as well as the form (coupon, registered) and denominations. Today practically all domestically issued corporate bonds are in registered form—i.e., the ownership is registered with the transfer agent (normally the trustee), and a check for the interest payment is sent to the registered holder. In late 1986, a form of registered corporate bond called *book entry* appeared. Ford Motor Credit Company issued $200 million of 7 ⅛% Notes due October 15, 1989, under a prospectus dated October 7, 1986. With the book-entry form, only one global registered note is issued; it is deposited with, and held by, the Depository Trust Company (DTC) in New York City and registered in the DTC's nominee name. The global note may be transferred in whole only to another nominee or successor of DTC. Buyers of the notes really acquire ownership of beneficial interest in them, records of which are kept by the participating firms (banks, brokers, dealers, and clearing corporations) and the depository.

The Depository Trust Company is a limited-purpose trust company established to hold securities and to facilitate the clearance and settlement of its participants' securities transactions through the electronic book-entry changes in their participants' accounts. Because of restrictions on the transfer of global notes, some investors may not hold book-entry-form securities These would be those who, by state law or other regulations, must have physical delivery in definitive form of the underlying securities they own. It is expected that as the book-entry method becomes more acceptable, these rules and regulations will be modified. It should be noted that as the Depository's nominee is the sole owner of the global note, owners of beneficial interests will not be considered owners or holders thereof under the indenture. The prospectus states that "neither Ford Credit, the Trustee [Chase Manhattan Bank] . . . has any direct responsibility or liability for the payment of principal or interest on the Notes to owners of beneficial interests in the Global Note." But it goes on to say, "Payments by Particpants and indirect participants to owners of beneficial interests in the Global Note will be governed by standing instructions and customary practices, as is now the case with securities held for the accounts of customers in bearer form or registered in 'street name,' and will be the responsibility of the participants and indirect participants."

The usual denomination of registered corporate debt is $1,000 and multiples thereof, although in some cases a minimum of $5,000 or $10,000 (and even $100,000) may be required. In cases of rights offerings and debt issued in exchanges or on emergence from bankruptcy, the indenture may provide for denominations of less than $1,000, such as $100 or $500 pieces. These lower-denominated issues are called "baby bonds." There have even been a few issues whose minimum denomination or par value was as low as $20 each. As the normal unit of trading is in multiples of $1,000, prices may vary for trades in units of other than that amount.

The third article also discusses the authentication, delivery, dating, registration, transfer, and exchange of the bonds, as well as mutilated, destroyed, lost, and stolen bonds. Finally, it sets forth the record dates for interest and the interest payment dates.

Remedies

There are several other articles common to both types of debt, although one might be, for example, article 12 in one indenture and article 8 in the other. Article 9 in the model mortgage indenture (article 5 in the model debenture indenture) concerns remedies,—the steps that are available in case the company defaults. The trustee is responsible for enforcing the available remedies; while only the debtholders' representative, the trustee ultimately is responsible to the majority of the bondholders. In this article, events of default are defined and may include the following: (1) failure to pay interest on the date due or within the grace period (usually 30 days); (2) failure to make a principal payment on the due date; (3) failure to make a sinking fund payment when due; (4) failure to perform any other covenants and the continuation of that failure for a certain period after the trustee has given notice to the debtor company;and (5) certain other events of bankruptcy, insolvency, or reorganization, which may include defaults of the company's other debt obligations.

If an event of default is continuing, either the trustee or the holders of 25 percent of the principal amount of the outstanding issue may declare all the bonds of that series immediately due and payable, along with unpaid and accrued interest up to the date of acceleration. This may pressure the obligor to cure the defaults (if able to do so) and thus rescind the acceleration or to seek waivers of the defaults while it is trying to find a solution. But such acceleration might force the debtor to seek protection of the bankruptcy courts; it thus might be better to work with the debtor along the path to recovery. The article also provides limits to lawsuits that individual bondholders may bring against the company with a default under the indenture provisions. However, no provision may impair the bondholders' absolute and unconditional right to the timely payment of principal, premium (if any), and interest on the bonds and to bring legal action to enforce such payment.

The Trustee

While the trustee's rights and duties are mentioned in various articles throughout the indenture, the next article (6 and 10 in the model indentures) gives certain specifics regarding the trustee and its activities, including resignation or removal. Note that the trustee is paid by the debt-issuing company and can do only what the indenture allows. The article may open with wording such as: " . . . the Trustee undertakes to perform such duties and only such duties as are specifically set forth in this Indenture, and no implied covenants or obligations shall be read into this Indenture against the Trustee. . . . " Further, " . . . the Trustee shall exercise such of the rights and powers vested in it by this Indenture, and shall use the same degree of care and skill in their exercise, as a prudent man would exercise or use under the circumstances in the conduct of his own affairs," or "No provision of this Indenture shall be construed to relieve the Trustee from liability for its own negligent action, its own negligent failure to act, or its own wilful misconduct. . . . " Of course, certain exceptions are listed.

One of the indenture trustee's duties as enumerated in this article is to notify bondholders of a default under the indenture (except in cases such as a cured default or in which the board of directors, "responsible officers" of the trustee, etc. determine in good faith that withholding notice is in the bondholders' "best interests"). Also, the trustee is under no obligation to exercise the rights or powers under the indenture at the bondholders' request unless it has been offered reasonable security or indemnity. This seems reasonable in this age of frivolous lawsuits. The trustee is not bound to investigate the facts surrounding documents delivered to it, but it may do so if it sees fit.

Another section of the article requires the issuer to pay the trustee reasonable fees for its services, reimburse it for reasonable expenses, and indemnify it for certain losses that might arise from administering the trust. A subsection of the article states that in cases of conflict of interest, the trustee will either eliminate the conflict or resign within 90 days from the date on which the existence of the conflict was determined. One often sees in the financial press legal advertisements of a trustee's resignation and the appointment of a successor. As there must always be a trustee, no resignation is effective until a new trustee has been secured. Such real or potential conflicts often occur when the trustee bank is also a creditor of the issuing company. For example, in 1984 Citibank, N.A., resigned as trustee for the first mortgage bonds of Long Island Lighting Company, citing a potential conflict of interest between its obligations to bondholders as trustee and as a creditor to Lilco. It can't very well serve the bondholders' interests and its own creditor interests at the same time.[8] There is also provision for a trustee's removal with or without cause, upon the action of a majority of the debtholders.

Reports

The next article (7 and 11 in the model debenture and mortgage indentures, respectively) is somewhat short but has caused many bond market participants some concern. It deals with debtholders' lists and reports by the trustee and issuing company. Under the article, the company must furnish the trustee with semiannual lists of bondholders and their addresses and preserve this information until a new list is available. This is to enable the requisite number of bondholders to communicate with other bondholders about their rights under the indenture. Unless specifically stated, companies are under no specific obligation to send bondholders any financial or other report on its operations or activities. But the trustee must submit to the bondholders certain brief reports concerning its continued eligibility as trustee, any advances made by the trustee to the corporation, any other indebtedness to the trustee by the company and any company property or funds held by the trustee. How many bondholders have actually received these reports or even seen them? Probably very few; perhaps many nominees, such as stockbrokers and banks, have failed to send them to the beneficial owners.

The bone of contention between some bondholders and issuers concerns financial reports by the company to its security holders. The indenture usually requires the company to file with the trustee copies of annual and other reports that it normally must file with the Securities and Exchange Commission. Unless specifically mentioned in a particular indenture, a company is not required to send these reports to debtholders. Many years ago bondholders might have been content with little or no information, but that is not so today. Although not spelled out, bondholders have a right to be treated fairly. All registered holders should automatically receive the same annual and quarterly reports that the company sends to its stockholders. Allied Supermarkets, Inc., in its May 7, 1986, prospectus for a debenture offering, said, "So long as the debentures are outstanding, the Company will furnish each Debentureholder and the Trustee with annual reports to its shareholders containing audited consolidated financial statements and any quarterly or other financial reports furnished to its shareholders, no later than the date such materials are mailed or made available to its shareholders." However, these annual and quarterly reports are normally written for shareholders and not bondholders. In most cases, they lack some of the information a knowledgeable bondholder needs. For example, a simple look at the debt part of the capital structure often will reveal the inadequacy of the financal reporting. Frequently the outstanding amount of a particular bond issue may not be clear from the financial statements. For instance, in a description such as "4⅜%–9⅛% sinking fund debentures due 1992–2007 . . . $258.5," what is the outstanding amount of the 4⅜s and each of the other issues in this bunching?

A couple of years ago, I wrote to the Ford Motor Credit Company and Dart & Kraft, Inc. requesting information about the amounts outstanding for individual issues, since the annual reports and 10K forms were unsatisfactory. Dart & Kraft's Director of Corporate Finance responded: "Regarding your requst . . . for principal amounts of Dart & Kraft's publicly issued debt, we presently do not disclose that information other than the amounts disclosed in our 1983 Annual Report." The Treasurer's office of Ford Motor Credit Company replied: "I regret to inform you that it is now our policy to not disclose detailed information on principal amounts outstanding on specific debt issues." A 1975 article in The New York Times said: "It is ironic that most public companies today, despite the importance of debt financing and the increasingly dynamic nature of the bond market, still regard holders of their debt as second-class citizens when it comes to giving them information."[9] This is still pertinent today.

Consolidation, Merger, Conveyance, and Lease

Common to indentures of secured and unsecured debt are model articles 12 and 8 dealing with consolidation and merger, or the conveyance, transfer, or lease of assets. Some indentures may expressly forbid the debtor company to merge or consolidate with another, but most indentures for public debt issues allow corporate mergers, consolidations, and the sale of substantially all of the corporation's assets if certain conditions are satisfied. Transfer or sale of less than substantially all of the corporation's property usually is not subject to this article's control. One such condition is that the company be the surviving party to the merger/consolidation or, if not, that the other party be organized and existing under federal and/or state laws. The new or surviving corporation must assume the terms of the indenture, including the timely payment or principal, interest, and premium (if any) on the subject debt securities; the successor company is substituted for the predecessor company in the indenture. Of course, if secured, the terms of the transaction (unless waived by bondholders) must provide for the preservation of the security lien and the trustee's rights and powers. The merger, consolidation, or asset sale cannot take place if it would cause an event of default under the indenture's various covenants. Some indentures might place other restrictions on these transactions, including tangible net worth tests of the surviving corporation.

Supplemental Indentures and Covenants

As times change, so may corporate laws and practices. An indenture that was satisfactory when entered into many years may not be so today. Thus, article 13 in the mortgage indenture and article 9 in the debenture indenture provide for supplemental indentures and amendments to the original indenture. The most common supplemental indenture is one issued under a blanket indenture for new and addtional series or issues of debt securities. The supplemental indenture sets forth the terms and conditions for the issuance of the new debt securities, including authorized amounts of the new issue, interest rate, maturity, and redemption provisions. It may also include restrictive provisions not found in the basic or blanket indenture, but, more often than not, it contains much less restrictive provisions. Of course, the more restrictive provisions of preceding and still outstanding debt issues remain in force until the debt is extinguished or the original indenture is changed or amended.

Certain provisions may be made without bondholders' consent. These include the addition of provisions for the debtholders' benefit or the surrender of company rights to correct inconsistencies or errors in the original indenture and to bring the original indenture into conformity with new and applicable laws concerning corporate trust indentures. Other provisions may require the assent of a two-thirds (or greater) majority of the debt outstanding; changes of a substantive nature require a 100 percent vote. The latter category includes changes in the maturity, interest rate, redemption premium, place of payment, currency in which the debt is payable, or any provision that would impair the right to start legal suit for enforcement of any defaulted payment. Some of the changes sought may include extension of the maturity and reduction of coupons or payment of interest in common stock at the company's options. In some cases, the company may seek amendments to the indenture and offer to exchange new securities for old. If the old indenture received the required number of votes, the indenture would be changed and would govern any old securities that were not exchanged for new ones. The new securities issued in the exchange would have a new indenture.

In order for Peoples Express, Inc. (PEI) to merge into Texas Air Corporation in late 1986, the debtholders of People Express Airlines, Inc., a subsidiary of PEI, were required to exchange their old securities for new ones with longer maturities and lower interest rates and to consent to amendments to the old indenture (66⅔ percent vote of the outstanding principal amount of each issue was required). The amendments included the elimination of provisions restricting the payment of dividends by the company and the acquisition of shares of common stock. Bondholders who did not tender and did not vote for the indenture amendments nevertheless would be bound by the new supplemental indenture concerning dividends and stock repurchases even if they kept their original securities.

The debtor seeking indenture amendments often will give consideration to the debtholders in the form of increased interest payments or one-time fee. Companies' solicitations will, of course, often carry boilerplate statements such as "Management of the Company believes that the proposed changes are in the best interests of the Company and the holders of each issue being asked to consent to the proposed indenture changes." Many of these proposed changes weaken some of the existing covenants. For example, in 1985 Houston Natural Gas (HNG) asked some of its debentureholders to eliminate the interest coverage test, which required available earnings to be at least 2.5 times annual interest charges on consolidated senior funded debt before it could issue new senior funded debt. The proxy statement said, "HNG wishes to change its debt incurrence tests to reflect current practice as it applies to corporate obligors of HNG's caliber and to improve HNG's financing flexibility in order to permit HNG to be able to respond to rapid changes in the business and financial environment in which it operates." With no change, HNG would have been permitted to issue about $240 million of additional debt on October 31, 1984, assuming a 12 percent interest rate. With the elimination of the restriction, it would have been able to issue $1,773 million of additional debt under a less restrictive capitalization test. As the proxy statement said, "to the extent that as a result of the proposed amendment HNG increases its leverage through the issuance of additional Senior Funded Debt beyond its ability to reasonably service such debt, the holders of the Debentures would be adversely affected thereby."

In 1977 and 1978, a number of electric utility companies sought changes in their indentures issued between 1928 and 1945. The reasons given were basically the same, namely, their desire to modernize their indentures by eliminating obsolete and unnecessary restrictions and to increase their financial flexibility. The changes allowed the companies to issue additional debt in greater amounts or at an earlier date than previously. Many dramatic changes had occurred in the economy since the indentures were written, and the high capital costs and rising fuel expenses caused by the runaway inflation of the seventies wrought havoc in the utility industry. Of course, weakening of debt restrictions may cause little problem in the short run—indeed, such changes usually will not in themselves cause a downgrade in the company's debt rating. But it is at times of crisis that investors probably wish that less restrictive covenants were not granted so freely. Investors should carefully review any proposed indenture changes. The relaxed restraint on corporate managements' financing activities might mean more problems for the debtholders.

Covenants

Articles 14 of the mortgage indenture and article 10 of the debenture indenture are concerned with certain limitations and restrictions on the borrower's activities. Some covenants are common to all indentures, such as (1) paying interest, principal, and premium, if any, on a timely basis; (2) maintaining an office or agency where the securities may be transferred or exchanged and where notices may be served on the company with respect to the securities and the indenture; (3) paying all taxes and other claims when due unless contested in good faith; (4) maintaining all properties used and useful in the borrower's business in good condition and working order; (5) maintaining adequate insurance on its properties (some indentures may not have insurance provisions since proper insurance is a routine business practrice); (6) submitting periodic certificates to the trustee stating whether the debtor is in compliance with the loan agreement; and (7) maintaining its corporate existence. These are often called *affirmative* covenants, since they call upon the debtor to make promises to do certain things.

    Negative covenants are those that require the borrower *not* to take certain actions. These are usually negotiated between the borrower and the lender or their agents. Setting the right balance between the two parties can be a rather difficult undertaking at times. In public debt transactions, the investing institutions normally leave the negotiating to the investment bankers, although they will often be asked for their opinions on certain terms and features. Unfortunately most public bond buyers are unaware of these articles at the time of purchase and may never learn of them throughout the life of the debt. Borrowers normally want the least restrictive loan agreement available, while lenders want the most restrictive. But lenders should not try to restrain borrowers from normal business activities and conduct, which could imperil the corporations. A company might be willing to include additional restrictions (up to a point) if it can get a lower interest rate on the loan. As we have seen, when companies seek to weaken restrictions in their favor, they are often willing to pay more interest.

What do some of these negative convenants cover? Obviously there is an infinite variety of restrictions that can be placed on borrowers depending on the type of debt issue, the economics of the industry and the nature of the business, and the lenders' desires, if any. Some of the more common restrictive covenants include various limitations on the company's ability to incur debt, since unrestricted borrowing can lead the company and its debtholders to ruin. Thus, debt restrictions may include limits on the absolute dollar amount of debt that may be outstanding or may require ratio tests— for example, debt may be limited to no more than 60 percent of total capitalization or to a certain percentage of net tangible assets. There may be interest coverage tests, requiring that the company maintain earnings available for interest charges at a given minimum level in order to do additional borrowing. There could be cash flow tests or requirements and working capital maintenance provisions. Certain captive finance companies have entered into supplementary agreements requiring them to maintain the fixed charge coverage at a level that will enable the securities to meet the eligibility standards for investment by insurance companies under New York State law. The required coverage levels are maintained by adjusting the prices at which the finance company buys its receivables or other financial assets from its parent company or through an income maintenance agreement with the parent. These protective provisions usually are not part of indentures, but they are important considerations for bond buyers.

Some indentures may prohibit subsidiaries from borrowing from all other companies except the parent. Indentures often classify subsidiaries as restricted or unrestricted. Restricted subsidiaries are those considered to be consolidated for financial test purposes; unrestricted subsidiaries (often foreign and certain special-purpose companies) are those excluded from the covenants governing the parent. Subsidiaries often are classified as unrestricted in order to allow them to finance themselves through outside sources.

Limitations on dividend payments and stock repurchases may

be included in indentures. Cash dividend payments often are limited to a certain percentage of net income earned after a given date (frequently the issuance date of the debt, called the "peg date"), plus a fixed amount. Sometimes the dividend formula might allow the inclusion of net proceeds from the sale of common stock sold after the peg date. In other cases, the dividend restriction might be worded so as to prohibit the declaration and payment of cash dividends if tangible net worth (or other measures, such as consolidated quick assets) declines below a certain amount. There are usually no restrictions on the payment of stock dividends. In addition to dividend restrictions, there often are restrictions on a company's repurchase of its common stock if such purchase might cause a violation or deficiency in the dividend determination formulae. Certain holding company indentures might limit the company's right to pay dividends in the common stock of its subsidiaries. For example, Citicorp, the holding company parent of Citibank, N.A. is restricted, under certain circumstancs, from paying dividends in shares of Citibank. The prospectus dated August 20, 1986, states,

Citibank covenants . . . as long as any of the notes which mature more than ten years after their issuance are outstanding, it will not declare or pay any dividends, or make any distribution to its stockholders ratably, payable in shares of stock of Citibank, if after giving effect thereto, the Adjusted Stockholders' Equity of Citicorp would be less than 200% of Senior Long-Term Indebtedness; *provided, however,* that Citicorp may declare and pay such dividends and make any other distributions without regard to the foregoing provisions so long as the aggregate amount . . . of the value . . . of the shares of Stock . . . does not exceed 20% of the Adjusted Stockholders' Equity of Citicorp. . . . "

Another part of the covenant article may place restrictions on the disposition and the sale and leaseback of certain property. In some cases, the proceeds of asset sales totaling more than a certain amount must be used to repay debt. This is seldom found in indentures for unsecured debt, but at times some investors have wished they had such a protective clause. At other times, this type of provision might allow a company to retire its high-coupon debt in a low interest rate environment, thus causing bondholders a loss of value. It might be better to have such a provision in cases where the company would have the right to reinvest the proceeds of asset sales in new plant and equipment rather than retiring debt or to at least give debtholders' the option of tendering their bonds. The April 15, 1986, indenture of CSX Corporation does not prohibit the sale by the company or any subsidiary of any stock or indebtedness of any restricted subsidiary. The main restricted subsidiaries of this transportation and energy company are Chesapeake and Ohio Railway Company, Baltimore and Ohio Railroad Company, CSX Transportation, Inc., Texas Gas Resources Corporation, American Commercial Lines, Inc., and Texas Gas Transmission Company. One hopes that management has the bondholders' welfare in mind in case they decide to dispose of a substantial operation that may provide some degree of security for eventual repayment of the debt. A sale/leaseback transaction involves the sale of and simultaneous leasing back of property for a fixed number of years. Restrictions on these transactions might be limited to certain property owned, the amount of property that can be included in the transaction, or the use of the proceeds therefrom.

Some indentures restrict the investments that a corporation may make in other companies, through either the purchase of stock or loans and advances. As *Commentaries* states:

> By restricting the amount of cash or property which the borrower may invest in other enterprises, it is expected that the available assets of the borrower will be applied and devoted primarily to the basic business and purposes of the enterprise. If the borrower does not need the money in that enterprise, it may then be encouraged to use it for accelerated debt repayment. Such a covenant is not commonly used but when used it is more often found in directly placed issues than in public issues.[10]

The May Department Stores Credit Company has a provision in the indenture for its 9% Debentures due 1989 stating that

> The Company will not . . . invest in a substantial part of its assets in securities other than Deferred Payment Accounts, certain governmental securities maturing not more than eighteen months after the date of purchase, prime commercial paper and securities of a Subsidiary of the Company or May engaged in a business similar to that of the Company. The Company may also acquire debt securities of May in certain circumstances.

Again, in this age of corporate raiders and lack of concern for debt investors, some consideration perhaps should be given to the resurrection of this type of restrictive provision.

Finally, there may be an absence of restrictive covenants. The prospectus of Transamerica Financial Corporation dated April 16, 1986, states forthrightly:

> The Indentures do not contain any provision which will restrict the Company in any way from paying dividends or making other distribution on its capital stock or purchasing or redeeming any of its capital stock, or from incurring, assuming or becoming liable upon Senior Indebtedness, Subordinated Indebtedness or Junior Subordinated Indebtedness or any other type of debt or other obligations. The Indentures do not contain any financial ratios or specified levels of net worth or liquidity to which the Company must adhere. In addition, the Subordinated and Junior Subordinated Indentures do not restrict the Company from creating liens on its property for any purpose.

Let the buyer beware! If corporate managements and boards of directors viewed themselves as fiduciaries for all of the investors in the company, from stockholders to bondholders, indentures with many restrictive covenants might be unnecessary. But in most instances, that is not the case; they strive to increase shareholder wealth (or their own), not the wealth of the total firm, and often at the expense of the senior security investor. As one observer of bondholders' rights summarizes,

> Contrary to popular belief, indentures do not have numerous detailed covenants that regulate the bondholder-stockholder conflict. Indeed, an indenture may have no restrictive covenants at all. Such covenants are costly. Other constraints on stockholder gain at bondholder expense are ineffective. Since fiduciary duties are a substitute for costly constracts, directors should have fiduciary duties to bondholders as well as to stockholders. The exclusive focus of corporate law on stockholders is too narrow for modern corporate finance. Bondholders and stockholders are all security holders in the enterprise and equally deserving of board protection.[11]

SECURED DEBT

Now that we have seen a general introduction to corporate bonds, let us get into some specifics. Our starting point will be bonds that are secured by some from of collateral, the first of the three Cs of credit:

the collateral, which is pledged to ensure repayment of the debt; the character of the borrower, which ensures that the obligation will be paid on a timely basis; and the capacity of the borrower, which ensures that it will have the means for repaying the debt.

Utility Mortgage Bonds

The largest issuers of debt secured by property, i.e., mortgage debt, are found in the electric utility industry. Of the major electric companies that periodically issue debt, there is but one—United Illuminating Company in Connecticut—that issues only unsecured debt; all the others have mortgage debt as the primary debt vehicle in their capital structures. Other utilities, such as telephone companies and gas pipeline and distribution firms, have also used mortgage debt as sources of capital, but generally to a lesser extent than electrics.

Most electric utility bond indentures do not limit the total amount of bonds that may be issued. This is called an *open-ended mortgage,* a contribution to American corporate finance credited to Samuel Insull, the pioneer of the electric utility business who once served as secretary to Thomas Alva Edison.[12] The mortgage generally is a first lien on the company's real estate, fixed property, and franchises, subject to certain exceptions or permitted emcumbrances owned at the time of the execution of the indenture or its supplement. The after-acquired property clause also subjects to the mortgage property the company acquires after the filing of the supplemental indenture. For example, the prospectus for Niagara Mohawk Power Corporation's 9⅛% First Mortgage Bonds due 1996 says that the "mortgage provides that substantially all after-acquired property of such character shall become subject to the lien thereof. . . . " Some indentures might state that it is a first lien on all the properties used or useful in the company's operations (Niagara Mohawk Power Corporation, for example). Property exempted from the mortgage lien may include nuclear fuel (often financed separately through other secured loans); cash, securities, and other cash items and current assets; automobiles, trucks, tractors, and other vehicles; inventories and fuel supplies; office furniture, and leaseholds; property and merchandise held for resale in the normal course of business; receivables, contracts, leases, and operating agreements; and timber, minerals, mineral rights, and royalties.

Permitted encumbrances might include liens for taxes and governmental assessments, judgments, easements and leases, certain prior liens, minor defects, irregularities and deficiencies in titles of properties, and rights-of-way that do not materially impair the property's use. For example, the mortgage for Indiana & Michigan Electric Company as supplemented for the issuance of 9 ⅝% First Mortgage Bonds due 2015 in 1986 is "(a) a first lien on substantially all of the fixed physical property and franchises of the Company . . . and (b) a lien, subject to the lien of IMPCo's mortgage, on the fixed physical property acquired in connection with the merger of IMPCo into the Company. . . . " Citizens Utilities Company 7 ⅞% First Mortgage and Collateral Trust Bonds due 1996 are secured by a direct first lien on substantially all of the public utility properties located in Arizona, Colorado, Idaho, and Vermont and a direct second lien on property located in Hawaii (there was a prior mortgage on the Hawaiian properties of $930,000 at the end of 1984).

Historically, bonded debt—at least for the electric utility industry—was viewed as permanent capital and, as such, was not expected to be repaid but only rolled over or refunded. This is the current view taken of the federal government debt. Prior to the mid-1970s, most of the new issues were long term with maturities of around 30 or more years. Sinking funds were either nonexistent or, if insignificant, usually could be satisfied with additions to property and not with actual debt retirement (Chapter 4 has more on debt retirement features). It made no sense to repay permanent debt if one only had to borrow the amount that was just repaid. Therefore, other protective measures had to be incorporated into the indenture in order to satisfy the lender that the mortgage property was being cared for.

To provide for proper maintenance of the property and replacement of worn-out plant, maintenance fund, maintenance and replacement fund, or renewal and replacement fund provisions were placed in indentures. These clauses stipulate that the issuer spend a certain amount of money for these purposes. Depending on the company, the required sums may be around 15 percent of operating revenues, as defined; in other cases, the figure is based on a percentage of the depreciable property or amount of bonds outstanding. These requirements usually can be satisfied by certifying that the specified amount of expenditures has been made either for maintenance and repairs to the property or by gross property additions. They can also be satisfied by depositing cash or outstanding mortgage bonds with the trustee; the deposited cash can be used for property additions, repairs and maintenance, or—to the concern of holders of high-coupon debt—the redemption of bonds. More will be said on this topic in Chapter 4.

Another provision for bondholder security is the release and substitution of property clause. If the company releases property from the mortgage lien (such as through the sale of a plant or other property that may have become obsolete or unnecessary for use in the business or through the state's power of eminent domain), it must substitute other property or cash and securities to be held by the trustee, usually in an amount equal to the released property's fair value. It may use the proceeds or cash held by the trustee to retire outstanding bonded debt. Certainly a bondholder would not let go of the mortgaged property without substitution of satisfactory new collateral or adjustment in the amount of the debt, as he or she should want to maintain the value of the security behind the bond. In some cases, the company may waive the right to issue additional bonds. Pennsylvania Power & Light Company's prospectus dated October 7, 1986, says: "Property may be released upon the bases of (1) the deposit of cash, or, to a limited extent, purchase money mortgages; (2) property additions, after adjustments in certain cases to offset retirements and after making adjustments for qualified prior lien bonds outstanding against property additions; and (3) waiver of the right to issue bonds without applying any earnings tests."

Although the typical electric utility mortgage does not limit the total amount of bonds that may be issued, there are certain issuance tests or bases that usually must be satisfied before the company can sell more bonds. New bonds are often restricted to no more than 60 to 66⅔ percent of the value of net bondable property. This generally is the lower of the fair value or cost of property additions after adjustments and deductions for property that had previously been used for the authentication and issuance of previous bond issues, retirements of bondable property or the release of property, and any outstanding prior liens. Bonds may also be issued in exchange or substitution for outstanding bonds, previously retired bonds, and bonds otherwise acquired. Bonds may be issued in an amount equal to the amount of cash deposited with the trustee. In August 1986, Central Hudson Gas and Electric Corporation sold $50 million of 8⅛% First Mortgage Bonds due 1994 against $44.465 million of bonds that had been issued under the mortgage and since retired and $5.535 million on the basis of 66⅔ percent of the net bondable value of property additions after December 31, 1940. The prospectus says, "The amount of net bondable value (unbonded bondable property) at June 30, 1986 was approximately $281 million; and the amount of additional mortgage bonds in respect thereto was approximately $187 million."

A further earnings test, often found in utility indentures, requires that interest charges be covered by pre-tax income available for interest charges of at least two times. The above Central Hudson prospectus states:

> ... additional mortgage bonds may be issued ... for purposes other than refunding outstanding mortgage bonds only if net earnings ... for twelve consecutive calendar months within the fifteen calendar months immediately preceding the date when the Trustee receives any application for authentication and delivery of mortgage bonds shall exceed two times the interest charges for one year on (1) all mortgage bonds outstanding ... , (2) the mortgage bonds then applied for, (3) all prior lien bonds to be outstanding ... , (4) all indebtedness secured by any lien prior to the lien of the Mortgage if the indebtedness secured thereby has been assumed by the Company or if the Company customarily pays the interest on such indebtedness. For the twelve months ended June 30, 1986, such ratio of net earnings to fixed charges was 3.60, and at such date the Company could have issued $349 million of additional first mortgage bonds ... assuming an annual interest rate of 8.75%.

Mortgage bonds go by many different names. The most common of the senior lien issues are *First Mortgage Bonds* as used by Cincinnati Gas & Electric Company, Long Island Lighting Company, Public Service Company of New Hampshire, and Consumers Power Company, among others. Baltimore Gas & Electric Company uses the title *First Refunding Mortgage Bonds,* while Canal Electric Company, a wholesale electric generating company, uses *First and General Mortgage Bonds.* The Baltimore issue is subject to a first mortgage lien (with certain exceptions) and secured by a pledge of 100,000 shares of Class B stock of Safe Harbor Water Power Company, an operator of a hydroelectric plant in Pennsylvania. The Canal Electric lien is broad-based, covering all of its property owned adjacent to the Cape Cod Canal, after-acquired property, and pledged contracts relating to a couple of its generating units. Texas Utilities Electric Company issues *First Mortgage and Collateral Trust Bonds*. These are secured by Class "A" Bonds, which are first mortgage bonds issued by former subsidiaries (now divisions), and a first mortgage lien on certain of the company's other property. In come cases (excluding prior lien bonds, as mentioned above), a company might have two or more layers of mortgage debt with different priorities. In most cases, this situation has occurred because the company could not issue additional first mortgage debt (or the equivalent) under the existing indentures. Often this secondary debt level is called *General and Refunding Mortgage Bonds (G&R)*. In reality, this is mostly second mortgage debt. Long Island Lighting Company first issued G&R bonds in June 1975.

Let us take a look at the mortgage debt issues of Public Service Company of New Hampshire, which, in addition to general and refunding mortgage bonds with varying degrees of security, has third mortgage bonds as well as publicly issued, unsecured debt. All in all, this amounts to four levels of claims against the company and its properties. Public Service Company, the largest electric utility in New Hampshire, supplies electricity to about 75 percent of the state's population. Along with a number of other neighboring utilities, it embarked on the construction of an ambitious nuclear project located in Seabrook, New Hampshire. As did many other nuclear facilities under construction during the late 1970s and early 1980s, it encountered rapidly increasing construction costs, skyrocketing financial costs, and regulatory delays due to consumer and other opposition to nuclear facilities, among other things. (In 1976, a prospectus estimated that Seabrook Unit #1 would be in service in 1981; at the time of this writing [late 1986], it had not yet been placed on stream.) The end result was a strain on the company's finances, especially internally generated cash flow, which resulted in a lack of financial flexibility. PNH finally omitted common and preferred stock dividends in May 1984.

Due to provisions contained in the indenture of the company's First Mortgage Bonds that restricted the issuance of additional senior mortgage debt, PNH entered into a General and Refunding

Mortgage Bond Indenture in August 1978. The terms of this indenture are somewhat similar to the first mortgage bonds except for the removal of the restrictions on the issuance of additional debt and a modification relating to the use of the allowance for funds used during construction in the earnings test. The G&R bonds have a lien on substantially all of the property and franchises owned by the company (as do the first mortgage bonds), "subject, however, to the payment of the Trustee's charges, to the lien of the First Mortgage, to the lien on after-acquired property existing at the time of acquisition or created in connection with the purchase thereof . . . and to Permitted Liens."[13]

The G&R indentures, as supplemented, also provide that the bonds are additionally secured by a pledge of the maximum amount of First Mortgage Bonds that may be issuable at the time of the issuance of the G&R bonds. Thus, the G&R constitutes a second mortgage on the company's property and, in some cases, backed up by a first mortgage. At the end of 1985, PNH had seven issues of G&R bonds outstanding, of which four had the additional backing of First Mortgage Bonds (see Table 1-5). The prospectus states that the principal benefit to the holders of G&R bonds that have first mortgage bonds pledged as additional security would be in reorganization or insolvency of the company when the allocation to the holders of these G&R bonds might be increased by reason of their participation

Table 1-5
Selected Data on General & Refunding Mortgage Bonds
Public Service Company of New Hampshire
at December 31, 1985 ($ Thousands)

G & R Bond Issue			G & R Amount Outstanding	Pledged First Mortgage Bonds	Percent of G & R Collateralized by FMB
"A"	10.125%	1993	$ 43,620	$ 9,727	22.30 %
"B"	12.00%	1999	60,000	9,185	15.31
"C"	14.50%	2000	30,000	None	0
"D"	17.00%	1990	23,000	None	0
"E"	18.00%	1989	50,000	24,135	48.27
"H"	Variable	1991	112,500	10,080	8.89

Source: Annual Report for 1985.

in the First Mortgage through the pledged bonds. Upon the retirement of all nonpledged First Bonds (2006 or earlier), the G&R bonds would become the equivalent of First Mortgage debt as the original first mortgage would have been discharged or satisfied.

The next level of debt in PNH's capitalization represents a third mortgage through the issuance in early 1986 of $225 million of Deferred Interest Third Mortgage Bonds Series A due 1996. The company had to resort to this level due to the G&R earnings test, which would have permitted the issuance of only about $26 million of G&R debt at December 31, 1985. The prospectus states, "The . . . Bonds, . . . are secured by a mortgage on substantially all of the Company's New Hampshire properties. The Third Mortgage is junior and subordinate to the liens of the First Mortgage and the G&R Indenture." While the Third Mortgage does not have an earnings test, additional bonds under the indenture may be issued only if the total of the outstanding First, G&R, and Third Mortgage Bonds does not exceed 90 percent of the book balue of the company's New Hampshire properties subject to the Third Mortgage. The final stratum of debt is the unsecured one consisting of promissory notes and debentures. PNH is a rare bird among electric utility companies (or even among non-railroad companies) due to its capital structure. Most companies might not have more than two—or at the most three—different types of debt on their books.

As stated earlier, electric companies utilize mortgage debt more than other utilities. However, other utilities, such as telephone and gas companies, do have mortgage debt. Among the telephone companies with mortgage debt are some of the subsidiaries and affiliates of the GTE Corporation system. Illinois Bell and New York Telephone issued first mortgage debt until the early 1970s, when they closed off the mortgage and started issuing unsecured debenture debt. Prior to the breakup of the Bell system, the mortgage bonds and debentures of the Bell subsidiaries carried the same rating. For example, the bonds and debentures of New York Telephone were assigned a Moody's "Aaa." After the divestiture, however, different ratings were applied to the secured and unsecured debt. In September 1986, New York Telephone's first mortgage bonds had a rating of Moody's "Aa2" and the debentures a rating of "Aa3."

Gas companies also have used mortgage debt to some extent. Again the issuance tests are similar to those for the electric issues, as are the mortgage liens. However, the pipeline companies may have an additional clause subjecting certain gas purchase and sale contracts to the mortgage lien.

Other Mortgage Debt

Non-utility companies no longer offer much mortgage debt; the preferred form of debt financing is with unsecured paper. In the past, railroad operating companies were frequent issuers of mortgage debt. In many cases, a wide variety of secured debt might be found in a company's capitalization. One issue might have a first lien on a certain portion of the right of way and a second mortgage on another portion of the trackage, as well as a lien on the railroad's equipment, subject to the prior lien of existing equipment obligations. For example, Chesapeake & Ohio Railway Company's Refunding and Improvement Mortgage Bonds, 3½% Series due May 1, 1996, have a direct lien on 2,406.59 miles of track (819.32 miles as a first lien, 1,354.88 miles as a second lien, and 232.39 miles as a third lien), on the company interest in 9 miles operated under leasehold agreements and 411 miles operated under trackage rights, on C&O's owned equipment, and on its leasehold interest in equipment subject to prior mortgage liens and outstanding equipment trust obligations. (Railroad equipment trust certificates will be more fully described later.)

In the general classification of industrial companies, only a few have first mortgage bonds outstanding; unsecured financing is the norm for large public corporations. In the steel industry, Inland Steel Company, National Steel Corporation, Youngstown Sheet and Tube Company, and Jones & Laughlin Steel Corporation have mortgage debt. The latter two are now part of the bankrupt J&L Steel complex. While electric utility mortgage bonds generally have a lien on practically all the company's property, steel company mortgage debt has more limited liens. The prospectuses for Inland and National Steel describe the particular steel properties subject to the mortgage lien and make special mention that "various other properties of the Company . . . are not now subject to the lien of the Mortgage."[14] The mortgages of Youngstown and Jones & Laughlin retained the respective liens on their respective properties after their own merger and their subsequent merger with Republic Steel. Mortgages may also contain maintenance and repair provisions, earnings tests for the issuance of additional debt, release and substitution of property clauses, and limited after-acquired property provisions. In some cases, shares of subsidiaries also might be pledged as part of the lien.

Some mortgage bonds are secured by a lien on a specific property rather than on most of a company's property as in the case of a utility or steel company. For example, Humana Inc. has sold a number of small issues of first mortgage bonds secured by liens on specific hospital properties. The 16½s of 1997 are secured by a first lien on a 267-bed hospital in Orlando, Florida, while the 16¼s of 1996 have a lien on a 219-bed hospital in St. Petersburg, Florida. Although technically mortgage bonds, the basic security is centered on Humana's continued profitable operations. Because the security is specific rather than general, investors are apt to view these bonds as less worthy or of a somewhat lower ranking that fully secured or general lien issues. As the prospectuses say, the bonds are general obligations of Humana Inc. and also secured by the first mortgage. Standard & Poor's has mentioned that "It is difficult to assure that debtholders secured by specific collateral such as a hotel or hospital will, following a bankruptcy and liquidation of assets, realize values which make them whole."[15] The ultimate realization under these adverse circumstances greatly depends on the value of the property obtained in liquidation or assigned as part of the reorganization process. In many cases, by the time a company must resort to bankruptcy action, the properties are not worth what they once were. Any deficiency between what is owed and the value of the property then becomes a general unsecured claim against the debtor.

Other Secured Debt

Debt can be secured by many different assets. Forstmann & Company, Inc. issued $60 million 11¾% Secured Senior Extendible Notes due April 1, 1998, secured by a first-priority lien on substantially all of its real property, machinery, and equipment and by a second-priority lien on its inventory, accounts receivable, and intangibles;

the first-priority lien on these latter assets is held by General Electric Credit Corporation (GECC) for its revolving credit loan. At August 3, 1986, the revolving credit amounted to nearly $44 million and may go to as much as $72 million in the future. The prospectus points out:

> There can be no assurance that the fixed assets of the Company are currently, or in the future will be, adequate collateral for the Notes. While the Fair Market Value of the Company's fixed assets (assuming a continuation of current operations) has been appraised by American Appraisal Associates, Inc., an independent appraising firm, at $89,616,000 and the Company believes the replacement value of those assets to be more than $150,000,000, the Orderly Liquidation Value of those assets (assuming a piecemeal disposition over a reasonable period of time) has been appraised at $38,481,000. In addition, there can be no assurance that the Company's current assets will, after satisfaction of the claims of GECC, provide any collateral for the Notes.[16]

But in the view of Forstmann's management, "It is highly unlikely that the assets of the Company would be sold in a liquidation situation because of the greater marketability of the Company if sold as a going concern."

Collateral trust debentures, bonds, and notes are secured by financial assets such as cash, receivables, other notes, debentures, or bonds and not by real property. Louisville and Nashville Railroad Company's 11% Collateral Trust Bonds due July 15, 1985, were secured by a pledge of L&N's 11% First and Refunding Mortgage Bonds, Series P, due April 1, 2003, in an amount equal to 120 percent of the collateralized bonds. The mortgage bonds were a direct first lien on 3,949 miles of road, a direct second lien on 1,373 miles, and a third lien on 512 miles. Hudson's Bay Oil and Gas Company Limited sold some 7.85% Collateral Trust Bonds due 1994 in the United States in 1969. These bonds were secured by an equivalent amount of U.S. dollar–payable First Mortgage Sinking Fund Bonds with the same maturity, interest rate, and payment dates and redemption and sinking fund provisions as the collateral bonds. The pledged securities, being nearly similar in every way to the collateralized bonds, are sometimes called "shadow bonds." Thus, the collateral bond indenture constitutes a first lien on the pledged bonds and an indirect lien ranking *pari passu* (equally) with the holders of the company's other first mortgage bonds on its property as described in the Deed of Trust and Mortgage dated May 1, 1955, and supplemented.

Collateral trust notes and debentures have been issued by companies engaged in vehicle leasing, such as RLC Corporation, Leaseway Transportation Corporation, and Ryder System, Inc. The proceeds from these offerings were advanced to various subsidiaries in exchange for their unsecured promissory notes, which in turn were pledged with the trustees as security for the parent company debt. These pledged notes may later become secured by liens or other claims on vehicles. Protective convenants for these collateralized issues may include limitations on the equipment debt of subsidiaries, on dividend payments by the issuer and the subsidiaries, and on the creation of liens and purchase money mortgages, among other things.

Finally, debt can be secured by the pledge of assets such as partnership notes (DCS Capital Corporation 12.20% Series A Notes due 1994 or Pembroke Capital Company Inc. 14% Notes due 1991). DCS Capital Corporation is owned by DCS Capital Partnership, whose general partners are Dow Chemical Company, Union Carbide Corporation, and Shell Canada Limited. The partnership note is secured by a cash deficiency agreement and performance guarantees with the three partners on a several basis, initially in the following proportions: Dow, 52 percent; Union Carbide, 27 percent; and Shell, 21 percent. These agreements and guarantees are not assigned directly to the holders of the Series A Notes, but the trustee has the right to enforce them if the notes are not paid when due. The Pembroke issue is secured by a partnership note of Pembroke Cracking Company, a partnership of Texaco Limited and Gulf Oil (Great Britain) Limited, wholly-owned subsidiaries of American corporations. If the Pembroke Capital Note is not paid on a timely basis, the general partners are severally obligated to make, or cause to be made, payments sufficient to cover the principal and interest if their respective subsidiaries fail to do so.

Sperry Lease Finance Corporation has issued lease-back notes primarily secured by receivables arising from the leasing of electronic data processing equipment and payments under letters of credit issued for the benefit of the trustee. Others have issued Lease Obligation Bonds and Serial Facility Bonds payable from, and secured by, rentals paid under leases relating to the generation and sale of power from electric generating units. In 1986, El Paso Funding Corporation, a subsidiary of El Paso Electric Company, sold $396 million of Lease Obligation Bonds due 1991, 1996, and 2013. In the same year, OPC Scherer Funding Corporation issued $182 million of Serial Facility Bonds due 1991–2011, with the lease rental payments to be paid by Oglethorp Power Corporation.

Private Export Funding Corporation (PEFCO) has sold Secured Notes with the pledged security being an equivalent principal amount of obligations backed by the full faith and credit of the United States of America, such as guaranteed importer notes, or cash. The interest on PEFCO's secured notes is unconditionally guaranteed by the Export-Import Bank of the United States, a U.S. agency. Various thrift institutions have secured their debt obligations in order to enhance their papers' credit standing. Some have issued securities backed by eligible mortgage collateral, such as mortgages and deeds of trust on real property, either federally insured or guaranteed, and by conventional mortgages. Other mortgage-related collateral includes mortgage participation certificates issued by various federal government agencies. These secured issues are obligations of the thrift, not of any special trust. The security is still owned by the thrift, although pledged for repayment of the created debt. Proceeds from the sale of the secured bonds and notes (rather than from the sale of mortgages) are used for the thrift's general purposes.

Equipment Trust Financing—Railroads

Railroads and airlines have publicly financed much of their rolling stock and aircraft with secured debt. The securities go by such names as equipment trust certificates (ETCs) in the case of railroads and secured equipment certificates, guaranteed loan certificates, and loan certificates in the case of airlines. We will look at railroad equipment trust financing first, for two reasons: (1) The financing of railway equipment under the format in general public use today dates back to the late 1800s, and (2) it has had a superb record of safety of principal and timely payment of interest, more traditionally known as dividends. Railroads probably comprise the largest and oldest group of issuers of secured equipment financing.[17]

Probably the earliest instance in U.S. financial history in which a company bought equipment under a conditional sales agreement (CSA) was in 1845, when the Schuylkill Navigation Company purchased some barges.[18] Over the years secured equipment financing proved an attractive way for railroads—both good and bad credits—to raise the capital necessary for financing rolling stock. Various types of instruments were devised—equipment bonds (known as the New York Plan), conditional sales agreements (also known as the New York CSA), lease arrangements, and the Philadelphia Plan equipment trust certificate (ETC). The New York Plan equipment bond went the way of the dodo bird in the 1930s. The Philadelphia Plan ETC is the form used for most, if not all, public financings in today's market.

The ratings for equipment trust certificates are higher than those on the same company's mortgage debt or other public debt securities. This is due primarily to the collateral value of the equipment, the instrument's superior standing relative to other claims in the event of bankruptcy, and its self-liquidating nature. The railroad's actual creditworthiness may mean less for some equipment trust investors than for investors in other rail securities or, for that matter, other corporate paper. However, that is not to say that financial analysis of the issuer should be ignored. Table 1-6 compares the ratings on equipment trust certificates of a number of railroad companies with the ratings on some of their other public debt. In some cases, the differences between the two securities are slight; in others, they comprise a complete rating grade.

Equipment trust certificates are issued under agreements that provide a trust for the benefit of investors. Each certificate represents an interest in the trust equal to its principal amount and bears the railroad's unconditional guarantee for the prompt payment, when due, of the principal and dividends (the term *dividends* is used because the payments represent income from a trust and not interest on a loan). The trustee holds the title to the equipment, which when the certificates are retired, passes to, or vests in, the railroad. But the railroad has all other ownership rights. It can take the depreciation and utilize any tax benefits on the subject equipment. The railroad

Table 1-6
Ratings of Debt Securities of Selected Railroad Companies
(October 1, 1986)

Company	ETC Rating			Senior Public Debt Rating	
	Moody's	S&P		Moody's	S&P
Atchison, Topeka	Aaa	AAA	General Mortgage	Aa3	AA
& Santa Fe			Adjustment Mortgage	A1	AA-
Baltimore & Ohio					
Railroad	Aa3	AA+	First Consolidated	A3	A+
Burlington Northern	Aa1	AAA	(RR) Consolidated	A1	AA
Inc. (RR)			(Inc.) Notes	A2	A-
Chesapeake & Ohio					
Railway	Aa1	AA+	General Mortgage	A1	AA
Gulf, Mobile &					
Ohio R.R.	A2	A-	Income Debentures	B1	B
Louisville & Nashville	Aa2	AA+	1st & Refunding Mtg.	A2	A+
Norfolk & Western					
Railway	Aaa	AAA	1st Consolidated	Aa1	AA
Southern Pacific					
Transport.	Aa3	A	1st & Refunding	A3	BBB
Union Pacific					
Railroad	Aaa	AAA	General Consolidated	Aa2	AA

Source: *Moody's Bond Record* and *Standard & Poor's Bond Guide,* October, 1986.

agrees to pay the trustee sufficient rental for the principal payments and the dividends due on the certificates, together with expenses of the trust and certain other charges. The railroad uses the equipment in its normal operations and is required to maintain it in good operating order and repair (at its own expense). If the equipment is destroyed, lost, or becomes worn out or unsuitable for use (that is, suffers a "casualty occurrence") the company must substitute the fair market value of that equipment in the form of either cash or additional equipment. It may use cash to acquire additional equipment unless the agreement states otherwise.

The trust equipment must be clearly marked to show that it is not the railroad's property. One equipment trust agreement states:

Section 4.6. The Railroad agrees that at or before the delivery to the Railroad of each unit of Trust Equipment, there shall be plainly, distinctly, permanently and conspicuously placed and fastened upon each side of such unit a metal plate bearing the words [Missouri Pacific Equipment Trust, Series No. 22, Chemical Bank, Trustee, Owner and Lessor] . . . , or such words shall be otherwise plainly, distinctly, permanently and conspicuously marked on each side of such unit, in either case in letters not less than one-half inch in height. Such plates or marks shall be such as to be readily visible and as to indicate plainly the Trustee's ownership of each unit of the Trust Equipment. In case . . . such plates or marks shall at any time be removed, defaced or destroyed, the Railroad shall immediately cause the same to be restored or replaced.

The Trust Equipment may be lettered "Missouri Pacific Railroad", "Missouri Pacific Lines", "M.P." or with the name, insignia, emblem or initials of any Affiliate which . . . is authorized to use the equipment . . . for convenience of identification of the leasehold interest of the Railroad therein. During the continuance of the lease . . . the Railroad shall not allow the name of any person, association or corporation to be placed on any of the Trust Equipment as a designation which might be interpreted as a claim of ownership thereof by the Railroad or by any person, association or corporation other than the Trustee.[19]

Immediately after the issuance of an ETC, the railroad has an equity interest in the equipment that provides a margin of safety for the investor. Normally, the ETC investor finances no more than 80 percent of the equipment's cost and the railroad the remaining 20 percent. The equipment typically is new, but good, used equipment can also be included. However, investors might want the railroad to invest somewhat more equity. The Union Pacific Railroad Company's Equipment Trust No. 1 of 1985, issued July 15, 1986, was for $35,055,000, equal to 80 percent of the original cost of the equipment financed. This equipment consisted of 25 diesel electric road freight locomotives with a cost of $30,155,375 (cost per locomotive, $1,206,215) and 384 trilevel auto racks with a cost of $13,664,960 ($35,386 each) for a total of $43,820,335. Although modern equipment is longer-lived than that of many years ago, the ETC's length of maturity has not been increased from the standard 15 years. Assuming a 20-year equipment life with straight line depreciation, there will be a positive margin of equity in the trust. Actually, however, many of the railcars can remain in service for 30 to 40 years without any major overhaul. Also, the structure of the financing provides for periodic redemption of the outstanding certificates.

The most common form of ETC is the serial variety: The ETC is issued in 15 equal serial maturities, each coming due annually from the end of the first year to the end of the fifteenth. The Union Pacific offering consisted of 15 serial maturities of $2,337,000 due each July 15 from 1987 through 2001. The dividend rates ranged from 6.5 percent for the first serial due July 15, 1987, to 7.875 percent for the tranches maturing on July 15, 1999 to 2001. There are also sinking fund equipment trust certificates that are retired through the operation of a normal sinking fund, one-fifteenth of the original amount issued per year. Thus, the Louisville and Nashville Railroad Company's 12.30% Equipment Trust Certificates, Series 10, due February 1, 1995 (original issue, $53,600,000), has an annual sinking fund of $3,575,000 designed to retire 93.4 percent of the issue prior to maturity.

Table 1-7 shows how the Union Pacific equipment trust will look over the years. The first column is the time span from acquisition to the end of year 20. The second column shows the depreciated value of the equipment using straight line depreciation over 20 years at 5 percent per year. The third column estimates what the equipment's liquidation or market value will be at the end of the various years. As with most equipment, the assumed liquidating value drops more rapidly in the earlier than in the later years. This table makes clear the increasing cushion between the amount of certificates outstanding (they are being retired at a rate of 6.67 percent a year) and the equipment's depreciated and liquidation values. At the end of year 20 the equipment, whose title reverted to the railroad at the end of the fifteenth year, has an estimated scrap value of $6,648,623 and is fully depreciated. In reality the scrap value may vary greatly, depending on the condition and type of the equipment, its estimated remaining usefulness, and the economic climate. Much of this rolling stock can be restored to good operating condition. Standard equipment is more generally useful than specialized stock with limited appeal and markets. Of course, we assume standard gauge equipment, which is the norm for most U.S. railroads.

The standing of railroad or common carrier equipment trust certificates in bankruptcy is of vital importance to the investor. As the equipment is needed for operations, it is likely that the bankrupt railroad's management will reaffirm the lease of the equipment because without rolling stock, it is out of business. One of the first things the trustees of the Penn Central Transportation Company did

Table 1-7
UNION PACIFIC RAILROAD COMPANY
Equipment Trust No. 1 of 1985
Estimated Value of the Security for an Equipment Trust Certificate
Relative to Outstanding Obligations over a 20-Year Period

Period	Value of Equipment		ETCs Outstanding	Cushion between ETCs Outstanding and	
	Depreciated	Liquidation		Depreciated Value	Liquidation Value
Acquisition	$43,820,335	$43,820,335	$35,055,000	$8,765,335	$8,765,335
End of year:					
1	41,629,318	35,056,268	32,718,000	8,911,318	2,338,268
2	39,438,302	31,550,641	30,381,000	9,057,302	1,169,641
3	37,247,285	28,711,083	28,044,000	9,203,285	667,083
4	35,056,268	26,414,197	25,707,000	9,349,268	707,197
5	32,865,251	24,301,061	23,370,000	9,495,251	931,061
6	30,674,235	22,356,976	21,033,000	9,641,235	1,323,976
7	28,483,218	20,791,988	18,696,000	9,787,218	2,095,988
8	26,292,201	19,336,549	16,359,000	9,933,201	2,977,549
9	24,101,184	17,982,990	14,022,000	10,079,184	3,960,990
10	21,910,168	16,724,181	11,685,000	10,225,168	5,039,181
11	19,719,151	15,553,488	9,348,000	10,371,151	6,205,488
12	17,528,134	14,464,744	7,011,000	10,517,134	7,453,744
13	15,337,117	13,018,270	4,674,000	10663,117	8,344,270
14	13,146,101	12,106,991	2,337,000	10,809,101	9,769,991
15	10,955,084	11,259,501	0	0	0
16	8,764,067	10,133,551	0	0	0
17	6,573,050	9,120,196	0	0	0
18	4,382,034	8,208,177	0	0	0
19	2,191,017	7,387,359	0	0	0
20	0	6,648,623	(scrap value)	0	0

after the firm filed for bankruptcy on June 21, 1970, was to reaffirm its equipment debt. On August 19, the court issued the required equipment debt assumption orders.[20] There was about $90.7 million of equipment trust certificate issues outstanding, $442.9 million of conditional sales agreements, and unexpired lease rental payments on other contracts of $594 million. It was not until the end of 1978 that investors started to recover something from their other Penn Central debt obligations. Cases of disaffirmation of equipment obligations are very rare. If equipment debt were disaffirmed, the trustee could repossess and then release or sell it to others. Any deficiency due the equipment debtholders would still be a claim against the bankrupt railway company. Standard equipment should not be difficult to release to another railroad.

The Bankruptcy Reform Act of 1978 covers railroad reorganizations in subchapter IV of Chapter 11 and grants them special treatment and protection. One very important feature in Section 77(j) of the preceding Bankruptcy Act was carried over to the new law. Section 1168 states that section 362 (the automatic stay provision) and section 363 (the use, sale, or lease of property section) are not applicable in railroad bankruptcies. It protects the rights of the equipment lenders while giving the trustees the chance to cure any defaults. Equipment debt of non-common carriers such as private car lines (Trailer Train, Union Tank Car, General American Transportation, etc.) does not enjoy this special handling.[21] Railroad bankruptcies usually do not occur overnight but creep up gradually as the result of continuous deterioration. New equipment financing capability becomes restrained. The outstanding equipment debt at the time of bankruptcy often is not substantial, and the outstanding portion contains a fair amount of equity.

ETCs have been issued even in reorganization. An interesting example due to the dividend rate (especially when compared with rates of only a few years ago) is the issue of Chicago & North Western Railway Company Trustees' Equipment Trust Certificate, 2½% of 1939. The $1,800,000 offering made on November 24, 1939, was sold at yields ranging from 0.45 percent for the December 15, 1940, maturity to 2.85 percent for the December 15, 1949, piece. The funds raised paid approximately 76.2 percent of the equipment's cost.

During this century, losses have been rare and delayed payments of dividends and principal only slightly less so. Detroit, Toledo and Ironton Railway Company defaulted in June 1908 on $40,000 of 4½% Equipment Notes. The face value less a small amount of expenses was eventually realized.[22] Seaboard Airline Railroad and Wabash Railway company required holders of maturing equipment obligations to either extend their maturities for a short period or exchange them for Trustees' or Receivers' Certificates of lower coupon. There were a couple of other delays of principal and/or dividend payments, but these were limited to the grace period. Due to the strong position of the lien on equipment and loans by the Reconstruction Finance Corporation (RFC) to some railroads, losses were minimal during the Great Depression. This is especially noteworthy in view of the sharp drop in commodity prices and traffic that resulted in a decline in equipment value. During the thirties, some railways even had surplus equipment.

One railroad that defaulted and caused investors a loss was Florida East Coast Railway Company (see Table 1-8). In most Wall Street literature on equipment financing, this case appears only as a historical footnote; however, it is interesting even though it is history and laws have changed.[23]

In the early 1920s, Florida experienced boom conditions. Florida East Coast Railway Company improved and extended its track and rolling stock. This resulted in excessive plant capacity for the business at hand. In 1922 the company operated about 765 miles of track, 131 locomotives, 147 passenger cars, and 2,791 freight and other cars. In 1926 FEC operated 849 miles of track plus 326 miles of extra main track, 250 locomotives, 321 passenger cars, and 3,428 freight and other cars. Table 1-9 presents some interesting company statistics from 1922 to 1933. Note the sharp increase and subsequent decline in revenues, the jump in debt from 1924 to 1926 and the concomitant rise in fixed charges, and the trends in passenger and freight density.

On September 1, 1931, the railroad entered receivership and defaulted on the interest payment due on its 5% Gold Series A First and Refunding Bonds due September 1, 1974 (issued September 1924, May, 1925, and March 1926). The March 1, 1932, $80,000 payment due on the 4½% Series E Equipment Trust Certificates was paid in May 1932. In April 1932 the Reconstruction Finance Corporation ap-

Table 1-8
FLORIDA EAST COAST RAILWAY COMPANY
(Selected Details)

Incorporated: May 28, 1892
Receivership: September 1, 1931
Trustees appointed: April 21, 1941
Emerged from receivership: January 1, 1961

Subject Securities

Equipment Trust Certificates, 5% Gold, Series D, due $125,000 each July 1, 1925 to July 1, 1939.

Original Issue: $1,875,000

Offered at 99.75 in June 1924 by J. P. Morgan & Company, First National Bank, and National City Company, New York.

Original Trustees: Bankers Trust Company

Successor Trustee: New York Trust Company

Security: 20   mountain-type locomotives
                     5   switching locomotives
                     3   steel passenger cars
                   200   steel underframe box cars
                    20   caboose cars
                   100   ballast cars

Cost of equipment: $2,387,400

Company equity: $512,400 (21.45 percent)

Rating history: Moody's: 1927   Aa
                                  1932   Baa
                                  1935   Ba
                                  1937   Not rated

proved a loan to the receivers of $918,373, of which $627,075 was taken down. The funds were used to meet maturities and interest payments due March 1 and October 1, 1932. The $125,000 Series D Certificates maturing on July 1, 1932, were extended to July 1, 1935, and the interest due was paid in August 1932. The July 1, 1933, maturity was extended to July 1, 1936, but interest was paid. The next two maturities, July 1, 1934, and July 1, 1935, were not paid, nor were interest payments due July 1, 1934, January 1, 1935, and July 1, 1935.

On July 9, 1934, the court authorized the receivers to disaffirm the Series D Equipment Trust Certificates. The disaffirmation was filed with the court on February 1, 1936, and the trustee declared the

Table 1-9
FLORIDA EAST COAST RAILWAY COMPANY
(Selected Statistics)*
($ Millions)

	1933[a]	1932[a]	1931[a]	1930	1929
Operating revenues	$6.694	$6.721	$9.379	$11.730	$13.446
Operating expenses	$5.539	$5.701	$6.860	$8.614	$9.438
Operating ratio	82.75%	84.82%	73.14%	73.44%	70.19%
Gross income (loss)	($0.060)	($0.184)	$0.753	$1.191	$1.738
Interest & rents	$2.971	$3.042	$3.048	$3.084	$2.975
Coverage of interest					
& rents	0	0	0.25×	0.39×	0.58×
Net income (loss)	($3.186)	($3.317)	($2.395)	($1.998)	($1.325)
Funded debt	$61.980	$62.160	$62.260	$62.775	$63.500
Capital stock					
& surplus	*$41.840*	*$45.488*	*$49.090*	*$51.626*	*$55.055*
Total capital	$103.820	$107.648	$111.350	$114.401	$118.555
Working capital	($5.962)	($3.658)	($1.712)	$0.573	$1.158
Average miles of					
track operated	839	859	865	863	855
Extra main track					
(second track)	326	326	326	326	326
Rolling stock:					
Locomotives	175	175	175	176	248
Passenger cars	168	168	168	170	198
Freight & other	1,868	1,868	1,886	1,886	3,137
Revenue density (000):					
Passenger[b]	66	61	84	113	130
Freight[c]	250	237	346	456	536

*Based on company reports to the Interstate Commerce Commission.

[a]1931 to 1933 excludes interest on First and Refunding 5s, due September 1, 1931, and subsequently unpaid, and matured Series D Equipment Trust Certificates.

[b]*Revenue passenger density*: This indicates the number of passengers carried per mile of road. It is found by taking the total number of passengers carried one mile divided by the average miles operated. This figure is reduced to a unit indicating nearer than any other figure the volume of passenger business done.

[c]*Revenue freight density*: This indicates the number of tons of freight carried one mile per mile of road and is found in the same manner as passenger density. Revenue freight density is also a barometer as long as mileage does not change drastically. These figures are valuable because their comparison from year to year indicates the trend in the volume of freight business.

Source: *Moody's Steam Railroads* and *Moody's Railroads*, various editions.

Table 1-9 *(continued)*

1928	1927	1926	1925	1924	1923	1922
$13.875	$17.860	$29.427	$29.133	$20.107	$16.024	$13.428
$9.889	$14.376	$20.407	$19.928	$13.270	$10.771	$9.432
71.27%	80.49%	69.35%	68.40%	66.00%	67.22%	70.24%
$1.577	$1.539	$5.906	$5.976	$4.785	$3.606	$2.769
$3.162	$3.197	$3.019	$2.043	$1.020	$0.840	$0.774
0.50×	0.48×	1.96×	2.93×	4.69×	4.24×	3.58×
($1.697)	($1.775)	$2.784	$3.840	$3.517	$2.758	$1.992
$64.245	$64.990	$65.835	$48.800	$30.975	$39.400	$37.500
$55.865	*$57.592*	*$59.177*	*$56.243*	*$52.315*	*$23.792*	*$20.958*
$120.110	$122.582	$125.012	$105.043	$83.290	$63.192	$58.458
$2.519	$3.780	$6.443	$13.578	$13.645	$1.917	$2.193
856	851	849	776	763	765	765
326	326	326	206	25	2	—
249	249	250	207	175	145	131
208	215	221	217	161	148	147
3,376	2,299	3,428	3,428	3,448	2,972	2,791
143	155	269	336	203	160	131
525	802	1,225	1,261	955	728	553

balance of the rentals due on February 24, 1936. At this time the un-matured certificates amounted to $1 million. A public sale of the equipment was held in Jacksonville, Florida, on April 29, 1936, and the trustee bought practically all of it. The equipment was resold in July 1937.

On December 22, 1936, the trustee obtained a deficiency judgment against the company for $820,657, which was allowed as a general claim under the receivership. On December 1, 1943, a judgment of $308,246 ($301,250 principal, $4,669 interest, and $2,326 costs) was awarded as compensation for the use of the equipment and failure to make repairs. The receiver had used the equipment from September 1931 to December 1934 but did not disaffirm the lease until February 1936. Judgment was paid on March 4, 1944, and distribution was made to certificate holders. The trustee received a final payment on March 6, 1950; it amounted to $120,000 in final settlement of its unsecured claim against the railroad.

The gross amount recovered in these various actions was over $892,000, or more than 89.2 percent of the par value of the remaining certificates. After all expenses and fees were paid, the net recovery by each holder was between 68 and 70 percent of the claim. The total principal loss was between $298,000 and $316,000. Some observers have placed the loss at $175,000; our records indicate otherwise. The distributions per $1,000 certificate were as follows:

July, 1937	$422.60	($440.58 to holders who did not sign the February 28, 1936, agreement covering indemnification and payment of expenses of the noteholders' committee)
March, 1944	$152.96	Representing net proceeds of the December 1943 judgment
May 15, 1951	$108.27	Proceeds of final judgment
Total	$683.83	/$701.81

In looking at this whole episode, we can see that the total loss is not that great compared to losses investors have taken in other railroad and corporate securities.

Airline Equipment Debt

Airline equipment debt has some of the special status held by railroad equipment trust certificates. Of course, it is much more recent, having developed since the end of World War II. Many airlines have had to resort to secured equipment financing, especially since the early 1970s. Like railroad equipment financing, much airline equipment debt, under section 1110 of the Bankruptcy Reform Act of 1978, is not subject to sections 362 and 363, namely the automatic stay and the court's power to prohibit repossessions of equipment.[24] Of course, it gives the airline 60 days in which to cancel the lease or debt and return equipment to the trustee. If the airline decides to continue using the equipment, payments resume, including those that were due during the delayed period. Thus, the creditor will get either the payments due according to the terms of the contract or the equipment.

The equipment is an important factor. If the airplanes are of recent vintage, well maintained, fuel efficient, and relatively economical to operate, it is more likely that a company in distress and seeking to reorganize would assume the equipment lease. On the other hand, if the outlook for reorganization appears dim from the outset and the airplanes are older and less economical, the airline could very well disaffirm the lease. In this case, releasing the aircraft or selling it at rents and prices sufficient to continue the original payments and terms to the security holders might be difficult. Of course, the resale market for aircraft is on a plane-by-plane basis and heavily subject to supply and demand factors. Multimillion-dollar airplanes have a somewhat more limited market than do boxcars and hopper cars worth only around $25,000.

Most of the publicly offered eqiupment loans in the 1969 to 1979 period financed approximately 70 to 75 percent of the cost of new aircraft and related parts. The 25 to 30 percent equity was invested mostly by outside financial institutions, which could take advantage of the depreciation deduction and the investment tax credit. These issues generally had maturities of 15 to 16 years. Some of the eqiupment deals of the 1980s had maturities out to 20 years, but in many cases the debt portion of the financing amounted to 50 to 60 percent of the equipment's cost. The lease agreement required the airline to pay a rental sufficient to cover the interest, amortization of principal, and a return to the equity participant. The airline was responsible for maintaining and operating the aircraft, as well as for obtaining adequate insurance.

In the event of loss or destruction of the equipment, the company has the option of substituting similar equipment or redeeming the outstanding certificates with the insurance proceeds. In 1975, a portion of the Trans World Airlines 10s of 1985 were redeemed due to the destruction of one of the Boeing 727–231 aircraft securing the loan. An important point to consider is the equity owner. If the airline runs into financial difficulty and fails to make the required payments, the owner may step in and make the rental payment in order to protect the investment. The carrier's failure to make a basic rental payment within the stipulated grace period is an act of default, but it is cured if the owner makes payment. The prospectus for American Airlines, Inc. Secured Equipment Certificates, Series B, says:

> The Owner Trustee may also cure any other default by American in the performance of its obligations under the Lease which can be cured by payment of money. The Indenture provides that nothing contained therein shall preclude the Owner Participant, the Owner Trustee or any other person from lending American the funds required for any annual basic rental payment or any other payments due under the lease.

Thus, a strong owner lends support to the financing, and a weak one adds little.

Airline equipment debt should be considered by many investors, but it pays to investigate before investing. Investors should look at the collateral and its estimated value based on the studies of recognized appraisers compared with the amount of equipment debt outstanding. As the equipment is a depreciable item and subject to wear, tear, and obsolescence, a sinking fund should be provided, in most cases starting within several years of the initial offering. Of course, the ownership of the aircraft is important, as mentioned above. Obviously investors must review the obligor's financials, as the paper's basic value depends on the airline's ability to service the lease rental payments. Failure to do adequate research and digest what has been studied could lead to a costly and possibly unwise investment.

Many investors have probably wished that they had more closely read the prospectus of Peoples Express Airlines, Inc. 14 ⅜% Secured Equipment Certificates due April 15, 1996, and dated April 17, 1986. It fully describes certain risk factors and shows the company's heavy leverage and recent lack of fixed charge coverage. It points out that the aircraft to be secured is used, ranging in age from 4.5 to 18 years and having estimated useful lives of 12 to 20.5 years, as well as the possible impairment to the trustee's right to repossess the aircraft in the event of default. All in all, investors were buying weak paper. The truth was revealed all too quickly. Less than six months later—before the first interest payment had been made—the company informed all its creditors that they had to make concessions in order for Texas Air Corporation to proceed with its acquisition of Peoples. Probably the most hurtful concession was that requesting the equipment certificate holders to exchange their old paper for new paper with interest rates of 2¼ percentage points less. Thus, the 14⅜ percent owners would get new certificates with a 12⅛ percent interest rate. While the buyers paid $1,000 per certificate on delivery on April 24, 1986, they were worth only about $700 each on September 12 and a somewhat better $800 on October 3. But that 14⅜ percent coupon had certainly been attractive in April!

A borrower can pledge any type of asset for a loan in order to obtain a lower cost of money if the security is satisfactory to the lender. In some cases, the lender's claim or access to the property is somewhat moot insofar as the debtor, even in bankruptcy, will continue to use the collateral under court supervision. A mortgage could be closed off and unsecured financing utilized, as with New York Telephone Company and some others. The expenses associated with issuing unsecured debt are usually less than those of secured obligations, and the mortgage may be considerd an anachronism to many observers of the financial scene. But in other cases, a borrower may be unable to get any money unless the security is adequate. Thus, it may be necessary for one to "hock the family ranch" in order to get the financing.

UNSECURED DEBT

We have discussed many of the features common to secured and unsecured debt. Take away the collateral and we have unsecured debt. In this connection, the remaining two Cs of credit—character and capacity—become increasingly important.

Unsecured debt, like secured debt, comes in several levels of claim against the corporation's capitalization. But in the case of unsecured debt, the nomenclature attached to the debt issues sounds less substantial. For example, "General and Refunding Mortgage Bonds" sounds much more solid than "Subordinated Debentures," even though both are basically second claims on the corporate body. In addition to the normal debentures and notes, there are junior issues; for example, General Motors Acceptance Corporation, in addition to senior unsecured debt, had public issues designated as senior subordinated and junior subordinated notes, representing levels 2 and 3 of the capital structure. The difference in a high-grade issuer normally may be considered insignificant as long as the issuer remains high grade. But in cases of financial distress, the junior issues usually fare worse than the senior issues. Only in cases of very well-protected junior issues will they come out whole—in which case, so will the senior indebtedness. Thus, many investors are more than willing to take junior debt of high-grade companies; the minor additional risk, compared to that of the senior debt of lower-rates issuers, is worth the incremental income.

Looking at General Motors Acceptance Corporation's Senior Subordinated Notes, 14⅜% due April 1, 1991, we see that they "are subordinate in right of payment . . . to all indebtedness for borrowed money . . . now outstanding or hereafter incurred, which is not by its terms subordinate to other indebtedness of the Company." The Junior Subordinated Notes, 8⅛%, of April 15, 1986, says that they are both subordinate and junior, with the remaining wording similar to that of the senior subordinate debt. The junior debt subordination wording further implies that in the event of bankruptcy or insolvency proceedings, liquidation, reorganization, or receivership, all principal, premium (if any), and interest on superior and senior subordinated indebtedness will be paid in full before any payment is made on junior subordinated indebtedness. Many of these legal proceedings actually involve negotiation and compromise among the various classes of creditors. Even junior creditors may receive some consideration, although, under strict interpretation of priority, they normally would be entitled to little or nothing at all. Chapter 11 gives some examples of the distributions made in reorganization to senior and subordinated debtholders of the same company.

Subordination of the debt instrument might not be apparent from the issue's name. This is often the case with bank and bank-related securities. Chase Manhattan Bank (National Association) had some 8¾% Capital Notes due 1986. The term "Capital Notes" would not sound like a subordinated debt instrument to most inexperienced investors. Yet capital notes are junior securities. The subordination section of the issues prospectus says, "The indebtedness . . . evidenced by the Notes . . . is to be subordinate and junior in right of payment to its obligations to depositors, its obligations under banker's acceptances and letters of credit and its obligations to any Federal Reserve Bank and (except as to any Long Term debt as defined ranking on a party with or junior to the Notes) its obligations to its other creditors. . . . " This issue was bank debt and thus had prior claim on the banks assets in the event of receivership, conservatorship, or the like over and above the claim of the bank's sole shareholder (and its creditors), the Chase Manhattan Corporation.

Some debt issuers have other companies guarantee their loans. Normally this is done when a subsidiary may issue debt and the investors want the added protection of a third-party guarantee. Some examples of third-party (but related) guarantees are U S West Capital Funding, Inc. 8% Guaranteed Notes due October 15, 1996 (guaranteed by US West, Inc.). The principal purpose of capital funding is to provide financing to U S West and its affiliates through the issuance of debt guaranteed by U S West. Citicorp has guaranteed the payment of principal or interest on a subordinated basis for some of the debt issues of Citicorp Person-to-Person, Inc., a management holding company that provides management services to affiliates offering financial and similar services. PepsiCo, Inc. has guaranteed the debt of its financing affiliate, PepsiCo Capital Resources, Inc., and Standard Oil Company (an Ohio corporation) has unconditionally guaranteed the debt of Sohio Pipe Line Company.

The use of such guarantees makes it easier and more convenient to finance special projects and affiliates. The guarantee statement in a prospectus might read as follows: "U S WEST will unconditionally guarantee the due and punctual payment of the principal, premium, if any, and interest on the Debt Securities when and as the same shall become due and payable, whether at maturity, upon redemption or otherwise. The guarantees will rank equally with all other unsecured and unsubordinated obligations of U S WEST." While a guarantee offers a debtholder some measure of protection, one should not throw caution to the wind. In effect, the job might even become more complex, as an analysis of both the issuer and the guarantor should be performed. In many cases, only the latter is needed if the issuer is merely a financing conduit. However, it both concerns are operating companies, it may very well be necessary to analyze both, as the timely payment of principal and interest ultimately will depend on the stronger party.

One of the important protection provisions for unsecured debtholders is what is know as the *negative pledge clause,* or a variation thereof. This provision is found in most senior unsecured debt issues and a few subordinated issues. It restrains the company from securing or pledging assets to secure its debt without equally securing the subject debt issue(s) (with certain exceptions). It is intended to prevent other creditors from obtaining a senior position at the expense of existing creditors, but "it is not intended to prevent other creditors from sharing in the position of debentureholders."[25] Again, it is unnecessary to have such a clause unless the issuer runs into trouble— but as with insurance, it is not needed until the dreaded time arrives.

One book on international lending says that "the chief value of such a clause is that no future loan can be secured without at the same time securing equally or ratably all other loans which contain the negative pledge clause. It is obvious that such a clause does not prevent the borrower from contracting other obligations in the future." It also points out a stronger version of the clause specifying that if the issuer pledges revenues as security for a new loan, the older loan will have priority as to the pledged security.[26]

One type of clause reads as follows:

> The Company will covenant that it will not, and will not permit any Restricted Subsidiary to create, assume, incur or guarantee any Secured Indebtedness without securing the Notes and Debentures equally and ratably with such Secured Indebtedness unless immediately thereafter the aggregate amount of all Secured Indebtedness . . . and the discounted present value of all net rentals payable under leases entered into in connection with certain sale and lease-back transactions . . . would not exceed 5% of Consolidated Net Tangible Assets.[27]

Another restrictive covenant has the following limitation on liens:

> FFC will not, and will not permit any Designated Subsidiary to, issue, assume, incur or guarantee any indebtedness for borrowed money . . . secured by a mortgage, pledge, lien security interest or other encumbrance upon any share of capital stock of any Designated Subsidiary unless the Securities . . . shall be secured equally and ratably with such Debt.[28]

A final example says:

> the Company will not and will not permit a subsidiary to . . . pledge, mortgage or hypothecate, or permit any mortgage, pledge or other lien upon, any proper-

ty at any time owned by the Company or any subsidiary . . . to secure any Indebtedness without making effective provisions whereby the Debentures will be equally and ratably secured, together with any other Indebtedness entitled to be so secured.

It goes on to list exceptions such as existing mortgage liens under the General Mortgage, permitted liens, and and purchase money mortgages.

Negative pledge clauses are not just boilerplate material added to indentures and loan agreements to give lawyers extra work. They have provided additional security for debtholders when prognoses for companies' survival was bleak. International Harvester Company and International Harvester Credit Company had negative pledge clauses that became effective when they obtained badly needed bank financing. (See Chapter 11 for additional details.)

As we have seen, corporate debt securities come with an infinite variety of features; yet we have merely scratched the surface. We will look at many more in subsequent chapters. For now, the reader should realize that participation in the corporate bond ring involves careful analysis and study. Failure to do one's homework—whether one is a trader, an investor, or a financial consultant—often leads to disaster. While prospectuses may provide most of the needed information, the indenture is the more important document.

NOTES

1. "See 'Hybrids' that Buoy Eurobonds," *Business Week*, August 3, 1982, 78. This interesting article, although about bonds sold in Europe, is relevant for debt sold in the U.S. market. Referring to these gimmicky debts, one investment banker said, "It's a sign of desperation. All these bastardizations are trying to get investors to take a long-term view when they really don't want to. It's an inflation induced madness." Another said; "We're scrambling to create gimmicks to get cash because most corporations don't want to pay today's [high] interest rates. Gimmicks do help; they're a function of trying to gain the investor's attention." Yet another claimed, "If plain vanilla can't be sold, you need to make tutti-frutti." There will be more about gimmicks in later chapters.

2. American Bar Foundation Corporate Debt Financing Project, *Commentaries on Model Debenture Indenture Provisions 1965 Model Debenture Indenture Provisions All Registered Issues 1967 and Certain Negotiable Provisions Which may be Included in a Particular Incorporating Indenture* (Chicago: American Bar Foundation, 1971). This work henceforth will be called *Commentaries* or *Commentaries on Indentures*.

3. Medium-term notes will be more fully discussed in Chapter 2. Normally issued in maturities ranging from 9 months to 15 years from the date of issue, they are offered on a best-efforts basis by some of the major investment banking firms acting as agents for the issuers.

4. For additional insight into listed bond trading, see Ben Weberman, "Comparison Shopping." *Forbes*, October 6, 1986, 203. See also David Henry, "Patience Rewarded," *Forbes*, May 19, 1986, 82.

5. Ann Monroe, "Big Broad Suspends Trading in Bonds of 3 Phone Firms," *The Wall Street Journal*, July 10, 1985.

6. See Robert I. Landau, *Corporate Trust Administration and Management*, 3d ed. (New York: Columbia University Press, 1985). This book is a good reference on corporate trust indenture trends and practices.

7. American Bar Foundation, *Mortgage Bond Indenture Form 1981*. (Chicago: American Bar Foundation, 1981).

8. On September 28, 1984, a notice appeared in *The Wall Street Journal* addressed to the holders of BankAmerica Corporation's Money Multiplier Notes due in 1987, 1990, 1991, and 1992. The indenture trustee, the Bank of California, had issued this notice, citing a conflict of interest under the indenture due to its merger with Mitsubishi Bank. Apparently, two years earlier a subsidary of Mitsubishi Bank had acted as underwriter for an overseas offering of BankAmerica notes that were now causing the conflict under the indenture and the Trust Indenture Act. The last paragraph of the notice is interesting:

> The Bank does not intend to resign from its position as Trustee, as we feel that this development in no way impairs our ability to perform the duties and obligations required by the Indenture. We at the bank will continue our efforts to provide the best possible service to you and will be happy to answer your questions. . . .

9. Harold Wolfson, "Tell It to the Bondholder, Too," *The New York Times*, May 18, 1975.

10. *Commentaries*, p. 458.

11. Morey W. McDaniel, "Bondholders and Corporate Governance," *The Business Lawyer*, vol. 42, no. 2 (February 1986): 413–460. This article shows the weak position of bondholders vis-à-vis stockholders in today's corporations when it comes to fair and equitable treatment.

12. Forrest McDonald, *Insull* (Chicago: University of Chicago Press, 1962).

13. Prospectus for $30,000,000 Public Service Company of New Hampshire General and Refunding Mortgage Bonds, Series C 14½% due 2000, dated January 22, 1980.

14. Prospectus for $125,000,000 Inland Steel Company First Mortgage 7.90% Bonds, Series R due January 15, 2007, dated January 12, 1977.

15. "Rating 'Secured' Industrial Debt," Standard & Poor's *CreditWeek*, August 16, 1982, 944.

16. Prospectus for 60,000 Units Forstmann & Company, Inc., dated September 26, 1986.

17. See Michael Downey Rice, *Railroad Equipment Obligations* (New York: Salomon Brothers, 1978). This book, privately published and sponsored by the investment banking firm of Salomon Brothers, gives a good historical and legal background on the instrument. It does not, however, incorporate the effects of the Bankruptcy Reform Act of 1978, which became effective on October 1, 1979.

18. Arthur Stone Dewing, *The Financial Policy of Corporations* (New York: Ronald Press, 1926), 178.

19. Missouri Pacific Railroad Equipment Trust Series No. 22, *Equipment Trust Agreement,* Dated as of October 15, 1982, between Chemical Bank Trustee and Missouri Pacific Railroad Company.

20. Rice, *Railroad Equipment Obligations,* 125.

21. *Bankruptcy Reform Act of 1978, P.L. 95-598* (Chicago: Commerce Clearing House). Section 1168 states in part,

> The right of a secured party with a purchase-money eqiupment security interest in, or of a lessor or conditional vendor of, whether as trustee or otherwise, rolling stock equipment or accessories used on such equipment, including superstructures and racks, that are subject to a purchase-money equipment security interest granted by, leased to, or conditionally sold to, the debtor to take possession of such equipment in compliance with the provisions of a pruchase-money security agreement, lease or conditional sale contract, as the case may be, is not affected by section 362 or 363 of this title or by any power of the court to enjoin such taking of possession. ...

22. Dewing, *The Financial Policy of Corporations,* 216.

23. See Rice, *Railroad Equipment Obligations,* 115, 119, 122.

24. Some secured issues are not affected by section 1110 of the Bankruptcy Reform Act and thus would be treated as any regular secured creditor. If the airline could use the aircraft, it could continue as a debtor-in-possession and the trustee would be prohibited from exercising its right of repossession. The secured creditor must be given "adequate protection," but this term has not been explicitly defined. It is generally meant to protect the secured debtor's interest in the collateral. This may be accomplished by cash payments or the granting of additional security. Peoples Express Airlines, Inc., in its offering circular and consent solicitation of October 8, 1986, explained why its secured equipment certificates likely would not qualify for treatment under Section 1110:

> In view of the fact that all of the aircraft were originally acquired by the Company with the proceeds of other financings, the Company believes that in the event of . . . seeking relief under the Federal Bankruptcy Code, . . . the . . . limitations on remedies available to the Trustee would not be affected by Section 1110 . . . which allows for repossession of Aircraft in certain instances. Accordingly, the Company does not believe that the Trustees will have the legal ability to realize upon the Aircraft collateral promptly after the institution of a bankruptcy case. Any delay in the exercise of the Trustees' legal remedies may adversely affect the collateral value of the Aircraft.

See also Louis B. Goldman, Michael J. Album, and Mark S. Ward, "Repossessing the Spirit of St. Louis: Expanding the Protection of Sections 1110 and 1168 of the Bankruptcy Code," *The Business Lawyer,* vol. 41, no. 1 (November 1985): 29–55.

25. *Commentaries,* 350.

26. John T. Madden, and Marcus Nadler, *Foreign Securities* (New York: Ronald Press, 1929), 162, 163.

27. Prospectus for $1,000,000,000 International Business Machines Corporation Notes and Debentures, dated October 4, 1979.

28. Prospectus for $150,000,000 Fireman's Fund Corporation 9⅝% Debentures due 2016, dated October 16, 1986.

CHAPTER 2

MATURITY
CHARACTERISTICS

The date stated in a bond's title may not always mean that the bond will mature as specified. This chapter looks at the maturity characteristics of corporate debt, from retractable and extendable issues to bonds with puts; these features allow the holder to alter the stated maturity date. We will also look at the trend of new-issue maturities over the recent past.

WHAT IS MATURITY?

Webster's defines maturity as being fully grown, ripe, or fully developed or as being perfect, complete, or ready.[1] While these definitions might apply to some bond market participants, we are interested in the financial definition: the coming due of a security, i.e., the termination or the end of a period of a note, debenture, bond, or other obligation. A debt issue's maturity is fully set forth in the indenture and is usually part of the issue's title. For example, we might refer to "Sears 12s of '94" for Sears, Roebuck and Co. 12% Notes due January 15, 1994, or the "long bond" to mean the most recently issued and longest-maturing bond of the U.S. Treasury. Most people assume that the issue's principal will be paid on the maturity date and interest will cease to accrue after that date. But this is not really so; the maturity is the latest date at which the principal amount will be paid. In the majority of cases (at least those of investment-grade or higher-quality issues), the maturity date probably should be taken with a grain of salt. Often the issuer can retire or redeem an issue prior to maturity (i.e., prematurely). In other cases, the bondholder can get the principal back upon request before the stated maturity date due to features in the bond contract.

Obviously, when working with time spans we can use all sorts of measurements. The bond world usually is concerned with short-term, intermediate-term, and long-term bonds. Some use these descriptions without fully understanding what they mean; various bond market practitioners and theoreticians might give different estimates of maturity. As a starting point, let us regard any debt obligation due within one year as the equivalent of cash items. Commercial paper is in this category, since its maturity cannot be more than 270 days from the date of issuance. Also included is any debt, regardless of its original time to maturity, that is scheduled to be retired within 12 months from the date of inquiry.

The author informally surveyed analysts, traders, salespeople, and debt portfolio managers to get their viewpoints on the time span for the maturity of bonds due beyond one year or more. To this select group, short-term debt meant issues with maturities of from one to five years, though several said that two years was their outside limit and one tolerated issues due up to seven years. A majority said that intermediate-term corporate debt matures within five to ten years of issuance. Some held out for 12-year issues, and one included issues with maturities as long as 15 years. Long-term bonds, then, would be those with maturities longer than those of intermediate-term issues. Some would include a category between intermediate- and long-term, but the market generally thinks in terms of only three maturity categories.

For our purposes, we will consider short-term corporate debt as that having maturities of from one to five years. Intermediate-term debt is debt that matures in more than 5 years and goes out no more than 12 years. Finally, long-term debt matures in more than 12 years.

LONG-TERM DEBT

What is considered long-term today may have been relatively short-term in another generation. Over the years investors' perceptions of bond maturity have undergone substantial changes. If one asked if any long-term bonds have been issued since 1980, the reply would be an emphatic yes; however, a generation or two ago, the answer may have been no. Dewing says this about bond maturity:

> The length of their life varies greatly according to the credit market at the time of issue, the prejudices of investors, the type of security behind the bonds, and the character of the business in which the issuing corporation is engaged. A classification of periods is little more than approximate; yet such phrases as "short-term" and "long-term" have crept into the vocabulary of finance. Without holding too rigidly to the limits given, one may say that obligations which mature in less than five years are the nature of notes, meaning by note merely a short-term bond in which the safeguards described in the indenture under which they are issued refer much more to the temporary credit of the corporation than to the ostensibly permanent character of its property. Bonds which run from five to fifteen years may be conveniently designated as short-term, while those that run from fifteen to forty years may be called medium-term bonds. Those which will not mature for more than forty years should be called long-term bonds and belong to a special class because of the difficulty of projecting conceptions of property value into the distant future.[2]

Probably no corporate bond market participant today would agree with Dewing's maturity classification. There is no doubt that a bond with a maturity greater than 40 years is in the long-term category, but most would take exception to Dewing's short- and intermediate-term views.

Today's bond investors are little aware of truly long-term bonds; they haven't seen or touched any, and only a few have read about them. Yet such bonds do exist. U.S. investors can buy a perpetual issue of Canadian Pacific Limited on the New York Stock Exchange. ("perpetual" means that the debt can be outstanding indefinitely and thus has no maturity). This issue is called 4% Perpetual Consolidated Debenture Stock. Despite the word "stock" in the title, however, it is debt. According to *Moody's Transportation Manual,* the debenture stock is a perpetual obligation of the company constituting " . . . a first charge on the whole of the undertaking, railways, works, rolling stock, plant, property and effects of the company." This issue is truly perpetual, as it is not subject to call or redemption by Canadian Pacific. As it has no maturity, there can be no yield to maturity; current yield (the 4 percent interest rate divided by the market price) is its common yield measurement.

In November 1986, Citicorp, a large bank holding and financial services company, sold a $500 million perpetual issue overseas. This supposedly was a first for a U.S. banking concern, although other foreign banks have sold similar undated debt securities. Citicorp can utilize the perpetuals as equity for regulatory capital purposes but as debt for Internal Revenue Service purposes. The tax authorities have viewed debt without maturity as equity and thus have not allowed interest expense to be deducted for income tax purposes. But this particular issue can be redeemed at Citicorp's option starting in 1991, at the option of the holder in 2016, and annually thereafter. On redemption in 2016 or later, however, the holder will get in exchange not cash but securities, such as common stock, perpetual preferred stock, or other marketable permanent capital. This optional redemption on the holder's part apparently will cause the Internal Revenue Service to view the issue as debt. In contrast to the Canadian Pacific perpetuals, the Citicorps are not viewed as truly infinite securities, since they can be redeemed by either party.

Is a perpetual security too long? The Green Bay & Western Railroad's Class "A" and Class "B" Income Debentures are due only when the railroad is sold or reorganized! At the end of 1985 only $2,000 par amount of Series "A" debentures were outstanding out of an originally authorized $600,000. Class "B" debentures outstanding were $6,298,000 out of an authorized $7,000,000. They are not perpetual issues, but they come pretty close. These are interesting items in several respects. First, they are not callable. Second, the disposition of the income is quite unique. After all operating expenses have been paid, then 2½ percent of the par value will be paid on the Class "A" debentures and then 2½ percent on the common stock (based on $100 par value). The two securities will then share, on a pro rata basis, up to an additional 2½ percent (5 percent in total). Any excess earnings may be delcared and distributed to the holders of the Series

"B" debentures with no limitation upon the director's approval. This is a case of a debenture that ranks behind common stock in the disposition of earnings and yet can receive a payment limited only by earnings and management's discretion. But of course, management is elected by the common shareholders, and they have the final say.

Between 1904 and 1934, payments on the "A" debentures and stock were between 2½ percent and 5 percent; in 1935 they were 2½ percent on the debentures and 1 percent on the stock; in 1936 and 1937, both issues received a payment of 7½ percent; nothing was paid in 1938; and 5 percent was paid on both securities from 1939 to 1978, the latest years for which payment information is available. As the Class "B" income debenture payments come from what is left over and also must be declared by management, they have been relatively meager, ranging from zero in 1921, 1932, to 1936, 1938 and 1939, 1946 to 1948, 1950, 1953, 1955, and 1961 to 3 percent in 1965. In most years, interest amounted to less than 1 percent of the par value.

The Class "A" debentures and the common stock share equally in liquidation on a pro rata basis up to their par value. Also, upon the sale of the railroad, 75 percent of the stockholders must agree to accept the par value ($100 per share) for their stock. Any remaining balance of liquidation proceeds go to the Class "B" debenture holders.[3] This capital structure has been described as the "English recapitalization" and "a railroad which cannot be placed in receivership or undergo financial difficulty as long as it can earn enough to pay its operating expenses."[4] Finally, the following poem (attributed to S.C. Barnett, a reporter from the *Green Bay Press-Gazette*) has been written about the Series "B" debentures:

> I've classed among my foolish ventures
> My purchase of "Class B: debentures";
> Those bonds which say in language deft,
> "With all else paid, you get what's left,
> (Unless the Board makes declaration
> It's needed for depreciation!)"
>
> But once in many years, I find
> The gloomy cloud is silver-lined;

The long-dead-ghost perambulates,
The eagle sh—er defecates,
And there I see, upon my desk
A Winthrop letter, labeled "Esq."

I feel a kinship, quite complete,
With mighty figures of "The Street:"
The railroads' thundering symphony
Earning dough for them—and me!
And midst its tones, like some great organ,
I'm one with Vanderbilt and Morgan!

I've got my bonds, I'm glad I've held 'em,
But payments STILL are goddam seldom.[5]

For investors who feel more confident with a definite maturity, financial history provides some examples. Still outstanding and paying (an example is in the author's scripophily collection) are the 4% First Mortgage Gold Bonds of the Toronto, Grey & Bruce Railway Company dated January 1, 1884, and maturing June 14, 2883. The bonds come only in coupon form in denominations of £100. The coupons (40 to a sheet and enough for 20 years) are payable in Montreal (in Canadian dollars, as payments in gold are restricted) or London (in sterling). According to *Moody's Transportation Manual*, the company's properties were leased to the Ontario and Quebec Railway Company for 999 years at an annual rental equal to interest on 4 percent first mortgage bonds. On Januay 1, 1884, the lease was transferred to the Canadian Pacific Railway Company (now Canadian Pacific Limited). The bonds are truly long-term, as they are not callable for life. Canadian Pacific reports that of the £719,000 outstanding, it owns £307,900.[6]

Of a somewhat shorter maturity (but at least of a U.S. company) are the Elmira and Williamsport Railroad Company's Income Bonds due October 1, 2862. The bonds were guaranteed as to interest by the Northern Central Railway but were assumed by the Pennsylvania Railroad Company in 1914 for 999 years from 1863 and eventually became an obligation of the Penn Central Transportation Company. While not subject to call, the bonds were paid in full in late 1978 upon the reorganization of Penn Central. The security for the issue was a first lien on the railroad's lease; the payment at reorganization was $1,468 in cash.

Another relatively long-term bond (at least by present-day reckoning)—and also involved in the Penn Central reorganization—is the West Short Railroad Company's 4% First Mortgage Bonds due January 1, 2361. The noncallable bonds were issued in 1886, guaranteed by the New York Central and Hudson River Railroad Company, and eventually assumed by Penn Central on February 1, 1968. The lien was on 306 miles of track from Weehawken, New Jersey, to Buffalo, New York, a line dating back to early American railroading. Upon the Penn Central reorganization, each $1,000 principal amount of West Shore 4s received $140 in cash, $131 principal amount of Penn Central Corporation's 7% Series "A" General Mortgage Bonds due 1987, $265 principal amount of Series "B" Bonds due 1987, 19.8 shares of Series "B" Convertible Preference Stock, and 8.92 shares of common stock.

The Decline of the Long-Term Bond Market

Today one will find few real long-term bonds such as those above in the marketplace. Certainly an occasional one might turn up in one of R.M. Smythe's auctions or on offering lists of collectible financial instruments, but American corporations probably will not be issuing them. Even the aforementioned Citicorp perpetual can be called. In 1985 one major business publication said, "The long-term corporate bonds is beginning to look like an endangered species. . . . The mainstay of the credit markets only ten years ago, fixed-rate issues with maturities of twenty years or more shrank . . . and shrivelled. . . . The long-term fixed rate sector is now speculative and not a financing market.[7] The decline is attributed to many factors, including the high inflation and soaring interest costs of the seventies, which wrought havoc on the values of long-term debt instruments. Investors wanted instruments of shorter maturity. For example, insurance companies changed their emphasis from the traditional whole-life policy, with its focus on the long-term investment of reserves and the buildup of cash values, to the more short-term-oriented term life and other policies, which are designed more for pure insurance purposes than for savings and investment.

Companies used to finance their long-term assets with long-term debt and short-term assets, such as receivables and inventories, with commercial paper and bank loans. If they borrowed long, they invested long; if they borrowed short, they invested short. In effect, corporate financial officers would try to match the maturities of their assets and liabilities. If they borrowed short and invested long, they could have faced a crisis at maturity. They might not have had the liquid assets available to pay the loan when due, and refinancing might have been very difficult due to adverse market conditions. A well-run and structured corporation with sound practices and financial policies will seldom face a crisis at maturity, as it will have managed its cash flow carefully and in accordance with solid principles.

One way to look at asset life is in terms of a company's depreciation policies. The lower the depreciation as a percentage of gross plant, the longer the assets' book life. Most new-issue debt of the Bell Telephone System, both before and after the divestiture, typically has had 40-year maturities. Of course, depreciation measurements may not tell the whole story. If the plant has been underdepreciated due to obsolescence, the debt's maturity may not match the asset's life. In the telephone industry, copper wire may last for 40 or more years—but with fiber optic cable available, will it continue to be used? Is the copper wire today worth what it is carried at in the company's financials? Perhaps telephone debt should have shorter and more conventional maturities.

If a company's long-term growth prospects are good, lenders may be more willing to lend to it on a longer-term basis. However, the 1970s' stagflation and low-to-no-growth attitudes of public officials and many big business leaders contributed to the shortening of maturity investors' preferences. Even if borrowers would be better served by longer-term loans, it is investor demand that must be satisfied if financing is to be obtained at relatively reasonable cost levels. There have been a number of times when the yield curve was inverted—that is, rates of shorter-term bonds were higher than those on longer-term securities. This has led to increasing investor preference for short-term debt.

With our society's great emphasis on the short-term—ranging from debt financing to managing corporate income statements for quarterly results to youngsters with newly minted degrees but little business experience wanting to become millionaires overnight—it is no wonder that government leaders and major businesses have failed to provide the inspiration needed for America's premier place in the world. The deficit is always going to be cured in the next few years. New laws will shortly lead to a better life (but will botch things up in the long run). The general attitude is "What are you doing for me right now? Let's get ours while we can." While people want action, what is needed is thought. Companies cannot adequately plan for the future if they must constantly be concerned with rolling over maturing debt. This short-term viewpoint does little to improve the soundness of one's bond investment.

Recent Changes

The 1970s witnessed many changes in the maturity characteristics of corporate bonds. In many cases, the stated maturity was shortened to suit the investors' needs. In others, the effective maturity could be shortened or retracted by the investor or the issuer. Still others permitted the parties to lengthen the maturity.

There are few truly extendible bonds in the marketplace, i.e., issues whose maturities may be extended at the issuer's option. Most investors would not buy bonds that gave the issuer the sole right to lengthen the maturity unless they got something in return. The few outstanding issues have been issued mostly by speculative-grade companies such as Turner Broadcasting and Texas Air Corporation. For example, Texas Air's Senior Increasing Rate Extendible Notes provide for their maturity on each interest payment date commencing August 15, 1986, unless the company extends the maturity to the next interest payment date. Issued in February 1986 with an initial interest rate of 12.5 percent, the rate is increased by 50 basis points per quarter during the first year (payments due on May 15, August and November 1986, and February 1987) and 25 basis points per quarter starting May 15, 1987. However, the final maturity can be no later than February 15, 1991.

The increase in the coupon rate is the extra consideration Texas Air pays for the right to extend maturity; the investor is getting something in return. However, since this can be pretty expensive money, Texas Air has the right to pay off the whole issue on any maturity date, extend the whole issue's maturity to the next interest payment date, or extend only part of the issue and redeem the balance of the bonds at the early maturity date. However, the minimum amount of bonds whose maturity may be extended is $25 million. The scheduled interest rate would be 14½ percent for the quarter starting February 15, 1987, rising to 15½ percent on February 15, 1988, and finally to 18¼ percent for the quarter starting November 15, 1990, and payable February 15, 1991. Turner Broadcasting has extended the maturity on only part of its increasing-rate extendible notes, and redeemed a large portion at the maturity dates in late 1986.

BONDS WITH PUTS

Most bonds with "extendible" (or "extendable") in their titles are likely mislabeled; they should be called retractable bonds, since the issuer has the right to shorten the maturity from that stated. This is, in effect, an exercise of the company's right to call the bonds. Many variable-rate issues give the company the right to call the bonds at a number of dates prior to the final maturity. For example, Ford Motor Credit Company has an extendible note issue with a final maturity of July 15, 2006. The coupon is 7⅞ percent to July 15, 1991, at which date Ford Motor Credit may redeem the bonds (retract the maturity) or determine a new interest rate, interest period, and redemption terms. This last action is generally referred to as "extending the maturity." But the terminology is not really important, as what is retractable to one is extendible to another.

This bond has another interesting feature, one that was not often used until the early seventies—a *put*. This provision gives the investor the option to either ask for repayment on a certain date(s) prior to the stated maturity or hold the bond to either the next put date (if any) or maturity. In the case of the Ford Motor Credit issue, the holder may put the notes back to the issuer on July 15, 1991 (the date at which the new interest rate and terms would commence), or hold them until the next put date, when he or she can elect to have the bonds redeemed once again. This option is not a separate instrument but part of the bond itself.

In most cases, bond investors are at the issuer's mercy. They have loaned money for what they expect to be a certain number of years, but this period could very well be shortened if the issuer decided to call the bonds. A call or premature redemption often occurs when the situation is advantageous for the borrower and less attractive for the lender, namely in periods of lower interest rates, when the lender would have to reinvest the proceeds at yields that more than likely would reduce the overall rate of return (or at least the rate of return promised at the time of the initial investment). In periods of high interest rates, when bond prices are depressed, few issuers have any interest in retiring their debt. However, holders of optional maturity bonds or bonds with puts can turn the tables in their favor. If the coupon rate is below the going market rate, investors need not hold the debt until maturity or even sell it in the market place; they can turn it back to the issuer for repayment at the principal amount and reinvest the proceeds in a security having a current market interest rate.

The right to put the bonds back to the issuer is an important option. Bondholders should be aware of the period during which the issuer or trustee must be notified. If the notification is not properly given, the holders will continue to own the bonds, which could be to their detriment. Besides a loss in value, they could be left holding a much less marketable security. Generally, the put option, once exercised, cannot be revoked. But there are some cases of floating rate notes that provide that if the interest coupon is increased after the bonds have been put but before the effective put date, the holder may request to have the bonds returned. The lead time for notification varies from four to fifteen days prior to the put date to six to eight months.

The importance of heeding the put date cannot be overstressed. For example, in 1979 Beneficial Corporation sold $250 million of debentures with a coupon of 11½ percent to January 15, 1984, and 9 percent thereafter to maturity on January 15, 2005. The put notification period was from September 15 through October 14, 1983. The notes were worth close to par at that time, as they could be redeemed on January 15, 1984. However, for those who did not exercise the put the market price plunged; a few investors were left holding a now 9 percent note due in 21 years. The 9 percent notes traded at about 71 in late 1984—quite a penalty for negligence. Only $15 million remained outstanding.

Straight Bonds with Puts

When analyzing a bond with a put option, the investor should price it to both the maturity date and the put date. With these two yields in hand, the greater yield is the one the holder gets. This is in contrast to bonds optionally callable by the issuer, in which case the lower yield is the least the investor may expect to receive.

In the example in Table 2-1, the investor controls the put and thus is assured of the yield to the put of 9.51 percent at the price of 97. But with the regular issue, the investor is not assured that the company will call the bond and thus must used the 9.22 percent yield to maturity for investment planning. In the case of the bond selling at a premium of 103, the owner of the put bonds would not ask the company to redeem the bond at par when it could be sold in the open market at 103 or held to maturity; therefore, the yield to maturity of 8.3 percent is the appropriate one in this case. In analyzing the regular bond selling at a premium, the investor would use the lower yield to call of 8.01 percent; he or she would not be assured of holding the bond to maturity, since the company may exercise its right to call it at par in 1991.

Table 2-1
Example of Pricing Put Bonds and Regular Bonds

Put Bonds	Regular Bonds
9.25% due 11/1/96 Put date: 11/1/91	9.25% due 11/1/96 Call date: 11/1/91
Price: 97 Yield to maturity: 9.22% Yield to put: 9.51%	Price: 97 Yield to maturity: 9.22% Yield to call: 9.51%
Price: 103 Yield to maturity: 8.3% Yield to put: 8.01%	Price: 103 Yield to maturity: 8.3% Yield to call: 8.01%

Of course, the put option is not without cost to the investor. Companies do not normally provide nice little gifts such as puts for free. Let us assume that we can buy three new issues of similar quality. Issue A is a ten-year note with an 8.75 percent coupon and a put at par in five years; Issue B is a five-year note with a 9 percent coupon; and Issue C is a ten-year note with a 9.25 percent coupon. None of the issues are callable by the company for their life spans. In the case of put bond A, we are obviously giving up yield in exchange for the option, since in five years we can either do nothing and let the put option expire unused or utilize the put option to retract the maturity from ten years to five. What is this option worth? If we take a five-year 8¾ percent issue and price it on a 9 percent yield-to-maturity basis, we will get a price of 99.01 ($990.10), or a put cost of .99 points ($9.90 per $1,000 note). We will be receiving 25 basis points less for Issue A than for Issue B (or paying $9.90 more) for the privilege of having additional investment flexibility relative to an alternative straight five-year issue. With a five-year note, we would have to make a reinvestment decision in five years. But the remaining choice is Issue C, the straight ten-year note with a 9.25 percent interest rate. Again, an 8.75 percent issue price to yield 9.25 percent in ten year is worth 96.782. Thus, the cost of the put option is 3.218 points, of $32.18 per $1,000 note.

We must determine whether or not the put option is worth the price. Obviously, the cheaper the price of the option, the better it is for us. If we could pay par for two bonds with the same coupon but one issue had a put and the other did not, then, other things equal, the bond with the put would be the more attractive. However, the market seldom provides such "freebies," and a decision has to be made. With Issue A, you must choose between hold and put in five years. With Issue B, we must reinvest the proceeds at maturity in five years. Issue C requires no decision. Whether the put of Issue A is exercised, its value depends on the level of interest rates and the slope of the yield curve at that time. Of course, if the put bond has more than one put option date (as some do), it is a more valuable piece of paper. Companies such as ITT Financial Corporation and Beneficial Corporation have issued straight coupon bonds with multiple put dates.

Let us look at two scenarios.

Case 1:   In five years the put will have no value if, at the
time the option can be exercised, market yields
on comparable bonds with five years to maturity
are less than the coupon on the puttable issue.

Let us assume that on November 1, 1991, a five-year note is worth
8.25 percent. Our note with a put would then be worth 102.015 (as a
five-year, 8.75 percent issue), and the 9.25 percent issue at a 8.25 percent yield to maturity would be worth 104.04. The put option would
be out of the money—i.e., worthless—as the strike or exercise price
of $1,000 (100 percent of par) would be less than the worth of a com-
parable bond. The holder would not exercise the put but would
either retain the bonds as a five-year investment or sell them,
depending on his or her needs and objectives.

   In this scenario, the investor's total income over a 10-year holding period (assuming a reinvestment rate of 8 percent) per $1,000
note would amount to $1,320.79, while the 9.25 percent issue would
have returned $1,377.24, a difference in favor of the straight bond of
$74.45. In the case of Issue B, the 9 percent, five-year bond, a rein-
vestment would have to be made at the end of year 5. Assuming the
reinvestment into the 9.25 percent Issue C, the total income would be
$1,333,51.

Case 2:   The put option will have value in five years if interest rates rise, since the strike or exercise price
will be worth more than the value of a com-
parable-maturity note.

Again assume that on November 1, 1991, five-year paper is selling
for a 10 percent yield to maturity. The note with a put is worth at
least $1,000 (even though an 8.75 percent five-year issue at a 10 per-
cent yield to maturity would be priced at only 95.173). The 9.25 percent note with five years to expiration is worth 97.104. Certainly the
investor would exercise the right to early redemption and reinvest
the proceeds into the higher-yielding issue, increasing his or her annual income from $87.50 per note to $95.26 (($1,000/$971.04) · $92.50).

   The investor with Issue A who exercised the put in the higher interest rate scenario and reinvested in the 9.25 percent issue at a 10

percent yield to maturity would then have a total interest income of $1,349.35, an increase of $45.56 per $1,000 note over merely holding onto the put bond. In addition, he or she would have 1.0298 bonds of the 9.25 percent issue, assuming even-dollar reinvestment. This would bring the total return to $1,379.91. In the case of the five-year bond, a rollover at maturity into the 9.25 percent Issue C would result in a total income of $1,401.38.

In actual practice, investors would likely make numerous calculations of what might occur and rank the probabilities of their occurrence. No one knows what the yield levels, yield spreads, and their relationships will be at any future date, not even tomorrow. Therefore, a holder of these issues should be constantly aware of their present value and estimated worth under various interest rate and spread assumptions.

We might wish to know the additional income or coupon needed on an alternative investment at the put date that would enable us to recover the premium paid. Recall that the lower of the two premiums at issue date for Series A was .99 points, or $9.90 per 8.75 percent note. Therefore, this is the amount that must be recovered over the remaining five years assuming an X reinvestment rate. In other words, what is the periodic deposit needed to grow to $9.90 over the 10 remaining semiannual periods assuming an 8 percent annual (4 percent semiannual) reinvestment rate? When we get this figure, we add it to the coupon on the puttable bond to arrive at the coupon required for the alternative par bond. (Most of the better calculators now have programs for computing compound and annuity functions.) The coupon required in order to make up the $9.90 cost of the put option is 8.91 percent, comprised of the basic 8.75 percent coupon and .16 of 1 percent (16 basis points) from the annual recovery calculations. Of course, few bonds have coupons with such odd amounts, and an 8.9 percent coupon would not provide for full recovery while an 8.95 percent coupon would provide too much. But again, the bond market can adjust prices, as all bonds are not par bonds. Prices adjust daily as interest rates change; coupons do not (except for variable-rate issues). And while perfect substitutes among bonds may at times be difficult to find, bonds that can satisfy the requirements at hand are often available.

In a rising interest rate environment, the put option ought to lend support to the issuer's price, and the closer the time to the exercise of the put option, the stronger ought to be the support, as the bond would be priced on a yield-to-put basis. While investors obviously would pay a premium for the option, this insurance can provide them with additional flexibility that could well be worth the price due to the volatile nature of the bond market and the wide swings in yields experienced over the past decade. Put bonds are not ideal instruments, but as few mortals are blessed with perfect foresight, they offer some insurance against major market moves in the wrong direction.

Put Bonds with a Morbid Touch

Some put provisions have certain restrictions on the holder's right to redeem the bonds. For example, a few issues provide that no more than a certain amount of bonds will be repurchased from any holder at any one put date. In addition, there may be an aggregate limitation on the total amount of bonds that may be redeemed at any one time. CP National Corporation's 15¼% Debentures due 1997 provide for an annual put subject to no more than $25,000 principal amount from any debentureholder and no more thant $500,000 principal amount in aggregate.

Some issues have a death redemption benefit; to enjoy this put, the holder must be deceased. The legal representative of the deceased holder or the surviving joint tenant may tender the bonds to the issuer for redemption. In some cases, these puts have priority over the put requests of living debtholders. In the case of Cato Corporation 10½% Subordinated Debentures due 1996, the death benefit is applicable only to the initial beneficial owner. The death benefit provisions are found mostly in smaller issues, generally underwritten by regional and local investment banking firms. It can provide an estate with a market for the bonds, which otherwise might be difficult to sell.

In reaction to the increased activity of corporate raiders and mergers/acquisitions, some companies have incorporated "poison puts" into their indentures. These puts are designed to thwart unfriendly takeovers by making the target company unpalatable to the acquirer. All too often in recent years, companies have been taken over or substantially restructured and their debt substantially increased, resulting in lower bond ratings and declining bond prices. The common shareholder may come out all right, but not the bondholders. Bondholders consider this an unfair transfer of wealth from one class of investors to another.

Basically these provisions might not entirely deter a proposed acquisition, but they could make it more expensive. In addition, they increase uncertainty, since in most cases the put payment is not made until 100 days after the change in control occurs. Thus, management has no way of knowing exactly how many bonds will be tendered for redemption. Of course, if the board of directors approves the change in control—i.e., the transaction is friendly—the poison put provisions will not become effective. To some, a friendly takeover probably means that upper management has acquired lucrative golden parachutes and other consulting contracts and can now let the lower echelons of management and workers, as well as bond investors, fend for themselves.

The designated event of change in control generally means either that continuing directors no longer constitute a majority of the board of directors or that a person, including affiliates, has become the beneficial owner, directly or indirectly, of stock with at least 20 percent of the voting rights. In a couple of cases (such as ITT Corporation's 7⅞% Notes due 1993 and Kerr-McGee Corporation's 9¾% Debentures due 2016), a rating change is also part of the requirement for setting the put in motion. Section 3.02 of the ITT indenture states:

> *Right to Require Repurchase.* In the event that (a) there shall occur a Change in Control of the Company and (b) the prevailing rating of the Securities by Standard & Poor's Corporation . . . or Moody's Investors Service, Inc. . . . on any date within 90 days following the occurrence of such Change in Control shall be less than the rating by such firm of the Securities on the date 30 days prior to the occurrence of such Change in Control by at least one Full Rating Category (the events referred to in the preceding clauses (a) and (b) being collectively called the "Repurchase Events"), then each Securityholder shall have the right . . . to require the Company to purchase, and upon the exercise of such right the Company shall purchase, all or any part of such Securityholder's Securities on the date . . . that is 100 days after the date of the last to occur of the Repurchase Events at par plus accrued and unpaid interest to the Repurchase Date.[8]

The prospectus for the ICN Pharmaceuticals, Inc. Debenture offering commented on the change-in-control put as follows:

> The Change-in-Control Put may deter certain mergers, tender offers or other present or future takeover attempts and may thereby adversely affect the market price of the Common Stock. Since a Change-in-Control Put may deter takeovers where the person attempting the takeover views itself as unable to finance the repurchase of the principal amount of Debentures which may be delivered to the Company for repurchase upon occurrence of such Change-in-Control. To the extent that the Debentures are repurchased pursuant to the Change-in-Control Put, the Company will be unable to utilize the financing provided by the sale of the Debentures. In addition, the ability of the Company to obtain additional Senior Debt based on the existence of the Debentures may be similarly adversely affected.[9]

MEDIUM-TERM NOTES

Medium-term notes (MTNs) are debt instruments offered on a continuous basis over an extended period by corporations and their designated agents. An extension of commercial paper issuance, maturities normally range from 9 months to 15 years, although some may be as short as 6 months. Prior to 1982, the major captive automobile finance companies accounted for most of the issues and offered their medium-term notes directly to the public. But with the advent of shelf registrations by the Securities and Exchange Commission and Rule 415, which provides the issuer of public securities considerably more flexibility than before, medium-term note programs took on a new life. The auto finance companies and other issuers made arrangements with the major Wall Street investment banking firms to market their medium-term notes as agents of the issuers on a best-efforts or reasonable-effort basis.[10] In addition, in order to broaden the market for the securities, the investment bankers started a secondary market in the MTNs of the issuers for which they acted as agents. Providing increased liquidity and needed marketability, this action gave investors another outlet for their MTN investments in the event circumstances changed; they would no longer be locked in until maturity.

Total MTNs outstanding at the end of 1986 were estimated at $35 to $40 billion. According to one observer, the growth of MTNs came at the expense of commercial banks' term loans. The cost to the issuer is often less than that of many term loans.

> Many large corporate borrowers have as good or better credit ratings than all but a very few of the banks lending in this market. Moreover, for large borrowers the banks no longer have any special expertise in assessing the creditworthiness of potential borrowers. Much of the relevant information is public and readily available to any potential investor.[11]

The cost of MTNs to the issuer is also less than that of conventional note issues. Agents' commissions typically range from .125 to .6 percent per $1,000 depending on the note's maturity. Costs of conventionally underwritten debt issues can run higher.

An issuer with an active MTN program posts the rates for the maturity ranges that it wishes to sell. Generally these are from 9 months to 1 year, 1 year to 18 months, 18 months to 2 years, and then annually out to 15 years. Depending on the issuer, the note may have either a fixed or variable rate. Fixed-rate interest payments normally are made semiannually and the interest payment dates are the same for all the notes of a particular series. Of course, the final interest payment is made at maturity. Floating-rate and variable-rate MTNs may have more frequent interest payments. If the interest rate market is volatile, posted rates may change, sometimes more than once a day. The notes are priced at par, which appeals to many investors because they need not concern themselves with amortizing premiums and accreting discounts. Any change in rates will not affect the rates on previously issued notes.

The purchaser usually may set the maturity date as any business day within the offered maturity range subject to the borrower's approval. This is a very important benefit of MTNs, as it enables lenders to match maturities with their own maturity requirements. Also, since MTNs are offered continuously, an investor can enter the market as needed and usually find suitable investment opportunities. The available supply of underwritten issues in both the new-issue and secondary markets, on the other hand, might not satisfy the investor's requirements. A particular series of medium-term notes may have many different maturities, but all will be issued under the same indenture. The bulk of the notes sold have maturities of less than five years, with the two-to-three-year range the most preferred. The notes generally are noncallable for life, although some issuers have the leeway to add redemption features to unsold notes.

The initial issuers were the automobile finance companies needing vast sums of medium-term funds with which to finance car sales. Soon other consumer and commercial finance companies entered the market, as they found it a good area in which to get immediate funds in specific amounts and maturities. Banks, bank holding companies, and thrift institutions also have borrowed through medium-term notes. Financial institutions probably account for about 75 to 80 percent of the issuers, followed by industrial companies, utilities, railroads, and international lending organizations.

On the investor side, banks and bank trust departments are the biggest holders of MTNs, followed by thrift institutions, insurance companies, and nonfinancial corporations. Commercial banks and thrifts have used medium-term notes as part of their arbitrage activities. They have borrowed in Europe or gotten funds through term certificates of deposit and reinvested the monies in higher-yielding MTNs with similar maturities, taking the spread between the two instruments. Of course, if they need funds to meet increased loan demand, the MTN secondary market provides an outlet. Although the maturity features of medium-term notes are very important, individuals have had little significance in this market. The minimum denomination is usually $25,000 and multiples thereof, although the majority of the issues seem to require a minimum purchase of $100,000. Also, the commissions on MTNs are less than on many competing investments, and individual salespeople would more than likely steer their clients to more profitable vehicles.

Not all medium-term notes are sold on an agency basis; some have been underwritten. C.I.T. Financial Corporation issued $200 million of 8% Medium-Term Notes due March 1, 1989, at a discount price of 99.875 percent on February 27, 1986. A few weeks later, through a different set of underwriters it issued $100 million of 7.75% Notes due April 15, 1993, redeemable at the issuer's option on and after April 15, 1991. Equitable Life Leasing Corporation sold 12.62% Medium-Term Notes with a final maturity of November 1, 1988. The interesting thing about this issue is that the company makes level monthly payments representing interest and principal repayment. Equitable has also issued serial medium-term notes with each series maturing every six months. Finally, United States Steel Corporation sold 9% Intermediate-Term Notes due in 1992, with the underwriting discounts and commissions ranging from .125 to .625 percent of par.

MATURITY DISTRIBUTION IN THE CORPORATE BOND MARKET

Over the years there have been a number of studies on the maturity distribution of the bond market. Of major importance is the work of Hickman covering most of the first half of this century.[12] Table 2–2 is condensed from his *Statistical Measures*. It is interesting to note that well over 50 percent of the outstanding corporate debt at the turn of the century had maturities of more than 30 years. About $3.5 billion out of the total of $5.9 billion had maturity dates of 1930 and

Table 2–2
Outstanding Issues Classified by Term to Maturity, 1900–1944
($ Millions/% of Total)

Year	Total Outstanding	Over 1, to 5 Years	Over 5, to 15 Years	Over 15, to 30 Years	Over 30, to 50 Years	Over 50 Years
1900	$5,882.7	$252.3	$775.0	$1,388.6	$2,149.5	$1,337.3
		4.29%	12.83%	23.62%	36.54%	22.73%
1916	$15,957.1	$1,116.8	$3,030.4	$4,949.8	$4,909.9	$1,950.2
		7.00%	18.99%	31.02%	30.77%	12.22%
1928	$25,352.0	$2,209.2	$6,110.9	$10.643.0	$3,853.6	$2,535.3
		8.71%	24.10%	41.98%	15.20%	10.01%
1936	$22,081.9	$1,376.3	$6,059.8	$8,941.1	$3,198.4	$2,506.3
		6.23%	27.44%	40.49%	14.48%	11.36%
1944	$19,687.0	$1,140.0	$5,092.3	$10,028.8	$1,538.5	$1,895.4
		5.79%	25.87%	50.90%	7.82%	9.63%

Note: Excludes issues due within one year and those for which information is lacking. Data are for January 1.
Source: W. Braddock Hickman, *Statistical Measure of Corporate Bond Financing Since 1900* (Princeton, N.J.: Princeton University Press, 1960), Table 40.

later, with nearly 23 percent due in more than 50 years. There were 96 issues amounting to $1,214.7 million due in 1975 and beyond, but the bulk of these consisted of railroad debt. By 1916, debt due more than 30 years out amounted to 43 percent of the total outstandings. In 1928, it was 25 percent, in 1936 about 26 percent, and in 1944 around 17 percent. (Hickman's study does not go beyond 1944.) Much of the decline in the extremely-long-term outstandings more than likely has been due to the extinguishment of debt through bankruptcy and reorganization.

Over the 1900 to 1943 period, the number of issues and par amount of super-long-term offerings (30 years and longer) declined. In the 1900 to 1907 period, Hickman tabulated 1,692 new super-long-term issues with a par value of $4,090.1 million. The length of maturity of new offerings generally declined in importance over each succeeding period (with the exception of 1924 to 1931). In 1940 to 1943, only 6.35 percent of the issues offered were 30 years or longer in maturity; this amounted to $674.7 million, or a bit more than 11 percent of the total par amount offered. The years in the 1900 to 1943 period having the greatest volume of super-long-term issues are shown in Table 2–3. Table 2–4 presents the par amount of offerings classified by term to maturity.

Maturity Composition of Today's Corporate Bond Market

The average maturity of the outstanding investment-grade corporate bond has declined over the past decade (see Table 2–5). The Merrill Lynch Taxable Bond Index, Corporate Master, which includes all investment-grade corporate issues with $10 million or more outstanding, had an average maturity of 20.08 years at the end of 1974. This steadily declined to under 19 years at the end of 1978, under 18 years at the end of 1981, and under 16 years at the end of 1983. The average maturity approximated 15 years and 1 month at December 31, 1985. The average maturity of new-issue investment-grade corporate issues declined as interest rates rose into the double-digit area starting in 1979. The low point was reached in 1984, when the average maturity was only 9.87 years.

Table 2–6 shows the breakdown of new-issue investment-grade

Table 2-3
Top Volume Years for Super-Long-Term Offerings, 1900–1943
(Par Amount, $ Millions)

Over 30, to 50 Years		Over 50, to 75 Years		Over 75 Years	
1927	$1,111.5	1903	$173.9	1922	$219.8
1928	902.8	1939	158.1	1930	125.3
1901	854.4	1936	106.6	1900	107.8
1931	770.3	1924	105.1	1915	101.5
1930	767.2	1930	88.3	1902	100.3

Source: W. Braddock Hickman, *Statistical Measures of Corporate Bond Financing Since 1900* (Princeton, N.J.: Princeton University Press, 1960), Table 94.

Table 2-4
Par Amount of Offerings Classified by Term to Maturity, 1900–1943
($ Millions/% of Total)

Period of Offerings	Total	Over 1, to 5 Years	Over 5, to 15 Years	Over 15, to 30 Years	Over 30, to 50 Years	Over 50 Years
1900–1907	$8,592.5	$659.1	$726.9	$3,116.4	$3,270.2	$819.9
		7.67%	8.46%	36.27%	38.06%	9.54%
1908–1915	$9,249.1	$1,510.4	$918.0	$3,651.8	$2,536.7	$632.2
		16.33%	9.93%	39.48%	27.43%	6.83%
1916–1923	$12,138.0	$2,076.0	$3,594.6	$4,676.7	$1,263.1	$527.6
		17.10%	29.61%	38.53%	10.41%	4.35%
1924–1931	$20,764.7	$1,565.0	$4,059.0	$9,415.7	$4,873.6	$850.5
		7.53%	19.55%	45.35%	23.47%	4.10%
1932–1939	$13,533.0	$610.1	$3,793.3	$7,888.1	$840.9	$400.6
		4.51%	28.03%	58.29%	6.21%	2.96%
1940–1943	$6,115.5	$55.3	$1,600.4	$3,785.1	$494.9	$179.8
		0.91%	26.17%	61.89%	8.09%	2.94%
1900–1943	**$70,392.8**	**$6,475.9**	**$14,693.1**	**$32,533.8**	**$13,279.4**	**$3,410.6**
		9.20%	**20.87%**	**46.22%**	**18.87%**	**4.48%**

Source: W. Braddock Hickman, *Statistical Measures of Corporate Bond Financing Since 1900* (Princeton, N.J.: Princeton University Press, 1960), Table 94.

Table 2-5
Average Maturity of Investment-Grade Corporate Bonds, 1974-1985
(Years)

Year	Corporate Master Index	New Issues	Moody's Composite Corporate Bond Average
1974	20.08	19.93	9.03%
1975	19.07	17.99	9.57
1976	18.80	20.39	9.01
1977	18.72	22.83	8.43
1978	18.52	23.10	9.07
1979	18.23	22.01	10.12
1980	18.16	18.42	12.75
1981	17.55	15.70	15.06
1982	17.42	12.90	14.94
1983	15.83	15.37	12.78
1984	15.50	9.87	13.49
1985	15.08	12.86	12.05

Table 2-6
Percentage Distribution of Corporate New-Issue Investment-Grade Offerings
by Maturity Classification, 1974-1985

Year	Short-Term	Intermediate Term	Long-Term
1974	5.64%	28.18%	66.18%
1975	1.73	41.80	55.47
1976	7.34	26.36	66.40
1977	6.39	14.70	78.91
1978	8.75	23.71	67.54
1979	2.78	25.27	71.95
1980	8.98	38.90	52.12
1981	7.02	51.01	41.97
1982	21.48	45.80	32.72
1983	28.00	31.55	40.45
1984	42.74	42.87	14.39
1985	30.26	38.34	31.40

volume by maturity classification. Until 1981, long-term issues (maturities of 12 or more years) constituted over half the volume. Short-term debt was really insignificant, accounting for under 10 percent of the volume for any year prior to 1982. In that year short-term offerings increased substantially, rising to 21.48 percent of the investment-grade offerings. In 1984, long-term new issues were only a mere 14.39 percent of all investment-grade corporates. It should be noted that in our calculations, if an issue has a put exercisable at the holder's option, the maturity is considered to be the first put date, not the maximum maturity. Also, medium-term note offerings under a best-efforts basis are not included in our figures.

Table 2-7 indicates the average maturity for new-issue investment-grade offerings by industry classification. The industry with the longest maturity debt on average is telecommunications. Bell System issuers traditionally have used relatively long-term bonds in their financing activities, with maturities out to 40 years. Electric utilities have issued debt with maturities in the 30- to 35-year range. But investor demand for shorter maturities has even affected the utility industries. In 1981, the average new telephone and electric issue was of considerably shorter maturity than that of several years prior. Industrial companies, also traditional users of long-term funds, have had to shorten the maturities of their new-issue offerings, from slightly under 20 years in 1974 to 14.25 years in 1985.

Table 2-7
Average Maturity of Corporate New Issues
By Industry Classification
(Selected Years)

Industry	1985	1981	1978	1974
Telecommunications	29.35	26.50	37.24	31.87
Electric	23.60	16.87	25.49	20.39
Gas and water	12.44	12.81	17.77	16.00
Industrials	14.25	17.79	19.79	19.87
Finance	6.41	11.55	16.82	10.48
Banks and thrifts	8.21	6.38	15.87	17.87
Transportation	15.29	17.28	18.00	19.85
International	12.72	11.35	17.83	22.69

It is interesting to note that the average maturity of bank issues has fallen by more than half, from 17.87 years in 1974 to 8.21 years in 1985 (after reaching only 6.38 years in 1981). Finance company issues have also experienced a sharp reduction in average maturity, especially since 1978. Is this because investors want shorter maturity issues due to the difficulties these financial institutions have faced in the eighties? Are they concerned about loans to oil companies, real estate loans in the oil belt, consumer loans to residents of troubled areas, loans to over extended farmers, or borrowings by Third World nations that may never be able to repay? Are these investors thinking that a shorter maturity may provide them with greater protection and peace of mind than a longer issue in the case of a troubled thrift or bank? Seeking refuge in a shorter maturity issue should not provide comfort to an investor.

The shorter maturity structure of corporate debt over the past decade increases pressures on corporate financial managers. The more frequent refinancings needed to replace a heavier volume of maturing debt also adds to management's burden and to the pressures and distortions in the corporate bond market. A greater portion of a corporation's cash flow might have to be redirected away from potentially profitable investments toward the repayment of obligations as they become due. We often hear corporations and other borrowers say that although their assets exceed their liabilities, they are in a temporary cash bind because of maturing debt obligations.

NOTES

1. *Webster's New Universal Unabridged Dictionary*, 2d ed. (New York: Dorset & Baber, 1983).

2. Arthur Stone Dewing, *The Financial Policy of Corporations* (New York: Ronald Press, 1941), 180.

3. In addition to the description of the issues in *Moody's Transportation Manual*, see Ray Specht and Ellen Specht, *The Story of the Green Bay and Western*, Bulletin 115, October 1966, Railway and Locomotive Historical Society.

4. Ibid., 28.

5. Ibid., 29.

6. Letter to the author, March 24, 1981.

7. Elizabeth, Kaplan, "The Waning of the Long-Term Bond," *Dun's Business Month*, June 1985, 40–42.

8. *Indenture between ITT Corporation and The Bank of New York, Trustee,* dated as of April 15, 1986, $100,000,000 7 ⅞% Notes due April 15, 1993.

9. Prospectus for $100,000,000 ICN Pharmaceuticals, Inc. 12 ⅞% Sinking Fund Debentures due July 15, 1998, dated July 17, 1986.

10. Prospectuses of issues for which Merrill Lynch Capital Markets is the agent contain wording such as "The Notes are being offered on a continuing basis by the Company through . . . who have agreed to use their best efforts to solicit purchasers of the Notes." Several of the issues for which Goldman, Sachs & Co. is the agent state that "Offers to purchase the Notes are being solicited, on a reasonable efforts basis, from time to time by the Agents on behalf of the Company." Is a best-efforts basis better than a reasonable-efforts basis?

11. Ben Weberman, "Watching $40 Billion Walk Out the Door," *Forbes,* October 20, 1986, 33–34.

12. Braddock Hickman, W. *Statistical Measures of Corporate Bond Financing Since 1900* (Princeton, N.J.: Princeton University Press, 1960).

CHAPTER 3

COUPON CHARACTERISTICS OF CORPORATE BONDS

There are numerous variations in the interest payments corporations set on their debt instruments. These range from zero and nominal interest rates to interest rates that fluctuate periodically based on an index or other measurement. A bond's value is chiefly determined by the payments it is expected to generate.

GENERAL CHARACTERISTICS OF INTEREST PAYMENTS

Investors lend money and in return expect to receive some form of consideration for its use, usually periodic payments in the form of interest. The most common form of interest rate is that fixed for the life of the issue—the so-called straight or fixed coupon. Since the early seventies, the floating-rate or variable-coupon bond has increasingly attracted investor demand; their coupons may fluctuate over the issues' life. Sometimes the debt instrument provides for no periodic interest payment but a lump-sum payment at maturity—the zero coupon issue. Bond market convention calls these payments "coupons" even though all bonds now sold in the United States are in registered form. "Interest payment" or "interest rate" would be more accurate. "Coupon," of course, comes from the time when bonds were sold with coupons attached representing the interest payments to be made over their lives. Thus, when you hear a trader ask "What's the coupon on that bond?", take it to mean "What is the interest rate?"

Timing of Interest Payments

Most debt issues sold in the United States provide for the payment of interest twice a year. If the interest rate on a $1,000 bond is 10 percent, the bond will have two $50 payments every year. In some cases, such as that of medium-term notes (discussed in Chapter 2), interest is paid semianually and at maturity. The payment at maturity will be less than $50 on a 10 percent issue if the maturity date does not coincide with the interest payment date; this is called a "short coupon." Another type of short coupon is found on some new issues on which the interest might accrue from the date the trade settles; that is, the date payment is made by the purchaser to the underwriter. For example, if a new issue is sold with a settlement date of September 15 but interest payment dates of March 1 and September 1, the bond's price may exclude interest from September 1. In this case, the first interest payment, on March 1, will represent interest on the use of the money for 5.5 months. If the offering terms call for the buyer to pay the offering price plus accrued interest from September 1 until the settlement date of the transaction, interest payment due on March 1 will be a full coupon payment. If this bond were sold in August and settled on August 22, the first interest payment would be called a "long coupon," as it would be for slightly more than six months' interest.

Thus, semiannual payments would be, say, each January and July 1 or March and September 15. These would be abbreviated in many debt publications as "J&J1" or "M&S15." The first or the fifteenth of the month are the most common interest payment dates. Some issues pay at the end of the month or some other date. For example, John Deere Credit Company has several issues with interest payments due on April 30 and October 31; the 11% Notes of Sun Trust Banks, Inc. pay interest on March 31 and September 30; Indiana Bell Telephone 10% Debentures due in 2010 pay interest on April 10 and October 10.

Bonds with only one interest payment a year (annual coupons) are popular overseas but are quite rare in this country. However, this does not mean that they don't exist. Ford Motor Credit Company has several issues in the public market that pay only annually. It sold four issues of annual adjustable-rate notes in 1984 and 1985, raising $475 million. Upon emerging from reorganization in 1984, Wickes Companies, Inc. issued 12% Debentures due January 31, 1994. The interesting feature of this debt is that interest is payable annually on January 31, 1986 (accuring from February 1, 1985), and 1987, then switches to semiannual payments commencing July 31, 1987. Bond issues with more than two interest payments a year are also fairly scarce. There are a number of domestically issued floating-rate notes with quarterly interest payments but not many with straight coupons. However, CP National Corporations 10.375% Debentures of 1991 and 16.50% Debentures due 1996 pay interest on the last day of May, June, September, and December.

Bonds paying interest monthly are rarely encountered. However, in August 1982 General Motors Acceptance Corporation sold $60 million of notes due September 1, 1997. The issues was divided into two tranches whose only differences were the interest rate and the frequency of interest payments. The 12.9 percent notes totaled $54,350,000 and paid interest March 1 and September 1; the balance of $5,650,000 consisted 12.5 percent notes with interest payable on the first of each month starting October 1. The prospectus said, "The lower stated interest rate on the Notes with interest payable monthly . . . reflects in part the earlier and more frequent payment of interest on the Monthly Notes than on the Notes with interest payable semi-annually."

The buyers of the monthly notes receive $10.41667 per $1,000 note each payment, or a total of $125 a year. The 12.9 percent semiannual issue pays $64.50 every six months, or $129 annually. Are the buyers of the monthly payment notes getting $4 less per note per year? The answer is yes—but the two yields are not equivalent. Compounding is a very important element when discussing bond returns. The whole concept of yield to maturity involves some basic assumptions, for examples, that the interest earned from an investment will be reinvested at a rate equal to its purchase or contract yield. In fact, interest on interest for long-term bonds can account for a substantial portion of their total return.[1] Of course, no one knows the exact reinvestment rates obtainable in the future. If the reinvestment rate averages more than the purchase yield, the effective total return will be greater. If it averages less than the purchase yield, the real total return will be less than that initially expected. Thus, promised rates of return as expressed through yields to maturity may not be the realized rates of return.

The semiannual investor can reinvest the $64.50 only once—when he or she receives it. Thus, in a six-month period this will grow by $4.16 to $68.16 assuming conventional compounding at the purchase yield of 12.9 percent (6.45 percent for six months). At the end of one year this will amount to $133.16, of which $4.16 is interest on interest and $129 from the two semiannual interest payments.

The monthly interest payment is compounded at one-twelfth the nominal interest rate of 12.5 percent (0.104167 percent). This results in total interest payments of $125 and interest earned on interest of $7.42, for a total of 132.42. The compounding makes up much, but not all, of the $4 difference. The monthly noteholder is still short by $0.74 per year. If the monthly pay note had a nominal annual coupon of 12.57 percent, the compounding effects would make this equivalent to the 12.9 percent semiannual issue. Of course, one should keep in mind that the issuer bears additional costs in making more frequent interest payments. Someone has to pay the cost, and in this case it is the bond buyer.

Normally, interest (as well as principal) payments due on a Sunday or holiday are paid on the next business day without additional interest for the extra period. Indentures might have a clause covering this in the covenant section or in the article of miscellaneous provisions. Beneficial Finance has the following provision:

Section 14.03. *Payments Due on Sundays and Holidays.* In any case where the date of maturity of principal or interest on any Securities or the date fixed for redemption of any Securities shall be a Sunday or legal holiday or a day on which banking institutions in the State of New York are authorized by law to close, then payment of interest or principal and premium, if any, may be made on the next succeeding business day with the same force and effect as if made on the date of maturity or the date fixed for redemption and no interest shall accrue for the period after such date.[2]

Payment and Record Date

Since most corporate bonds are now in registered form, interest is paid by check to the holder of record on the interest payment date. The interest check normally is mailed on the business day preceding the interest payment date. The record date normally is 15 days prior to the payment date; this is the date on which the trustee prepares the list of bondholders who are entitled to the upcoming interest payment. The interest on the General Motors Acceptance Corporation issues described above is payable to holders of record on the fifteenth of the month preceding the interest payment date; the record dates for the semiannual payments are February 15 and August 15. Interst payments for bonds in coupon or bearer form are collected in a fashion similar to the clearance of checks. The investor deposits the coupons with his or her bank for collection through the banking system from the issuer's bank or paying agent. The agent checks the coupons to see that they are in order and then credits the depositor's bank or correspondent for eventual credit to that account.

Sometimes corporations with shaky credit standings will be unable to make the interest payment on the due date. In such a situation, the established record date for that interest payment becomes void, and anyone who purchases the bond after that date will have the right to receive that interest payment when paid and if still the holder of the bond. When the company obtains the necessary funds, a new record date for that interest payment will be established. Let us assume that August 31 is the original record date and September 15 the interest payment date. Fund are not on hand, and thus the interest payment is not made on September 15. Several weeks later monies become available, allowing payment to be made. A new, special record date will be set for the late interest payment, generally no more than 15 or fewer than 10 days prior to the new payment date. Holders of record on that *new* date will be entitled to the interest payment. Section 307 of the registered version of the Model Debenture Indenture provides for the payment of defaulted interest.

Accrued Interest

The purchase of a bond usually requires payment in an amount equal to the agreed-upon sales price plus another sum for the interest that has accrued between the last interest payment date and the settlement date on the transaction (and possibly a commission charge as well). If the bond is an income bond or in default—that is, not currently paying interest—no interest will have accrued and none will be paid. The bond is said to "trade flat" when it does not trade with accrued interest. Some bonds of less than desirable credit standing have provisions allowing the company to make the interest payment in the form of common stock based on a formula that utilizes the stock's price and trading activity. Such issues also trade flat. The seller is entitled to accrued interest only if the bond is in good standing. If the bond is sold so that the transaction settles after the interest record date and before the interest payment date (i.e., the seller is still a holder of record), the purchaser will have paid the seller accrued interest up to the date of settlement. As the purchaser is entitled to the full interest payment on the payment date, the seller (or his or her broker/dealer) will attach a due bill to the bond that assigns the rights to the upcoming interest payment to the purchasers.

For the sake of argument, let us assume that the accrued interest for the trade settling after the record date is $55 and that a full six months' interest is $60. The purchaser has paid the holder of record the proper amount accrued, namely $55. The seller's broker gives a due bill for the $60 interest payment to the purchaser so that the latter will be paid when the seller receives the interest payment. Thus, the seller will receive the $55 interest and the buyer the $5 owed for the rest of the interest ($60 due bill less the $55 accrued interest paid at purchase). If the corporation fails to make payment after the record date, the due bill will become void and the new holder will be entitled to receive payment not from the seller but from the company.

Many holders of speculative-grade bonds have discovered a hard fact of life: They bought bonds and paid accrued interest only to have the company default on the next interest payment. The seller received payment (including accrued interest) from the buyer at the time the transaction took place, but if the new holder subsequently sold the bonds the price would probably be lower and there would be no accrued interest. This can add substantially to the cost of a junk bond, in both monetary and psychological terms. It is often difficult to acknowledge that one has been double duped. For one, the timing on the investment was wrong, as it went into default shortly after being purchased, and the buyer lost more than the stated purchase price because the accrued interest is now part of the claim, which may or may not be settled. Second—and probably even more grating to many—the old seller got a higher price plus the accrued interest!

While a year has 365 days (or 366 days, in the case of a leap year), the corporate bond year for purposes of computing interest is comprised of only 360 days. Each month in a corporate bond calender is 30 days whether it be February, April, or August. A 12 percent corporate bond will pay $120 per year, or $10 per month, and interest will accrue in the amount of $0.33333 per day. Thus, the accrued interest on a 12 percent bond for 3 months is $30; for 3 months and 25 days, $38.33; and so forth. But there are some issues in which an actual number of days and a year of 365 or 366 days are used in computing accrued interest.

TYPES OF INTEREST PAYMENTS

Most corporate bonds that one encounters are the "plain vanilla" type—just a semiannually paying issue with the same interest rate throughout its life. But in the 1970s, as the financial markets lost their hold on the past and tumbled into the future, the finance industry became globalized, and computers became a common tool for the new wizards of finance, complexity seemed to take the upper hand.[3] To some, the more complex the instrument, the better it was.[4] An increasing number of variations in corporate bond structures began to appear on the financial scene. Some of these were good and others dubious. In some cases only one or two issues could be sold, as they apparently did not fulfill investors' current needs. In those instances where the unconventional features made financial sense, the market responded warmly. In the former category were such issues as money market notes, dual coupon debentures, and maximum-reset notes and debentures; the latter included some types of floating- and variable-rate securities and zero coupon bonds. We will look at a number of these modern-day creations.

Currencies

Most bonds sold in the United States by American corporations are denominated in good old legal tender dollars and pay interest in dollars. This make sense, since the funds raised are mostly used to finance domestic activities. Monies required for financing of foreign subsidiaries and other nondomestic purposes can be raised overseas in international and local markets and through banks and other lending institutions. Even dollars can be raised outside the United States in the Eurodollar market. But in the early eighties, some American companies sold issues in the United States denominated in foriegn curriencies and "faux-currenices," as both straight coupon and floating-rate issues. For example, in March 1985, Hercules Incorporated sold 10 1/8% Bonds due March 15, 1992, for 50 million european currency units (ECUs).[5] The issue's trustee is an American bank. The purchasers can pay for the bonds in ECUs or U.S. dollars; if made in dollars, such payments must be converted into ECUs through underwriters' the agent.

The ECU bonds were issued in registered form to U.S. buyers; foreign buyers could get bonds in coupon form. Only bearer (coupon) bonds can be exchanged for registered bonds; registered bonds cannot be exchanged for the coupon form. Registered bonds are not callable for life, but coupon bonds can be called at the issuer's option at any time in the event of changes in the U.S. tax laws that would cause the company to pay additional amounts with respect to bearer bonds. If called, the holder can avoid having the bonds redeemed by exchanging coupon for registered bonds. Principal and semiannual interest payments are in ECUs but may be paid in dollars for registered bonds at the holder's option. The actual dollar amount to be received will depend on the exchange rate prevailing two business days preceding payment. The indenture provides that if the ECU ceases to exist, payment will made in its dollar equivalent as determined by a bank selected by the trustee; this would be based on the ECU's composition on the last day it was used.

Bonds have also been issued in the United States in real foreign currencies, such as the New Zealand dollar (NZ$), the Australian dollar (A$), and the Canadian dollar (C$), by Chrysler Financial Corporation, Citicorp, Security Pactific Corporation, and several other industrial and bank holding companies. Generally, interest and principal payments will be converted into U.S. dollars unless the holders want to receive the foreign currency. The holders bear any costs in connection with the currency conversion, which are deducted from the payments. Semiannual interest payment dates are not the usual first or fifteenth of the month but odd days such as the third, nineteenth, or twenty-second, and the record dates are 15 days earlier. Holders of large amounts may receive their payments by wire transfer from the trustee instead of by check. The governing law for these issues is New York statutes. In the event of a legal action, any judgment likely would be made in U.S. dollars. However, the prospectuses state that it is unclear whether or not the exchange rate between the foreign currency and the U.S. dollar would be taken into account.

Some individual investors (and probably a few institutional ones) think it is chic to own foriegn currency financial instruments. While these certainly may make nice cocktail conversation, investors who follow fads rather than their intellect are often burned. In most cases, foreign currency issues are poorly suited for individual investment. Like speculative-grade corporate issues, foreign currency issues of even investment-grade credit standing require professional management. In addition to the normal credit or business risk and the interest rate risk, they introduce currency risk. Knowledgeable professionals have the staffs and resources needed to follow and research international economic and political activity and the resulting effects on the currency markets. They can engage in hedging transactions to reduce the exchange risk.

The high nominal interest rates on some of these issues should not disguise the currency risk. If the currency depreciates, it will be converted into fewer dollars. The Australian dollar was equal to U.S. $.90 in December 1983, U.S.$0.83 in 1984, U.S.$0.68 in 1985, and U.S. $0.65 in December 1986. The decline has not been steady; there have been rallies. Skilled professionals might be able to survive in these markets, but most individuals probably will fail.

Of course, there may be a time when a currency appreciates in value. If you hold a financial instrument denominated in that currency, you might enjoy increasing interest payments as the foreign payment is converted into more and more U.S. dollars, and at maturity you may receive more for the bond than you paid for it. But we live in a world of paper currenices (not solid, like gold) that are widely accepted media of exchange in financial transaction settlements. Confidence is essential in order for people to accept these pieces of paper; when that is gone, the currency may both buy and be exchangeable for little. Throughout history politicians have been know to depreciate and debase their currencies when things got rough, and it could happen again. Some may wonder if investors are again playing with the greater fool theory. Most Americans do not have foreign currency liabilities and thus usually do not need foreign-currency-dominated assets. Holding such assets is a form of speculation, not investment. In addition the marketability of many issues sold in the United States is less than adequate for individuals due to the small amounts issued relative to those overseas. Also, they are unlisted. Individual and smaller institutional investors should use large investment organizations for their international debt transactions. There are mutual funds available for that purpose. Many of these are relatively new, however, and the jury is still out as to whether their performance will match their promise and investors' expectations.

COUPON VARIETIES

With the exception of floating-rate debt, whose interest payment might vary as often as weekly due to changes in some financial benchmark, most bonds have one interest rate for life. However, a few have been issued with interest payments that automatically change after the bonds have been outstanding for awhile. In Chapter 2 we mentioned Beneficial Corporation's Debentures due 2005 that had an 11½ percent interest rate to January 15, 1984, and a 9 percent rate thereafter. But that was an issue with a stepped-down interest rate. Others have been issued with increasing interest rates; these are known as *dual coupon* or *stepped-up coupon* issues. In September 1982, Charter Company proposed to issue $100 million of Dual Coupon Subordinated Debentures due 2002. Preliminary pricing talk indicated that the interest rate for the first 5 years would be 7 percent, increasing to 9½ percent for the final 15 years. The bonds were to be priced at 50 percent of face value, raising $50 million before underwriting fees. Instead of this offering, Charter sold $60 million face amount of 14¾% Subordinated Debentures due 2002; it defaulted on its interest payments two years later. Another dual coupon issue resulted from the reorganization of Wickes Companies. It issued 20-year debentures due January 31, 2005, with interest accruing at 7½ percent from February 1, 1985, until January 31, 1994, and at 10 percent thereafter to maturity.

In February 1986, the herd instinct resurfaced on Wall Street as American Express Credit, Gannett Company, Hertz Corporation, and Household Finance Corporation each sold a $100 million issue with stepped-up coupons. These noncallable issues had interest rates of 8.4 to 8.5 percent for the first five or six years, stepping up in 1990 or 1991 to 9.3 to 9.55 percent up until the maturity date. A few companies, including Texas Air and Turner Broadcasting, have sold increasing-rate or progressive-rate notes whose interest rate is raised by a fixed number of basis points each quarter. As mentioned in Chapter 2, this can become pretty costly and thus encourage the debtor to redeem the notes at the earliest possible time.

Participation Bonds

One type of bond that has been publicly issued may participate in any appreciation of certain real estate. In 1982 the Koger Company, a real estate operating concern, sold $30 million of Real Estate Appreciation Notes due June 1, 2000. The notes have a fixed 9 percent coupon rate to June 1, 1988. The fixed rate will be reset on June 1, 1988 and 1994, to the greater of 8 percent or the capitalization rate used by the independent appraiser of the company's properties. In addition, on these dates the principal amount of the notes may be increased by the amount of additional interest accrued to the preceding December 31 based on an increase in the appraisal of the company's properties. Fixed interest is payable on this increase in the principal amount.

Finally, there are bonds that participate in the fortunes of the company not through an increase in the common share price, as with convertible securities, but through an increase in the company's earnings or participation in certain assets. Few have been issued, but one, the Union Pacific Railroad Company/Oregon Short Line Railroad Company 4% Participating Gold Bonds due Agust 1, 1927, was called prematurely due to its involvement with the historic antitrust case of the Northern Securities Company, a railroad holding company. The bonds, dated August 1, 1902, were secured by this company's common stock. Besides an annual 4 percent interest payment beginning in 1903, the holders were to receive an additional amount equal to any dividends and interest in excess of 4 percent paid on the collaeral, namely the common stock of Northern Securities. On March 14, 1904, the U.S. Supreme Court rendered a decision in the Northern Securities case under the Sherman Antitrust Act, which prohibited the company from receiving dividends from its railroad stock. The decision also put "an end to the holding company as a legal instrumentality for the attainment of monopoly [powers]."[6] Therefore, Northern Securities could not pay dividends on its shares, making the participating feature of the bonds meaningless. They were redeemed at 102.50 on February 1, 1905.

In a more current vein, Hovnanian Enterprises, Inc. has some 16⅞% Participating Senior Subordinated Debentures due May 15, 1994, issued in 1982. The fixed rate is paid quarterly, but on each May 15 an additional sum may be paid based on a percentage of the company's pre-tax net income, as defined. As long as Hovnanian Enterprises has earnings and the bonds are outstanding, an additional amount will be paid. In the case of Northern Pacific's 15% Subordinated Participating Debentures due February 15, 1998, and issued in 1985, additional interest is payable if the company's adjusted earnings exceed certain levels, and only up to an additional $60 per debenture. The excess amount may be paid in cash or additional debentures.

Income Bonds

Much maligned and seldom encountered are income bonds, a hybird security superior in capitalization ranking to preferred equity but generally of a subordinated status in the debt classification. Today one would think that with all the varieties of debt instruments being created and the burgeoning market for speculative-grade bonds, the positive features of income bonds would appeal to at least some issuers and investors. As time passes, the income bond likely will become financial history, but it could be resurrected at some future time. Most of the outstanding income bonds have been issued as a result of financial reorganization. Some observers feel that this is the reason they have been shunned by issuers and investors alike; they carry with them the stigma of financial failure.

In the United States, income bonds came out of the railroad reorganizations of the nineteenth century. Interest payments were contingent rather than fixed and would be paid only if earned. But earnings can be juggled, and "interest disbursements often depended on the judgement of the board of directors who were likely to reflect the interests of the stockholders who elected them rather than the income bondholders who were creditors of the corporation. As a result, the board might favor directing earnings towards enlarged expenditures for maintenance of property and equipment rather than toward income bond payments."[7] Because of this, a carefully worded definition of earnings and a requirement that interest be paid if earned are necessary protective features. Also, interest payments, if not earned and paid, should be cumulative without limitation.

Failure to pay interest (if unearned) on an income bond is not an act of default and would not, in and of itself, be a cause for bankruptcy. Failure to pay interest on other obligations or to meet other terms of the income debt agreement may be grounds for legal proceedings. It is this factor that is important to both parties to the contract; it lessens the financial burden on a company in times of stress. By not being required to pay interest while it has no earnings, the company's management may be able to gain enough time to straighten things out for the benefit of the creditors and equity owners. It is this feature that makes income bonds similar to preferred stocks; failure to pay preferred stock dividends, whether or not earned, is not an act of default, although it does indicate financial problems. Dividends can be suspended at management's whim. While they are payable from after-tax net income, income debt interest, although contingent, is payable from pre-tax income, thus reducing the net cost to the issuer. But income bonds occupy a creditor position in case of bankruptcy, while preferred shares retain an equity position.

There are only a score or so if income bonds in the public markets today. Most are railroad issues, a number of which are in arrears on their payments. About half have annual interest payments and the rest semiannual or even quarterly payments. The bonds trade flat and have a record date for registered holders. Like preferred stocks, they will trade "ex-interest" a week prior to the record date. Some companies will publish interest payment notices in the financial press prior to the interest payment date, but these often escape notice. A reliable source for income bond payments is the *Standard & Poor's Called Bond Record,* which has a special section on these payments.

Besides being issued as part of financial reorganizations, income bonds and debentures have been issued to replace preferred stock, refund higher interest rate income bonds, and raise capital for general corporate purposes. They have been issued with warrants, with the income debenture usable in lieu of cash of the warrant's exercise price. One major issuer in the sixties and seventies was Gamble-Skogmo, Incorporated, which sold them first through its own securities sales organization and then through an outside organization, mostly on a best-efforts basis, to thousands of people in Middle America. Traditional investment bankers were reluctant to offer these securities; thus, the company relied on a small, regional firm.

Income bonds can be used in mergers and acquisitions instead of preferred stock and junior debt. They can have convertible or participating features. They can be designed with features such as sinking funds and call provisions and be of any priority as to other types of debt. An income obligation of a creditworthy issuer certainly should find a receptive market and be generally evaluated like any other senior security. The income obligation of a speculative-grade issuer should be viewed as no worse than most of the similar debt outstanding. While the certainty of interest payment is less than with conventional debt, the investor may receive at least some cash flow from the investment, which is more than can be said for low-grade zero coupon issues. But as with all securities, it is important to know the terms of the issues so that a proper bond analysis can be made.

Missouri Pacific Railroad Company (MoPac) has several issues of income paper outstanding: the 4¼% General Income Mortgage

Bonds Series A due January 1, 2020, the 4¾% General Income Mortgage Bonds Series B due January 1, 2030, and the 5% Income Debentures due January 1, 2045. While income bonds generally have been associated with troubled companies, MoPac is no longer in that category—the bonds were rated "A3" and the debentures "Baa1" by Moody's Investors Service at the end of 1986; Standard & Poor's ratings were "AA−" for all three issues. These securities were issued in the 1956 reorganization of the company, which had filed for bankruptcy in 1933. They are secured by a general mortgage on all of the railroad's properties and assets, subject to the rights of the first mortgage. Interest has been paid on a timely basis to date; it is payable to the extent earned from available net income (as defined) up to the stated amount and cumulative up to 13.5 percent (three years of unpaid interest).[8] But the board of directors, at its own discretion and subject to the limitation that the funds are not required for needed and desirable improvements, may, out of lawfully available monies, pay the accumulated and accrued interest on the bonds. However, past-due interest on the Series B bonds cannot be paid unless the unpaid interest on the Series A bonds has been paid or set aside for payment. The interest on the debentures is not cumulative but again may be paid at the board's discretion whether or not earned, provided that the senior issues have been taken care of.

Hudson & Manhattan Railroad Company issued an interesting income bond in 1913, called the "Five Per Cent Adjustment Income Bonds due February 1, 1957," with interest payable April 1, October 1, and at maturity. Issued under a plan for readjustment of the company's debt, each $1,000 principal amount can also be paid in pounds sterling in London at the rate of £205-11s per $1,000 bond (a dual currency bond). Interest was noncumulative prior to January 1, 1920, but cumulative after that date. The company entered bankruptcy proceedings in December 1954, and a reorganization plan became effective at midnight, December 31, 1961. The income bondholders received only 3.5 shares of Class B stock. But in September 1962, the company was taken over by the Port of New York Authority through condemnation proceedings, which resulted in the eventual payment of $531.60 per Class B share.

In October 1981, the trustee of Curtis Publishing Company's 6% Subordinated Income Debentures due 1986 notified the company that it was in default since it had not made the interest payments due

April 1 and October 1, 1981 (plus some earlier payments), even though it had net income for 1979, 1980, and 1981. In fact, the unpaid principal amount for the debentures at the end of 1981 amounted to $943,000 and the accrued interest to $870,000. The company claimed that because it had an accumulated deficit it could not pay interest on the debentures even if earned unless ordered to do so by a court of competent jurisdiction. The company's counsel opined that it would violate Pennsylvania law to pay the interest as debt issued in exchange for stock, is considered stock for purposes of the law and any interest payments would be considered dividend payments. Also, dividends were prohibited so long as there was an accumulated deficit.

In 1983, Curtis reached an agreement with the trustee under which a standby letter of credit of a national bank was issued covering interest obligations on the debentures for 1980 through 1983. It also agreed to build up cash reserves for the purpose of paying the principal at maturity. At the end of 1986, the company informed the author that the debenture and all accrued and unpaid interest were paid in full at the October 1, 1986, maturity. The payments due during the disputed time—from the beginning of 1980 through April 1, 1983—were paid with interest on the past-due amounts. It is interesting to note that although payments due from October 1, 1983 (coupon number 54), to the April 1, 1986, coupon were earned and available for payment, most holders, according to a company spokesperson, did not send in their coupons for collection.

Original-Issue Discount Bonds with Coupons

In this section we discuss bonds that underwriters have deliberately priced at discounts to their face value due to interest rates at below current market levels; these are original-issue discount bonds (OIDs). We do not cover bonds that have been previously issued and, due to increases in interest rate levels, are now trading below par (called market discount issues).

Original-issue discount bonds are issues that, for one reason or another, are issued at prices less than the par value. For tax purposes, the OID may be ignored if it is less than 0.25 percent of the par value times the number of years to maturity. If a 5-year bond is originally offered at 98.75 or higher, no OID is deemed to exist. The cutoff point for a 10-year bond is 2½ points or 97½ or higher, 95 for a 20-year issue, and so on. In the case of many speculative-grade issues, the interest coupons may appear fairly current, but if the issuer were to sell a bond priced at par, the coupon actually would have to be even higher. In some cases, management's reluctance to have such a high coupon on the books may be the reason for issuing a bond at an original—issue discount. In addition, the actual out-of-pocket cash outlay for interest expense obviously would be less for an OID than for a bond with a full coupon.

While original-issue discount bonds aren't a phenomenon of the eighties, they took the market by storm in 1981 and 1982, especially in the investment-grade area. Prior to this time, most original-issue discount bonds were issued by speculative-grade companies. While some investment-grade OIDs were issued on a private placement basis in 1980, the first public issue in this era was offered on March 10, 1981: $175 million par value of Martin Marietta Corporation's 7% Debentures due March 15, 2011, sold at 53.835 to yield 13.25 percent to maturity. This was quickly followed by several issues of General Motors Acceptance Corporation, J. C. Penney Company, and Transamerica Financial, among others. By the end of the year, nearly $7 billion par value ($3.3 billion of proceeds) was being traded. In the first five months of 1982, another $1.6 billion of par value ($745 million of proceeds) was issued. Most of these had interest rates in the 5½ to 7 percent range.[9] However, certain changes in the tax laws made issuance after May less attractive to many companies, and volume fell drastically. Since then, the majority of original-issue discount bonds have been issued by companies with debt quality ratings below investment grade.

Original-issue discount debt offered corporations a number of advantages. The interest cost was less than that on full coupon debt for several reasons; some have put the savings over conventional fixed coupon debt at 50 to 100 basis points. Investors were willing to make this yield sacrifice because it enables them to lock in the return on the discount portion of the investment and reduce the reinvestment risk on the coupon portion in the event interest rates declined. Most OIDs were currently callable, but this provision was not too meaningful. Thus, these issues afforded considerable protection from premature redemption compared with current coupon issues, for no company would want to call a 6 or 7 percent coupon bond at 100, especially when rates were higher than the coupon rate. In addition, the issuer could amortize the original-issue discount for tax purposes on a ratable or pro rata basis over the issue's life and utilize the compound interest or economic interest method for financial reporting purposes.

Thus, in the early years of an issue, the amount deducted or amortized for tax purposes exceeds that of the economic method. The company reduces its nearby tax burden and increases cash flow; the amortization of the discount, although called "interest expense," is not a cash outlay. Cash flow is important to the issuer, and the issuer has the use of this additional money until the debt must be repaid. The 1982 tax law change made the tax and financial reporting methods the same for the original-issue discount for subsequent issues, namely the economic or true interest basis. Under this method, the amortization of the original-issue discount steadily increases over the years by the rate at which the bond was issued. It reduces the cash flow benefit in the early years from original-issue discount bonds, but it does not eliminate it. The accretion of the discount is still a non-cash charge to the income statement.

Some have said that because the interest imputed by the discount is taxable, it will discourage many potential buyers. This is true for individual investors who, unless in a low marginal tax bracket, must pay taxes on the accreted discount even though it is not cash interest. Individuals generally would be better off with tax-advantaged investments such as municipal bonds.[10] However, one must not overlook the fact that the main buyers of taxable corporate bonds are not taxable individuals for their own accounts but institutions with little or no tax liabilities such as pension funds, including individual retirement accounts, and other self-directed plans. These original-discount issues have provided those investors with a debt instrument well suited to their needs.

While the 1982 tax changes dampened the incentive of investment-grade companies to issue new discount bonds, there were several other reasons. In times of high interest rates, investors look for ways and instruments with which to lock in yields and their promised returns. Interest rates peaked in mid-1982, making subsequent OID investments somewhat less appealing to many investors. In a lower interest rate environment, compounding or interest on interest is less important than when yields are high. Investors may hesitate to invest in what seems like a relatively low-guaranteed rate of return if they think that rates will rise again in the future and thus enable them to reinvest at higher yields. Also, the lower interest rates reduce cash flows for corporate issuers and the resulting tax advantages, making OIDs less attractive from their viewpoint. Finally, we can expect even less future interest in original-issue discount bonds due to lower marginal tax rates as the after-tax cash flow advantages are further reduced. However, some undoubtedly will continue to be issued.

Zero Coupon Bonds

The ultimate in original-issue deep discount bonds is the bond with no coupon or periodic interest payment. This is really just a principal portion of an issue, similar to stripping away the coupons from a coupon bond. There is nothing special about a zero coupon bond. It has all the advantages of the original-issue discount bond and more. It offers complete freedom from reinvestment risk, as there is nothing to reinvest. Call protection is even greater than with coupon OIDs.A number are not callable at all, but most are currently callable at par. The designers did not even make the bonds callable at a premium to accreted value as did those of some municipal zero coupon bonds. While most are bullet issues—that is, bonds with one maturity—a few issuers have opted for serial maturities. For example, PepsiCo Capital Resources, Inc. sold $850 million of zeros due annually from April 1, 1988, to April 1, 2012. Fluor Corporation, ITT Financial Corporation, and Hospital Corporation of America have also issued serial zero coupon bonds.

It was only a matter of weeks after the first OID was issued for the zero coupon corporate OID to hit Wall Street. On April 22, 1981, J.C. Penney Company, Inc. offered $200 million principal amount of zero coupon notes due May 1, 1989. The offering price was 33.247 for a yield to maturity of 14.25 percent. (Six days earlier, it had issued $200 million of 6% Debentures due in 2006 for a 14.85 percent yield.) Two months later, the next issuer stepped into the market.

One June 24, General Motors Acceptance Corporation issued $750 million principal amount of discount notes due July 1, 1991. The price was 25.245 for a 14.25 yield to maturity. In 1981, the company issued $2.475 billion par value ($778 million of proceeds) of zeros and another $6.89 billion ($1,652 million of proceeds) in 1982. Since then, new-issue activity has greatly diminished as it did for coupon OIDs.

While these issues were new to the corporate bond market, the concept of a zero coupon debt instrument is no stranger to American investors. They have bought U.S. savings and war bonds for years. These are non-interest-bearing issues that pay all the interest due at maturity. Many term savings certificates and accounts can be viewed as just another form of zero coupon bond. An investor buys the certificate or makes a deposit at a stated interest rate for a certain time period. The interest is not paid out but allowed to be reinvested and compounded until maturity. Overseas they might call these "capitalization certificates" or bonds or deposits with capitalized interest. Toward the end of the Civil War, the federal government issued circulating legal tender compound interest Treasury notes in denominations of $10, $20, $50, $100, $500, and $1,000. The notes accrued interest at a rate of 6 percent compounded every six months (3 percent per period) and were repayable at the end of three years. The obverse of the note stated, "Three years after date the United States will pay the bearer . . . dollars with interest at the rate of six per cent compounded semi-annually." The reverse side said, "By Act of Congress this note is a legal tender for . . . dollars but bears interest at six per cent compounded every six months though payable only at maturity as follows [here is found the accrued interest and the worth of the note at the end of six semiannual periods]. . . . The sum $ . . . will be paid the holder for principal and interest at maturity of note three years from date." In April 1879, the Treasury issued refunding certificates in $10 denominations that accrued interest at a 4 percent annual rate for an indefinite period. But in 1907, Congress stopped the accrual of interest when it reached $11.30 for each $10 certificate.

In bankruptcy, the claim of an original-issue discount bond, whether or not it has a coupon, is not the principal amount of $1,000 but the accreted value up to the date of bankruptcy; this consists of the original offering amount plus accrued and unpaid interest. These bonds, especially zero coupon issues, have been sold at deep discounts, and the issuer's liability at maturity may be substantial. Thus, there is the accretion of the discount, but this is not put away in a special retirement fund. There are no sinking funds on these issues. One would hope that corporate managements properly invest the proceeds and run the companies for the benefit of all investors so that there will be no cash crisis at maturity. The potentially large balloon repayment creates a cause for concern among investors. It is most important to invest in higher-quality issues so as to reduce the risk of a potential problem. If one wants to speculate in lower-rated bonds, that investment should throw off some cash return.

Many investors have been confused by yields and returns of zero coupon bonds. There is no current return, as zero divided by the price is zero. Yet the author has heard from many bond market participants who bought zeros with current returns of 20 or 25 percent. That can't be. Where they went wrong was in assuming that the accretion of the original-issue discount is a dollar return or yield and dividing that amount by the security's price. This is a bookkeeping matter only, not cash in the pocket. A $500 investment that will grow to $1,000 in five years produces a gain of $500, or 100 percent of the original amount invested. Some might say that the annual return is 20 percent. This method of calculation is specious and out of step with generally accepted bond world conventions. Some investors confuse simple interest with compound interest, the traditional investment measurement. While the results may look good, they are incorrect and could lead to false conclusions.

The following formulae may be helpful to some investors in zero coupon bonds. There also are many fine bond calculators available that can calculate exact yields and prices for odd time periods.

Formula for Finding the Present Value of 1

$$Pn = 1/(1 + i)^n$$

where P = present worth of $1

n = number of time periods
i = interest rate per period (in decimal form)

Let us solve the formula for a zero coupon bond due in five years. We know that the future worth at maturity will be $1,000. We also know that the yield to maturity, or rate of return based on semianuual compounding, is 10 percent. Thus, for the number of time periods we get 10 (5 years × 2) and for the interest rate per period 5 percent (10 percent ÷ 2). Therefore, the present worth of $1 due in five years based on a 10 percent annual rate of interest is

$$Pn = 1/(1 + .05)^{10}$$
$$= 1/1.62889$$
$$= .61391.$$

To get the present worth of a $1,000 zero coupon note due in five years, we multiply $1,000 by the value of Pn (0.61391) and arrive at $613.91.

Formula for Finding the Interest Rate

$$i = [(FV/PV)^{1/n}] - 1$$

where   i = interest rate
         FV = future value
         PV = present value
         n = number of time periods

Solving for i for a five-year zero note selling at $613.91 gives us

$$i = [(1,000/613.91)^{1/10}] - 1$$
$$= (1.6289)^{.1} - 1$$
$$= 1.05 - 1$$
$$= .05$$

or 5 percent per semiannual period, which is equal to a 10 percent nominal annual interest rate.

Before purchasing a zero coupon bond, the investor must decide whether the total cash flow or return from a zero will be greater or less than that from a coupon bond over the same time span. To make this determination, the investor must estimate what he or she can earn on the reinvestment of the coupon payments. If the estimated return on the coupon bond is greater than that for the zero, the coupon issue may be the preferred investment. Obviously, in high interest rate markets, the zero, with its automatic compounding, is probably the more attractive investment. In low interest rate markets, where the compounding effect is less and the probability of higher interest rates greater, the coupon bond might be the better. While forecasting is one of the more difficult tasks to do with any degree of accuracy, it is necessary for making intelligent investment decisions. As with all senior security investments, forecasting decisions must be continually made and monitored as circumstances change. In general, bond portfolios should not be static but changed as time and outlook dictate. Individual issues and sectors get overvalued and undervalued from time to time, and zero coupon securities are no exception. Historical analysis of yield spreads and relationships may be useful.

Zero/Coupon Deferred Interest Bonds

The combination zero/coupon bond ("zero *slash* coupon"), or deferred interest bond, made its debut in 1984. Issued through exchange offers, leveraged buyouts, and recapitalizations or mergers, as well as being conventionally underwritten, these generally are subordinated issues of lower-quality issuers and have titles such as subordinated discount debentures, junior subordinated discount debentures, and the like. They have been issued by companies such as Owens-Corning Fiberglas Corporation, Metromedia Inc., and National Gypsum Company. Even the Deferred Third Mortgage Bond of Public Service Company of New Hampshire is included in this group. Most of the issues pay no interest for the first five years or so but then make conventional interest payments, ranging from 13 to 16 percent, until maturity. The deferred interest feature allows newly restructured, highly leveraged, and other companies with less than satisfactory cash flows to defer the interest payment over the bond's early life. It is hoped that when cash interest payments start, the company will be able to service the debt.

Zero/coupon securities have been issued with original-issue discounts for tax purposes, and thus income taxes must be paid on the accretion of the discount by taxable investors even though cash interest has not been received. Of course, tax laws, regulations, and their interpretations change over time; investors would therefore be wise to consult with their tax consultants for appropriate advice.

FLOATING -AND ADJUSTABLE-RATE DEBT[11]

Late in 1973, a new security variation crossed the seas from Europe to our shores: the floating-rate note. Rather than being a fixed coupon rate, the interest rate fluctuated at 1½percent (150 basis points) over the prime lending rate of specific banks, subject to the minimum rate of 8 percent and a maximum rate of 12 percent. Only two issues, for a total of $35 million, were issued in the national markets. The next year, 11 issues, totaling some $1.3 billion, were readily absorbed by investors before offerings dried up until 1978. Ten of these issues were based on the secondary market for 3-month U.S. Treasury bills. One $200 million issue was sold in 1978, followed by a jump to 18 issues for $2.7 billion in 1979. A few other benchmarks for rate determination purposes were tried. Again volume slipped, until 1982, when it resurged. By this time, investor demand was being stimulated by increasingly volatile bond markets. Market participants wanted an instrument with an income stream that would rise when other interest rates increased, one that offered some protection against any sustained downturn in market prices through the use of puts. Investors liked the terms, including the various financial benchmarks these securities offered. Some investors with floating-rate liabilities could match them against these floating-rate assets.

The term "floating-rate note" or "floaters" covers several different types of securities that have one common feature: Interest will vary over the instrument's life. It may be based on a financial benchmark such as the London Interbank Offering Rate (LIBOR) or the U.S. Treasury bill auction rate, or it can be determined at the issuer's discretion. Some have been based on nonfinancial benchmarks, such as the price of oil or the volume on the New York Stock Exchange. Floating-rate debt usually has coupons that are based on a short-term money market rate or index and reset (changes) more than once a year, such as weekly, monthly, quarterly, or semiannually; there are no known daily adjustments. One of the earliest and largest issues is based on the interest yield equivalent of the 3-month U.S. Treasury bill: Citicorp's Floating Rate Notes due June 1, 1989, issued in July, 1974. Interest is reset and payable each June 1 and December 1; in addition, investors have the right to have the company redeem the notes at par on those dates. Another example is Wells Fargo & Company's Floating Rate Extendible Note due February 1, 1988. Based on the one-month commercial paper rate, the coupon is reset weekly and paid quarterly. Wells Fargo's Floating Rate Subordinated Capital Notes due August 1, 1996, have a weekly reset feature of 1/16 of 1 percent over the 3-month LIBOR rate payable quarterly. This is an example of what the market calls a "mismatched" floater, that is, the interest reset dates differ from the interest payment dates.

"Adjustable-" or "variable-rate debt" includes those issues with coupons based mostly on a longer-term index and that reset no more than annually. In this category are those issues based on the one-year and longer Treasury constant maturity rate as published by the Board of Governors of the Federal Reserve System (Chapter 6 discusses the Treasury constant maturity.) Some issues may have terms such as the interest rate, interest period, and redemption features set by the issuer periodically during the note's life. In effect, the corporation issues a series of short- to intermediate-term securities of which only the first has known provisions. All have puts available to the holder, for without them the investors would be at the issuer's mercy.

Volume

More than 340 issues with at least 60 debt titles have been sold in this country. The appendix to this chapter lists the various types used to date. Table 3–1 shows the volume of floaters issued in the United States by issuer type since 1973. More than $54 billion has come to market, and an estimated $45 billion or so were outstanding and paying at the end of 1986. Some have matured, some have been converted or exchanged for other types of securities, some have been called, and some have entered the realm of bankruptcy courts (or are just about to). Banks and bank holding companies have issued the greatest amount of floaters, slightly more than $20.7 billion, or 38 percent of the total. This shouldn't be surprising considering that these floating-rate liabilities are a partial match for some of their corresponding floating rate assets. In second place with $15.9 billion are industrial and transportation companies, accounting for 29 percent of the amount issued to date. Close behind are finance companies, such as captive automobile finance companies and investment brokerage firms. International issuers have sold slightly more than $3 billion in the U.S. market; these include sovereign nations, international financial institutions such as the International Bank for Reconstruction and Development, and branches of foreign banks. Utility companies have not been active in this market. About three-quarters of the more than $54 billion were issued in 1984, 1985, and 1986.

Table 3–2 shows the distribution of the issues by benchmark or the interest determination basis. The Treasury constant maturity is the benchmark used for the greatest amount of issus—slightly more than $12 billion. Close behind are those based on the 3-month London Interbank Offering rate and those based on the 91-day Treasury bill auction rate. Other popular interest-rate-setting mechanisms are the 3-month Treasury bill secondary market rate and the one allowing the issuer to determine the rate at its own discretion.

Review of Terms and Features

Because financial designers have created debt instruments with a variety of terms, investors and other market participants should carefully review the prospectus and offering documents of issues that interest them, especially floaters.

Only a few issues have sinking funds requiring the periodic

Table 3-1
Floating-Rate Debt Issues by Issuer Type, 1973–1986
($ Millions)

	Banks	No. of Issues	Finance & Related	No. of Issues	Inter-national	No. of Issues	Industrial, Transpor-tation, Etc.	No. of Issues	Utilities	No. of Issues	Total $ Amount	Total No. of Issues	% of Total $ Amount Issued	% of Total Number of Issues
1986	$3,518.6	18	$2,514.2	16	—		$1,436.3	8	—		$7,469.1	42	13.73%	12.24%
1985	3,934.8	38	4,375.0	30	553.5	4	7,630.6	22	$575.0	5	17,068.9	99	31.38	28.86
1984	5,295.0	42	3,315.0	26	2,500.0	5	5,052.0	30	275.0	3	16,437.0	106	30.22	30.90
1983	3,710.0	20	1,025.0	9	100.0	1	300.0	4	100.0	1	5,235.0	35	9.62	10.20
1982	350.0	3	1,890.0	13	—		775.0	7	—		3,015.0	23	5.54	6.71
1981	250.0	1	25.0	1	—		85.0	1	—		360.0	3	0.66	0.87
1980	250.0	1	250.0	1	—		52.0	1	—		552.0	3	1.01	0.87
1979	2,041.5	14	250.0	2	—		400.0	2	—		2,691.5	18	4.95	5.25
1978	200.0	1	—		—		—		—		200.0	1	0.37	0.29
1974	1,160.0	8	10.0	1	—		157.5	2	—		1,327.5	11	2.44	3.21
1973	—		35.0	2	—		—		—		35.0	2	0.06	0.58
Total	$20,709.9	146	$13,689.2	101	$3,153.5	10	$15,888.4	77	$950.0	9	$54,391.0	343		
% of total	38.08%		25.17%		5.80%		29.21%		1.75%		100.00%			

Table 3-2
Floating-Rate Debt Issues by Benchmark, 1973–1986
($ Millions)

Benchmark	Amount	Percent of Total	Number of Issues	Percent of Total
Prime rate, commercial paper, and other short-term rates	$ 2,632.5	4.84%	11	3.21%
Money Market notes	100.0	0.18	1	0.29
1-month LIBOR	300.0	0.55	2	0.58
3-month LIBOR	10,612.4	19.51	63	18.37
6- and 12-month LIBOR	2,075.0	3.81	15	4.37
91-day T-bill auction rate	10,098.5	18.57	59	17.20
3-month T-bill secondary market rate	5,332.0	9.80	39	11.37
6-month T-bill auction rate	475.0	0.87	3	0.87
6-month T-bill secondary market rate	2,641.5	4.86	18	5.25
Treasury constant maturity	12,181.0	22.40	81	23.62
Issuer-determined rate	5,455.0	10.03	29	8.45
ANZAC dollars	497.0	0.92	6	1.75
Stepped-up coupons	400.0	0.74	4	1.17
Non financial and other	1,590.3	2.92	12	3.50
Total	$54,391.0	100.00%	343	100.00%

retirement of a portion of the bonds. Unlike conventional debt, many have call features that permit the company to redeem the bonds only on specific dates, often that on which the holder may put the bond. Others have fairly standard call features, and a fair number are not callable at all. The put features vary. Some permit the holder to require the company to redeem the bonds on any interest payment date, while others permit a put to be exercised only when the coupon is adjusted. In cases of extendible notes where the new terms, including the coupon and the length of time it will be in force (the interest period), are reset only every few years, the put may be used only on those dates. Of course, the time required for prior notification to the issuer or its agent varies from as little as four days to as much as two months. For example, Ford Motor Credit Company's 12% Extendible Notes due February 1, 1999, have interest reset dates of February 1 in

1989 and 1994. The notes are redeemable by the company at par and may be put by the holder only on those dates. Approximately 15 to 30 days prior notice is required for exercising the put. GTE Corporation's 5-year 11% Extendible Notes due March 15, 1993, can be put only on March 15, 1988. However, GTE may call the notes at par from March 15, 1987, through March 14, 1988, and again on and after March 15, 1992, to maturity. In addition, the notes are callable at 104 on September 15, 1988, if no more than $10 million is outstanding.

A few of the issues offered in 1979 are convertible or exchangeable at the holder's option into bonds with fixed coupons, generally in the 8½ percent area. For some, the conversion privilege has lapsed with little or no conversion for the simple reason that during most of the time they were outstanding, that privilege was valueless. Interest rates rose rapidly, and it wasn't until 1986 that a few investors started to look at the convertible right of these issues as possibly having some value. Others are exchangeable into fixed-rate notes only at the issuer's option.

Most of the issues sold in the United States are payable in U.S. dollars. But again there are issues denominated in ECUs, Australian dollars, and New Zealand dollars (also called ANZAC issues). In most cases, the coupon is set at a certain premium to the base or benchmark rate. For those based on the Treasury constant maturity, it might be set at a minimum percentage of the base rate (and may be set higher at the issuer's discretion). For example, BarclaysAmerican Corporation's Extendible Notes due July 1, 1996, had an interest rate change on July 1, 1986. On June 13, a notice appeared in the newspaper of record announcing an 8.1 percent rate for the next five years—at least 101 percent of the 5-year Treasury constant maturity. Investors could put the bonds on July 1 with 10 to 20 days' prior notice. Apparently a number of notes were sent in for redemption or the holders threatened to put the notes, for on June 26 another notice appeared increasing the coupon by 10 basis points to 8.2 percent. The notice stated, in part, "Any Holder of an Extendible Note due 1996 who has exercised the option to elect repayment thereof may revoke such election by telegram, telex, facsimile transmission or letter to be received by the Corporate Trust Offices . . . not later than 5:00 p.m., New York City time, on Friday, June 27, 1986." In other cases, the rate might be set at a certain number of basis points above or below the base rate. The rates of many 3-month LIBOR-based issues are set at LIBOR plus ⅛ or ¼ of 1 percent (12.5 or 25 basis points), while those of some 3-month Treasury bill–based issues are spread from 100 to as much as 450 basis points over the base rate. The higher the spread, the poorer the issuer's credit quality, all things being equal. Some issues provide for a change in the spread from the base rate at certain intervals over the floater's life. For instance, Citicorp's floater due September 1, 1998, has a coupon based on the interest yield equivalent of the market discount rate for 6-month Treasury bills plus 120 basis points from March 1, 1979, through August 31, 1983, then at 100 basis points over the base rate to August 31, 1988, and thereafter 75 basis points over until maturity. Some are on an either-or basis. Trans World Airlines' Subordinated Exchangeable Variable Rate Notes due September 15, 1994, are exchangeable at the company's option on or before September 15, 1989, for fixed-rate notes due 1994. The notes have an interest coupon that is reset and payable quarterly based on the higher of the 3-month Treasury bill plus 375 basis points or the 3-month LIBOR plus 250 basis points. The interest rate on American Express Credit's Money Market Notes due 1992 is set every fifth week based on bids submitted at an auction; this is similar to auction market preferred stocks, described in Chapter 6.

One usually expects that when interest rates rise, the interest rate on the floater will increase, and when rates fall, the coupon will decrease. This makes sense to most people, but there are some issues the might confuse even many bond professionals. Several companies issued yield curve notes early in 1986. The interest rate is reset and payable twice a year based on a certain percentage rate (depending on its issue) *minus* the 6-month LIBOR rate. For example, General Motors Acceptance Corporation's Yield Curve Notes due April 15, 1993, and noncallable for life, are based on 15.25 percent minus the 6-month LIBOR. If LIBOR is at 8 percent, the rate on the notes will be 7.25 percent; if LIBOR increases to 10 percent, the rate will drop to 5.25 percent; and if LIBOR falls to 6 percent, the rate will rise to 9.25 percent. It appears that only those investors who are positive on interest rates would care for these issues. Other types of issues for a bull on interest rates are the maximum reset note and debenture. One of each type came to market in late 1985, but neither was heartily received, according to some traders. The coupons on both initially were set at 10.625 percent. Interest is adjusted and payable semiannually. If the 6-month LIBOR exceeded 10.5 percent at the interest determination date, the interest rate for the period would be reduced from 10.625 percent by the amount of the excess, with the minimum rate being 0 percent. With LIBOR at 12 percent, the rate would decline to 9.125 percent. At least, if LIBOR exceeds 21⅛ percent, the holder will not have to pay the issuer anything.

Some issues have floors, or minimum interest rates. A number of the LIBOR-based issues have minimum rates of 5.25 percent. Others have declining minimums, such as the Citicorps due September 1, 1998; the minimum rate is 7.5 percent through August 31, 1983, then 7 percent through August 31, 1988, and then 6.5 percent to maturity. Certain issues have ceilings, or maximum rates, often because of state usury laws. Many issues say that the maximum rate is 25 percent due to New York State's usury law, but holders of $2.5 million or more of an issue are exempt from this. Some issues of Texas bank holding companies have had a 17 percent maximum rate. In 1974, Crocker National Corporation sold $40 million of floating-rate notes due 1994 with a 10 percent maximum rate due to vagaries of California law. For several years the coupon rate was below the ceiling, but in 1979 interest rates shot up, restricting the interest to 10 percent. As the notes had a put feature, many investors put the bonds back to the company and reinvested the proceeds in more attractive instruments. Had there been no put feature, those investors would have been out of pocket for a number of years. One should certainly relate the ceiling rate to the spread over the base rate: Is the spread sufficient to compensate for the limit on the income stream in the event rates rise, or is the ceiling too close to the base rate?

Several floating-rate issues have both a floor and a ceiling, collectively called collars. In 1985, Baltimore Gas & Electric Company issued a couple of floaters with collars. Based on the 91-day Treasury bill auction rate (bond equivalent basis), the spreads are 110 basis points for one and 112.5 basis points for the other; the collars are 8 and 12 percent and 7.9 and 11.9 percent, respectively. These appear to be relatively narrow bands within which the interest rate may vary, but the lower ceiling is offset to some extent by the higher floor. Other issuers of collared floaters include California Federal Savings and Loan Association, Citicorp, and the Student Loan Marketing Association.

The Market for Floaters

The first floating-rate notes, issued in 1974, had great appeal for individual investors even though certain features, such as the delayed put, were incorporated in order to reduce the competitive threat to many thrift institutions. They were initially viewed as, at worst, no longer than two-year instruments and then as six-month instruments once the puts became effective. Price fluctuations were relatively narrow. The second batch of floaters hit the market in 1979 and were warmly received by investors. Many did not care that the new generation of floating-rate paper had no put features. They thought that as long as the coupon rate was adjusted every six months, the bonds automatically would stay around par. How mistaken they were! There was nothing to keep the bonds at par; they had no puts and, as interest rate movements became increasingly volatile later in the year, their prices sank. These new issues were just intermediate-to longer-term securities with coupons that happened to fluctuate. If the issuer's credit quality deteriorated, prices would be reduced. Because of rapid interest rate movements, the interest rates, when reset, were often below the market rates, making it necessary to adjust bond prices. The semiannual coupon failed to provide the needed support. In the January 1980 to June 1981 period, based on end-of-week prices on the New York Stock Exchange, Citicorp's June 1, 1989, floater with a put had a price range of only 96 to 103¼. In contrast, floaters without puts had wider price fluctuations. Manufacturers Hanover's floating-rate notes of May 1987 moved between 86¼ and 101½, while Chase Manhattan's notes due 2009 had a low of 82 and a high of 100½.

In early 1980, interest rates fell sharply. The floaters that had been hurt the most in the preceding few months moved up rapidly toward the par area from the low 80s and 90s; for example, the Chase Manhattan 2009s went from 86 to about 100 in 15 weeks. But holding back some prices were the investors who wanted to get even—they wanted to get rid of an investment that had not measured up to their unreal performance expectations. After the rally, prices took another tumble as interest rates rose once again. This history shows how important a put feature may be for some investors. Of course, it also helps if they know the risks and rewards of what they are buying.

Many investors in the floating-rate note market are financial institutions with some type of floating-rate liability. Other investors use floaters as substitutes for money-market instruments, although those without put features are not perfect substitutes for short-dated instruments. Floaters have been used as hedges against rising interest rate markets. If interest rates are thought to be increasing, floaters with frequent resets should provide increasing income. Their defensive characteristics should lend them price stability. A mismatched floater might be more suitable. Resetting weekly to increasingly higher levels with interest payable quarterly or semiannualy, the holder is not locked into one rate for three or six months. LIBOR historically has been at higher levels than Treasury bill rates, and investors should analyze this relationship. If the spread between them is relatively narrow and one's interest rate outlook is cautious, one might consider LIBOR-based floaters so as to take advantage of a possible widening of the spread.

If an investor thinks that rates might be heading down, he or she might prefer floaters with less frequent resets (such as extendible notes) and deferred resets (that allow the higher coupon to be maintained as long as possible). Of course, large investors need not limit themselves to only domestic floaters; the supply of floating-rate paper in the foreign markets is considerable, and the major investment firms, with their worldwide trading capabilities, participate in these markets 24 hours a day.

Yields and Evaluation of Floaters.[12]

Yield calculations and evaluation methods for floating-rate notes are complex procedures, and no one method is entirely satisfactory for all. The simplistic current yield method (dividing the coupon rate by the price) does not take coupon changes into account. All we know is what the coupon is now and its relationship to the present price; we do not even know what the next coupon will be—we can only guess. Of course, this method does not take into account the bond's accretion of the discount or the amortization of the premium over the issue's life; it just assumes that the coupon and the price remain the same. But bond life isn't that way. Both floater prices and floater coupons change. Yield computations are complex, and one should have some idea of the cash flow from the investment and the interest rate on the reinvested cash flow. The timing of cash flows is also important. It is this uncertainty with respect to floating-rate-securities that makes their evaluation more difficult than other securities'.

With many extendible notes and similar paper, conventional yield and evaluation methods are more than likely satisfactory. After all, if you own a note with a fixed coupon to a put date, you can figure a yield to put on the same basis as a yield to maturity. You know the current price, the coupon that is fixed until the put date, the put date, and the put price (usually par). Thus, using the put date as a maturity date, you can easily obtain the yield to put with a standard bond calculator. However, the computations for issues whose coupon payments may vary over the period to put or the time to maturity are more confusing, especially when trying to compare issues with dissimilar characteristics. Nevertheless, you should try to reach the most well thought out decisions possible. With this in mind, we will discuss various methods of yield comparison and calculation. But remember that these are, to some extent, little better than educated guesses, as we lack much of the information available to a fixed-coupon investor.

Obviously, one will make better judgments when comparing similar issues. As mentioned above, current yields, while frequently used, are not particularly satisfactory; different issues may have different interest reset dates, a variable that current yields do not take into account. However, adjusting the coupon of both issues to the same refixing or resetting date may add some credibility to their evaluation; this is similar to the dividend reset procedure for adjustable-rate preferred stocks.

Table 3-3 gives selected details of a hypothetical floating-rate debt instrument. With today's assumed base rate at 5.75 percent, the adjusted reset coupon will be 5.75 percent plus the reset spread of 100 basis points, or 6.75 percent. This more clearly reflects the

Table 3-3
Selected Details of a Hypothetical Floating-Rate Debt Issue

Current coupon and maturity	7.5%/December 1, 1998
Coupon reset and payment dates	June 1 and December 1
Reset spread	+100 basis points (1%)
Base rate	6-month U.S. Treasury bills, interest yield equivalent of the secondary market rate.
Price	97.50
Today's assumed base rate	5.75%
Adjusted reset coupon	6.75%
Time remaining to maturity (assuming today is 11/1/86)	12 years, 1 month (12.0833 years)
Simple current yield	7.69%
Adjusted reset current yield	6.92%
Adjusted spread to base	117 basis points
Zero coupon basis/spread from base	138 basis points
Simple or positive margin	124 basis points
Reset or adjusted yield to maturity	7.06%
Spread or reset yield to maturity over base rate	131 basis points

current market, eliminating some of the ambiguity that may result from comparing similar issues with different reset dates and coupon rates. But it still doesn't consider any premium or discount on the bonds or the time period to maturity or redemption. However, in basing the current yield on the adjusted reset coupon, the adjusted current yield is 6.92 percent versus 7.69 percent for the actual present coupon of the issue.

The contractual reset spread is plus 100 basis points over the base rate. However, as the notes are selling at a discount from par (97.50), the investor is getting an even larger spread. We subtract the assumed base rate (5.75 percent) from the adjusted current yield (6.92 percent) and end up with 117 basis points as the adjusted spread to base. If the notes were selling at a premium to par, the adjusted spread to base would be lower than the contractual reset spread. Of course, at par the spread is 100 basis points.

Most of the floating-rate notes (and all in the domestic market as of the end of 1986) are not perpetual securities, and thus the discount or premium has to be accounted for through other calculations. The next yield method is the zero coupon basis/spread from base. Here we treat the note as a zero coupon instrument, determine the yield to maturity based on the zero coupon status, and add that yield to the reset spread. This gives us what is called the "locked-in spread." Thus, we have a zero coupon bond due in 1998 and priced at 97.50; this provides a yield to maturity of 0.38 percent. We add this to the reset spread of 100 basis points and arrive at a locked-in spread of 138 basis points. By purchasing this note at 97.50 (and assuming no change in the reset spread), we have solidified the spread at 138 basis points over the base rate.

Another method investors use is the simple or positive margin, also called the "spread for life," which gives a margin or spread over the base rate taking into account the issue's time to maturity and the discount or premium. The formula is:

$$\frac{\left(\dfrac{100 - \text{Price of note}}{\text{Time to maturity}} \right) + 1}{\left(\dfrac{\text{Price of note}}{100} \right)} \times 100$$

The spread for life (simple or positive margin) is 124 basis points.

The reset or adjusted yield to maturity method, also referred to as the "discounted cash flow to maturity method," is still another way of looking at floaters. One must assume what the base rate (and thus the coupon) will average over the bond's life. We use this figure as the coupon in a regular yield-to-maturity calculation. Our hypothetical bond (see Table 3–3) at due on December 1, 1998, gives us a reset yield to maturity of 7.06 percent assuming that the base rate averages 5.75 percent and the coupon 6.75 percent. Now that we have obtained this yield, we can get the spread or reset yield to maturity over the base rate by subtracting the base rate from this yield. Thus, 7.06 minus 5.75 equals 1.31, or 131 basis points spread across the base rate.

None of these methods is perfect, but the reset or adjusted yield-to-maturity method seems to be gaining more adherents. With so many different ways of analyzing floating-rate securities, consistency is important.

NOTES

1. For a full discussion of yield concepts, see Sidney Homer and Martin L. Leibowitz, *Inside the Yield Book* (Englewood Cliffs, N.J.: Prentice-Hall and New York Institute of Finance, 1972).

2. *Indenture dated as of June 15, 1983 between Beneficial Corporation and Bankers Trust Company, Trustee, Providing for the Issuance of Debt Securities.*

3. "Globalization" was the buzzword of Wall Street in 1986. The tying together of worldwide markets is of major importance to financial industry leaders (even though some haven't gotten their own houses in order).

4. In its December 8, 1986, issue, *Barron's National Business and Financial Weekly* carried an interview with James Rogers, a private investor and professor of finance at the Columbia University Graduate School of Business. Rogers said, in part,

> But since no economy in the world is near as strong as the financial markets, all this money has been flowing into financial assets all over the world. Investment bankers are staying up late, trying to come up with and invent new financial instruments to soak up all this money that's sloshing around. I keep up a little bit with these things, even in my retirement, but there are financial instruments now that I have never heard of. Some of the things they have created in the Eurodollar market—I just don't know what's going on anymore. And I've got former students who are out there trading interest-rate swaps and mortgage-backed securities and foreign currency swaps, and they don't have a clue as to what they're doing. They don't have a clue on the ultimate ramifications, or who the ultimate creditor is, or anything else about these things. All they know is it's trading and they're making a lot of money.

5. The European currency unit (ECU) is a "faux-currency" in that it is not money in circulation within a country, as is the pound sterling or the U.S. dollar. There is no central bank for issuing ECU notes, although financial institutions issue traveler's checks and other financial instruments denominated in ECUs, and this currency is receiving recognition in international transactions. The ECU is a synthetic or composite currency, consisting of specific amounts of the currencies of each of the 10 member nations of the European Economic Community (EEC). In mid-1986, it consisted of the following amounts of currencies:

3.71	Belgian francs	0.719	German marks
0.219	Danish kroner	0.00871	Irish pounds
0.256	Dutch guilders	140.00	Italian lire
1.31	French francs	0.14	Luxembourg francs
1.15	Greek drachmas	0.0878	United Kingdom pounds

6. William Z. Ripley, *Trusts, Pools and Corporations* (Boston: Ginn, 1916), 491.

7. Sidney M. Robbins, *An Objective Look at Income bonds* (Boston: Envision Press, 1974), 6–7. Another interesting article endorsing the use of income bonds in corporate capital structures is Leo Barnes, "A Do-It-Yourself Way to Cut Taxes," *Business Week*, May 5, 1975, 21–25.

8. For a fairly complete definition of available net income and the disposition of income, see *Moody's Transportation Manual*, 1986 ed. (New York: Moody's Investors Service, Inc.), p. 172.

9. *Moody's Bond Survey*, August 19, 1985, p. 3007, reported that Ford Motor Credit Company issued $100 million of 1% Original-Issue Discount Notes due August 15, 1990, at 63.52 to yield 10.571 percent to maturity. The current yield was a not too substantial 1.574 percent. They were in fully registered form in denominations of $5 million and multiples thereof.

10. To the author's knowledge, there are only three issues of zero coupon bonds called deferred interest debentures on which taxable holders pay no taxes on the accreted interest, although they could incur some capital gain tax liability. Issued in 1982 through recapitalizations under the tax code, these issues are Exxon Shipping Company's Guaranteed Deferred Interest Debenture due September 1, 2012, and General Motors Acceptance Corporation Deferred Interest Debentures due December 1, 2012, plus another issue due June 15, 2015. The debentures are callable at any time, in whole or in part, at the principal amount plus accrued interest computed on a straight line basis.

11. A complete discussion of floating-rate securities, including domestic and foreign Eurodollar bonds, mortgages, preferred stocks, and certificates of deposit, may be found in Frank J. Fabozzi, *Floating Rate Instruments: Characteristics, Valuation and Portfolio Strategies* (Chicago: Probus, 1986). Part of this section is adapted from this book.

12. This section is adapted from the author's chapter in Fabozzi, *Floating Rate Instruments*. More detailed analysis is found in Chapter 9, "Evaluating Floating Rate Notes," and Chapter 10, "Evaluating Floating Rate Notes: II."

APPENDIX

SECURITY ABBREVIATIONS AND ACRONYMS

AARN	annual adjustable-rate note
AREN	adjustable-rate extendible note
ARN	adjustable-rate note
ARPSD	adjustable-rate participating subordinated debenture
CD	certificate of deposit
CFRMBN	collared floating-rate mortgage-backed note
CP	commercial paper
CvFRN	convertible floating-rate note
CvSVRN	convertible subordinated variable-rate note
EFMB	extendible first mortgage bond
EFRN	extendible floating-rate note
EN	extendible note
ESN	extendible senior note
FMBES	first mortgage bond, extendible series
FRADD	floating-rate Australian dollar debentures
FRADN	floating-rate Australian dollar notes
FRMBES	first and refunding mortgage bond, extendible series
FREN	floating-rate extendible note
FRESN	floating-rate extendible subordinated note

FRESSN	floating-rate extendible senior subordinated note
FRGSCN	floating-rate guaranteed subordinated capital note
FRJr.SN	floating-rate junior subordinated note
FRMBB	floating-rate mortgage-backed bond
FRN	floating-rate note
FRNZDN	floating-rate New Zealand dollar notes
FRSCN	floating-rate subordinated capital note
FRSD	floating-rate subordinated debenture
FRSN	floating-rate subordinated note
FRSr.N	floating-rate senior note
FRSr.SN	floating-rate senior secured note
FVRETC	fixable variable-rate equipment trust certificate
GDS	guaranteed debt security
JD	junior debenture
MRD	maximum rate debenture
MRN	maximum rate note
MMN	money market note
RN	reset note
RSN	resettable subordinated note
SEN	senior extendable note
SEVRD(N)	subordinated exchangeable variable-rate debenture (Note)
SIREN	senior increasing-rate extendible note
SN	senior note
SPD	subordinated participating debenture
SRN	senior reset note
SSEN	senior secured extendible note
Sr.SEVRN	senior subordinated exchangeable variable-rate note
Sr.SFRN	senior subordinated floating-rate note
Sr.SRN	senior subordinated reset note
SSr.RN	springing senior reset note
SVRN	subordinated variable-rate note
VCRN	variable coupon renewable note
V/FRD	variable/fixed-rate debenture
VRDCSr.N	variable rate deferred coupon senior note

VRJr.SN	variable rate junior subordinate note
VRN	variable-rate note
VRSD	variable-rate subordinated debenture
VRSN	variable-rate subordinated note
VRSSD	variable-rate senior subordinated debenture
VSFRN	variable-spread floating-rate note
YCN	yield curve notes

CHAPTER 4

DEBT EXTINGUISHMENT

Most bonds do not remain outstanding until maturity. Some bonds are retired because the issuers went bankrupt, causing all the funded debt to become immediately due and payable. In other cases, the debt issue was modified in some manner, with the interest rate, maturity, and other terms changed to effectively give rise to a new debt. Often, however, bonds are redeemed prior to maturity because declining interest rates make is economical for the issuer to substitute new, lower-cost debt for older issues with higher interest rates; this may lead to improved earnings and cash flow. Other reasons include the issuer's desire to eliminate restrictive or onerous covenants from its indenture and to improve or change its capital structure. This chapter examines the many ways in which corporations prematurely extinguish debt.

THE IMPORTANCE OF KNOWING A BOND ISSUE'S REDEMPTION TERMS

Many investors have no sense of financial history and thus are unprepared when events occur in the market that are similar to past events. This is especially true when interest rates decline, particularly from lofty levels. Being unfamiliar with the financial past, such investors cannot understand what may happen under present or future conditions. They have often structured their portfolios based on considerations that were appropriate at the time but inadequately restructured when conditions changed. In many cases, investors' eagerness for increased yield makes their bond holdings vulnerable to premature retirement. This, coupled with an unfamiliarity with the issue's terms, makes bond investment riskier than it need be. Investors should read the prospectuses and indentures of the issues they own, especially for the higher-coupon bonds. Provisions vary from issue to issue, even among those of the same company and under the same general indenture. How often do you hear someone say, "I don't have time to read a prospectus"? Investors must diligently study their holdings in order to be able to take action at the appropriate time.

The importance of knowing the terms of bond issues, especially those relating to redemption, cannot be overstressed. Yet in financial and other publications there have appeared numerous instances of investors, professional and otherwise, who acknowledged that they don't read the documentation. For example, the following statements were attributed to some stockbrokers: "But brokers in the field say they often don't spend much time reading these [official] statements," "I can be honest and say I never look at the prospectus. . . . Generally, you don't have time to do that", and "There are some clients who really don't know what they buy. . . . They just say, 'That's a good interest rate.'"[1] The following passages are from legal decisions involving debt redemptions:

> Although she received prospectuses for her investment, plaintiff . . . never read any FPL [Florida Power & Light Company] prospectus or other description of the 10⅛ bonds before she purchased the 10⅛ bonds on. . . .

> . . . did not possess or read any FPL prospectus describing the 10⅛ bonds before he purchased the . . . bonds . . . in the after market.

> . . . did not read or rely on prospectuses when buying bonds in the after market. . . .

As the Fifth Circuit Court also pointed out in *Alabama Power*:

> . . . it is reasonable (for the issuer) to assume that investors who (purchase) their bonds would familiarize themselves with the conditions under which

they were issued, and particularly the terms of redemption, by reading the few short paragraphs on the face of the bonds.

The plaintiffs offered little, if any, evidence of their own due diligence in making their investment decisions, which respectively involved a reckless disregard for, or deliberate inattention to, the contents of the FPL prospectus, which none of them read or consulted, as well as an apparent and knowledgeable willingness to "gamble" on the part of the more sophisticated investor. . . . [2]

We note initially that bondholders are charged with knowledge of the contents of the trust indenture where the bond certificate refers to the terms of the indenture.[3]

A professional analyst's journal has this to say:

To infer that all money managers and other analysts do not read prospectuses is a quantum and incorrect leap, yet uneasy feelings exist about the number that do. Why read a prospectus, 10K or any other fully disclosed information? Is someone out there saying something and analysts not listening? One would surmise that, if prospectuses contained value, they would be read. Is there a delusionary safe harbor in believing too strongly that all known information is reflected in market prices and well diversified portfolios insure against all but market risks?[4]

Retirement of debt before the stated maturity is not a new phenomenon. James Grant said, "At the turn of the century the risk to bondholders was default . . . or the early redemption of sound securities."[5] It occurs periodically whenever interest rates decline. Hickman stated:

During periods of rising interest rates few issues are called, many are paid off at maturity, and though realized yields may rise with money rates, call premiums may be insufficient to offset default losses, and substantial capital losses may result. In periods of falling money rates the reverse appears to be true: few issues are paid off at maturity, many are called, and even though default losses may be substantial, call premiums may be more than sufficient to offset them, and capital gains may occur.[6]

Recent periods of major debt redemption activity include 1963, 1975 through 1978, and 1983 to the present. Times of generally declining interest rates, they provided ample opportunity for companies to rid themselves of high-coupon debt. Bond calls are common, and yet they have caused the unwary investor much consternation over the years. Investors have suffered unwarranted losses of principal that they might have avoided had they heeded one warning: Know the terms of the bond contract. Remember that investors are parties to the bond contract even though they may have purchased the issue in the secondary market long after the bonds were first publicly offered. The subsequent buyer is as much a party to the bond contract as is the initial purchaser; he or she succeeds to the contract.

It is common knowledge that bond market participants are unaware of indenture provisions, especially those relating to redemption and the options given to the issuer. Bondholders often have mistaken ideas as to what a corporation may do when it comes to debt retirement. It should always be kept in mind that corporate managements generally do not have bondholders' interests at heart; they are elected by, and beholden to, the owners of the business, namely the common shareholders. Recently, however, it seems that some no longer care even for stockholders' interests. One often hears that a company's actions regarding debt redemption were not taken in good faith or that it wasn't the company's intent when it issued the debt. Unfortunately, however, "good faith" may have meant something more in the past than it does today. Bond investors should rely only on what is in the bond indenture (and court decisions and law relating to the debt). A corporation's "intent" is not an article in a bond indenture, and it is difficult to know what that intent was when the bonds were first issued. Both managements and intents change, especially in situations where it is in the shareholders' best interests for the company to retire the debt. Perhaps the intent attributed to the corporation never existed but was merely a reflection of the bondholders' hopes. Until corporate managements take all investors' interests into consideration and act as fiduciaries, the bond investor should not be caught napping.

Concern over Premature Redemption

Some might ask, "Why all the concern about premature bond redemption? After all, we get our money back and can reinvest it." But that is the concern: In most cases, a company will call its high-coupon bonds when interest rates are low; therefore, investors lose their high income and must reinvest the bond proceeds in a lower interest rate environment. The expected promised yield at the initial purchase will have been reduced. While lower interest rates may reduce the interest-on-interest component of the expected total return from a bond, many investors still expect to get the relatively high interest payment coming in. But corporations are run by managements who do what individuals often try to do. If they see an opportunity to reduce their expenses by calling high-coupon debt, they usually will do so. If homeowners rush to refinance their home mortgages when rates drop, why can't companies refinance their outstanding high-cost debt?

Besides suffering a decline in interest income and the resulting interest-on-interest, investors often have the bonds called at prices lower than recent market prices. The call price may be at a premium to par, but the redemption price may be only par. Examples of calls at levels well below the bonds' prevailing market price are presented later in this chapter.

Yield-oriented investors are among those often hurt by premature bond redemptions. They are attracted by the relatively high yield to maturity without realizing that this is most likely due to one of two reasons: increased risk of default or increased risk of call. Very seldom is the high yield due to inefficiencies in the market. Whenever a bond offers an above-average yield, the investor should ask why. One does not usually get something for nothing in the financial markets.

Call and Refunding Provisions

A company wanting to retire a debt issue prior to maturity usually must pay a premium over the par value for that privilege. The initial call premium on long-term debt traditionally has been the interest coupon plus par or the initial reoffering price (or, in some cases, the higher of the two). Thus, a 30-year bond initially priced at 100.25 with an 8.75 percent coupon may have a call price of 109 for the first year, scaled down in relatively equal amounts to par starting in year 26 to maturity. In late 1986, Wisconsin Natural Gas Company offered 9.25% First Mortgage Bonds at 99 percent of par with a maturity date of September 15, 2016. Table 4-1 shows the redemption schedule for the bonds. Note that the initial call price equals the coupon plus the reoffering price. Subsequent redemption prices are in decrements of 33 basis points (0.33 of 1 percent) to par starting September 15, 2011. Some issues will give just the call premium, such as 8.25 percent or 7.92 percent, instead of the whole price.

Table 4-1
Redemption Schedule for Wisconsin Natural Gas Company
9.25% First Mortgage Bonds due September 15, 2016

If Redeemed During the 12-Month Period Ending September 14	Redemption Price	If Redeemed During the 12-Month Period Ending September 14	Redemption Price
1987	108.25%	2002	103.30%
1988	107.92	2003	102.97
1989	107.59	2004	102.64
1990	107.26	2005	102.31
1991	106.93	2006	101.98
1992	106.60	2007	101.65
1993	106.27	2008	101.32
1994	105.94	2009	100.99
1995	105.61	2010	100.66
1996	105.28	2011	100.33
1997	104.95	2012	100.00
1998	104.62	2013	100.00
1999	104.29	2014	100.00
2000	103.96	2015	100.00
2001	103.63	2016	100.00

Redemption: The New bonds will be redeemable in whole or in part at any time or from time to time prior to maturity upon at least thirty days' notice at the election of the Company, at the Redemption Prices applicable to the respective periods set forth . . . in each case with interest accrued to the redemption date; provided, however, that prior to September 15, 1991, no New Bonds may be so redeemed, directly or indirectly, from the proceeds of or in anticipation of any refunding operation involving the incurring of debt which has an effective interest cost to the company, computed in accordance with generally accepted financial practice, of less than 9.44% (the effective interest cost of the New Bonds).

Source: Prospectus dated September 10, 1986.

The prices shown in Table 4-1 above are called the *regular* or *general redemption* prices. There are also special redemption prices for debt called through the sinking fund and for bonded debt called through provisions such as the maintenance and replacement fund, the proceeds from the confiscation of property through the right of eminent domain, and the release and substitution of property clauses. The special redemption price is often par, but in the case of some utility issues it may initially be the public offering price, which is amortized down to par (if a premium) over the bonds' lives. Carolina Light & Power Company's 9¾ percent bonds due May 1, 2004, have a special redemption price that is a discount. The bonds were issued in 1974 at 99.75. The special redemption price starts at 99.75 and accrues to par for the year ending April 30, 2004. This price can be used for redemptions for the improvement fund, for the maintenance and replacement fund, or with the proceeds of released property. In other instances, the special redemption price is the same as the regular redemption price. This makes the debt redemption somewhat more expensive for the corporation and gives the bondholder an additional premium. Rules of thumb for corporate bond characteristics applicable a generation ago cannot be safely used today; there are too many exceptions for one to be able to ignore the documentation. In the case of shorter-maturity debt, the initial call price usually is not the full coupon but some fraction thereof, scaled down to par; it may even be par for the issue's life.

The Wisconsin Natural Gas bond is currently callable—that is, the company may redeem it at any time at the above prices (or par, in the case of the sinking fund). Other issues may not be called for any reason for a certain number of years. For example, there is usually a five-year noncallable period for long-term debt of the former members of the American Telephone and Telegraph Company family. Therefore, the call price at the time the bond may first be called is not par plus the coupon but the amortized price in five years obtained by the par plus the coupon calculation. If the telephone bond had the same coupon and reoffering price as the Wisconsin Natural Gas issue, the initial call price would be 106.60 for the 12 months beginning September 15, 1992.

In the latter half of 1979, some of the Bell System companies attempted to change the call price formula. Instead of basing the premium on the initial coupon, it arbitrarily set it at half the coupon rate. On August 21, 1979, Northwestern Bell Telephone offered $300 million of 9½ percent bonds due in 37 years at 99.7, with the initial call price after five years starting at 104.75. Several other affiliates tried the same call pricing over the next couple of months, but investors did not care for it. The lower call price meant that interest rates did not have to decline as much in order for the company to profitably redeem the debt, and thus vulnerability to call was increased. In addition, if the bonds were called, investors would receive substantially less than under the old formula. The unsuccessful experiment was stopped and the more traditional call pricing resumed.

If a debt has no protection against early call, it is said to be a currently callable issue, as is that of Wisconsin Natural Gas. But most new bond issues, even if currently callable, usually have some restrictions against certain types of redemption. The most common restriction is that against the refunding of the bonds for a certain number of years. Aware of the dangers of generalizations, industrial company long-term debt issues often have ten years of refunding protection and electric and gas utilities five years.[7] Many telephone, bank, and finance issues provide deferred call provisions. Both call and refunding prohibitions may be for a certain number of years or for the issue's life. Bonds that are noncallable for the issue's life are more common than bonds that are nonrefunable for life but otherwise callable.

Many investors are confused by the terms noncallable and nonrefundable. Hess and Winn said, "The terms 'non-callable' and 'nonrefundable' are often used rather loosely as interchangeable entities, although from a technical standpoint they have different meanings."[8] Call protection is much more absolute than refunding protection. While there may be exceptions to absolute call protection in some cases (such as sinking funds), it still provides greater insurance against premature and unwanted redemption than does refunding protection. Refunding prohibition prevents debt redemption only from certain sources, namely the proceeds of other debt issues sold at a lower money cost. The holder is protected only if interest rates decline, and the borrower can obtain lower-cost money to pay off the debt. The Wisconsin Natural Gas bonds cannot be redeemed prior to September 15, 1991, if the company has raised the funds from a new issue with a cost of 9.44 percent or less. There is nothing to prevent the company from calling the bonds from debt sold at a higher rate (although it normally wouldn't do so) or, as we shall see, from funds obtained through other means.

Some companies issue prospectuses that specifically clarify refunding and redemption; it is to be hoped that more will do so. Cincinnati Gas & Electric Company's prospectus for the 15¾% First Mortgage Bonds due in 1992 states,

> The New Bonds are redeemable (though CG&E does not contemplate doing so) prior to July 1, 1987 through the use of earnings, proceeds from the sale of equity securities and cash accumulations other than those resulting from a refunding operation such as hereinafter described. The New Bonds are not redeemable prior to July 1, 1987 as a part of, or in anticipation of, any refunding operation involving the incurring of indebtedness by CG&E having an effective interest cost (calculated to the second place in accordance with generally accepted financial practice) of less than the effective interest cost of the New Bonds (similarly calculated) or through the operation of the Maintenance and Replacement Fund.

Refunding means to replace an old bond issue with a new one, often at a lower interest cost. In the Florida Power & Light case, the judge said:

> The terms "redemption" and "refunding" are not synonymous. A "redemption" is simply a call of bonds. A "refunding" occurs when the issuer sells bonds in order to use the proceeds to redeem an earlier series of bonds. The refunding bond issue being sold is closely linked to the one being redeemed by contractual language and proximity in time so that the proceeds will be available to pay for the redemption. Otherwise, the issuer would be taking an inordinate risk that market conditions would change between the redemption of the earlier issue and the sale of the later issue.[9]

Corporations prefer to issue callable bonds, as they give them flexibility in their financial planning. If rates decrease or other circumstances change, they can get out of the debt contract with minimal cost. Investors, on the other hand, prefer noncallable bonds for their guarantee of certain cash flow for a fixed number of years, which allows them to plan accordingly. But borrowers and lenders often must compromise; thus, we get the bond that is noncallable or nonrefundable for only part of the issue's promised life span. In the early sixties, electric utilities offered issues with five years refunding protection at rates of 15 to 25 basis points less than issues with no refunding protection, other things equal. Investors were willing to reduce their yield for the additional protective feature.

In early 1986, a number of industrial companies issued long-term debt that was noncallable for the issue's life. Dow Chemical Company sold 8⅝ percent debentures due in 2006 and Atlantic Richfield a 9⅞ percent offering due in 2016. The prospectuses for both issues expressly prohibit redemption prior to maturity. According to *Standard & Poor's Creditweek*, "The first wave of noncall long-term bonds gave issuers 20 to 25 basis points savings on their financing costs. . . . Now companies are lucky if investors give up 10 to 15 basis point for a noncall feature."[10] Of course, interest rates dropped considerably in early 1986. Call protection is a valuable option when interest rates are high, which is precisely when lenders prefer noncallable issues. When interest rates are low, call protection is less meaningful, making fully call-protected bonds less attractive.

Redemption dates usually are stated as "on or after" a certain date. In some cases, however, bonds may be redeemed only on certain dates, often the interest payment dates. Prior notice must be given—usually 30 to 45 days preceding the redemption date. Of course, if the bonds are listed on a securities exchange, the exchanges must also be notified. For a fully registered bond, the redemption notice is sent directly to the registered holders; a printed notice in the financial press is not required, although this would aid market participants. If the bonds are in coupon form, a printed notice in the financial press listing the serial numbers of the bonds to be called is required.

Bonds can be called in whole (the entire issue) or in part (only a portion of it). A few issues, such as those of Alaskan Housing Finance Corporation, permit optional redemption only in whole. The method of redemption is usually stated as "by such method as it shall deem fair and appropriate" or "fair and equitable" and is left to the discretion of the trustees. Most directly or privately placed and unregistered issues provide for pro rata redemption in the event of partial calls. This means that all holders will have the same percentage of their holdings retired (subject to the restrictions imposed by the minimum denominations). Very few—if any—publicly issued bonds have pro rata redemption features; rather, the redemption is done "by lot." This is, essentially, the random selection of bonds through the use of computer programs.[11] Often, there is a clause in the documentation stating that the redemption is subject to the deposit of the redemption monies with the trustee on or before the redemption date. If funds are not on hand, the redemption notice becomes void and has no effect.

According to the New York Stock Exchange, trading in nonconvertible bonds that have been called in whole ceases when funds are available for payment with the trustee. In the case of a partial call, bonds called for redemption are no longer "good delivery" for the settlement of trades. The exception is when the trades are in the called bonds. Once a bond has been called, the few that do trade are, in effect, substitutes for very-short-term paper. Active bond portfolio managers should be alert as to which of their bonds have been called so that trades will settle promptly and without any problems caused by the delivery of "bad" bonds.

Refunding is the primary cause of bond redemptions, as companies can increase their shareholders' wealth by substituting lower-cost for higher-cost debt. There are many different ways in which issuers estimate the savings to be attained through refunding, but refunding is basically a capital budgeting procedure. One calculates, on an after-tax basis, the net present value of the expected savings over the life of the issue to be refunded and subtracts from that the costs of the transaction to obtain the net advantage for the refunding transaction. In all cases, the discount rate used is the after-tax yield on the new debt based on semiannual payments. It should be noted that the issue's call premium and related expenses are deductible from the current year's income taxes, thus reducing the cost of the refunding. Expenses associated with the new or refunding issue must be amortized over the issue's life. If the net advantage of the refunding is greater than zero, a refunding opportunity exists.[12]

Because the call premium and certain other costs are written off for financial purposes in the year incurred, the transaction may result in a loss for reported net income purposes. But that should not override the economics of the transaction. Many utility companies have been urged by their regulators to use all available means for reducing their interest costs. As further encouragement they should be assured that they will not have to absorb the loss on the transaction in the year incurred but can amortize it and related costs (net of the tax benefits) over the new securities' lives for rate-making and reporting purposes. However, as a member of the staff of the Public Utilities Commission of the State of California stated in 1983, "If there is a clear-cut opportunity for a utility to effect substantial interest savings through refinancing and it fails to act promptly, there is ample justification for a ratemaking adjustment imputing a lower interest rate as a penalty."[13] The optimal timing of a refunding may be difficult to determine, for once done the opportunity to effect further savings is gone; the issuer will have given up the call option. An issuer should decide whether to refund now or wait until rates are lower. If the rates are expected to be lower, the issuer must determine whether they will be low enough to make the delay worthwhile. If a refunding is done now, the costs of the new bond issue are locked in until the refunding-protected period has expired (in five or ten years).

The refunding of high-cost debt in a lower interest rate environment should come as no surprise to any investor. Any one who faithfully reads the financial press should be aware of current interest rate levels as compared to those on the bonds he or she owns. Also, some companies have issued press releases and other reports outlining vulnerable issues. On March 18, 1986, Public Service Electric and Gas Company issued a release titled "PSE&G Announces Potential Redemption of High Interest Rate Debt Issues." It lists seven issues with coupons of 12 percent or more and an outstanding principal amount of $482.28 million and the dates on which they are eligible for redemption. The release said, in part,

> The Company estimates that $132 million of interest costs would be saved through these refundings over the remaining lives of the redeemed bonds ($38 million on a "present value" basis) based on a 9% refunding rate. Another benefit would be a reduction in the embedded cost of long-term debt by about 65 basis points. The interest coverage ratio would also be improved, thereby enhancing the credit standing of the Company.

OUTRIGHT REDEMPTIONS

For want of a better term, we will use *outright redemptions* to mean the retirement of debt at the general redemption price. The proceeds for the outright redemption need not come from lower cost borrowings, nor is the redemption triggered by the maintenance and replacement fund, the sinking fund, or the release and substitution of property provisions found in bonded debt. Outright redemptions are also known as "cash calls," but this term could be applied to other types of debt calls. The point to remember is that they can occur at any time unless there are call prohibitions; the investor should not be lulled by a nonrefunding provision.

In the spring of 1973, Bristol-Myers Company called for redemption at 107.538 one-third, or $25 million, of its 8⅝ percent debentures due 1995. The debentures were issued in 1970. Trading as high as 111 in 1972 and about 108–109 when the call was announced, capital losses were incurred. A number of holders, including institutional investors and at least one Wall Street corporate bond dealer, were confused by the call, having mistaken "nonrefundable" for "noncallable." The bonds were nonrefundable for 10 years but currently were callable. In 1977, NCR Corporation redeemed all of the outstanding amount ($75 million) of it 9¾ percent debentures due 2000 at 107.88. Still within the 10-year nonrefunding period, the bonds were trading at 111 to 111.5 at the time the call was announced. NCR was in a strong cash position, with projected cash flow substantially in excess of expected capital spending plans. This redemption helped to improve NCR's balance sheet and reduced leverage. In the opinion of these companies' managements, their debt offered them better returns than did investment in plant and equipment.

Then there is the case of Archer-Daniels-Midland Company (ADM). On May 12, 1981, the company sold $250 million of 7 percent debentures due May 15, 2011, and $125 million of 16 percent sinking fund debentures also maturing on May 15, 2011. Both issues were currently callable; the original issue discounts at par and the full coupon issue at a premium. The 16 percent debentures also had the standard 10-year prohibition against lower-cost refunding. Subsequent to these offerings, ADM raised money in 1982 and 1983 through lower-cost borrowings. It also sold common equity on January 28, 1983, raising more than $131 million, and again on June 1, 1983, raising another $15.45 million. At approximately 6:19 p.m. on June 1, 1983, the Dow Jones Capital Markets Newswire Service announced that the company would redeem on August 1, at 113.95 plus accrued interest of $33.78, all of its outstanding 16 percent sinking fund debentures due May 15, 2011.

This caused an uproar in the markets. This call was well within the 10-year refunding-protected period. One investment banking firm sued to bar the redemption, claiming that "investors expected the debentures to continue on the market until 1991 [which] kept the trading value of the debt at about $1,250 per $1,000 face value and misled investors into believing that the debentures would continue to be traded. . . . it wouldn't have purchased the debentures if it believed Archer-Daniels would redeem the bonds so soon."[14] People don't often sue in debt redemptions unless they stand to lose money. Here, the plaintiff did lose money. Several weeks before the call, it had purchased $15,518,000 face amount of the debentures at 125.25 per bond, and the day before, another $500,000 principal amount of bonds at 120.[15] If these bonds were held to the call cate, the principal loss would be nearly $1,784,000.

The company said that the proceeds for this redemption came from the sale of the common stock. The shelf registration prospectus dated March 22, 1983, may have indicated that the high-coupon debt might be in jeopardy when it said, in the use of proceeds section, "The proceeds will be used, as required, for general corporate purposes, including working capital, capital expenditures and possible acquisitions of, or investments in, businesses and assets, and *the repayment of indebtedness originally incurred for general corporate purposes* [emphasis added]." The prospectus for the called debentures said that "The proceeds will be used, as required, for general corporate purposes." This is part of the standard boilerplate found in many financing documents. The plaintiff claimed that ADM was not allowed, by the issue's terms, to call the bonds from lower-cost funds and pointed to the 1982 and 1983 debt financings. It contended that the money raised from the common stock sales was little more than a subterfuge for circumventing the refunding protection provided in the indenture. It also alleged securities fraud by ADM, as the company did not reveal its own interpretation of the redemption language and would contemplate redemption if it felt that doing so was in its own best interest.

The court upheld ADM's right to call the sinking fund debentures with the proceeds from the sales of comon shares, saying that the redemption was within the company's legal rights and in accordance with the indenture. It pointed to the strict "source" of funds argument which had come up several years earlier in the case of the redemption of a preferred stock with the proceeds of common stock.[16] The Archer-Daniels decision was an important event in the modern corporate bond world, as it substantially eroded the effectiveness of standard refunding provisions.

But the story didn't end with the 1983 call. Investors don't readily forget the times they lost money, especially if they feel that they might have been "bamboozled." One year later, on August 6, 1984, ADM sold $100 million of 13 percent sinking fund debentures due August 1, 2014, at a price of 97.241. The new bonds also came with the standard 10-year refunding protection. The offering wasn't too successful, since only about 70 percent of the bonds were sold at that price. When the manager of the offering released the issue from syndicate underwriting restrictions, the bonds immediately sold off. As *Bondweek* (August 13, 1984) said, "A-D-M Re-enters Market with a Thud," and, " . . . the offering never really got off the ground. Street officials said that without a doubt A-D-M's controversial move last year was a factor in the poor reception of its issue last week in the midst of an otherwise bullish market." On January 9, 1986, ADM sold $100 million of 10¼ percent debentures due January 15, 2006. In this case, the bonds were noncallable for the issue's life. The price the company had to pay to reenter the corporate bond markets and the good graces of institutional investors was that the bonds were noncallable for life. In April, 1986, the company attempted to rid itself of the then high-coupon 13s. Instead of calling the bonds at below-market prices as it had nearly three years earlier, it tendered for them with a bid above the market. Archer-Daniels probably had had enough of Wall Street lawyers for a while.

SINKING FUNDS AND PURCHASE FUNDS

A *sinking fund* is a provision in a loan agreement that allows for the periodic retirement or amortization of a debt over its life. It can also be the periodic deposit of funds or property into a reserve for the debt's eventual retirement or the maintenance of the value of the collateral securing it; this is called an *improvement fund* or a *sinking and improvement fund*. Nowadays it is more common to have the sinking fund applied to the current extinguishment of debt than to have the funds build up for use at maturity.

Were debt viewed as permanent, sinking funds would not be needed. Thus, the debt of the U.S. government appears to be a permanent cancer on the nation's escutcheon and is provided with no sinking fund. Of course, some might say that with bills rolling over every week and with the frequent note and bond maturities, a sinking fund, even if desirable, would be unnecessary. To reduce debt, the Treasury would only have to sell a smaller amount at each auction. However, much corporate debt generally has been viewed as less than permanent. Early U.S. railroad issues came with sinking funds, but in the last half of the nineteenth century, railroads sold many secured and very long-term issues with no sinking funds. Railroad promoters and managements (as well as investors) apparently viewed the properties as lasting forever. But starting in the early twentieth century, as industrial corporations became more prominent in the financing world with unsecured debt, the importance of sinking funds increased. Investors thought that providing for the periodic retirement of their debt before the assets became economically worthless would be preferable. This would strengthen issuers' credit by prohibiting an unwieldy sum to become due and payable all at once. The security tangible assets provided was less important, as investors realized that much corporate property depreciates, deteriorates, depletes, and becomes obsolete and that debt service would be better provided from operations and cash flow or, in some cases, from the pledging of unfunded property in lieu of the debt retirement.

Sinking funds of one type or another have probably existed for as long as people have borrowed money from one another and worried about the ultimate repayment. A sinking fund was proposed for government debt during the kingship of William III, Prince of Orange, in the late seventeenth century.[17] References to measures for reducing the Crown's public debt are found in Mackay's narrative of the South-Sea Bubble scandal:

> Upon the 22d of January 1720, the House of Commons resolved itself into a committee of the whole house, to take into consideration that part of the king's [George I, the Elector of Hanover] speech at the opening of the session which related to the public debts, and the proposal of the South-Sea Company towards the redemption and sinking of the same.[18]

In George Washington's administration, the first Secretary of the Treasury, Alexander Hamilton, developed a scheme for reducing the country's debt. But many government attempts at using sinking funds for debt reduction purposes fell short of the goal.

There are many types of sinking funds found in publicly issued corporate debt. The most common is the *mandatory specific sinking fund*, which requires the periodic redemption of a certain amount of a specific debt issue. This type is found in most longer-term industrial issues and some electric utility bonds. Bell System debt has no sinking funds, while much of the debt of the independent companies has sinking funds of varying types. A typical mandatory specific sinking fund might read as follows:

> The Company will provide for the retirement by redemption of $7,500,000 of the principal amount of the Offered Debentures on December 1 of each of the years 1997 to and including 2015 at the principal amount thereof, together with accrued interest to the date of redemption. The Company may also, at its option, provide for the redemption of up to an additional $15,000,000 principal amount . . . annually, . . . such optional right being noncumulative. The Company may, at its option, (1) deliver outstanding Offered Debentures (other than Offered Debentures previously called for redemption) and (2) apply as a credit Offered Debentures which have been redeemed either at the election of the Company or through the application of a permitted optional sinking fund payment, in each case in satisfaction of all or any part of any required sinking fund payment, provided that such Offered Debentures have not been previously so credited.[19]

The above paragraph tells us that for this $150 million issue, the company must retire 5 percent each year starting December 1, 1997 (one year after the refunding protection expires). Four or 5 percent is customary for longer-term industrial bonds, but it can be more. Owens-Corning Fiberglas Corporation's 11¾% Senior Subordinated Debentures due 2001 have an annual 20 percent sinking fund requirement starting in 1997. (Utility issues may have smaller sinking

funds.) The above payments will retire 95 percent of the issue prior
to maturity, leaving $7,500,000 at maturity. Many investors would
call this a 100 percent sinking fund. The company has the right to increase sinking fund payments by another $7,500,000. This is called a
"double up" option. Some issues allow the retirement of up to 200
percent or more of the minimum required amount; this option normally would be used in periods of lower interest rates. Usually the
company may deliver debentures acquired by it instead of paying
cash and calling the required bonds at par. In high interest rate
periods, when the bonds are trading below par, companies normally
prefer to buy their bonds through open market purchases instead of
calling them at the higher price; this can lend price support to the
bonds. In times of lower interest rates, open market purchases are
unnecessary and costly. The company can merely deposit cash with
the trustee for a par call; which may tend to depress the bond's
price.

Over the years, a number of institutional investors have played
the "sinking fund game": these have become known as "sinker
sockers." In this scheme, one or a few investors might try to control
an issue, i.e., buy up the available floating supply of a deep discount
bond with a currently operating sinking fund or with one due to start
in a couple of years. This does not mean that they must own 100 percent of the bonds, only a substantial portion of the available supply.
Many bonds may be "locked up" in certain investment accounts due
to restrictions on their sale at prices lower than their cost. These investors have often purchased the bonds at the time of the original offering at much higher prices. Even if they do not control every
outstanding bond, they can make life difficult for corporate financial
managers. This is because after a company has cleared the market of
tradable bonds for the sinking fund, the only ones remaining are
those cornered by the sinking fund collectors. Therefore, if a company needs bonds to satisfy the sinking fund, it must strike a bargain
with the bonds' owners at a price at or close to the sinking fund call
price. Thus, the investor stands to reap an extra reward.

Of course, things can go wrong. Investors may have to sit with
an underperforming asset for several years until its scarcity becomes
known. During that time, their credit quality may deteriorate or their
objectives may change. One portfolio manager with a major mid-
Atlantic bank reportedly tried to corner some bonds of a steel com-

pany. However, the steel company, which was an important account of the bank, became aware of the scheme, was perturbed, and stopped doing business with the bank. A number of companies have become painfully aware of sinking fund collectors and, as a result, try to keep their sinking fund activities and related information (amounts outstanding and to be retired) as secret as possible.

There is also the *nonmandatory specific sinking fund*, the most prevalent type in electric utility issues. The $100 million, 12⅛ percent bonds of Public Service Electric and Gas Company due on December 1, 2012, require the retirement of $1 million of bonds each December 1, 1983, through 2011. The company may satisfy the sinking fund, in whole or in part, by delivering bonds acquired through open market purchases or other means, by paying cash to the trustees, who will call bonds for redemption at 100, or by utilizing unfunded property additions or improvements at 60 percent of their cost. Property credits so utilized cannot be further employed under the mortgage.

Utilities generally are considered consumers of capital, for they engage in large, ongoing construction projects. Because they need to borrow fairly regularly, the application of property credits helps to reduce their demands on the capital markets. (It makes no sense to pay off debt on the one hand only to have to go back to the market to raise the money that was just paid out.) The utilization of property credits conserves cash and still helps maintain the integrity of the collateral behind the bonds. In some cases, the company may be able to authenticate and simultaneously cancel new bonds specifically authorized for this purpose. This usually is done against unfunded property additions and thus reduces the amount of new debt that the company can issue.

A slight variation of the property sinking fund is found in the indenture of Continental Telephone Company of California's 7⅝% First Mortgage Bonds due December 31, 1997. The requirement is 1 percent annually of each outstanding series of bonds. The funds must be held by the trustee as part of the mortgaged property and paid back to the company as reimbursement for 100 percent of the amount of available net property additions. If not paid out, the funds may be used to repurchase or call bonds. Any funds remaining in the trust after five years must be used to retire debt.

One cannot always believe what is stated in a company's financial reports. In May, 1977, some holders of New England Power Company's 10⅞ percent bonds due 2005 were surprised when the company announced the redemption on the following July 1 of $2.4 million of the $80 million outstanding at 101.55. The issue had the usual utility sinking fund provisions, namely 1 percent annually, cash, bonds or property credits at 60 percent. In addition, the indenture provided that an additional 2 percent ($1,600,000) could be retired. Surprised investors, having read the company's 1977 annual report, would have concluded that property credits would be used and bonds would not be called. A footnote to the financials said that "the company may elect to satisfy its annual sinking fund obligations of $3,850,000 . . . by evidencing to the Trustee net additional property in amounts not less than $6,417,000 in 1977. . . . For the sinking fund requirement due in 1977 the company intends to so elect." Because of declining interest rates, the company did a complete about-face in less than four months. Thus, the sinking fund obligation was satisfied with the high-coupon bonds and property additions. In 1978, the company also retired $2.4 million of the 10⅞s. High-coupon bonds in a lower interest rate environment are vulnerable to call even if the issuer promises not to do so.

Specific sinking funds apply to just the named issue. There are also *nonspecific sinking funds* of both the mandatory and nonmandatory variety. The nonspecific sinking fund, also known as a *funnel, tunnel, blanket,* or *aggregate* sinking fund, is based on the total outstanding amount of a company's bonded indebtedness. If mandatory, the sinking fund must be satisfied by bonds of any issue(s) selected by the company. If nonmandatory, the company may utilize certain property credits to fulfill the sinking fund requirement. Nonspecific sinking funds are found in the indentures of 17 companies. Three of these—Baltimore Gas & Electric, Ohio Edison, and Pacific Gas & Electric—have mandatory funnel sinking funds. The other 14, including the subsidiaries of the Southern Company and Northeast Utilities, have nonmandatory funnel sinking funds.

In most cases the redemption price for bonds called under the funnel sinking fund is par, but Pacific Gas & Electric's and Southern California Edison's operate at the general redemption prices. However, Pacific Gas has chosen to retire its low-coupon discount issues. The funnel sinking fund may be deceptive. It is usually 1 percent of all bonds outstanding, but this can amount to a large requirement, especially if the total amount is applied against a single issue. If bonded debt of $3 billion consists of issues ranging from $50 million to $200 million, the annual requirement is $30 million; this equals 15 to 60 percent of any one issue. When interests rates and cash needs are high, companies normally utilize unfunded property additions. But when interest rates are down, this provides a way to redeem high-coupon debt, usually at par. In some cases, however, a maximum of 1 percent of a specific issue may be retired within five years of issuance (the refunding-protected period). The Southern Company (among others) had to place this restriction in its subsidiaries' indentures after the funnel calls of the early 1970s. Thus, while there is a limit on the amount of bonds that can be redeemed in the first five years, once that period has expired, investors should be careful. An issuer could apply the maximum amount possible to the retirement of the bonds at par and then call any remaining ones at the regular redemption prices.

Most sinking funds operate annually, but some, such as Pacific Gas & Electric's are effective semiannually. Again, most sinking funds are based on a specific percentage of the original amount issued or an amount of bonds that remains the same until the entire issue is retired. But other issues' sinking fund payments increase periodically. Each payment may be higher than the preceding one, or payments might be level for several years, then step up for another few years, and so forth. Some sinking funds even increase for several years and then decrease for a few years.

Because of the risk of exhausting gas supplies, some mortgage and debenture indentures of gas pipeline companies provide for the acceleration of the sinking fund in the event that estimates of the reserve lives of the companies' proven gas reserves decline. ANR Pipeline Company (formerly Michigan Wisconsin Pipe Line Company) has such a provision. The prospectus for the 10⅝% First Mortgage Pipe Line Bonds due April 15 1995, states,

> Indenture will provide in substance that in the event that an independent engineer's certificate of reserve life, which the Company is required to file with the Trustee prior to May 1 of each year, shows a reserve life for the Company's controlled proven gas reserves of less than eight years and a date of exhaustion of reserve life earlier than any sinking fund payment date then in effect, the next two sinking fund installments shall each be increased. . . . However, if the reserve life shown in any such certificate is less than four years, all sinking

fund installments falling due subsequent to the year in which such certificate is filed shall become payable on December 31 of such year.

Thus, the sinking fund payments can be increased, but if future certificates consequently show an improvement in the gas supply, the sinking fund will be adjusted once again. In the 1970s, Transcontinental Gas Pipe Line Corporation was required to accelerate the sinking funds of at least five of its mortgage bond issues and one debenture issue for at least five years in a row.

There are other types of sinking funds seldom seen in public U.S. corporate debt. Sinking funds can be on a contingent basis, i.e., based on a certain level of corporate earnings or expressed as a percentage of earnings or cash flow. This type may be found in some financially weaker companies (such as one emerging from bankruptcy or reorganization), requiring that part of the cash flow be directed toward debt retirement. If the earnings aren't there, there is no sinking fund requirement. Missouri-Kansas-Texas Railroad Company's 5% Prior Lien Series E Bonds due 1990 has a 1 percent sinking fund with the deposits to be made from earnings in excess of $1 million. That company's 5½% Subordinated Income Debentures due 2033 have a noncumulative sinking fund payable from available income, if any. Normally, failure to make a sinking fund payment when due is an event of default.

Another type of sinking fund, found in the issues of Canadian provincial debt sold in the U.S. market, is what is called the *invested* or *Canadian* variety. This is really a fund that is set aside in order to provide some monies for the retirement of debt at maturity. Usually the funds can be invested in the same bonds, other bonds of the issuer, Canadian government bonds, and certain other permitted investments. Some issuers have utilized this type of fund to help support the market for existing bonds at the time of sale of a new issue. In effect, they have bought the outstanding bonds from some holders at an attractive spread from the new issue when the proceeds were to be placed in the new bonds.

A few issues may have a *purchase fund*. In some cases, it may operate prior to the start of the sinking fund; in others, there may be no sinking fund. Although the purchase fund may seem like a sinking fund, it does not operate when the debt's market price is above par. The purchase fund may require that the issuer, through its agent, attempt, on a best-efforts basis and in good faith, to purchase a certain amount of bonds at par or less, in public and private transactions, each year. This may lend market support to the bonds and encourage some investors to buy the bonds who ordinarily might not do so.

A purchase fund found in Harnischfeger Corporation's 15 percent notes due April 15, 1994, requires an annual purchase fund of 5 percent of the original issue in the event the notes' market price is less than par for 60 consecutive calendar days. This purchase fund is cumulative and remains in effect until satisfied, but there may be no more than one such purchase obligation in any one year. The prospectus says,

> The purchase agency arrangements have been designed to provide a limited measure of market liquidity for the Notes and in certain circumstances to result in the retirement prior to stated maturity of a portion of the outstanding Notes. There can be no assurance that such arrangements will, in fact, support market liquidity for the Notes or result in the retirement of any Notes. The purchase agency arrangements are not equivalent to a sinking fund, mandatory redemption feature or similar provision. . . . In the event that the market price of the Notes is equal to or greater than 100% of the principal amount thereof for even one day within each 60 consecutive calendar day period, the purchase agency arrangements of the Note Indenture will not become operative. Prospective purchasers should be prepared to hold any Notes to be purchased by them until maturity in 1994, optional redemption, if any, by the Company or sale in the open market or otherwise.

In 1986, the *annuity note* appeared. This is basically a level debt service arrangement similar to a home mortgage; each periodic payment is applied to interest and principal. Ford Motor Credit Company issued Series 1 of its Annuity Notes in September 1986. The minimum denomination was $100,000, repayable in 20 equal quarterly installments of $5,933.28 each March 1, June 1, September 1, and December 1 starting December 1, 1986. The first installment consisted of $1,791.45 of interest and $4,201.83 of principal. The last installment, on September 1, 1991, will consist of only $105.47 of interest and $5,887.81 of principal. This type of security eliminates a large balloon payment at maturity and helps the company to better match its liabilities to its automobile receivables. Some investors needing periodic return of principal, especially those pension funds with heavy payments to retired beneficiaries, have been thought to be among the purchasers of these notes.

MAINTENANCE AND REPLACEMENT FUNDS

Until March 23, 1977, hardly anyone in the investment community knew—or cared—what a *maintenance and replacement fund (M&R)* was. On that date the exact nature of this little known, never used, but standard provision was made abundantly clear when Florida Power & Light Company announced its intention to deposit cash in the amount of $64.8 million with the trustee of its 10⅛ percent bonds due March 1, 2005 (issued March 13, 1975), to satisfy the maintenance and replacement fund requirement. (The maintenance and replacement fund is also known as the *maintenance and renewal fund,* the *maintenance fund,* and the *replacement fund.*) The cash was used for the redemption on September 2, 1977, of $63.7 million of the outstanding $125 million of bonds at the special redemption price of 101.65. The regular redemption price at that time was 110.98, and the refunding-protected period would not expire until March 1, 1980, when the regular redemption price would be 109.76. Prior to the March announcement, the bonds were trading around 111; afterward, they immediately fell to 101.

The M&R provision was first placed in bond indentures or electric utilities subject to regulation by the Securities and Exchange Commission under the Public Utility Holding Company Act in the early 1940s. It remained in the indentures even when some of the companies no longer were subject to regulation under the act. Property is subject to wear and tear, and the replacement fund supposedly helps maintain the integrity of the property securing the bonds. One writer said, "A replacement fund is designed to force actual annual expenditures for new property or the reduction of bonded indebtedness."[20] It differs from a sinking fund in that it only helps maintain the value of the security while a sinking or improvement fund is designed to improve the security behind the debt. The M&R is similar to, but more complex than, a provision in a home mortgage requiring the homeowner to maintain his or her property in good repair.

A maintenance and replacement fund requires a company to determine, after the close of the fiscal year, the amount that is needed to satisfy the fund and the amount of any shortfall. (Not all utilities provide for them, and some companies have eliminated or sharply modified them in recent years.) The requirement is based on a formula; this is usually 15 percent or so of adjusted gross operating revenues, but some funds are based on a much smaller percentage (such as 2 to 2.5 percent) of depreciable mortgaged property or a percentage of bonded debt. The difference between what is required and the actual amount expended on maintenance is the shortfall. The shortfall usually is satisfied with unfunded property additions, but it can be satisfied with cash or, in some cases, maintenance and replacement fund credits from prior years. The cash can be used for the retirement of debt or withdrawn upon the certification of unfounded property credits.

Inflated fuel costs in the 1970s increased the M&R requirements of those funds based on a percentage of revenues beyond what normally would have been adequate. In some cases, the unfunded property additions might be insufficient to satisfy the shortfall. Companies may be unable to obtain the necessary operating permits and other licenses for some nuclear plants, which would make such property ineligible for use as unfunded property. Also, the amount of available property additions may be inadequate due to declining construction outlays resulting from reduced demand for electric power. But the M&R certainly grants most companies the right to retire debt. Some issues restrict the amount of bonds that may be redeemed through the M&R fund. While investors sometimes hear that company X has no intention of retiring debt through the M&R provisions, this is doubtful—it may be forced to by the economics of the situation, as Florida Power & Light was. Of course, the company's cash position is an important determinant of whether or not it is financially able to call the bonds. As we have seen, cash can be raised if doing so makes sense, and refunding limitations almost always relate to redemptions at the general, not the special, redemption prices. Also, some companies may be reluctant to utilize an M&R call for fear of angering their investors. But again, if a company is being pressured by regulatory authorities, it may have no choice. Also, the initial trauma of the M&R calls of the late 1970s is over; investors today are more aware of the possibility of such calls and usually can position themselves accordingly.

How did the Florida Power & Light call come about? In January, 1977, rate hearings began with the public service commission, which was interested in FP&L's cost of debt and ways to reduce it. One way, suggested the company's financial people, was through the maintenance and replacement fund. This testimony was given on March 23 and a press release issued, but the right to not redeem the bonds was reserved. In June, an order was issued granting FP&L a $195.5 million rate boost, based on the assumption that half of the 10⅛s would be retired and substituting a 9 percent rate. It projected that annual interest savings of over $500,000 would be passed through to customers. "Once the Florida Public Service Commission factored these retirements into its cost of capital calculations, the company had little choice but to go ahead and exercise the special redemption option."[21] The 1983 court decision said that all the benefits from the redemption would be passed through to the ratepayer whether or not the bonds were called. The company's shareholders received none of the savings.

Florida Power & Light's redemption broke the ice. Several others followed, most notably Carolina Power & Light Company's. In 1977 and 1978, the company deposited nearly $79 million with its trustee under similar provisions. In June 1978, it called for the redemption of $46 million of the privately held 11⅛ percent bonds due 1994 and $32.7 million of the publicly held 11s of 1984 at the special redemption price of par. The company was sued by its bondholders, including an institutional bondholder who had negotiated the first Carolina Power & Light Mortgage dated May 1940, which contained an improvement fund and a maintenance and renewal fund that could be satisfied with fundable property or bonds. The courts have upheld the companies' rights to redeem debt through such provisions. But issuers must ensure that their offering documents clearly spell out special redemption features to avoid accusation of concealing important information. On the other hand, it is incumbent on bond buyers to know the terms of the issues they own.

After the 1977 to 1978 period, maintenance and replacement fund calls receded into the background as interest rates rose. It wasn't until 1985 that these redemptions reappeared to any noticeable degree. By that time investors were at least somewhat familiar with these provisions, or at least should have been, even though they still disliked them. The legal considerations were out of the way, and the provisions had become a fact of life: "Investors, beware! We have the right to redeem our debt in any way that our contract allows. We will do it in the cheapest way in order to benefit our ratepayers and shareholders." Most of the calls came at par. On May 5, 1986, Houston Lighting & Power Company redeemed $117,056,000 of its 12⅜% First Mortgage Bonds due March 15, 2013, through the replacement fund provisions, leaving about $8 million outstanding. The call price was par, but the bonds were trading at 115 or so just before the redemption was announced in early April.

REDEMPTION THROUGH THE SALE OF ASSETS AND EMINENT DOMAIN

Bondholders want the borrower to maintain and preserve the value of the collateral securing the debt. The fact that the debt may be overcollateralized does not necessarily mean that management has free rein over the use and disposition of the excess collateral and any proceeds therefrom. But the lender has no right to impose undue restrictions on the borrower's ability to sell plant and property if doing so is deemed desirable from the standpoint of sound business practice. The secured lender has the right to adequate protection. If a company has $100 million of bonded debt outstanding secured by $200 million of plant, property, and equipment, the $100 million surplus collateral provides additional protection for the bond owner. If the company feels that it is prudent to sell some of the property securing that debt, it should be allowed to do so (release the property from the mortgage lien) and substitute either cash or other property so that the total value of the collateral will not be reduced. The cash can be used to retire bonds or buy additional collateral. This type of situation is covered by *release and substitution of property clauses.* Obviously notes and debentures, being unsecured, have no release and substitution of property clauses.

The release and substitution of property clause of Arizona

Public Service Company as described in its prospectuses is fairly clear:

> When not in default under the Mortgage, the Company may obtain the release from the lien thereof of (a) property that has become unserviceable, obsolete or unnecessary for use in the Company's operations, provided that it replaces such property with, or substitutes for the same, an equal value of other property and (b) other property that has been sold or otherwise disposed of, provided that the Company deposits with the Trustee cash in an amount, or utilizes as a credit net Property Additions acquired by the Company within the preceding five yars and having a fair value (not more than Cost), equal to the fair value of the property to be released.[22]

The company has utilized this method of debt redemption a couple of times. In late 1984, it retired $100 million of its 16% First Mortgage Bonds due 1994 at 100, with the proceeds from its gas distribution assets. In early 1987, it redeemed $150 million of its 11½% Mortgage Bonds due June 1, 2015, at par. The proceeds for this redemption came from the sale and leaseback of its portion in Unit #2 of the Palo Verde nuclear power plant. These bonds had been issued only in June 1985.

There have been cases in which companies sold plant, deposited the funds with the trustee, and then later decided not to redeem debt. In March 1984, Georgia Power Company sold some property and deposited funds with the trustee. It could have used the funds to purchase or redeem bonds or could have withdrawn them against delivery of bonds or shown that unfunded property additions existed after withdrawal. The fear of a high-coupon bond redemption hung over the market for a couple of months until, on May 31, the company said it would not redeem any debt. Georgia decided against the call because of uncertainties in the financial market. It pointedly stated that if it had future asset sales, its options regarding the use of the funds would remain open.

Of course, investors are hurt most when their high-yield bonds are called at par or the special redemption price. But unsecured debt usually has no special redemption prices or requirements for prepayment in the event of asset sales. However, redemptions of unsecured debt do occur within the refunding-protected period if the funds came from the sale of assets. On December 13, 1983, Internorth, Inc. announced a February 1, 1984, call of $90.5 million out of $200 million of its 17½ percent debentures due August 1, 1991, at the regular redemption price of 112.32. The refunding-protected period ran until September 30, 1988. However, the proceeds were obtained from the sale of its Northern Propane Gas Company unit. On October 1, 1984, it redeemed another $23,875,000 of these 17½ percent debentures at 109.86 with funds obtained from the December 1983 sale of two tanker ships.

Wisconsin Michigan Power retired $9.9 million of its 9¼ percent bonds due 2000 on February 28, 1977, at 100.97. On the preceding June 30, the company had sold its gas business for $16.9 million to an affiliate, Wisconsin Natural Gas Company. The gas company got some of the money through bank borrowings. Of the proceeds, $16.5 million was deposited with the trustee under the release and substitution of property clause and a portion of the funds released to the company against certified property additions. The balance was used to redeem the high-coupon 9¼s, as interest rates had declined to the point where management thought it was in the company's best interest to do so.

Another somewhat similar transaction between affiliated companies occurred eight years later and resulted in Southern Carolina Electric and Gas Company's (SCE&G) redemption of its 16% First Mortgage Bonds due June 1, 2011, at par on March 1, 1985. At the end of 1984, the company formed a holding company called SCANA that had two subsidiaries, SCG&E and the South Carolina Generating company. South Carolina Electric & Gas Company sold a coal-fired generating plant to its affiliated generating company for $80 million. They used these funds to call the 16% bonds, which recently had been trading at 116. Some might call this unfair dealing and maybe even a sham transaction, but it does not appear to be much different from the preceding Wisconsin Michigan Power transaction. Both of these redemptions naturally angered a number of sophisticated institutional investors.

Many utility bond issues contain provisions concerning the taking of assets by a government body through its right of eminent domain or the disposition of assets by order of or to any government authority. In a number of cases, bonds must be redeemed if the company receives more than a certain amount in cash. Washington Water Power Company must apply the proceeds of $15 million or more to the retirement of debt, while the Southern Company subsidiaries' indentures require redemption of debt if the amount received is more than 10 percent of the principal amount of bonds outstanding. Again the redemptions would be made at the special redemption price. The author is not aware of any major calls due to eminent domain, but state takeovers of utility properties are bandied about from time to time. A recent example that was still up in the air at the end of 1986 is Long Island Lighting Company; many disgruntled ratepayers and politicians have urged the state to take over Lilco's facilities.

Sales of property and plant to government units are slightly more common. In 1984, Pacific Power & Light Company sold an electric distribution system to the Emerald People's Utility District for $25 million. It applied these proceeds to the redemption of half of the outstanding 14¾% Mortgage Bonds due 2010 at the special redemption price of 100. This issue was not the highest-coupon one outstanding in the company's capitalization. There were some 18s of 1991, but these were exempt from the special provision for the retirement of bonds with the proceeds from property sold to government authories.

NET WORTH, MERGER, AND OTHER REDEMPTIONS

The great increase in merger and acquisition activity, including leveraged buyouts, has caused some corporations to include other special debt redemption, extinguishment or retirement features in their indentures. For example, the *maintenance of net worth clause* has been included in the indentures of many of the lower-rated bond issues of the mid-1980s. In this case, an issuer covenants to maintain its net worth above a certain level. If its net worth falls below that specified amount for (usually) two consecutive quarters, the company must begin redeeming the debt at par. The redemptions, often 10 percent of the original issue, are mostly on a semiannual basis and must continue until the net worth recovers to an amount above the stated figure. In many cases, the company is required only to "offer to redeem" the stated amount. An offer to redeem is not mandatory on the bondholders' part; only those holders who want their bonds redeemed need do so. In a number of instances in which the issuer is required to call bonds, the bondholders may elect not to have the bonds redeemed. This is not much different from an offer to redeem. It may "protect" bondholders from the redemption of the high-coupon debt at lower interest rates. However, if a company's net worth declines to a level low enough to activate such a call, it probably would be prudent to have the debt redeemed.

The minimum net worth requirement typically is approximately 45 to 55 percent of the net worth at the time the debt was issued. But the definition of net worth, or net tangible assets, is not the same for all issuers. The prospectuses talk about generally accepted accounting principles and frequently include only common shareholders' net worth, but some also include preferred stock. Intangible assets, such as goodwill, patents, trademarks, and unamortized deferred charges, normally are excluded from the calculation of tangible net worth. But again definitions may vary among issues. The prospectus for Coastal Corporation's 11¾% Senior Debentures due June 15, 2006, defines consolidated net worth as:

> . . . the total consolidated stockholders' equity (exclusive of any Mandatory Redemption Preferred Stock) of such person and its subsidiaries determined on a consolidated basis in accordance with generally accepted accounting principles, except that there shall be deducted therefrom all intangible assets (determined in accordance with generally accepted accounting principles) including, without limitation, organization costs, patents, trademarks, copyrights, franchises, research and development expenses, and any amount reflected as treasury stock; provided, that goodwill arising from acquisitions and unamortized debt discount and expense, whether existing on the date of the indenture or arising thereafter, shall not be deducted from total consolidated stockholders' equity.

Many investors view goodwill as an intangible item.

Obviously the definition is very important, and one cannot always rely on the prospectus since it may include no definition or only an incomplete one. This was very important for the holders of the 14⅞% Senior Subordinated Notes due 1995 of Minstar, Inc. The $300 million issue was publicly sold in April 1985. One year later, the company announced the June 30 call of $30 million at par due to the net worth clause. The notes were trading around 113 ($1,130 each) prior to the call announcement. Minstar also bought an additional $60 million of notes in the open market, recording an extraordinary loss of $7.9 million on the debt extinguishment. Here again an indenture provision was used to retire some high-cost debt and caught investors off guard. Analysts and investors relying on the prospectus could come up with no close approximation of tangible net worth. The prospectus stated "Tangible Net Worth generally means consolidated shareholders' equity, less, among other things, goodwill, patents, trademarks, service marks, trade names, copyrights, organization or developmental expenses and other intangible items."

The indenture for the notes defines tangible net worth as follows:

> "Tangible Net Worth" means the consolidated equity of the common stockholders of the Company and its consolidated subsidiaries less their consolidated Intangible Assets, all determined on a consolidated basis in accordance with generally accepted accounting principles. For purposes of this definition "Intangible Assets" means the amount (to the extent reflected in determining such consolidated equity of the common stockholders) of (i) all write-ups (other than write-ups resulting from foreign currency translations and write-ups of tangible assets of a going concern business made within twelve months after the acquisition of such business) subsequent to December 31, 1984 in the book value of any asset owned by the company or a consolidated subsidiary, (ii) all investments in unconsolidated subsidiaries and in persons which are not subsidiaries, and (iii) all unamortized debt discount and expense, unamortized deferred charges, goodwill, patents, trademarks, service marks, trade names, copyrights, organizational or developmental expenses and other intangible items, all of the foregoing as determined in accordance with generally accepted accounting principles.[23]

Note item (ii) above and the reference to investments. Minstar had substantial investments in marketable equities with value, yet the indenture was written so as to make them valueless. They had to be eliminated in the calculation of tangible net worth. It is interesting to note that the use of proceeds section of the prospectus stated that the monies "will be added to the Company's general funds to be used for acquisitions, investments and general corporate purposes." It said that the company "makes significant investments in securities of other companies." Thus, investors who initially purchased the bonds were effectively reducing tangible net worth to the extent that investment securities were purchased with the proceeds. Also, this could allow a company with a similar definition and operations to rid itself of some high-coupon debt at par just by making more investments! Of course, Minstar's published annual report made no mention of what tangible net worth amounted to according to the indenture's definition at December 31, 1985.

There are a few other ways by which companies can (or must) extinguish debt prior to maturity. The issues of some finance companies and others with a considerable amount of accounts receivable have a provision allowing the issues to be redeemed if the amount of receivables declines below a certain figure. While not mandatory, this provision can protect debtholders from weakening of credit due to a substantial decline in the issuer's asset base. It may allow the issuer to reduce its debt burden, assuming that it still has the wherewithall to do so, by calling the debt. Of course, if the company elects to redeem debt, it will most likely choose from the higher-coupon issues. This provision has been infrequently invoked—if ever—by major debt issuers. A call could occur if there were a serious recession and receivables declined by a substantial amount. If could also be activated if a company sold or transferred receivables to another corporation as part of a reorganization, restructuring, or liquidation.

The debt of some foreign companies sold in the United States may be subject to premature redemption in the event of certain situations that normally would not affect conventional domestic issues. In December 1983, Swan Brewery Company Limited sold US$135 of 14⅞% Limited Subordination Debentures due December 15, 1998. The issue has a provision requiring Swan to redeem a specific percentage of the outstanding debentures (subject to certain credits) if the average of the U.S. dollar noon buying rates for Australian dollars over certain six-month periods is less than those stated in the prospectus. The redemption is on a pro rata basis, but holders may elect not to have their bonds redeemed. Another provision, also subject to election by the debtholder, allows the company to offer to redeem in whole if the Australian government requires the withholding of taxes and other government charges from payments to the debentureholders.

PSA, Inc's. 12½% Senior Notes due 1996 are subject to mandatory redemption in whole if at any time the common stock or assets of its Pacific Southwest Airlines subsidiary is sold to, or if the airline merges with, an unrelated entity for more than $115 million. Another special mandatory redemption—which is limited, as holders may elect not to have their notes redeemed—appears in the USG Corporation's senior notes due in 1991 and 1996 and issued December 1986. It basically says that if a "designated event," including certain mergers, recapitalizations, or a concentration of the shares (20 percent or more) in the hands of one person, occurs within one year, and if the ratings are lowered to below investment grade because of it, the company must redeem the notes. This is somewhat similar to the poison put mentioned in Chapter 2.

TENDERS

A more pleasant method of debt retirement—at least for the bondholders—is the tender. While it may be more costly for the borrower than a straight cash call, it allows debt to be retired even if its is noncallable. Also, tenders don't force the holder to give up the bonds. In order to induce the submission of bonds under a tender, the issuer must offer a price above what others are willing to offer, namely a buyback price above the market. According to Finnerty, the premiums offered in the 1977 tenders for some Bell System subsidiary issues "were determined by calculating the respective tender prices that would provide a yield-to-first-call comparable to the yield an investor could realize by investing in U.S. government agency issues over the same time horizon."[24] Today investors would rather compare the resulting yield to direct government paper in view of the numerous concerns about some of the agencies' viability.

Tenders are not limited to issues selling above par. In 1983, Diamond International Company tendered for its 8.35 percent debentures due in 2006 at 77½, and Black & Decker Manufacturing Company tendered for its 8.45 percent notes due 1985 at 98. In 1985, Burlington Northern Railroad Company made an unsuccessful tender at 53½ for Northern Pacific Railway Company's 4% Prior Lien Railway and Land Grant Gold Bonds due 1997 and at 39 for Northern Pacific's 3% General Lien Railway and Land Grant Gold Bonds due 2047. The bonds, issued in 1896, are not callable for life. The mortgages do not provide for their modification or for the release of certain collateral, namely some valuable natural resource–laden properties that Burlington Northern wanted to commercially develop. The tender was part of a plan to obtain the property's release by substituting government bonds in a trust to ensure the payment of principal and interest when due for the remaining untendered bonds; this is an example of an in-substance defeasance (discussed shortly). Bondholders sued, as they thought a higher price should have been offered. A federal judge barred Burlington from proceeding, and the company withdrew the offer.

Transworld Corporation sold $250 million of 8 ¾ percent notes due 1993 and 9.85 percent debentures due 2016 under a prospectus dated October 2, 1986. The notes were not redeemable for life and the debentures not redeemable prior to 2006. Shortly thereafter, Transworld became the target of a corporate raider. Deciding that liquidation or corporate suicide was a better path to take, the company quickly formulated a liquidation plan. Currently callable company debt was called by year's end. The nonredeemable issues were tendered for at par, giving holders a golden opportunity to stay whole. Those who did not tender would have the bonds assumed by a new subsidiary organized from the company's remaining operations.

From late 1984 through 1986, a fairly substantial number of tenders occurred as interest rates declined. A tender allows a company to retire debt at a predetermined price, and rather quickly since they usually are open for only a couple of weeks. A simple open market bond purchase usually occurs over a longer period, leaving the purchaser subject to changes in market conditions. This may prove cheaper than a tender offer if interest rates rise and prices decline, but it is less likely to permit the company to achieve its debt retirement goals. Of course, the market can also go against the company using a tender offer, with the result that few bonds will be repurchased. As with cash calls, net present value savings now are made under successful tenders, the average coupon of the outstanding debt is reduced, and certain expenses are currently deductible for income tax purposes. But like other debt retirement transactions, tenders may result in accounting or financial reporting losses.

With the Dutch auction tender, the sellers rather than the buying company set the prices they wish to receive. At the end of the tender period, the buyer reviews all the bids received and determines the highest price it is willing to pay. It then buys all the bonds tendered to it at or below the maximum acceptable tender price. The Dutch auction allows the market to set the tender price.

Proceeds for a tender can come from any source. On December 3, 1986, May Department Stores Company sold $150 million of 9⅛ percent debentures due 2016. The use of proceeds section says that the new funds will be used to retire some short-term debt that had a weighted average interest cost of 5.8 percent and matured before January 1, 1987. Yet, on December 11 the company announced the tender for $100 million of its 11⅞ percent debentures due April 15, 2015, at 112.04. Holders need not tender their bonds, and the company is within its rights to offer to repurchase them even within the refunding-protected period.

In general, it makes good sense for most investors to consider tender offers because if enough bonds are repurchased, the few remaining could very well become virtually unmarketable, or at least very illiquid. If listed, they could be delisted. Traders ordinarily will not take into their positions bonds that cannot be readily resold. Also, with fewer bonds outstanding the holder is more likely to lose a greater percentage of its holdings through the sinking fund. In September 1983, Northern States Power Company (Minnesota) received tenders at 119.75 for about $65.6 million out of $75 million of its 15¾ percent mortgage bonds due 2011. Some $9.4 million remained in public hands. The sinking fund was 1 percent, or $750,000 each year, cash, bonds, or property additions. On October 31, 1983, the company called for the December 1 sinking fund $750,000 of the bonds, or nearly 8 percent of the then outstanding amount. Thus, in less than two months holders lost some 19¾ points—the difference between the tender price and the sinking fund call price. Similar amounts were retired in subsequent years at par and the remaining balance on December 1, 1986, at 112.21.

DEFEASANCE

Defeasance is included as a type of debt extinguishment even though the bonds remain outstanding. It is one of the few methods of premature debt extinguishment in which bondholders are basically unaffected. There are two types of defeasance: economic, or in-substance, defeasance and legal defeasance, or novation. Until recently defeasance was rarely used for public corporate debt obligations. There had been cases of privately placed debt in which the issuer reached an agreement with all of the lenders under which they would release the borrower from the indenture in return for ample consideration, typically an acceptable securities package. There was little that a corporation with public debt could do to defease its obligations, although municipal obligations provided for legal defeasance for a number of years.

In November 1983, the Financial Accounting Standards Board (FASB) approved by a four-to-three vote the *Statement of Financial Accounting Standards No. 76*, "Extinguishment of Debt, An Amendment of APB Opinion No. 26," providing for the economic, or insubstance, defeasance of corporate debt.[25] This became effective for transactions entered into after December 31, 1983, and applies only to debt with specific maturities and fixed interest rates. In this type of defeasance, an irrevocable trust is established to service the principal and interest payments on the debt issue being defeased. The assets of the trust must consist of essentially risk-free monetary assets in the currency in which the debt is denominated and with a cash flow timed to very closely match that of the defeased obligation. For U.S.-dollar-payable debt, these qualified assets include cash, direct obligations of the U.S. government, debt guaranteed by the U.S. government, and securities backed by U.S. government obligations as collateral under an arrangement in which the collateral's interest and principal payments flow directly to the security holder. As some securities can be paid prior to the stated maturity or have partial principal payments that may be paid before the final maturity, they are not essentially risk free from a timing standpoint and thus are ineligible for inclusion in the trust assets. Many agency issues also would be ineligible, as they are not guaranteed by the United States. The debtor must be virtually guaranteed that it will not be required to make any future payments in regard to the defeased debt.

An economic defeasance removes the debt from the corporation's balance sheet but leaves the borrower still liable under all of the indenture provisions until the debt is actually extinguished. It must abide by any covenants, as economic defeasance is not provided for in indentures. Because of the debtor's continuing obligation under the indenture, the transaction must be disclosed in the notes to the financial statements for as long as the debt remains outstanding. The debt remains liable for tax reporting purposes, since it pays income tax on the income of the trust and takes a deduction for the interest expense. Also, when the trust terminates upon maturity of the defeased debt, taxes also must be paid on the increase in value between the cost of the trust's assets and the maturity value. But any fees paid to investment bankers for advice and any trustee fees normally will be considered tax-deductible expenses at the time they are incurred.

A novation, or legal, defeasance removes the debt from the balance sheet for financial reporting purposes, frees the corporation from any indenture terms (with a few minor exceptions), and eliminates any further tax consequences. In order to obtain this, the indenture must provide for legal defeasance. In January 1981, Union Carbide Corporation registered a proposed $200 million offering whose indenture contained this provision. The issue never came to market. Investors were confused and thought this was another method by which a company could prematurely retire debt. However, after in-substance defeasance got the nod of approval from the Securities and Exchange Commission in 1983, indentures of publicly offered corporate bonds with legal defeasance provisions started to appear. The provision mentioned in the debt securities prospectus for Dayton Hudson Corporation (dated October 16, 1986) says that after payment of the necessary funds has been made to the trustee,

> ... the Indenture will cease to be of further effect ... (except for certain obligations to compensate, reimburse and indemnify the Trustee, to register the transfer or exchange of Debt Securities, to replace stolen, lost or mutilated Debt Securities, to maintain paying agencies and to hold monies for payment in trust), and the Company will be deemed to have satisfied and discharged the indenture. ... In the event of any such defeasance, holders of Debt Securities of such series would be able to look only to such trust fund for payment of principal and premium, if any, and interest, if any, on their Debt Securities.

While the trusts are irrevocable they are not inviolable, as a considerable number provide for withdrawal of collateral and substitution of cash and other satisfactory collateral sufficient to satisfy the payment obligations in a manner consistent with the defeasance provisions. Withdrawals reportedly were made in late 1986, when some companies bought back and retired portions of their defeased debt and sold corresponding shares of government securities withdrawn from the trusts. This was an economical way of taking advantage of the tax laws, which would shortly change. The loss taken on the repurchase would be partially offset by the high 46 percent income tax rate, while the capital gain on the sale of the Treasuries would be taxed at 28 percent. This caused some accounting experts to consider whether the whole issue should be reexamined. The initial FASB bulletin took into account the possibility of the repurchase of defeased debt and said that it should be viewed as though "the debtor is making an investment in the future cash flows from the trust and should report its investment as an asset in its balance sheet. The debtor should not be considered to be reextinguishing its debt. Thus, no gain or loss should be recognized from such purchase of those debt securities."[26] It did not consider that the "irrevocable" trusts could be violated even if provided for.

In 1982 there were several economic defeasance transactions. Kellogg Company defeased its 9⅝ percent notes due October 1, 1985, by paying $65.6 million in cash to the Morgan Guaranty Trust Company, which arranged for a group of companies to assume the principal and interest payments for the $75 million issue. The transaction was also guaranteed by a Morgan Guaranty letter of credit. Exxon Corporation defeased its 6 percent debentures due 1997 and 6½ percent debentures due 1998. The trust portfolio consisted of federal government and agency securities. These transactions were allowed to stand as economic defeasances, since they occurred before FASB No. 76 took effect. Since the beginning of 1984 a number of other companies have defeased debt, including Atlantic Richfield Company, Cincinnati Gas & Electric Company, and City Investing Company (as part of its liquidation plan). Du Pont Company announced in December 1984 that on December 1, 1988, it would redeem its 14 percent notes due 1991 and set up a trust arrangement to service the defeased issue.

Defeasance transactions normally occur when interest rates are high, a company has lower-coupon debt outstanding, the prices of Treasury securities are depressed, and the issuer is in an ample cash position. Also, the benefits of investing in a trust full of Treasury securities should be viewed as better than investing in new plant and equipment. Among the advantages of defeasance is the boost it can give to the company's reported earnings due to the difference between the par value of the defeased bonds and the cost of the trust assets. United States Steel Corporation (now USX Corporation) issued an earnings release on July 30, 1985, stating that it retired $192 million of debt in the first half of the year, including defeasance of $168 million of the 4⅝ percent subordinated debentures due 1996. The total extinguishment resulted in an extraordinary gain of $38 million net of income tax of $32 million. These earnings are "below the line" and should not be used in calculating the financial ratios popular with corporate bond analysts; they are nonoperating, non-cash, and nonrecurring.

The debt is removed from the books, leverage should decrease and other debt-related measurements should show improvement. This could lead to a better credit evaluation for the company, especially if the defeasance is a novation. The repayment risk formerly associated with the predefeased debt is, to all intents and purposes, eliminated. The defeasance reduces the chance of the issue's price being run up in a repurchase program, but at times it may be more expensive. Obviously it should be undertaken only after all alternative methods of debt redemption have been analyzed. The benefits to the balance sheet and income statements are one-time occurrences and may be only temporary (which should not fool knowledgeable bond investors). Also, with an in-substance defeance nothing will really have changed, since the company is still liable for the debt.

How have the rating agencies reacted to defeasance transactions? When the previously mentioned Union Carbide issue was proposed, Moody's Investors Service, in its *Bond Survey* of February 2, 1981, stated, "When and if such a transaction [defeasance] occurs, payment of the bonds becomes assured, Moody's would raise the rating for these debentures from Aa to Aaa." Standard & Poor's Corporation commented that it would rate legally defeased issues "AAA" in consideration of the quality of assets in the trust and the matched flow of funds to debt service requirements. However, getting the highest possible rating for an in-substance defeased issue would require overcoming concerns about corporate bankruptcy and the effects on the trust estate pledge to service the debt. S & P said,

Therefore, in order for S & P to rate in-substance defeased debt "AAA", opinions of counsel are required indicating that:

—The automatic stay provisions of the Bankruptcy Code (Section 362 (a)) would not apply in the event of the company's bankruptcy.

—Section 549 of the code, which could void or impair the timely use of escrowed funds to pay debt service, would not apply in the event of the company's bankruptcy.

—Deposit of assets into the escrow account will not constitute a preference with respect to the company in the event of the company's bankruptcy within 90 days after such deposit.

In addition, S & P must be assured that the defeased debt will be free from any risks associated with cross-default provisions that would tie the default and acceleration of the defeased issue to a default on other debt of the company.[27]

But why would an issuer go to the extra expense of the procedure even if it could get opinions satisfactory to Standard & Poor's? The debt is outstanding, and a "AAA" rating would benefit not the issuer but only the debtholder. Even if the ratings of economically defeased and nondefeased issues of the same issuer are the same, many investors will prefer the defeased one. The risk of default exists for both types, and the trust arrangement may not hold up in bankruptcy, thus placing the two issues on a parity. Only time and a court decision will settle the question. If the company does not go into bankruptcy, the gains from buying the defeased issue will be dubious. One should not overpay for economically defeased debt.

Some students of finance believe that economic defeasance is a "non-event." At the beginning of 1984 investment bankers were excited about defeasance, namely because they stood to earn some additional fees. But now, only a few years later, the subject arouses little interest from anyone except, perhaps, a few academics preparing their annual research papers. One reason possible is that interest rates had come down substantially by the end of 1986, thereby increasing the cost of the Treasuries to be used in these transactions and reducing potential accounting profits.

CONCLUSION

The level and trend of interest rates are among the more important factors in a company's decision as to whether or not to retire its debt, be it through a sinking fund, refunding, or defeasance. An issuer will redeem its debt when doing so will to its own advantage, not the debtholder's. If necessary, the issuer may use the protective provisions of an indenture against the bondholder. Other factors considered are the company's cash position and ability to raise the needed cash, its future cash requirements and financing plans, and, in the case of some utility companies, its ability to certify property additions or specifically authenticated bonds as credits for certain redemptions. The company must consider the impact of any call on its relationships with its creditors, the investment community, the regulatory authorities, and, most important, its shareholders and customers. Circumstances and attitudes do change. Just because a firm has established a pattern for satisfying sinking fund and other indenture provisions and may have waited until the redunding-protected period passed does not mean that it will continue to follow these patterns and methods. The greater the difference between the interest costs on the outstanding debt and the present level of interest rates (and the savings to be achieved), the more the company is compelled it to use whatever means it can to retire debt, especially high-coupon debt.

NOTES

1. "The Lessons of a Bond Failure," *The New York Times*, August 14, 1983.

2. Samuel Lucas, et al. Plaintiffs V. Florida Power & Light Company, Defendant. Final Judgment, 77-4009-Civ-SMA, United States District Court, Southern District of Florida. October 31, 1983.

3. Judgment, Harold Harris, Continental Casualty Company and National Fire Insurance Company of Hartford, etc. Plaintiffs–Respondents V. Union Electric Company, Defendant–Appellant, St. Louis Union Trust et al., Defendant–Cross Appellant, Missouri Court of Appeals, Eastern District, June 16, 1981.

4. "When's the Last Time You Read a Prospectus?" *Financial Analysts Journal* (September/October 1983): 10.

5. James Grant, Bernard M. Baruch: *The Adventures of a Wall Street Legend* (New York: Simon and Schuster, 1983), 55.

6. W. Braddock Hickman, *Corporate Bond Quality and Investor Experience* (Princeton, N.J.: Princeton University Press, 1958), 87.

7. On May 8, 1969, the Securities and Exchange Commission issued a release modifying its policy on refunding protection provisions for first mortgage debt of

companies subject to its jurisdiction under the Public Utility Holding Company Act of 1935. Prior to that date, those issues had to "be redeemable at the option of the issuer at any time upon reasonable notice and with reasonable redemption premiums, if any." The modification allowed issuers to include in their indentures provisions prohibiting the refunding of those new bonds with the proceeds of lower-cost debt securities for a maximum period of five years. These companies had to pay higher interest costs than other utility companies due to the lack of refunding protection. This SEC modification placed the utility holding company subsidiaries on a more equal footing with non–holding company operating utilities. The release also stated:

> Heretofore, the general redemption prices of first mortgage bonds have been considered reasonable . . . whenever such redemption prices commence, immediately following the issuance of such bonds, at an amount equal to the sum of the coupon rate plus the public offering price and decline each year thereafter by equal amounts to the principal amount at the beginning of the last year prior to maturity. No change in this policy is authorized. Therefore, when the five-year period of non-refundability authorized herein expires, the general redemption price at which the bonds may then be called will be the same as it would have been if there had been no restriction on refundability.

8. Arleigh P. Hess, Jr., and Willis J. Winn, *The Value of the Call Privilege* (Philadelphia: University of Pennsylvania, 1962), 24. This publication presents as interesting historical background of bonds calls, including corporate, government, and municipal.

9. Lucas et al. V. Florida Power & Light Company, Final Judgment, paragraph 77.

10. " 'Vanilla' Bonds Suit Investor Tastes," Standard & Poor's *CreditWeek*, August 4, 1986, 16.

11. Brief descriptions of the bond selection process may be found in Robert I. Landau; *Corporate Trust Administration and Management* (New York: Columbia University Press), 1985, 161–163, and *Commentaries on Indentures* (Chicago: American Bar Foundation, 1971), 497–499.

12. A comprehensive review of debt retirement and the associated math can be found in John D. Finnerty, *An Illustrated Guide to Bond Refunding Analysis* (Charlottesville, Va., Financial Analysts Research Foundation, 1984). The book covers refunding of premium and discount debt, sinking fund issues, tenders, exchange offers, defeasance, and preferred stock.

13. Letter dated June 13, 1983, to Members and Conferees, National Association of Regulatory Utility Commissioners (NARUC), from John J. Gibbons, Chairman, NARUC Staff Accounting Committee. Mr. Gibbons was also the Assistant Director and Chief Accountant of the Revenue Requirements Division of the California Public Utilities Commission.

14. "Morgan Stanley Sues Over Archer-Daniels' Plan to Redeem Debt," *The Wall Street Journal*, July 11, 1983.

15. Morgan Stanley and Company, Incorporated, Plaintiff v. Archer-Daniels-Midland Company, Defendant, Opinion 83 Civ. 5113, United States District Court, Southern District of New York, July 29, 1983.

16. The Franklin Life Insurance Company v. Commonwealth Edison Company, United States District Court, Southern District of Illinois, May 19, 1978. See Chapter 7 for a brief discussion of this case.

17. F. Corine Thompson and Richard L. Norgaard, *Sinking Funds: Their Use and Value* (New York: Financial Executives Research Foundation, 1967).

18. Charles Mackay, *Extraordinary Popular Delusions and the Madness of Crowds* (New York:Harmoney Books, 1980 reprint), 49. Originally issued in 1841, this book became popular after its recommendation by Bernard M. Baruch a half-century ago. In discussing the speculative madness of the time, Mackay comments on one of the "bubbles" as follows:

> But the most absurd and preposterous of all, and which shewed, more completely than any other, the utter madness of the people, was one started by an unknown adventurer, entitled, *"A company for carrying on an undertaking of great advantage, but nobody to know what it is."* (p. 55)

This appears to be similar to the blind pools of the mid-1980s.

Mackay also wrote something that could have appeared in today's financial press after the insider-trading scandals and relating to today's "90-day wonders" from some prestigious business schools:

> The public mind was in a state of unwholesome fermentation. Men were no longer satisfied with the slow but sure profits of cautious industry. The hope of boundless wealth for the morrow made them heedless and extravagent for to-day. A luxury, till then unheard of, was introduced, bringing in its train a corresponding laxity of morals. The overbearing insolence of ignorant men, who had arisen to sudden wealth by successful gambling, made men of true gentility of mind and manners blush that gold should have power to raise the unworthy in the scale of society. The haughtiness of some of these "cyphering cits," as they were termed by Sir Richard Steele, was remembered against them in the day of their adversity. In the parliamentary inquiry, many of the directors suffered more for their insolence than for their peculation. One of them, who, in the full-blown pride of an ignorant rich man, had said that he would feed his horse upon gold, was reduced almost to bread and water for himself; every haughty look, every overbearing speech, was set down, and repaid them a hundredfold in poverty and humiliation. (pp. 71–72)

19. Prospectus for The May Department Stores Company's $150 million of 9⅛% Debentures due 2016, dated December 3, 1986.

20. John M. Stuart, "A Re-examination of the Replacement Fund," *Public Utilities Fortnightly,* May 23, 1968, 3.

21. "Early Redemption of Outstanding High Coupon Bonds—A Welcome Relief for Ratepayers" (Speech by William D. Talbott, Director, Accounting Depart-

ment, Florida Public Service Commission, presented at the Fifth Institutional Investors Bond Conference, New York, October 21, 1977).

22. Prospectus for $100 million of Arizona Public Service Company First Mortgage Bonds, 11½% Series, due November 1, 2015, dated November 21, 1985.

23. Minstar, Inc. $300 million of 14⅞% Senior Subordinated Notes Due 1995, Indenture, dated as of April 1, 1985, Norwest Bank Minneapolis, N. A. Trustee.

24. See Finnerty, An Illustrated Guide.

25. Statement of Financial Accounting Standards NO. 76. "Extinguishment of debt, An Amendment of APB Opinion NO. 26," November 1983. The three dissenting members said that

> . . . they do not believe the extinguishment of debt accounting and resultant gain or loss recognition should be extended to situations wherein the "debtor is not legally released from being the primary obligor under the debt obligation." They believe . . . that "a liability once incurred by an enterprise remains a liability until it is satisfied in another transaction or other event or circumstance affecting the enterprise." . . . Dedicating the assets might ensure that the debt is serviced in timely fashion, but that event alone just matches up cash flows; it does not satisfy, eliminate, or extinguish the obligation. For a debt to be satisfied, the creditor must be satisfied. (p. 5)

26. Statement of Financial Accounting Standards No. 76, 14.

27. Roy Taub and Neil Baron, "Bond Defeasance Nears FASB Approval," Standard & Poor's Creditweeks, November 28, 1983, 550.

CHAPTER 5

CONVENTIONAL PREFERRED STOCKS WITH FIXED DIVIDEND RATES

In this chapter we review conventional preferred stocks, those issues that have fixed dividend rates and are not convertible into common stock.[1] Convertibles and variable-rate dividend issues are covered in subsequent sections. However, much of what is discussed here applies to the other types of preferred stock. The various ways in which preferred stock can be redeemed are found in Chapter 7.

INTRODUCTION

Preferred stock is part of the invested capital of a corporation, ranking senior to common equity but junior to debt capital. As equity, it has an ownership interest in a company's earnings and assets subject to the priorities of securities senior to it. However, its status is superior to that of common shares, which are residual in nature; i.e., the common shareholder gets what remains after payments are made to or reserved for the holders of senior securities. Preferred stock has certain priorities and limitations that common shares do not. Generally, these include limits as to participation in the earnings and/or assets of the corporation, whether it is fully operational or in liquidation, and restrictions on voting rights for general corporate purposes.

Thus, preferred stock is a hybrid security, possessing some of the attributes of both equity and debt.

One might wonder why companies issue preferred stock. In the case of a newly established concern the issuer may need equity but not want to give up voting control of the company. Thus, it sells preferred shares, giving holders a preference for dividends but not allowing the shares full voting rights. The common shareholder can therefore maintain control of the company. From the issuer's point of view this is less risky than selling debt, because missing dividend payments will not force it into bankruptcy proceedings as skipping interest payments might. In the case of established corporations, important reasons for the issuing preferred stocks might include the desire for a balanced capital structure (especially in the electric utility industry) and the availability of funds from other investors for investment in the preferred shares of the issuer that otherwise might not be accessible. As we shall see later, most preferred stock investors can take advantage of the tax laws and receive greater after-tax income from a corporation's preferred than from its debt.

Since preferred is considered by creditors as part of a company's equity, it provides an issuer with a greater borrowing base. For example, if a finance company is limited to borrowings of eight times its equity base, the addition of preferred stock will allow it to increase its borrowings by many times the amount raised by the sale of preferred. In the case of an insurance company, a greater level of equity capital will increase statutory capital and surplus, thus enabling it to expand its volume of business. Further, increased equity may help the company maintain the ratings on its debt by not overburdening the senior layer of capital with increased interest charges.

SIZE OF THE MARKET

The total amount of publicly issued preferred stock outstanding at the end of 1985 was approximately $36.2 billion. There were approximately 1,270 issues in the market, of which 995 (78.35 percent) were electric utility shares and, in a distant second place, 116 (9.13 percent) of industrial and transportation companies. The par value of the electric utility issues was around $23.5 billion, compared with

Table 5-1
Size of the Public Preferred Stock Market
(as of December 31, 1985)

	Number of Issues	Percent	Total Par or Stated Value ($ Billions)	Percent
Electric utility	995	78.35	23,449	64.85
Industrial/transportation	116	9.13	7,537	20.84
Telephone	47	3.70	1,630	4.51
Banking and finance	31	2.44	2,363	6.53
Gas and water	81	6.38	1,180	3.26
Total public market	1,270	100.00	$36,871	100.00

$7.5 billion for the industrial/transportation sector. Table 5-1 summarized the market at the end of 1985.

In recent years, the issuance of new public preferred stocks of the conventional variety has been below the levels of the 1970s. In the author's opinion, this is due to the trend by many issuers toward the use of adjustable-rate and auction-rate preferred stocks since 1982. Also, electric utility companies, traditionally the heaviest issuers of preferreds, have demonstrated overall improvement in their finances over the past few years. Many companies have completed or are near completing major construction programs and thus require less external financing, both debt and equity. Table 5-2 shows the financing volume from 1971 through mid-1986. Figures provided by the Securities and Exchange Commission include convertible and adjustable-rate issues. Table 5-3 shows Securities and Exchange Commission data by industry (including convertible and adjustable-rate issues) for 1971 through June 30, 1986.

Let us now look in greater detail at the complexion of the preferred new issue market over the past few years. In the 1982 to mid-1986 period, 112 conventional preferreds were brought to market with a total par or stated value of nearly $6 billion. Electric utilities accounted for 86 issues with a par value of $3,668 million, equal to 61 percent of the total preferred financing. Companies in the banking and insurance fields offered eight issues for $702 million, followed by industrial concerns with seven issues for $666 million.

Table 5-2
Conventional Preferred Stock, New Issue Volume, 1971-1986
($ millions)

Year	Volume	Year	Volume
1986*	$ 525.0	1978	$1,394.5
1985	1,066.6	1977	1,921.0
1984	463.0	1976	1,949.1
1983	1,609.5	1975	2,508.5
1982	2,308.7	1974	1,725.5
1981	1,220.3	1973	2,328.5
1980	1,960.5	1972	2,324.4
1979	1,317.5	1971	1,900.8

*To June 30

Gas companies offered eight issues, raising only $340 million. Bringing up the rear were the telecommunications industry with two issues and transportation companies with one issue, accounting for $90 million each.

An increasing number of new issues have provided holders with sinking funds designed to retire the shares over periods ranging from 5 to 30 years. A few have no sinking funds per se but require redemption of all of the shares six years or so after their sale. Another novel feature for three of these issues gives the issuing company the right to exchange the preferred shares for debt with similar features. These shares were sold by companies with little or no taxable income. Once such a company progresses to a taxable net income position, it can turn the dividends (which are paid from after-tax net income) into a pre-tax interest expense, thus increasing net income available for common shareholders.

Sinking funds are an important consideration for fire and casualty insurance companies. In 1978, the National Association of Insurance Commissioners changed the accounting procedures for valuing qualified sinking fund preferreds on the books of these companies. The rule change allowed the companies to value the stock at cost rather than marking the shares to the current market price. This brought the valuation of these securities in line with their economic reality. It also benefited both issuers and buyers by broadening and strengthening the market for, these issues. It reduced the impact of

Table 5-3
Gross Proceeds from Primary Public Preferred Stock Offerings
By Industry, 1971-1986
($ Millions)

	Total Business	Manufacturing	Extractive	Electric, Gas, and Water	Transportation	Communication	Sales and Consumer Finance	Financial and Real Estate	Commercial and Other
1986*	$6,054	$1,411	$ 66	$ 683	$295	$1,148	$150	$2,020	$281
1985	6,224	1,230	217	430	175	75	75	3,561	461
1984	4,219	826	165	613	67	127	0	2,017	404
1983	7,693	1,243	363	1,900	571	0	80	3,270	266
1982	4,953	507	186	2,106	111	32	0	1,996	15
1981	1,633	467	0	978	12	0	0	125	51
1980	3,194	653	142	1,675	204	50	0	336	135
1979	1,966	239	194	1,184	47	93	0	96	156
1978	1,755	306	75	1,076	443	28	0	129	92
1977	2,423	72	0	1,307	0	92	2	293	216
1976	2,353	266	140	1,743	0	70	0	133	1
1975	3,089	379	75	2,390	0	45	0	125	75
1974	1,745	28	0	1,647	0	63	0	0	7
1973	2,400	2	1	1,237	0	1,104	0	54	2
1972	2,408	69	2	2,278	0	52	0	5	2
1971	3,556	212	12	1,901	7	1,395	0	22	7

*To June 30, preliminary.
Figures may not add due to rounding.
Source: U.S. Securities and Exchange Commission, SEC Monthly Statistical Review, various issues.

market fluctuations of the companies portfolios to the extent that they utilized sinking fund preferreds. The issuers could now sell stock with lower dividend rates than if the issues had been of the conventional variety without sinking fund provisions.

A qualified sinking fund issue is one that is subject to a 100 percent mandatory sinking fund with annual installments that commence no later than 10 years from the date of issue and are no less than 2.5 percent annually, thus providing for its retirement no later than 40 years after issue. Certain issues outstanding on December 31, 1978, were "grandfathered" as meeting these qualifications.

LISTING AND TRADING OF PREFERRED STOCKS

At the end of 1985, there were approximately 526 issues of straight preferred stocks listed on the New York Stock Exchange and the American Stock Exchange, the two major U.S. stock exchanges. Preferreds are also listed on the regional exchanges, although the volume of trading is not significant. There are no minimum criteria for a New York Stock Exchange listing, but the issue should be large enough and have a sufficient number of shareholders to justify trading there. If the market value of the publicly held preferred is less than $2 million and the number of shares less than 100,000, the Exchange will consider delisting the issue. Also, listed preferred shares (with some exceptions) normally will have voting rights, be preferred as to dividends and upon liquidation, and have certain redemption rights. These rights include a minimum of 30 (and a maximum of 90) days' prior notification of the proposed redemption; partial redemptions are to be by lot or pro rata.

The American Stock Exchange has somewhat similar criteria, with listing considered on a case-by-case basis. If the issuer's common stock is already listed, the preferred must have a minimum market value of $2 million and at least 100,000 shares publicly held. Preferred stock of nonlisted companies must have an aggregate market value of at least $4 million and a minimum of 400,000 shares held by no fewer than 800 round lot holders.

The normal unit of exchange-traded stock is 100 shares, a so-called round lot. However, many of the smaller issues are allowed to trade in units of 10 shares. In the financial pages of the newspaper, these 10-share lots are denoted by a "z" in the volume column; this means the number of shares traded in full. Otherwise, the volume of trading in this column is the number of 100-share units. For example, Alabama Power Company has issues listed on the New York Stock Exchange that trade in round lots of 100 shares and lots of 10 shares. The 8.72 percent Depositary Preferred trades in units of 100 shares, while the 11.00 percent issue trades in lots of 10 shares. Transactions of less than the standard unit of trading, i.e., 1 to 99 shares or 1 to 9 shares, are odd lots and may be subject to an odd lot differential. This differential is added to the cost of the shares when purchased or subtracted from their price when sold. However, there are exceptions to the imposition of the odd lot differential, depending on a number of factors: the timing of the transaction, whether multiple odd lot orders are bunched into a round lot, and whether the firms executing the odd lot orders are doing so in their own trading departments for their own account or position.

Rule 390 of the New York Stock Exchange requires that shares listed on that exchange be traded there, with a few exceptions as denoted in section (c), subsection (viii):

> (c) The provision of this Rule shall not apply to any of the following transactions:
> (viii) any purchase or sale of any of the guaranteed or preferred stocks included within the listing of such stocks as may from time to time be issued by the Exchange, provided, however, that every proposed transaction in any such security by a member, member organization or affiliated person should be reviewed in light of the factors involved, including the market on the floor of the Exchange, the price, and the size, so that whenever possible the transaction may be effected on the floor.

Nearly 200 issues have received this exemption from Rule 390. In most cases, the real market for professional investors is off-the-board (in the over-the-counter market). It is in this marketplace where transactions can be more readily negotiated, especially in the less actively traded issues.

WHO BUYS PREFERRED STOCKS?

In the main, the buyers of preferred stocks are taxable corporations, those institutional investors that can take advantage of the tax features of preferred dividends in order to achieve after-tax yields higher than those from fully taxable investments.[2] Such investors include corporations that purchase preferreds for their own account as part of their cash management activities. Straight preferreds, both perpetuals and those with sinking funds, are appropriate for part of a company's longer-term cash reserves. We do not have data on the preferred stock holdings of nonfinancial corporations, but it is probably a significant amount. To cite just one example, at the end of 1985 Dominion Resources, Inc. (formerly Virginia Electric & Power Company) purchased all of the common stock of Rincon Securities, Inc., a wholly owned subsidiary of Tucson Resources, Inc. Rincon invests in financial assets and owns preferreds worth approximately $260 million, most of which are sinking fund issues of other electric utility companies.

According to A.M. Best Company, at the end of 1984 preferred stock investments (both publicly and privately issued) of property and casualty insurance companies were nearly $9 billion, equal to 4.3 percent of their total investments and 25 percent of their total investments in all equities.[3] Preferred stock activity of these companies is greatly influenced by profits and losses from their underwriting activities. When they are in a low tax or loss part of the underwriting cycle, they tend to invest in corporate and other fully taxable securities; when the cycle changes to profitable underwriting activity, they tend to increase their investments in tax-exempt and tax-preferred instruments.

Life insurance companies, historically long-term investors, also own a considerable amount of preferred stocks, either convertible preferreds as common stock alternatives or straight preferreds. The American Council of Life Insurance has reported that at the end of 1984 preferred stock holdings of U.S. life insurance companies amounted to $11 billion but only 1.5 percent of total assets and 17.4 percent of total stock investments.[4] Total assets were $723 billion, and total stock investments were $63 billion.

TAXATION AND COMPARISON WITH
ALTERNATIVE INVESTMENTS

Enacted into law in 1939, the intercorporate dividends received exclusion now allows corporate investors to exclude 85 percent of the income dividends received from their taxable income if they have held the shares for at least 46 days. Therefore, those dividends that meet the qualifications are subject to a minimum tax of only 6.9 percent (for those in the highest marginal tax bracket of 46 percent). It should be noted that the exclusion is not fully allowed for corporate shareholders if the preferred investment has been financed by debt that is directly attributable to the investment in such shares. The deduction is not allowed for dividends on stock not held with substantial risk of loss for a specified period; this reduces the advantages of hedging stock investment portfolios. Also, there are special regulations covering "extraordinary" dividends if the shares have been held for one year or less. These preferred dividends are those that equal or exceed the adjusted cost by 5 percent or more; the non-taxed portion must be used to reduce the shareholder's cost basis of the stock.

Individuals, on the other hand, are not much of a factor in the preferred stock market, except, possibly, for some of the lower-rated, higher-yielding issues. The dividends on preferred stock held by individuals investors are taxed like any other dividends, namely at the marginal income tax rate. Thus, an individual in the 40 percent tax bracket will pay $4 in taxes for every $10 of taxable dividends received, keeping only $6. If the dividend received is a return of capital or a "nontaxable" distribution, the cost basis of the stock will be reduced by the amount of the dividend. If the cost basis is reduced to zero, the dividend will be treated as one subject to the capital gains tax.

Preferred shares of utility companies may be classified as either "old money" or "new money" shares. "New money" preferreds are those issued after October 1, 1942, for purposes other than refunding. "Old money" preferreds are those that were issued prior to that date or, if issued since then, had the proceeds directed to the refunding of older issues. A few outstanding issues are considered "part new money–part old money." As previously stated, qualified dividends are allowed the 85 percent intercorporate dividends received deduction. However, "old money" shares qualify for a dividend deduction of only 59.13 percent; thus, the investor keeps only 81.2, rather than 93.1, percent of the dividend.

The formulae for computing the current yield, the after-tax yield, and the pre-tax or taxable equivalent yield are as follows:

ATY	=	after-tax yield
CY	=	current yield
DD	=	dollar amount of dividend
DT	=	percent of dividend subject to income tax
P	=	price of preferred stock
PEY	=	pre-tax equivalent yield
TR	=	marginal tax rate

1. Current Yield

$$CY = DD/P$$
$$= \$10 / \$100$$
$$= 10\% \text{ (pretax basis)}$$

2. After-Tax Yield

$$ATY = CY[1-(TR \cdot DT)]$$
$$= 10[1-(.46 \cdot .15)]$$
$$= 10[1-(.069)]$$
$$= 10 \cdot (.931)$$
$$= 9.31\%$$

3. Pre-Tax Equivalent Yield

$$PEY = ATY(1/1-TR)$$
$$= 9.31(1/1-.46)$$
$$= 9.31(1/.54)$$
$$= 9.31(1.85185)$$
$$= 17.24\%$$

Let us look at a "new money" preferred with a 10 percent dividend selling at $100 per share. The pre-tax current yield is 10 percent; this equates to 9.31 percent on an after-tax basis for an investor in the 46 percent marginal tax bracket. A more dramatic way of looking at these yields is to see what pre-tax yield is needed on a fully taxable investment to match the preferred's after-tax return. Formula 3 shows that at the 46 percent tax rate an investor would need an alternative investment yielding 17.24 percent to match the preferred's 9.31 percent after-tax return. A fully taxable security yielding 10 percent pre-tax yields only 5.4 percent after federal income taxes.

Table 5–4 shows the pre-tax dividend rate, the after-tax yield based on the 85 percent dividends received deduction (DRD) and a 46 percent corporate tax rate, the equivalent needed from a fully taxable investment, and the after-tax yield on a fully taxable investment with the pre-tax yield shown in column 1. Again, a preferred with 10 percent dividend yield provides the corporate investor with a 9.31 percent after-tax yield. To match this yield, the investor would need

Table 5–4
Comparison of Preferred Stock and Other Yields
("New Money" Issues)

Pre-Tax Preferred Dividend Rate	Current 85% DRD After-Tax Yield (46%)	Pre-Tax Needed to Equal Preferred (46%)	Fully Taxable Instrument After-Tax Yield (46%)
5.00%	4.66%	8.62%	2.70%
5.50	5.12	9.48	2.97
6.00	5.59	10.34	3.24
6.50	6.05	11.21	3.51
7.00	6.52	12.07	3.78
7.50	6.98	12.93	4.05
8.00	7.45	13.79	4.32
8.50	7.91	14.65	4.59
9.00	8.38	15.52	4.86
9.50	8.84	16.38	5.13
10.00	9.31	17.24	5.40
10.50	9.78	18.10	5.67
11.00	10.24	18.96	5.94
11.50	10.71	19.83	6.21
12.00	11.17	20.69	6.48
12.50	11.64	21.55	6.75
13.00	12.10	22.41	7.02
13.50	12.57	23.28	7.29
14.00	13.03	24.14	7.56
14.50	13.50	25.00	7.83
15.00	13.97	25.86	8.10
15.50	14.43	26.72	8.37

another investment yielding 17.24 percent before taxes. If a fully taxable investment yields 10 percent before taxes, the after-tax return is only 5.4 percent. These calculations leave out the effects of any state or local income taxes.

Since the tax status of dividends is so important to corporate investors, we will now look at selected yields for various types of preferreds and other investments on both a pre-tax and after-tax basis (see Tables 5–5a and 5–5b). Pre-tax yields are just the starting point; it is what you keep that is important, and relying on pre-tax yields and spreads can be misleading.

Looking at the "A" utility perpetual preferred averages for 1985, we can see that the average pre-tax yield of 11.33 percent was 71 basis points less than the pre-tax yield on an "A"-rated long-term utility bond. However, on an after-tax basis the preferred returned 404 basis points more than the utility bond. Note that in some instances the after-tax spread between sinking fund issues and the long-term public power bond favors the tax-free power bond. This is because investors are willing to pay more for issues with sinking funds than for those without. Preferred investors consider the effect of the sinking funds on their shares using the yield-to-average-life rather than the conventional current yield. The yield-to-average-life is an internal rate of return measurement that takes into account the cash flow expected to be received through the sinking fund payments with the final payment used as the maturity date; this final date is called the payout date.

Yield spreads are helpful in analyzing the relative value of one investment over another. Investors compare present spreads and levels (both absolute and relative) to historical ones in order to determine whether an issue is overvalued, undervalued, or fairly valued in the market. For example, if spreads are relatively narrow between a preferred and an alternative investment, the investor might avoid the stock, hoping that the yield relationship will return to wider levels at which the preferred would represent a more attractive opportunity. Other investors, while recognizing the narrow spread relationship, might still want the stock for its after-tax yield, as it satisfies certain portfolio objectives. It is these differences in investment philosophy that contribute to the markets; what seems rich to one person might appear fairly valued to another.

Table 5-5a

Comparison of Selected Yields—Pre-Tax and After-Tax

(Percent)

| Average For Year | "A"-Related Preferred Average | | | | | | U.S. Treasury 30-year | | Utility Bonds Long Term | | "A" 30-Year General Obligation | | "A" 40-Year Public Power | |
| | Industrial Sinking Fund | | Utility Sinking Fund | | Utility Perpetual | | | | | | | | | |
	Pre	After	Pre	After	Pre	After	Pre	After	Pre	After	Pre	After	Pre	After
1985	10.33	9.62	10.13	9.43	11.33	10.54	10.70	5.78	12.04	6.50	9.19	9.19	9.85	9.85
1984	12.14	11.30	11.82	11.00	13.31	12.39	12.41	6.70	13.61	7.35	10.17	10.17	10.84	10.84
1983	11.15	10.38	10.88	10.13	12.17	11.33	11.25	6.07	12.78	6.90	9.55	9.55	10.13	10.13
1982	13.40	12.47	12.72	11.84	14.14	13.17	12.60	6.80	15.44	8.34	11.68	11.68	12.60	12.60

Note: Marginal tax rate of 46 percent used.

Table 5-5b
Comparison of Spread Relationships—Pre-Tax and After-Tax (Basis Points)

"A" Industrial Sinking Fund Preferred
versus

Average for Year	U.S. Treasury		Utility		General Obligation		Public Power	
	Pre	After	Pre	After	Pre	After	Pre	After
1985	−37	+384	−171	+312	+114	+ 43	+ 48	− 23
1984	−27	+460	−147	+395	+197	+113	+130	+ 46
1983	−10	+569	−163	+348	+160	+ 83	+102	+ 25
1982	+80	+567	−204	+413	+172	+ 79	+ 80	− 13

"A" Utility Sinking Fund Preferred
versus

Average for Year	U.S. Treasury		Utility		General Obligation		Public Power	
	Pre	After	Pre	After	Pre	After	Pre	After
1985	−57	+365	−191	+293	+ 94	+24	+28	−42
1984	−59	+730	−179	+365	+165	+83	+98	+16
1983	−37	+406	−190	+323	+133	+58	+75	0
1982	+12	+504	−272	+350	+104	+16	+12	−76

"A" Utility Perpetual Preferred
versus

Average for Year	U.S. Treasury		Utility		General Obligation		Public Power	
	Pre	After	Pre	After	Pre	After	Pre	After
1985	+ 63	+476	− 71	+404	+214	+135	+148	+ 69
1984	+ 90	+569	− 30	+504	+314	+222	+247	+155
1983	+ 92	+526	− 61	+443	+262	+178	+204	+120
1982	+154	+637	−130	+483	+246	+149	+154	+ 57

Note: Marginal tax rate of 46 percent used.

Preferred Dividend Stripping, or the Evening Up Process

In comparing one preferred stock issue with another, it becomes necessary to do what is known as the "dividend strip," or the "evening up" process. Unlike most bonds, preferred stocks trade flat, i.e., without accrued dividends; yet a purchaser of the shares is entitled to the dividend when it is declared. As most preferred stocks pay dividends quarterly, investors can get four dividends a year. Holders on the record date are entitled to the dividend. Thus, if the record date for a dividend payable on May 31 is May 15, buyers of the stock on May 8 (five business days preceding the record date) will get the dividend, but buyers on May 9 will not. On May 9 the shares will trade "ex-dividend"; that is, their price will decline by the amount of the dividend. To summarize, if the record date for a dividend is Monday, the stock will trade ex-dividend four business days earlier, or the preceding Tuesday; if the record date is a Tuesday, the ex-date will be the preceding Wednesday; and so on.

While preferreds trade without the accrual of dividends, in reality their price will reflect the accretion of dividends from one ex-dividend date to the next. The stripping procedure is a process designed to reduce the distortion on the current yield caused by the dividend accrual (or buildup) in order to allow for a comparative evaluation of yields. As the ex-dividend date approaches, the price of the stock reflects this accrual. Let us look at two examples. The shares are of equal quality and have similar terms except for the dividend and the dividend payment date.

Issue A

Dividend: $ 6 (monthly accretion of $0.50; $1.50 quarterly)
Stock price: $75.50
Dividend payment dates: 15th of January, April, July, and
                             October
Ex-dividend dates: last day of December, March, June,
                             and September

Issue B

Dividend: $4 (monthly accretion of $0.333; $1.00 quarterly)
Stock price: $50
Dividend payment dates: 15th of February, May, August, and
                             November
Ex-dividend dates: last day of January, April, July, and
                             October

The current yield level for stocks of this caliber is 8 percent. It is now February 1, and the yield on Issue B is 8 percent ($4/$50). However, the current yield on Issue A is 7.95 percent ($6/$75.50). There is no dividend buildup in Issue B as it just went ex-dividend. However, the price of Issue A reflects a one-month accrual of the dividend, or $0.50 a share. Therefore, we must adjust its price for the dividend accrual to arrive at the adjusted or stripped price in order to make a comparison between the two issues. We subtract the dividend accrual of $0.50 from the $75.50 share price and get $75 as the stripped price. This results in a current yield on Issue A of 8 percent. Now assume that a month later, on March 1, the shares have moved in price: Issue A is now trading at $76 a share and Issue B at $50.625. We must adjust the price of each for the two-month accrual in Issue A and the one-month accrual in Issue B. The adjusted price for A is $75, resulting in a stripped current yield of 8 percent. The adjusted price of B is $50.625 minus the one-month accrual of $0.333 a share, or $50.292. This results in an adjusted current yield of $7.95 percent. Assuming all other things equal, Issue A now represents a better value than Issue B.

Next, assume that on April 1 Issue A has gone ex-dividend by $1.50 and is trading at $74 a share, resulting in a current yield of 8.11 percent. Supposed that the preferred investors now want issues like this on an 8.10 percent yield basis. Issue B, with a full two months of dividend in its price, should trade at about $50 to give a stripped yield of 8.10 percent. A price of $50 less the accrued dividend of $0.666 results in an adjusted price of $49.334. This produces a current yield of 8.11 percent, which is just about in line with prevailing dividend rates and also comparable to Issue A. Any higher price would mean that the B shares are relatively overvalued vis-à-vis the A shares; conversely, any lower price would make it relatively undervalued.

Therefore, a preferred stock investor must know some of the details about the issue, namely the dividend rate and amount, the ex-dividend date, and the payment date. The dividend stripping process is fairly simple and requires only a few calculations. Investors would do well to observe this procedure. This type of information can be obtained from most stock guides, investment manuals, and the specialized dividend record books published by firms such as Standard & Poor's Corporation.

THE DIVIDEND ROLLOVER PROGRAM, OR CAPTURE-THE-DIVIDEND

Many corporations involved in investment in preferred shares have long practiced trading for dividends, also known as the dividend rollover program or capture-the-dividend. Many also have applied this investment technique to qualified common stock issues. However, as preferred stock prices generally are less affected by company fundamentals and are more sensitive to interest rate developments in the short run (especially those of the higher-rated issues), the greatest investor interest has been in the preferred market. In late 1985, the financial press had several articles on capture-the-dividend plays involving common shares. As one article put it, "The idea is for a corporation to buy a stock just before the dividend is paid, hold it for a while, and sell it without taking a loss. Because companies pay almost no tax on dividend income, the game can yield two to three times the after-tax return on Treasury bills."[5]

While it sounds easier than it is, the purpose of the exercise is to maximize yield over the short run, not to become a long-term investor. Under the tax laws in effect at the end of 1985, investors must hold stock at least 46 days in order to take the dividends received deduction. Theoretically, one can buy seven dividend payments a year. The shares are purchased prior to the ex-dividend date, after which they are sold and another issue is purchased. Investors continually roll over their investments. They get a full quarter's dividend by holding shares for the minimum required period. If preferreds provide a current return of 8 percent, the dividend roll increases the return to 14 percent. On an after-tax basis, the return is increased from 7.45 percent to 13.03 percent.

Of course, this assumes a level or stable market. However, in the real world markets fluctuate. Stocks do not always decline on the ex-dividend date by the full amount of the dividend to be paid; the drop may be more or less depending on other market factors. In actual practice, there will be short-term capital gains and short-term capital losses. Currently, short-term capital losses may be offset against short-term capital gains. An investor's tax status is of great importance in dividend capture programs; gains and losses must be carefully monitored and qualified tax counsel sought.

Investors must be flexible in their choice of preferred investments—the wider the acceptable quality range, the more alternatives
will be available. After all, there are a finite number of preferred
stocks that one can trade at any point in time. Characteristics that investors look for in dividend capture preferreds include stable or improving credit quality of the issuer and adequate size and distribution of the stock in order to facilitate transactions. While the
dividend rollover program is not for everyone, professional corporate money managers should consider its advantages and dis-
advantages.

TERMS OF PREFERRED STOCK ISSUES

We have discussed the size of the preferred market and why certain
investors look to preferred stocks. Now we will look at the features
of this instrument, such as dividend and asset preferences and voting
rights. The retirement features of preferred stock are covered in
Chapter 7.

Par Value

Preferred shares may have an arbitrarily set designation known as
par value.[6] They may carry a high par value, a low par value, or no
par value. From an investor's viewpoint, this is normally of little
concern. However, from an issuer's perspective, par value might
mean a great deal. In the organization of corporations, states may
impose franchise or organizational taxes based on the par value of
the shares. Further, some jurisdictions discriminate against no par
value shares. The choice of par value is thus dictated by state corporation statues and by tax considerations. Recent examples of par
and no-par designations include Gulf States Utilities Company
$12.92 Dividend Preferred Stock, $100 Par Value; Hartford Fire Insurance Class A Preferred Stock, 8.95% Series 3, $50 par value;
SCIPSCO, Inc. Cumulative Redeemable Exchangeable Preferred
Stock, $0.01 par value; and Commonwealth Edison's $9.30 Cumulative Preferred Stock, no par value. Often, low or no par value shares

will be given an arbitrary stated value. Forest Oil Corporation's $15.75 Preferred with a par value of $0.01 a share has a stated value of $100 per share, and Georgia Power's $3 Class A Preferred with no par value has a stated value of $25.

Some companies have preferred shares outstanding with varying par or stated values. For example, Georgia Power has some preferred with stated values of $25 and others with stated values of $100. Preferreds with a par or stated value of $50 are sometimes referred to as "half-stock." A majority of the preferred shares outstanding have par or stated values of $100 each. Preferred stock may not be sold for less than the par or stated value. Any proceeds in excess of that amount may be credited to capital surplus, while the par or stated value is credited to the capital stock account.

Over the past decade, there have been numerous issuances of lower-priced shares. In some cases, electric utility companies found that due to restrictions placed on them by the preferred stock agreements, they could no longer issue new preferred stock. Thus, they created a second class of preferred, called preference stock, without the issuance restrictions. Often these shares had a lower par or stated value that made them attractive to smaller investors—for some reason, 100 shares at $25 is more appealing to less sophisticated investors than 25 shares at $100 each.

Another way round the prohibition against selling preferred stock at less than par value has been the creation of depositary preferred shares. In this case, the depositary preferred share represents a fractional interest in a full preferred share with a higher par value. For example, Philadelphia Electric Company is authorized 10 million shares of $100 par value preferred stock. In 1984 it sold 5 million Depositary Preferred Shares, each representing one-tenth of a share of 14.15% Preferred Stock (par value, $100 per share). The Depositary Preferred was sold at $10 per share. Philadelphia Electric deposited 500,000 shares of the $100 par preferred with a bank acting as the share depositary. Each owner of a Depositary Preferred Share is entitled, proportionally, to all the rights and preferences of the underlying preferred stock, including an annual dividend of $1.415 payable quarterly.

Many depositary preferred shares are listed on one of the major stock exchanges, which gives them greater marketability than a smaller number of the underlying preferred shares would have. At times, these lower-cost shares can become overpriced relative to the higher-priced preferred shares of the same issuer. Investors should study the terms of the various issues carefully so as not to overpay for an issue just because of the lower price.

The cost to a preferred issuer of low-valued preferred stock (or depositary shares) is substantially higher than for $100 par or stated value shares. Of the 81 electric utility issues sold in the 1982 to 1985 period, 30 had par values of $50 or $100, 47 were issued at $25 or $27.50, and 4 were offered at $10 a share. In the $100 category, the underwriting discounts and commissions averaged 1.116 percent of the offering price, with a range of 0.1 to 5.88 percent; excluding the extremes, the average of these expenses was 0.982 percent. For preferreds with initial offering prices of $25 to $27.50 a share, the expenses averaged 3.663 percent (range of 0.382 percent to 5.138 percent) which, excluding the minimum and maximum expenses, gave an average of 3.703 percent—nearly 3.8 times that of the higher-priced stock. In the $10 share price category, the average expense was 4.675 of the offering price, with a range of 4 to 6.50 percent.

One reason for the greater expenses of lower-priced issues might be the increased selling effort and expenses required on the part of investment bankers. In the above cases, many of the lower-priced issues had lower-quality ratings than the higher-priced issues, which in some instances might have reduced the interest of institutional investors. The underwriters had to go to the retail or individual and small corporation market, where salespeople often receive larger commissions. Also, the cost of processing many smaller orders is greater than that for processing fewer, but larger, sales. In addition, with diminished institutional demand the price risks to the underwriters in volatile markets is increased. If the issue is not adequately priced initially—i.e., if the yield is not sufficient to entice buyers to part with their investment dollars—investment bankers face the possibility of having to sell their shares at lower prices in the secondary or after market. Thus, the increase in underwriting discounts and commissions to some extent provides the brokerage firm with a cushion against poor pricing or a turn for the worse during the marketing period.

Dividend and Liquidation Preferences

Dividends on preferred shares have priority or preferences over dividends on other junior stock; they usually must be paid before subordinate equity holders receive any dividends on their shares.[7] Eastern Air Lines, for example, has three issues of public preferred stock: $3.20 Cumulative Preferred Stock, $2.69 Cumulative Preferred Stock, and $3 Cumulative Convertible Junior Preferred Stock. The company suspended dividends on all of its shares with payments due November 15, 1983, as it incurred large losses in the first nine months of that year. No dividends were paid in 1984 and the first quarter of 1985. However, dividends on the senior preferreds were resumed on June 15, as earnings showed improvement, but dividends were not paid on the junior stock.

By this time, accumulated and unpaid dividends were $4.80 for the $3.20 Preferred, $4.035 for the $2.69 shares, and $4.50 for the $3 junior issue. Payments made in 1985 amounted to $4.20 and $5.331 respectively, per preferred share, but none were made on the junior preferred. By the end of 1985, dividend arrearages were reduced to $3 for the $3.20 shares, $2.5215 for the $2.69 shares, and $6.75 for the junior stock. Earnings once again came under pressure, and the company once more suspended dividend payments. Until all dividend obligations with respect to the two senior issues are cleared up, cured, or fully satisfied, no dividend may be paid on the junior issue of stock, The prospectus for the $3 junior preferred states:

> The certificate of designation for the Senior Preferred Stock provides that no dividends (other than dividends payable in the Company's capital stock ranking junior to the Senior Preferred Stock) on, or any distribution in respect of, any class or classes of stock of the Company ranking junior to the Senior Preferred Stock, including the preferred shares offered hereby, may be made unless there are no arrearages on any dividend or sinking fund payments on the Senior Preferred Stock.[8]

The payment of dividends is subject to being declared by the company's board of directors out of funds legally available for this purpose. State corporation laws define what constitute legally available funds, as do the articles of incorporation and bylaws of the issuers. The corporate charter of Consumers Power Company prohibits the payment of dividends on stock junior to the preferred if the company is in default in the payment of senior preferred dividends or if, immediately after the payment of such dividends, there will not remain to the credit of retained earnings at least $7.50 per share on all of its outstanding stock. Under the New York Business Corporation Law, dividends may be paid only from surplus. Also, debt agreements may determine when and in what amount dividends may be paid. While a company might have adequate means with which to pay preferred dividends, it may be unable to do so because of prohibitions contained in bond indentures or bank loan agreements. In 1983, Eastern Air Lines had to obtain consent from its mortgage lenders in order to pay preferred and junior preferred dividends.

Dividends normally are payable in cash on a quarterly basis, but there are a few exceptions. For example, Beneficial Corporation has three issues that pay dividends on a semiannual basis, while Harnischfeger Corporation's Series B $3.402 Depositary Preferred Shares pay monthly. Recently some preferreds have been issued that provide for the dividend payment in cash, common stock, preferred stock, or a combination thereof. These shares usually have been issued by companies of lower credit standing, those involved in financial reorganization outside of the bankruptcy courts, and those special-purpose companies involved in leveraged buyouts, mergers, and acquisitions. Turner Broadcasting Systems, Inc. issued Series A Preferred Stock in its 1986 merger with MGM/UA Entertainment Company. The stock will not begin to accrue dividends until one year after the effective date of the merger; the dividend rate thereafter will be $1.4459 per share per annum payable in either cash or shares of Turner common or Series A Preferred Stock. However, cash payments are prohibited unless Turner's outstanding debt is below $1.1 billion—and even then the debt indentures would restrict cash payments.

SCIPSCO Inc.'s preferred provides that for the first six years dividend payments will be made in additional shares of preferred stock valued at $35 a share for dividend determination purposes. Thereafter, dividends will be paid at the rate of $4.725 per share in cash and $0.875 per share in additional preferred stock. The option to pay dividends in stock enables the company to better service its creditors through the retention of cash.

The dividend determination formulae for these stock dividends usually value the shares to be paid at a discount to their market price for a certain number of business days preceding the dividend payment date. Of course, the value of the shares received in lieu of cash dividends might be more or less when received than when declared. To obtain cash, the preferred holder will have to sell the dividend shares, which could depress the market. Also, brokerage commissions might have to be paid and, if the shares being sold constitute an odd lot (from 1 to 99 shares), the price received might be below that for round lots (units of 100 shares).

Most of the preferred stocks in the marketplace are *cumulative* preferreds. If the dividend is not paid, it accumulates, or builds up, until the payments are made, as in the case of Eastern Air Lines. The accrued and unpaid dividends are known as arrearages. There have also been *noncumulative* preferreds in the past but, to the author's knowledge, none are outstanding at the present time. A noncumulative preferred is one whose dividend, once passed by the board of directors, is gone forever. The company might have earnings, but if its management feels that they could put the cash to better use than for the payment of a preferred dividend, they might do so. This type of stock generally would get a low valuation in today's market, and its issuer would probably be a company emerging from reorganization. Many current state corporation laws require that dividends be cumulative if there are earnings but no dividend is declared.

Cumulative-to-the-extent-earned preferreds are rare. While somewhat better than noncumulative preferreds, they don't offer the investor much solace if the company runs into a period of losses instead of earnings. With "run-of-the-mill" cumulative preferred, if the corporation suffers losses and does not declare a dividend, at least the dividend accumulates and will be paid if and when the company regains its financial strength. With cumulative-to-the-extent-earned preferred, however, the shareholder is entitled to receive dividends only if the company earns them; a loss would mean that the investor could kiss the dividends goodbye for good. The $8 First Preferred Stock of Uniroyal, Inc., is one such example. Shareholders were entitled to receive all net earnings up to 8 percent of the $100 par value each year before any dividend could be declared on any other stock. The stock was issued in 1892 by the old United States Rubber Company. The dividend record through 1985 is as follows.

1892	Nil	1902–03	Nil	1939	$12.00
1893	$ 4.00	1904	$ 4.50	1940–41	$ 8.00
1894	$ 9.33⅓	1905	$ 9.00	1942	$ 4.00
1895–96	$ 8.00	1906–27	$ 8.00	1943–77	$ 8.00
1897	$ 6.00	1928	$ 2.00	1978–79	$ 6.00
1898–1900	$ 8.00	1929–37	Nil	1980–81	Nil
1901	$ 1.00	1938	$ 4.00	1982–85	$ 8.00

In those years in which dividends paid were more than $8 per share, the excess came from the preceding year's earnings and represented the earned accumulation. Dividends on the common stock were not paid in 1892, 1896, 1898, 1901–1910, 1916–1918, 1922–1940, 1942, and 1979–1983. In 1985, Uniroyal was taken private in a leveraged buyout. After some litigation by preferred shareholders who thought that their stock should have been redeemed, a compromise was reached that changed the status of the dividends to cumulative.

Preferred stocks are generally *nonparticipating*, i.e., they are entitled to dividends at only the stipulated amount and do not share in any further company earnings. The SCIPSCO preferred, while nonparticipating, has a bonus of sorts for it holders. The annual dividend rate will be increased by a maximum of $0.35 a share if the rate on U.S. Treasury bonds with a 10-year constant maturity exceeds 10.15 percent. Thus, if the 10-year Treasury issue is at a 10.50 percent yield on the dividend determination date, the dividend will be increased by $0.1225 [$35 × (.1050 − .1015)]. If the Treasury yield is 11.15 percent or greater, the maximum of $.035 a share will be paid.

A few participating preferreds provide for dividends based on the net income of the issuer. Holders of ENSTAR Indonesia Participating Preferred Stock are entitled to semiannual per share cash dividends of .00000125 percent of the company's consolidated net income for the two calendar quarters prior to the quarter in which the dividend is declared and paid. (The company is a subsidiary of ENSTAR Corporation, formerly Alaska Interstate Company.) In 1985 the Federal Home Loan Mortgage Corporation ("Freddie Mac") issued a participating preferred that was available only to members of the Federal Home Loan Bank System and by Freddie Mac. In early 1986, however, it was considering eliminating this restriction so that the general public could buy shares as well. No dividends may be paid on the common shares in any calendar year until dividends have been paid on the preferred aggregate $10 million. Thereafter, the preferred shares in the aggregate will be entitled to receive $90 of dividends for every $10 of dividends paid on the common stock in the aggregate.

Another good example of a participating preferred is Southern California Edison's 5% Original Cumulative Participating Preferred. The par value was originally $100 per share but, through stock splits (quite uncommon for preferred stock) in 1926 and 1962, was reduced to $8.33. This nonredeemable stock has preference to cumulative dividends of 5 percent annually before dividend payments on preferred and common shares. Moody's *Public Utility Manual,* 1986, states that it is also "entitled to participate in any distribution to holders of preferred to the extent that such distribution shall as to any series exceed 5%, such participation being cumulative and also entitled to participate with common to the extent that such distribution shall be greater than the highest dividend rate paid on any preferred stock outstanding." Since 1910, it has continually paid dividends at a minimum of 5 percent of the original or adjusted par value; though there have been a few times when the dividend was lower than in the prior year, it has not been less than the common dividend. When the company increased the rate on the common dividend, it increased the rate on this senior preferred issue. Thus, the stock shares in the increasing fortunes of the common dividend holders, has priority in the event of liquidation, and has two votes per share. This preferred's price on the American Stock Exchange at the end of 1985 was $51, providing a current return of 8.47 percent on the indicated dividend rate of $4.32. The common's closing price of 26⅝ provided a current yield of 8.11 percent on its indicated dividend of $2.16 a share. All signs point to the better value offered by this preferred stock. However, with only 480,000 shares outstanding, the available supply is limited.

Not only do some preferred stocks participate in the earnings and common dividends of a company; some may also participate in its liquidation. The previously mentioned Freddie Mac preferred has a liquidation preference of $10 per share. In addition, after payment upon liquidation to holders of the common stock of the par value thereof, preferred holders in the aggregate will be entitled to a further distribution of $90 for every $10 further distributed to the common holders in aggregate. The Southern California Edison 5% preferred is entitled to participate with the common in any balance after preferred and preference shares have been paid in full and par has been paid on the common. Southern California Gas Company has a 6 percent, $25 par value issue with a liquidation value of $25 per share. After that amount has been paid and the other preferreds taken care of, the remaining funds and assets of the company will be divided on a pro rata basis among the preferred and common holders. The common shares have no par value.

Finally, Public Service Electric & Gas Company had an interesting Dividend Preference Common Stock. This was retired in 1986 through an exchange of $18 of cash or the conversion into one-half of a share of common stock as the company reorganized itself into a holding company. This stock had preference over the common shares, subject to the rights of the preferred, in the fixed amount of $1.40 annually. It had the right to two votes per share and twice as much per share as the common stock upon liquidation.

Voting Rights

Shareholders normally have one vote per share of stock, unless the articles of incorporation or the specific agreement governing the shares state otherwise. A majority of preferred stock issues do not have general voting rights, i.e., the right to vote on the same issues as common shareholders. Instead, because of the preferences accorded senior equity holders, the voting privilege is usually restricted to certain occurrences. Illinois Power Company gives preferred holders the right "to one vote per share on all matters submitted to the vote of shareholders, with the right to cumulate votes in the election of directors and the right to vote as a class on certain matters."[9] The shares also have the right to vote on matters concerning the issuance of unsecured debt and parity or senior preferred stock under certain circumstances. Texas Utilities Electric Company's preferred generally is without voting power. The prospectus reads: "Except for those purposes for which the right is expressly conferred upon the New Preferred under the Articles of Incorporation or by statute, no holder thereof is entitled to notice of or vote at any meeting of shareholders."[10] The shares have the right to vote on certain matters affecting the expressed terms of the outstanding preferred shares if the proposed changes are "substantially prejudicial to the holders thereof."

Nonpayment of preferred dividends is what usually brings the voting right into force. Typically, after a company has missed four to six preferred dividend payments, the preferred shareholders, voting as a class, have the right to elect a portion of the board of directors. Sometimes the corporate charter or bylaws provide that the board will be increased by a certain number of directors (two in the case of United States Steel Corporation), elected by the preferred stockholders voting as a class. In many cases, the preferred holders may elect a majority of directors, who serve until the dividend arrearages have been fully paid. Usually the voting is scheduled to take place at the next regular annual shareholders' meeting; in a few instances, however, the company must call a special meeting for this purpose. The effectiveness of preferred voting in the case of passed dividends varies. Often the company will pick nominees; occasionally the preferred holders will fight to elect their own people. In late 1985, several preferred holders of Long Island Lighting Company started a proxy fight in an attempt to install their own slate of candidates.

While nonpayment of dividends is a serious matter for preferred stock owners, it does not in and of itself result in bankruptcy, although it may be a precursor to it. Often, by the time management decides to pass on dividend payments, the company might already be in default of some provisions of its debt agreements. Such an action indicates that a company is in financial distress, although it might not be counted down and out. As the end of 1985, Standard & Poor's *Stock Guide* listed 26 companies with preferred stocks in arrears (undoubtedly there were others omitted). Of these, seven companies were in the bankruptcy courts. Obviously, most of the other issuers were flirting with financial reorganization in one way or another.

Of course, nonpayment of dividends can help a corporation on the path to recovery. For one thing, it conserves cash. For another, it demonstrates to creditors (and to regulators) that the company's owners are willing to sacrifice current income in order to assist in recovery. The improvement of retained cash flow can be used for needed capital expenditures and for debt service. For example, Western Union Corporation and its subsidiary, Western Union Telegraph Company, had each missed six preferred stock dividend payments by early 1986. In the case of the parent corporation, preferred holders were entitled to elect, as a single class, two directors until the arrearages were cured. The subsidiary shares allowed the election of two directors for each of its series of preferred outstanding, for a total of eight new directors. Prior to the annual meeting on May 15, 1986, the company proposed a financial reorganization or restructuring that would merge the parent into the subsidiary, with the latter the survivor. There would be an exchange of new Telegraph preferred for the outstanding preferreds of both companies and, as the dividend arrearages were taken into account when determining the exchange ratios, the accumulated and unpaid dividends would be satisfied. Therefore, the preferred holders would lose their right to elect part of the new board. This was an ingenious way for management to pay for arrearages and avoid having new, and possibly hostile, board members. The reorganization scheme was rejected by the security holders in September 1986.

When Is a Preferred Not a Preferred?

This might seem like a silly question, but it did come up in early 1986. Fox Television Stations, Inc. sold 1,148,000 shares of Increasing Rate Exchangeable Guaranteed Preferred Stock at $1,000 per share, raising over $1 billion. This was part of the financing that allowed Fox to purchase some television properties from Metromedia Broadcasting Corporation. The prospectus stated:

> There are substantial uncertainties regarding the Federal income tax treatment of the Transaction, the exchange pursuant to the Exchange Offer and the holding of the Fox Television Preferred Stock, in the case of exchanging holders of Debt Securities who receive Fox Television Preferred Stock or a combination of Fox Television Preferred Stock and cash. In particular, the issue of whether the Fox Television Preferred Stock is treated as debt or equity for Federal income tax purposes is likely to be the subject of controversy between the Internal Revenue Service (the "Service") and Fox Television, particularly if Fox Television and the holders of the Fox Television Preferred Stock take inconsistent positions with respect thereto. Counsel for Fox Television is unable to

opine as to the classification of the Fox Television Preferred Stock as debt or equity for Federal income tax purposes. Fox Television views the Fox Television Preferred Stock as debt, rather than as equity, for Federal income tax purposes and, accordingly, will deduct dividend payments on the Fox Television Preferred Stock as interest. If this position is correct, a holder must include dividends paid by Fox Television in income as interest, and such holder, if a corporation, will not be entitled to the dividends received deduction. Furthermore, if the Fox Television Preferred Stock is treated as debt, it is likely that the position of the Service would be that the exchange constitutes a taxable transaction in which exchanging holders of Debt Securities recognize gain or loss.

If the Fox Television Preferred Stock is treated as equity for Federal income tax purposes, (i) it is likely that the exchange of Debt Securities for Fox Television Preferred Stock will qualify as a tax-free exchange, except to the extend that an exchanging holder receives cash or property in addition to Fox Television Preferred Stock, and (ii) distributions on the Fox Television Preferred Stock would be taxable dividends to the extent of Fox Television's current and accumulated earnings and profits.[11]

This is a very complex matter, and its resolution appears to be several years in the future. One can only imagine the confusion at tax time when some holders might view the preferred as what its title implies—namely preferred stock—while others might take the position of the company.

NOTES

1. In this chapter we will use the term "preferred stock" to mean nonconvertible preferreds with fixed as opposed to variable dividend rates. On Wall Street these issues might be referred to by the cliché "plain vanilla.

2. This section is based on the tax laws in effect in mid-1986. At the time this chapter was being written, Congress was considering a revision of the tax laws that could slightly change the tax treatment of dividends received for corporate investors. Investors are advised to contact their tax advisors for counsel on the taxability of dividends.

3. *Best's Aggregate & Averages*, 46th annual ed. (Oldwick, N.J.: A. M. Best, 1985).

4. *Life Insurance Fact Book Update* (Washington, D.C.: American Council of Life Insurance, 1985).

5. Jeffrey M. Laderman, "Capture-the-Dividend: The Street's Hottest Game." *Business Week*, December 2, 1985, 129–130.

6. See Harry G. Henn and John R. Alexander, *Laws of Corporations and Other Business Enterprises*, 3d ed. (St. Paul, Minn. West Publishing, 1983). This book is a

one-volume text that is quite useful to participants in the corporate senior securities markets. It covers many legal aspects of preferreds and bonds that will help the layman understand these instruments.

7. An interesting exception to this time-honored statement is provided by the SCIPSCO, Inc. cumulative redeemable exchangeable preferred Stock, issued in 1985 to raise funds for the merger with Storer Communications, Inc. SCIPSCO is a wholly owned subsidiary of SCI Holdings, Inc. The prospectus dated November 1, 1985, states:

> Shares of the Preferred Stock shall have priority as to the payment of dividends over Scipsco's common stock and other series of preferred stock of Scipsco ranking junior with respect to either dividends or upon liquidation, dissolution or winding up. Except as provided below, no dividends may be paid on any junior series of Scipsco's preferred stock or on Scipsco's common stock unless full cumulative dividends have been paid (or declared and a sum sufficient for the payment thereof set apart for such payment) on the Preferred Stock for all dividend payment periods terminating on or following the date of payment of such dividends. When dividends are not paid in full upon the Preferred Stock and any other preferred stock ranking on a parity as to dividends with the Preferred Stock, all dividends declared upon shares of Preferred Stock and any other preferred stock ranking on a parity as to dividends shall be declared pro rata so that in all cases the amount of dividends declared per share on the Preferred Stock and such other preferred stock shall bear to each other the same ratio that accrued dividends per share of Preferred Stock and such other preferred stock bear to each other. **Notwithstanding the foregoing, dividends may be paid on the common stock, junior series of preferred stock or any other securities of Scipsco held by Holdings** [SCI Holdings, Inc.] **in an amount sufficient to permit Holdings to pay principal of, premium, if any, and interest on all of Holdings' outstanding indebtedness and to pay Holdings' expenses.**

8. Prospectus of Eastern Air Lines, Inc., $3 Cumulative Convertible Junior Preferred Stock, February 15, 1983, p. 23.

9. Prospectus of Illinois Power Company, 8.52% Cumulative Preferred Stock, January 28, 1986.

10. Prospectus of Texas Utilities Electric Company, $9.48 Cumulative Preferred Stock, January 17, 1986.

11. Prospectus of Fox Television Stations, Inc., Increasing Rate Exchangeable Guaranteed Preferred Stock, February 27, 1986. An interesting article on this transaction appeared in *Forbes* (Allen Sloan, "Understanding Murdoch—the Numbers Aren't What Really Matters," *Forbes,* March 10, 1986, 114–118). It stated: "To compound the confusion, Murdoch is telling the U.S. IRS that the Fox preferred stock is really debt and he will deduct the dividends. In Australia he will carry the preferred stock as equity on his balance sheet. In the one case he is enhancing his balance sheet, in the other case his cash flow." Only a few months later, 460,000 shrares were redeemed at $1,000 plus accrued dividends. The proceeds for the redemption were obtained from an overseas sale of convertible preferred stock and an offering of Swiss franc bonds.

CHAPTER 6

ADJUSTABLE-RATE AND AUCTION MARKET PREFERRED STOCKS

This chapter looks at preferred stock issues whose dividends usually fluctuate from payment to payment. The dividend rates are based on various financial benchmarks or are determined by an auction or remarketing procedure. First we discuss adjustable-rate preferred stocks; then we look at auction market preferreds.

ADJUSTABLE-RATE PREFERRED STOCKS

Straight adjustable-rate preferred stocks (ARPs), also known as floating-rate preferred stocks, first came to the public market in 1982.[1] By the end of June 1986, some 135 issues had been underwritten or issued in mergers and acquisitions for total gross proceeds of nearly $11.9 billion. Of these, 111 issues were conventional ARPs, 8 convertible adjustable-rate stocks (CVARPs), 11 collateralized ARPs (CARPs), 2 LIBOR-based shares, and 3 in the miscellaneous category. Banks have been the largest issuers, with $5.3 billion divided among 54 issues. The industrial category accounts for 12 issues for nearly $1.5 billion, followed by electric utilities with 34 issues for approximately $1.5 billion. Table 6–1 shows the volume by type of issue and Table 6–2 by industry classification.

Table 6-1

Adjustable-Rate Preferred Stocks: Financing Statistics
($ Millions/[Number of Issues])

Type of Issue	1982	1983	1984	1985	1986 (to 6/30)	Total
ARP	$2,823.21 [24]	$4,225.94 [45]	$1,422.36 [17]	$1,276.34 [15]	$513.00 [10]	$10,260.85 [111]
CVARP	—	$150.00 [3]	$253.03 [5]	—	—	$403.03 [8]
CARP	—	—	$887.50 [10]	$50.00 [1]	—	$937.50 [11]
LIBOR	—	—	—	$160.00 [2]	—	$160.00 [2]
Other	—	—	$110.00 [2]	$75.00 [1]	—	$185.00 [3]
Total	$2,823.21 [24]	$4,375.94 [48]	$2,672.89 [34]	$1,561.34 [19]	$513.00 [10]	$11,946.38 [135]

Table 6-2

Adjustable Rate Preferred Stocks: Financing Statistics

($ Millions/[Number of Issues])

Industry Type	1982	1983	1984	1985	1986 (to 6/30)	Total
Banks	$1,847.00 [16]	$2,221.95 [22]	$727.36 [10]	$426.34 [4]	$125.00 [2]	$5,347.65 [54]
Electric	$40.00 [1]	$460.00 [11]	$371.25 [7]	$510.00 [10]	$158.00 [5]	$1,539.25 [34]
Finance	—	$460.00 [4]	—	—	—	$460.00 [4]
Gas	$185.00 [3]	$50.00 [1]	$100.00 [1]	—	—	$335.00 [5]
Industrial	$200.00 [1]	$493.02 [6]	$366.54 [3]	$415.00 [2]	—	$1,474.56 [12]
Insurance	$551.21 [3]	$200.00 [2]	$135.00 [1]	$160.00 [2]	$230.00 [3]	$1,276.21 [11]
Savings & loan	—	$134.03 [1]	$887.70 [10]	$50.00 [1]	—	$1,071.73 [12]
Transportation	—	$356.94 [1]	—	—	—	$356.94 [1]
Telephone	—	—	$85.04 [2]	—	—	$85.04 [2]
Total	2,823.21 [24]	$4,375.94 [48]	$2,672.89 [34]	$1,561.34 [19]	$513.00 [10]	$11,946.38 [135]

223

1983 was the peak volume year for these securities. The decline in new-issue activity is due to the increased popularity of auction rate preferred stocks, which were introduced in 1984. This investment medium is discussed later in the chapter.

What Are ARPs?

In general, adjustable-rate preferred stocks are so-called "perpetual" equity securities (some of which have sinking funds) whose dividends are adjusted quarterly at a fixed basis point spread or a fixed percentage (dividend reset spread) above, at, or below the highest of three points on the Treasury yield curve. These benchmark rates are (1) the per annum market discount rate for 3-month Treasury bills, (2) the 10-year Treasury constant maturity, and (3) the 20-year Treasury constant maturity (TCM). This provides the investor with income that rides the crest of the yield curve, as it is not fixed to either a short-term or long-term rate (as is the case with most floating-rate debt securities). Fixing on the basis of only one rate could prove disadvantageous when the shape or slope of the yield curve changes. ARPs are redeemable at the issuer's option, in most cases starting five years after issuance at 103 percent of par or stated value and dropping to par in another five years. The dividends, being equity, qualify for the intercorporate dividends received deduction under federal tax laws, thus making the after-tax return quite favorable compared to many other fully taxable financial instruments.[2]

There are some exceptions to the above dividend-setting procedures. Aetna Life & Casualty Company's Class C, Series A and Series B Single Point Adjustable Rate Stock (SPARS) dividend rates are based on the "AA" 60-day commercial paper rate with the dividends payable every seventh Thursday. The dividend for AFF Capital Corporation is fixed at 11 percent through September 30, 1988, when it will start to float (unless, of course, the shares are called at that time). The Series C shares of Bank of Boston have the dividends based on the 3-month Treasury bill and the five-year or ten-year Treasury constant maturity (TCM). Dividends for Citicorp's "4th Series" (PARS) and Phillips Petroleum Company are based only on the 3-month Treasury bill, while Bowater Incorporated's and

Hartford Fire Insurance Company's dividends are based on 3-month LIBOR (London Interbank Offering Rate).

One of the features of adjustable-rate preferred stock is the minimum and maximum rates (known as "collars") that the issuer is permitted to pay. In times of rising interest rates the cap, or maximum rate, may become effective; in periods of falling interest rates the minimum rate, or floor, may be activated. In mid-1984, eight issues became "capped out," i.e., the maximum rate was activated. At least five others came within 15 basis points of hitting the maximum rate. Just one year later the tables were turning, as interest rates declined and the minimum rates, or floors, were being set.

The dividend cap obviously restricts an investor's yield on the stock. In a rising interest rate environment, dividend rates cannot rise above the maximum rate. Therefore, to counter the effect of the lid and keep rates in line with noncapped adjustable-rate preferreds, the markets will value these shares at a lower price (and a higher yield). In 1984, the eight issues that were capped out at rates between 12.5 and 14 percent would have had dividend rates of 13.05 to 14.45 percent without the ceilings. On the other hand, when interest rates declined to the levels prevailing in early 1986, for many issues any additional decline in rates would not show up when their new dividend rates were determined. The shares started to act somewhat like fixed-rate preferred stocks, with investors willing to pay higher prices for these issues than if they had had no floors. Of course, investors had to assess the vulnerability of the shares to redemption on the part of the issuer (the market price of stock must be compared to its call price at the time of purchase, and the time remaining to the redemption date must also be considered).

ARPs are *not* money market instruments and are *not* substitutes for short-dated paper. They possess more of the characteristics of equities than of debt. They do not enjoy the "magnet" of an approaching maturity as does floating-rate debt. (However, Aetna Class C Series A stock has a mandatory redemption feature designed to retire all of the shares in 1995, and the Series B shares will be retired in whole in 1996.) None of the issues gives the holder the right to "put" the stock back to the issuer even though the issuer has the right to call the shares at its option. Thus, unless selling above the call price, ARPs normally will be valued on a current yield basis like any perpetual instrument.

Some market participants might have the impression that these securities should trade around the par level at the dividend adjustment date regardless of the direction in which interest rates are headed. However, it should be remembered that the dividend determination spreads are set in place when the shares are first issued. Interest rate levels, the creditworthiness of the issuer, and/or the tax laws could change, with the result that investors may demand a different relationship to the base rate. Senior securities trade not in a vacuum but in a marketplace that continually scrutinizes relative values. Shares are valued based on many factors, including the terms of the particular issue, alternative investments available, market conditions, and investor's perceptions of quality and liquidity.

Convertible Adjustable-Rate Preferreds

Adjustable-rate convertible preferred stocks should not be confused with convertible adjustable-rate preferreds.[3] The former are convertible into a fixed number of a company's common shares, but the rate-setting procedures are similar to those for ARPs. This type of issue would have more appeal to the typical buyer of convertible securities. Here we are interested in convertible adjustable-rate preferred stocks (CVARPs).

Eight CVARPs have been issued, of which seven were outstanding on March 31, 1986. CVARPs are similar to regular adjustable-rate issues except that they are convertible into a *fixed-dollar* amount of common stock (usually $50 worth) on any quarterly dividend payment date at the holder's option, subject to a maximum number of shares per preferred share. This type of preferred is *not* an alternative way to invest in the company's common, as it does not participate in the price movements of the underlying common shares. The issuing company has the right to pay cash in lieu of issuing shares. If it pays cash for less than all the shares that have been tendered for conversion, it must make payment on a pro rata basis. In April 1986, GATX Corporation redeemed 660,300 shares of an 800,000-share issue that were tendered for conversion. The company paid $50 per share in lieu of issuing stock. Ohio Edison took a different course when its convertible ARPs were tendered: It issued common shares in lieu of cash. Out of 2,050,000 shares of its Class A convertible adjustable preferred issued on July 26, 1984, there were under 60,000 shares outstanding only two years later. The issuers have the right to change the maximum number of shares that may be issued on conversion. The conversion feature serves as a floor for the price risk that an ARP investor assumes, as the stock can be turned in for common shares worth $50 in the marketplace. However, the floor can disappear if the common price falls below the point at which the number of shares to be issued is worth less than $50 and if the company does not increase the number of shares upon conversion. Let us assume that a CVARP share is convertible into $50 market value of common subject to a maximum of four common shares for each share of CVARPs. If the common is worth $50 at the conversion date, the ARP holder will receive one share. If the common is worth $20, each CVARP share will get 2.5 common shares. The breakeven point in this example is a common price of $12.50. At $10, the conversion worth would be only $40 per ARP.

Collateralized Adjustable-Rate Preferreds

Collateralized adjustable-rate preferreds, also known as controlled adjustable rate issues, have the acronym CARPs. These issues have been sold by special-purpose subsidiaries of various thrift institutions organized for the purpose of issuing CARPs and managing a portfolio of permitted investments. This structure was devised to enable the parent to raise funds at a lower cost than if it did the financing directly.

Special-purpose corporations (SPCs) are permitted to acquire, hold, dispose of, and invest in certain mortgage-related securities, short-term investments, and U.S. Treasury securities that qualify as required assets. These are basically Government National Mortgage Association mortgage-backed pass-through certificates, Federal Home Loan Mortgage Corporation mortgage participation certificates, Federal National Mortgage Association mortgage-backed pass-through certificates, and U.S. Treasury securities, including obligations fully guaranteed by the federal government. Also, short-term investments (those with maturities no longer than 90 days) include certificates of deposit, demand deposits, banker's acceptances, and repurchase agreements subject to certain credit-rating criteria.

These investments normally are valued monthly. At that time, the issuer will determine (1) the market value and the discounted value of each asset, (2) the aggregated discounted value of all the required assets, and (3) whether the required asset coverage is being met. The required asset coverage test is satisfied if the company has assets with a discounted value, reduced by all accrued and unpaid expenses and liabilities and accrued and unpaid dividends to the date of the evaluation, equal to or greater than the current liquidation value of the preferred.

The market value of any asset may not exceed 100 percent. The discount factors applied to the assets depend on the type of asset and the volatility of its market prices. These factors are based on the worst price declines recorded by these instruments in the past and therefore allow their market value to withstand a decline in value of about twice the historical decline. As a result of the application of the discount factor, the market value at a specific date will be greater than the discounted value.

If the required asset coverage test is not met, the issuer has a short period in which to bring it in line. This can be done by purchasing additional assets and/or repurchasing the preferred in the open market. The company may also give notice for the redemption of the number of shares of preferred stock that, had they been redeemed before the computation of the coverage on the evaluation date, would have satisfied the coverage requirement on a pro formal basis.

One possible concern of investors is the insolvency of the parent thrift institution and the effect on the special-purpose corporation. The SPC is structured so as to insulate it from the effects of the parent's insolvency. If the preferred stock were issued directly at the parent company level, the holders would stand behind all creditors in the event of bankruptcy. By structuring these limited-purpose (so-called "bullet-proof") subsidiaries, the consequences of the parent's troubles are thought to be removed. It is distinctly possible that a creditor or receiver of the thrift would attempt to get a court to order the SPC's assets and liabilities to be considered along with the bankrupt's estate, on the theory that the two are really one entity, and thus make the SPC's assets available for claims against the parent.

However, the issuers will have received opinions of their counsel essentially stating that in the event of the parent's insolvency no creditor, receiver, claimant of the thrift, or the Federal Deposit Insurance Corporation, Federal Savings and Loan Insurance Corporation, or governmental agency with authority over the thrift, can order the consolidation of the SPC's assets with those of its parent. The opinions are based on assumptions that include maintenance of the SPC's separate existence, records, and operations, separation of the subsidiary's and parent's funds and assets, and holding of appropriate subsidiary board meetings.

In 1984, the general counsel of the Federal Home Loan Bank Board, the operating body of the Federal Savings and Loan Insurance Corporation (FSLIC), issued a letter opinion on these special-purpose corporations and their parent's financial distress. It is based on certain assumptions concerning corporate procedures, fairness of financing, business purpose of the SPC, and adequate disclosure in the prospectus. It states: "It is my opinion that, assuming the foregoing facts and conclusions, a court would not uphold the receiver's attempt to disregard the separation of the subsidiary."[4] In 1986, the general counsel of the Federal Deposit Insurance Corporation (FDIC) issued a similar letter to Standard & Poor's Corporation giving his opinion on the separate status of special-purpose subsidiaries of FDIC-insured organizations. The opinion, based on assumptions similar to those in the FSLIC case, states: " . . . a court would not uphold an attempt by the FDIC as receiver of the insured institution to disregard the separateness of the subsidiary."[5]

Market Review

The early ARP issues were well received by investors. The dividend rates on the first four offerings, issued in May 1982, were set at premiums of 50 to 75 basis points to the benchmark rate. In the secondary market, they rose to 3 or 4 points above the initial offering prices soon after the next batch of issues started to come to market in late July 1982. Dividend reset spreads were reduced for high-grade issues to a range of −30 to −100 basis points between July 22 and October 15, 1982, and then dropped to −200 basis points with the late October sale of BankAmerica Corporation Series A stock and

−225 basis points with Irving Bank's November issue. Investor demand was broad enough to accept medium-grade issues, with 10 stocks selling between the end of August and mid-December.

At the beginning of 1983 the market appeared to be in good shape, willing to take on an additional supply of stock. An index based on seven of the first adjustable-rate preferreds issued ended 1982 at 116.357 and by mid-February was a record 122.286 (see Table 6–3). This proved to be the turning point, as investor enthusiasm quickly cooled due to 13 issues with a par value of $1.8 billion being rushed to the offering table in a short period. Reset rates went to even larger discounts: −300, −400, −412½ basis points on the high grades and −450, −487½ basis points on the prime-rated names. Medium-grade issues also benefited from underwriters' ebullition, with reset spreads between −275 and −250 basis points. Collars were also reduced, declining to as low as 5 to 11.5 percent on the J.P. Morgan & Company issue. Some issuers also reduced the call protection period from the typical five years to three years, as in the case of Morgan and Student Loan Marketing Association issues.

By April 1, 1983, the ARP index had dropped 9.94 percent to 110.143 as investors and issuers withdrew from the market. The Morgan offering, as well as some other aggressively priced issues, remained mostly unsold on underwriters' shelves until the market settled down to more realistic levels. For the rest of the year and into the spring of 1984, demand for and issuance of the shares slowly improved as investor confidence was restored. Then the second tidal wave occurred: On May 18, 1984, the index was 113.393 and seven weeks later, on July 6, it was 95.321, a decline of 15.94 percent. Investors expecting stafety of principal certainly were dismayed!

In the author's opinion, the 1984 decline was caused by a number of simultaneously occurring events. Rising interest rates brought a general malaise to all sectors of the senior securities markets, with investors and dealers lowering bids and cutting back on positions. It was no time to assume an aggressive market stance. Also, higher interest rates created additional pressure on ARPs with low dividend ceilings as the maximum dividend rates started to become effective in mid-May for a number of issues. Further, for a number of months corporate investors were concerned about the effects of the proposed changes in the tax laws on preferred stock investments. Some investors thus postponed purchases, which further weakened the market. Probably the greatest influences on investor psychology were the problems at Continental Illinois Corporation and loans to Argentine and other Latin American borrowers. Large money center bank holding company shares generally suffered the greatest declines, although most issues were affected. Some ARPs declined even more than common shares; price drops of 20 percent or more were not uncommon.

In our view, this decline was, to a great extent, based more on emotion than on intellect, as is often the case in the securities markets. The main symptom was fear—fear of the loss of market value, that dividends would be omitted, of bankruptcy, and that the ARP concept was not viable. But the market recovered again, although not to the previous high levels. At the end of June 1986, the seven-share ARP index was 102.821.

Adjustable-Rate Preferred Stock Index

Table 6-3 and the accompanying chart summarize the adjustable-rate preferred stock index. The index, comprised of one insurance

Table 6-3
Summary of Adjustable Rate Preferred Stock Index

		ARP Index	Current Yield (Percent)
1982	High	117.464	10.72
	Low	100.000	14.20
	Last	116.357	10.82
1983	High	122.826	8.63
	Low	109.393	9.85
	Last	109.607	10.81
1984	High	113.393	10.94
	Low	95.321	13.96
	Last	100.929	12.40
1985	High	109.643	9.57
	Low	101.786	11.50
	Last	104.964	10.21
1986	High	106.679	9.32
(to 6/30)	Low	104.214	9.52
	Last	102.821	8.00

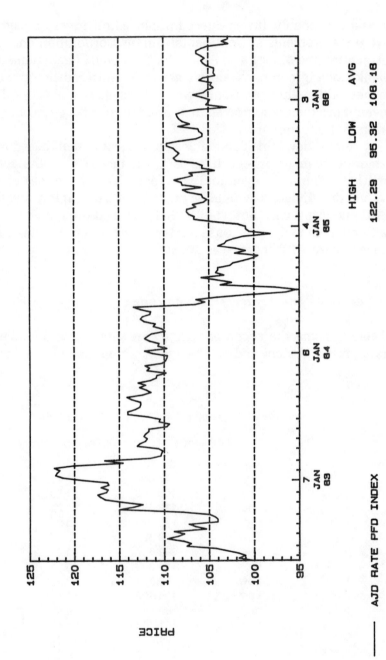

WEEKLY PRICE COMPARISON

PRICE

125
120
115
110
105
100
95

7
JAN
83

8
JAN
84

4
JAN
85

3
JAN
86

HIGH   LOW   AVG

122.29   95.32   108.18

———— AJD RATE PFD INDEX

company issue, five bank holding company issues, and one industrial issue, has an average dividend determination spread of −4 basis points and a composite rating of "A+". The spreads range from −90 to +50 basis points. Table 6–3 shows the high, low, and last index values since the inception of the index based on end-of-week prices on the New York Stock Exchange.

Returns of ARP

In each of the periods for which data are available, the annual after-tax total return (principal gain or loss plus dividend income, excluding reinvestment of the dividend) from a portfolio based on the ARP index has been positive even though there were capital gains in five periods and losses in six periods. Table 6–4 shows the total returns for the ARP index and for a straight A-rated 10 percent, generic perpetual preferred. The two are not exactly comparable. In the author's view, an ARP portfolio should be considered an intermediate-term (three-to-five-year) investment, while a straight preferred hold-

Table 6–4
Adjustable-Rate Preferred Index: Total Returns

12-Month Period Ending	ARP Index	After-Tax Total Return	A-Rated Preferred Index*	After-Tax Total Return
9/30/83	112.714	15.87%	81.97	20.92%
12/30/83	109.607	4.36	77.22	8.27
3/30/84	110.964	10.06	73.53	1.12
6/29/84	96.464	0.07	70.92	−1.25
9/28/84	101.143	2.29	76.34	6.07
12/28/84	100.929	4.57	76.92	11.76
3/29/85	105.679	6.81	81.97	20.92
6/28/85	105.643	18.83	93.02	35.56
9/27/85	105.643	14.01	88.89	24.04
12/27/85	104.964	13.26	99.01	32.78
3/28/86	104.357	8.29	114.94	40.32
6/27/86	102.821	6.70	109.29	22.60

*10 percent perpetual preferred.

ing should be viewed in the longer term. Investors with an even shorter-term outlook might well consider opportunities available in the auction market preferred market. Be that as it may, out of the twelve 12-month periods in Table 6–4, there were only two in which ARP registered superior total returns. In the three months between the end of March and the end of June 1984, interest rates rose sharply and straight preferreds suffered greater price erosion than did ARPs. Based on the quarterly index prices, ARPs have shown less volatility than the straight perpetual generic preferred for the period under review; ARP prices have had a standard deviation of 5.10, while the straight preferreds has been 7.64. The relative volatility is even greater considering the differences in the average prices. The standard deviation as a percentage of the average ARP price is 4.778 percent, compared to 9.356 percent for the straight preferred. So, for greater market risk, a straight issue ought to return more than an adjustable issue.

In Table 6–5, the after-tax current dividend yield on the ARP index are compared to those of various municipal yields with several maturities. While ARPs are not without market risk, the author believes they should be considered for inclusion in many corporate investment portfolios. The yields compare most favorably with those of many alternative investments.

Dividends and Dividend Determination Period

The dividend rate for most adjustable-rate preferred stocks is determined from data published in the *Federal Reserve Statistical Release H.15(519) Selected Interest Rates* (see Figure 6–1) during what is called the dividend determination period (DDP). The DDP is generally, but not always, 14 calendar days (the calendar period) immediately prior to the last 10 calendar days of the month prior to the dividend period for which the dividend rate on the ARP is being determined. Release H.15 is normally issued on Monday and is obtainable through the various Federal Reserve banks and by subscription from the Board of Governors of the Federal Reserve System.

The index basis for the dividend rate calculation is the highest of the two-week average of the following rates as published in H.15 during the DDP:[6]

Table 6-5
Comparison of After-Tax ARP Yields with Municipal Yield Indices

Date	End-of-Period After-Tax ARP Yield	Annual After-Tax Dividend ARP Yield	"A"-Rated Municipal General Obligations		
			3-Year	5-Year	7-Year
9/30/82	12.19%	n.a.	7.50%	8.50%	9.00%
12/31/82	10.07	n.a.	6.50	7.15	7.65
3/31/83	8.91	n.a.	6.50	7.15	7.60
6/24/83	9.07	n.a.	6.75	7.25	7.75
9/30/83	9.16	10.11%	6.50	7.20	7.60
12/30/83	10.06	8.83	7.00	7.60	8.10
3/30/83	10.04	9.61	7.00	7.75	8.25
6/29/84	11.97	9.89	7.75	8.45	8.85
9/28/84	12.31	10.19	7.45	7.95	8.40
12/28/84	11.54	10.67	6.95	7.70	8.20
3/29/85	10.23	10.48	6.60	7.45	7.95
6/28/85	10.56	11.98	6.20	6.95	7.45
9/27/85	9.25	10.80	7.50	7.50	7.90
12/27/85	9.51	10.38	6.40	7.00	7.20
3/28/86	8.87	9.54	5.60	6.00	6.10
6/27/86	7.45	8.75	5.60	6.20	6.45

- 3-month Treasury bills—market discount rate
- 10-year Treasury constant maturity rate
- 20-year Treasury constant maturity rate

To this index, base, or benchmark rate (usually rounded to the nearest five-hundredths of a percentage point—.05—although some issues provide for rounding to the nearest .01) an adjustment is made so as to arrive at the applicable dividend rate for the preferred. Such an adjustment or spread is the addition of the premium or the subtraction of the discount. For example, if the base rate is determined to be 8.5 percent, an issue with a dividend determination spread of a premium of 50 basis points will result in a dividend rate of 9 percent. Likewise, if the spread is a discount of 50 basis points, the dividend rate will be 8 percent. Normally, this applicable rate is published in a

FEDERAL RESERVE statistical release

These data are released each Monday. The availability of the release will
be announced, when the information is available, on (202) 452-3206.

H.15 (519)

For immediate release

SELECTED INTEREST RATES

SEPTEMBER 22, 1986

Yields in percent per annum

Instruments	1986 SEPT 15	1986 SEPT 16	1986 SEPT 17	1986 SEPT 18	1986 SEPT 19	This week	Last week	1986 AUG
FEDERAL FUNDS (EFFECTIVE) 1/	5.97	5.88	5.82	5.84	5.80	5.88	5.82	6.17
COMMERCIAL PAPER 2/3/								
1-MONTH	5.76	5.80	5.77	5.77	5.79	5.78	5.72	6.02
3-MONTH	5.71	5.74	5.73	5.72	5.75	5.73	5.67	5.92
6-MONTH	5.66	5.66	5.66	5.64	5.70	5.66	5.60	5.83
FINANCE PAPER PLACED DIRECTLY 2/								
1-MONTH	5.76	5.79	5.77	5.77	5.76	5.77	5.77	5.98
3-MONTH	5.57	5.58	5.57	5.57	5.58	5.57	5.56	5.94
6-MONTH	5.50	5.50	5.50	5.50	5.50	5.50	5.48	5.90
BANKERS ACCEPTANCES (TOP RATED) 2/								
3-MONTH	5.59	5.60	5.60	5.70	5.70	5.64	5.62	5.80
6-MONTH	5.55	5.57	5.56	5.68	5.68	5.61	5.58	5.71
CDS (SECONDARY MARKET)								
1-MONTH	5.72	5.75	5.77	5.76	5.82	5.76	5.73	5.97
3-MONTH	5.70	5.74	5.76	5.74	5.81	5.75	5.71	5.92
6-MONTH	5.73	5.75	5.76	5.74	5.83	5.76	5.72	5.92
BANK PRIME LOAN 1/4/	7.50	7.50	7.50	7.50	7.50	7.50	7.50	7.90
DISCOUNT WINDOW BORROWING 1/5/	5.50	5.50	5.50	5.50	5.50	5.50	5.50	5.82
U.S.GOVERNMENT SECURITIES								
TREASURY BILLS								
AUCTION AVERAGE 2/ 6/								
3-MONTH	5.16					5.16	5.24	5.57
6-MONTH	5.34					5.34	5.35	5.58
1-YEAR								5.82
AUCTION AVERAGE(INVESTMENT) 6/								
3-MONTH	5.30					5.30	5.39	5.72
6-MONTH	5.57					5.57	5.58	5.82
SECONDARY MARKET 2/								
3-MONTH	5.17	5.13	5.12	5.23	5.25	5.18	5.20	5.53
6-MONTH	5.35	5.33	5.32	5.42	5.44	5.37	5.36	5.55
1-YEAR	5.45	5.44	5.44	5.53	5.53	5.48	5.46	5.60
TREASURY CONSTANT MATURITIES 7/8/								
1-YEAR	5.77	5.76	5.77	5.87	5.86	5.81	5.79	5.93
2-YEAR	6.39	6.38	6.37	6.47	6.52	6.43	6.35	6.35
3-YEAR	6.69	6.66	6.64	6.75	6.81	6.71	6.64	6.49
5-YEAR	7.00	6.99	6.93	7.02	7.10	7.01	6.96	6.80
7-YEAR	7.36	7.35	7.28	7.41	7.50	7.38	7.30	7.01
10-YEAR	7.53	7.53	7.46	7.62	7.67	7.56	7.46	7.17
20-YEAR	7.62	7.63	7.58	7.70	7.77	7.66	7.57	7.28
30-YEAR	7.66	7.67	7.64	7.74	7.83	7.71	7.63	7.33
COMPOSITE								
OVER 10 YEARS(LONG-TERM)9/	8.19	8.16	8.11	8.24	8.35	8.21	8.07	7.72
CORPORATE BONDS								
MOODY'S SEASONED								
AAA	8.91	8.91	8.91	8.98	9.03	8.95	8.85	8.72
BAA	10.24	10.23	10.20	10.25	10.29	10.24	10.21	10.18
A-UTILITY 10/					9.72	9.72	9.59	9.51
STATE & LOCAL BONDS 11/				7.14		7.14	7.15	7.21
CONVENTIONAL MORTGAGES 12/					10.07	10.07	9.96	10.20

1. WEEKLY FIGURES ARE AVERAGES OF 7 CALENDAR DAYS ENDING ON WEDNESDAY OF THE CURRENT WEEK;

MONTHLY FIGURES INCLUDE EACH CALENDAR DAY IN THE MONTH.
2. QUOTED ON BANK-DISCOUNT BASIS.
3. RATES ON COMMERCIAL PAPER PLACED FOR FIRMS WHOSE BOND RATING IS AA OR THE EQUIVALENT.
4. RATE CHARGED BY BANKS ON SHORT-TERM BUSINESS LOANS.
5. RATE FOR THE FEDERAL RESERVE BANK OF NEW YORK.
6. AUCTION DATE.
7. YIELDS ON ACTIVELY TRADED ISSUES ADJUSTED TO CONSTANT MATURITIES. SOURCE: U.S. TREASURY.
8. SEE REVERSE FOR A DESCRIPTON OF THE CONSTANT MATURITY SERIES. THE TREASURY ANNOUNCED ON APRIL 30,
   1986 THAT IT NO LONGER WILL ISSUE 20-YEAR BONDS. CONSEQUENTLY,THE 20-YEAR CONSTANT MATURITY RATE IS
   NOW AN INTERPOLATION BETWEEN THE RATES ON 10- AND 30-YEAR SECURITIES.
9. UNWEIGHTED AVERAGE OF ALL ISSUES OUTSTANDING OF BONDS NEITHER DUE NOR CALLABLE IN LESS THAN 10 YEARS,
   INCLUDING ONE VERY LOW YIELDING "FLOWER" BOND.
10. ESTIMATE OF THE YIELD ON A RECENTLY-OFFERED, A-RATED UTILITY BOND WITH A MATURITY OF 30 YEARS AND CALL
    PROTECTION OF 5 YEARS; FRIDAY QUOTATIONS.
11. BOND BUYER INDEX, GENERAL OBLIGATION, 20 YEARS TO MATURITY, MIXED QUALITY; THURSDAY QUOTATIONS.
12. CONTRACT INTEREST RATES ON COMMITMENTS FOR FIXED-RATE FIRST MORTGAGES. SOURCE: FHLMC.

NOTE: WEEKLY AND MONTHLY FIGURES ARE AVERAGES OF DAILY RATES, EXCEPT FOR STATE & LOCAL BONDS,
      WHICH ARE BASED ON THURSDAY FIGURES, AND CONVENTIONAL MORTGAGES AND A-UTILITY BONDS,
      BOTH OF WHICH ARE BASED ON FRIDAY FIGURES.

Figure 6-1

general-circulation newspaper in New York City prior to the commencement of the dividend period to which it applies. Also, the company will send a notice of the new rate with the dividend payment check to holders of record.

The dollar amount of dividends payable for each dividend period is computed by dividing the applicable rate by 4 in the case of $100 par or stated value issues, by 8 in the case of $50 par issues, and by 16 in the case of $25 par issues. The dividend is based on a 360-day year, four 90-day quarters and twelve 30-day months.

Once the dividend rate has been determined, it cannot be paid until another step has been taken: The company's board of directors must declare the dividend out of assets legally available for payment. If the dividend is not declared, it accumulates. If there are arrearages, the adjustable-rate preferred may not be redeemed in part and the company may not purchase or acquire any shares of the preferred unless pursuant to a purchase or exchange offer made on the same terms to all holders of the stock. Obviously, if the dividends are not paid on the ARP stock, cash dividends may not be paid on the common shares or any other stock ranking junior to the preferred.

While voting rights vary among issues, most generally are not entitled to vote except in special circumstances. Usually, if the issuer is in arrears for six quarterly payments, the preferred stockholders may vote for some members of the board of directors until all dividend arrears have been paid. Continental Illinois Corporation deferred payment of five dividends normally payable between September 30, 1984, and September 30, 1985. The arrearages and the sixth payment due December 31, 1985, were paid on that date. Arrearages totaled $6.925, and the regular payment was $1.225.

Searching for Relative Values: the Dividend Strip and Yield to Call

In order to evaluate the various ARP issues, we must place them on a more comparable footing through some minor adjustments to the price and dividend. The reason is that as the ex-dividend date approaches, the price of the stock reflects the accrual, or buildup, of the dividend from the last ex-dividend date, just as with straight preferred stocks. In contrast, bonds normally trade on a price basis with the accrued interest added on. Equities trade flat, i.e., without the dividend accruals. In addition, the dividends for different issues are set at various dates throughout the year, and even if the dividend rates were the same, the prices would reflect different amounts of accrued dividends.

The first step is to remove the effect of the accrual of the dividend—to "strip" the dividend from the price of the stock. If the quarterly dividend on a $100 par value stock is 9 percent, or $2.25, and it is one month after the ex-dividend date and two months prior to the next ex-dividend date, we should subtract $0.75 ($2.25 × ⅓) from the preferred price as it presently reflects this accrual. One month from now the price will reflect two-thirds of the $2.25 dividend payment, or an accrual of $1.50 per share. Table 6–6 gives five examples of the dividend strip assuming that it was done on February 1. Issue A, selling at 54, has a dividend accrual of $0.69 per share that, when subtracted from the market price of 54, gives an adjusted price of 53.31.

Now that we have eliminated the effect of the dividend buildup, we must reset the dividend rates on a comparable basis. This step is obviously not necessary with fixed-rate or straight preferreds. For our purpose, we assume that the base rate on February 1 is 9.55 percent. From this we get the adjusted or reset dividend rate, and by dividing the reset or assumed dividend rate by the adjusted price we get the new, adjusted current yields. Thus, both the numerator and the denominator of the equation have been adjusted to the current day's level. This makes comparison among the issues easier and helps us determine which issues offer more attractive values (of course, taking quality and other factors into consideration).

Looking at Issues B and C, we note that the initial reset rates are −200 and −400 basis points, respectively, a difference of 200 basis points. However, the market has greatly narrowed the reset spreads. If we subtract the adjusted current yield from the new base rate, we find that the adjusted reset spread for Issue B is +123 basis points compared with the original −200. Likewise, for Issue C, the effective spread has changed from −400 to +106 basis points. The difference between the two issues is now only 17 basis points. For the issues that went to a premium over the par or stated value, the adjusted reset spreads have widened since they were first determined. They

Table 6–6
Example of Adjustable Rate Preferred Dividend Strip
(Assuming Current Date of 2/1/86 and Current
Benchmark Rate of 9.55 Percent)

	A	B	C	D	E
Current dividend rate	9.05	8.30	6.30	10.45	9.30
Quarterly dividend amount ($)	1.1313	1.0375	1.575	1.30625	1.1625
Next dividend date	3/31	2/18	2/18	3/31	3/31
Next ex-dividend date	3/6	2/7	2/7	3/9	3/9
Current price	54	36	58	54	53
Pretax current yield (%)	8.38	11.53	10.86	9.68	8.77
Estimated dividend accrual:					
Dollar amount	0.69	0.97	1.47	0.75	0.67
Number of days	55	84	84	52	52
Adjusted price	53.31	35.03	56.53	53.25	52.33
Reset spread (basis points)	−90	−200	−400	+50	−65
Adjusted or reset dividend rate (%)	8.65	7.55	6.00*	10.05	8.90
Pre-tax current yield based on adjusted price and dividend (%)	8.11	10.78	10.61	9.44	8.50

*6.00 percent is the minimum rate; without the floor, the rate would be 5.55 percent.
Note: Estimated dividend accrual is based on 30-day months, actual number of days in month, from last ex-dividend date. Adjusted price is current price less the accrual. Adjusted dividend rate is based on the assumed rate on 2/1/86 of 9.55%.

are now −144, −11, and −105 basis points for Issues A, D, and E, respectively, compared with −90, +50, and −65 basis points at issuance.

Another very important calculation must be made for issues selling above their call prices, and that is to obtain an estimate of the yield to call. The current yields for Issues A, D, and E effectively overstate their current returns. If things remain unchanged, the stocks will be vulnerable to call at the issuer's first opportunity, and the investor can lose the difference between the market price and the call price. The issuer has the option to call the stock; thus, shareowners can be assured of their holding the preferred only until the call date. The lesser of the current yield or yield to call is the appropriate one to use.

In the case of Issue A, the call price is $51.50 starting August 1, 1987, 2.5 points below the current market price and 1.81 points below the adjusted price. We must also assume that the 8.65 percent adjusted dividend rate will remain unchanged for the life of the issue. Most professional investors have bond calculators available and normally use them to calculate the yield to call. Adjusting the prices to make them comparable with bonds—i.e., on a percentage of par basis—we input 106.62 as the market price and 103 as the call price with 8/1/87 as the call date. The stripped yield to call for Issue A is 6.86 percent. The yields to call for Issues D and E, with slightly different call dates, are 6.76 and 7.69 percent, respectively.

AUCTION MARKET PREFERRED STOCKS

In 1984, designers of financial instruments developed a new variety of variable-rate preferred stock—auction market preferreds (AMPs)—for corporate money managers. Other names and acronyms have been affixed to this type of security, such as "Cumulative Auction Market Preferred Stock" ("CAMPS"), "Dutch Auction Rate Transferable Securities Preferred Stock" ("DARTS"), "Market Auction Preferred Stock" ("MAPS"), "Short-Term Auction Rate Preferred Stock" ("STAR"), and "Money Market Preferred Stock" ("MMP").[7] The instrument is generally not for the small or unsophisticated investor, as the shares are priced from $100,000 to $500,000 each; one issue came to market with shares priced at $5,000.

Table 6–7 lists the issuers as of August 31, 1986, arranged by the par or stated value of the shares. The manager of "temporarily" idle corporate funds might well find this to be an attractive alternative to money market instruments and other types of preferred stock. The dividends, payable every seven weeks in the case of most issues, are determined by bids from current holders and potential buyers and ought to reflect the money markets at the time of the bidding auction.[8] Dividends on the regular adjustable-rate preferreds (ARP) described earlier are determined quarterly. The more frequent dividend-fixing mechanism, as it is not set on any predetermined spread from a base rate, will allow the dividends (subject to certain minimum and max-

Table 6-7
Issuer Arranged by Par Value of Shares

$5,000

MidFed Capital*

$100,000

AFS Financial	International Paper
American International Group	Kroger Co.
Arlington Finance*	Lincoln National
Buckeye Capital Corp.	Marine Midland Banks
CNA Financial	Meritor Capital
Cen Trust Finance	Meritor Finance (I, II & III)
Com Fed Funding	Mid-America Capital Corp.
Crossland Funding	Mid-America Capital Corp. II
Crossland NY Funding (I, II, & III)	Midwest Financial
Dime Funding Corp. I	Newmont First Capital Corp.
Dollar Finance	Pathway Capital
East River Capital Corp.	Proctor & Gamble
Empire Funding	Republic New York Corp.
Empire of America	Ryder System
First American Capital Corp.	Seamen's Capital Corp.
First Federal Capital Funding*	Talman Finance Corporation
FFM Finance Corp.	Texas Instruments
FFM Finance Corp. II	Transamerica Corporation
Fulton Capital	USAT Finance
Goldome Florida Funding Corporation	Wells Fargo & Company
Goldome Florida Funding II	Weyerhauser Company

$250,000

AmCap Capital

$500,000

American Express	GLENFED Finance II
Central Power & Light	Household Finance Corporation
Citicorp	Manufacturers Hanover
Citizens & Southern (Ga.)	MCorp
City Capital	Security Pacific Corporation
Coast Credit	Union Bancorp
GLENFED Finance	USX Corp.

*Remarketable issue.

imum rates) to be based on the current credit perceptions of the issuer. All purchases and sales conducted through the auction or remarketing process are at the liquidation value, so far $5,000, $100,000, $250,000 or $500,000 per share, as the case may be. Of course, as with any security, investors are advised to refer to the prospectuses for more complete information about the various issues.

The Current Market

American Express Company issued the first AMP shares in August 1984, followed by United States Steel Corporation's Series A stock in early November. By the end of the year, seven issues totaling $550 million had been offered. Investors caught on to the new securities as another 56 issues amounting to slightly more than $3.9 billion were publicly sold in 1985. By the end of August 1986, there were 107 issues outstanding (one had been completely tendered for) with a par or stated value of more than $8.4 billion. Table 6–8 summarizes the volume of auction market preferred stock issues.

Further growth in the issuance of AMP stock is expected from both corporations raising new equity capital and the possible refunding of some outstanding adjustable-rate issues over the next couple of years.[9] Investors apparently like the maintenance of the stock at the par or liquidation value even though it comes at a cost (but at a

Table 6–8
Auction Market Preferred Stock Financing as of 8/31/86
($ Millions [Number of Issues])

Type of Issuer	1984	1985	1986	Total
Banks	—	$1,162.5 [16]	$1,217.5 [11]	$2,389.0 [27]
Financial services	$225.0 [3]	150.0 [2]	75.0 [1]	455.0 [6]
Industrial	75.0 [1]	850.0 [13]	775.0 [9]	1,700.0 [23]
Insurance	100.0 [1]	475.0 [7]	150.0 [2]	725.0 [10]
Thrift (collateralized)	150.0 [2]	1,280.0 [18]	1,605.0 [21]	3,035.0 [41]
Electric utilities	—	—	75.0 [1]	75.0 [1]
Total	$550.0 [7]	$3,917.5 [56]	$3,897.5 [45]	$8,365.0 [108]

savings to the issuer). If these offerings were conventional adjustable-rate preferred, the dividend rates would probably be 200 to 300 or more basis points higher. However, AMP shares are for the temporary, or short-term, investment of corporate cash, while a longer-term view should be taken of ARP.

Because of the 85 percent dividends received deduction, the after-tax return on AMP shares exceeds that of alternative short-term investments, all other things being equal. Table 5–4 in Chapter 5 shows the pre-tax preferred yield, the after-tax yield, the pre-tax return needed on an alternative investment to equal the preferred's after-tax return, and the fully taxable alternative investment yield. In October 1985 there were 25 dividend-setting auctions, with the AMP dividend rate averaging 6.171 percent; this was equal to 5.745 percent on an after-tax basis (46 percent marginal tax rate). The pre-tax 60-day commercial paper rate for "AA" corporate issuers averaged 7.924 percent at the time of the auctions; the after-tax commercial paper rate was 4.279 percent. The municipal commercial paper rate (60 to 89 days, A1+/P1 rated) was 4.947 percent, and the rate on "MIG1/AA" 30-day municipal variable-rate put bonds was 5.226 percent. While the pre-tax yields for the subject preferreds averaged 78 percent of the corporate commercial paper rate, it was 34 percent higher when adjusted for income taxes. AMPs provided a 16 percent higher return than municipal commercial paper and a 10 percent better yield than 30-day municipal put bonds.

A few months later, the spread relationships changed as interest rate levels continued to fall. In March 1986, the average dividend was 5.053 percent for 39 auctions (excluding new-issue pricings), or 4.704 percent on an after-tax basis. The 60-day corporate commercial paper rate averaged 7.381 percent, or 3.986 percent for a fully taxed corporate investor. The 60-day municipal commercial paper rate was 4.578 percent, and the 30-day municipal variable-rate put bonds were 4.861 percent. Thus, the auction rate preferred dividend on a pre-tax basis was 68.5 percent of the commercial paper rate but still provided an 18 percent greater yield when income taxes were considered. The incremental yield over municipal commercial paper averaged only 13 basis points, or 2.8 percent, while the municipal put bonds returned 16 basis points more than the subject preferreds.

There have been a number of instances since this market got started in which the auction rate preferred yielded less than some quoted alternative municipal yields. There are several possible reasons for this, including market inefficiencies, the transaction costs of switching from one instrument to another, and possible unfamiliarity with some of the municipal instruments.

Redemption Features

All AMP shares currently are redeemable at the issuer's option, in whole or in part, on or near any interest payment date. The initial call price is generally 103 percent (although an increasing number have call prices starting at 101.5 percent) of the offering price for the first year, 102 percent (101 percent) for the second year, 101 percent (100.5 percent) for the third year, and 100 percent thereafter. Some issues have call prices of 101 percent for the first year and either 100.5 or 100 percent for the second. These premiums are in line with the regular ARP issues but, because there is expected to be less incentive for refunding AMP shares, the deferred call period has been abandoned. However, the issuer does have an out in the event the dividend rate reaches certain levels. If the dividend rate equals or exceeds the "AA" commercial paper rate, the AMP may be redeemed in whole or in part at 100 percent on any interest payment date. Notice of redemption must be given at least 30 days and not more than 45 to 60 days prior to the redemption date. The collateralized issues also have provisions for mandatory redemption in the event the minimum asset coverage test is not satisfied or restored or the distributions made in any calendar year exceed the current and accumulated earnings and profits of the company for federal income tax purposes.

First Nationwide Capital Corporation issued $100 million of Short Term Auction Rate Preferred Stock ("STAR" Preferred) in April 1985. Toward the end of the year, the company became a subsidiary of Ford Motor Company. Because of this merger it was no longer able to use the signficant tax-loss carryovers of its parent, First Nationwide Savings, against its operating income for federal income tax purposes. As a result, it issued bonds with a 10.25 percent coupon and asked for tenders for the stock. All shares were tendered at the price of $101,500. If holders did not tender the stock, dividends on the shares in the future might be considered nondividend distributions and thus ineligible for the dividends received deduction. Also, marketability would be diminished, and the dividends set at future auctions might be different than they otherwise would be. If the dividend rate equaled or exceeded the commercial paper rate, the shares would have likely been called by the company at $100,000 each. In the view of many observers, holders had little choice but to tender their shares and go on to the next investment.

Stock Certificates, Securities Depositories, and Settlement

All existing holders and prospective purchasers of AMP must sign a "Purchaser's Letter" that states, among other things, that as long as the dividends are determined by auction, the ownership of the shares will be maintained in book entry form by a securities depository and no certificates will be issued. Currently, the Depository Trust Company is such a depository and Cede & Company is its nominee and the holder of record of such shares. Cede & Company maintains the records of the beneficial owners. Settlement of purchases and sales of shares are made on the first business day following the dividend auction or remarketing date through the securities depository. In cases where the dividend is not determined at auction, beneficial owners may obtain certificates for their shares.

Dividends

Dividends, payable every seven weeks in most instances, are determined by a Dutch auction process (or remarketing process in the case of AmCap Corporation and MidFed Capital Corporation) conducted on the first business day prior to the start of a dividend period. The current dividend period is 49 days (although the initial dividend period may be somewhat longer) in compliance with the 46-day holding period requirement under which a corporate stockholder is entitlted to take the 85 percent dividends received deduction. In many instances, if the dividend payment date is not a business day, dividends will be paid on the next business day with the payment date reverting to the original schedule for the next payment date. In others, the dividend date will be moved ahead to two business days prior to the "normal" date. If the law changes the minimum holding period, the issuer may change the dividend period to equal or exceed (but not by more than nine days) the new holding period requirement up to a maximum of 98 days. Any new dividend period must be evenly divisible by seven.

The amount of the dividend for each period is obtained as follows:

$$\frac{\text{Number of days in dividend period}}{360} \times \text{dividend rate} \times \text{Share price}$$

Many nonthrift issues provide that if the issuer does not pay the full amount of the dividend and/or the redemption price to the dividend paying agent on time, the auctions will then be discontinued and the rate will be equal to LIBOR (London Interbank Offering Rate) plus a premium. Some collateralized issues provide for a reserve fund for dividends. This provision requires the company to deposit with the dividend paying agent on each dividend payment date, and to maintain on deposit to the next dividend date, sufficient cash and/or short-term securities to pay the dividends that will accrue on the stock during the period. Others have a dividend coverage provision, which requires the company to value, as of each evaluation date (each dividend payment date and each 25 days preceding the next dividend payment date), its cash and short-term securities maturing by the next dividend payment date in order to ensure that the total value will be at least equal to the dividend amount due at the current applicable rate.

The maximum dividend rates are of the floating variety, not fixed as with adjustable-rate preferred stock—that is, they are based on a percentage of the "AA" composite commercial paper rate. This rate is the interest yield equivalent of the 60-day rate on commercial paper issued by corporations whose bond ratings are "AA" or equivalent. It is made available by the Federal Reserve Bank of New York on a discount basis. Provisions are included in the terms of the preferred for alternate commerical paper rates if the Federal Reserve

Bank does not make such rates available. Also, if the dividend period is increased, the commercial paper rate definition will be changed accordingly.

Some issues, such as American Express and Lincoln National Corporation, require that the maximum rate through the auction dividend pricing mechanism be no more than 110 percent of the commercial paper rate. For collaterilized thrift issues, the maximum dividend is 125 percent (120 percent in the case of Transamerica Corporation) if the applicable rate for the prior auction was 110 percent of the commercial paper rate. Several other issues, such as Citicorp, Manufacturers Hanover, MCorp, Security Pacific, United States Steel, and Weyerhauser, base the maximum dividend on the rating of the preferred stock—110 percent of the commercial paper rate if the prevailing rating on the stock is "aa"/"AA" or above, 120 percent if "a"/"A," 130 percent if "baa"/"BBB," and 150 percent if lower than "baa"/"BBB."[10] Minimum rates can be no lower than 58 to 59 percent of the commercial paper rate with the exception of AFS Financial, whose minimum rate is 80 percent.

Auction Procedures

The auction for the determination of the dividend takes place on the first business day prior to the start of a dividend period (except when the auction day or dividend payment day is a bank holiday). Each existing holder or prospective purchaser must sign a "Purchaser Letter" requiring the signer to abide by the procedures set forth in the prospectus. The issuer has also entered into an agreement with a trust company (Manufacturers Trust Company or Bankers Trust Company, in most cases), which will run the auction, determine the applicable dividend rate, and so forth. The three types of orders that may be entered are:

Hold order—the number of shares that an existing holder wishes to continue to hold without regard to the applicable rate for the next dividend period.

Bid—the number of shares that an existing holder wishes to continue to hold provided that the applicable rate for the next dividend period is not less than the rate specified by the holder. Also, an order by a potential holder willing to purchase shares, and by an existing holder who wishes to purchase additional shares, at a dividend rate no lower than that specified.

Sell order—the number of shares that an existing holder wishes to sell without regard to the applicable rate for the next dividend period.

On or prior to the auction date, the existing holders will submit their hold orders, bids, and sell orders to a broker-dealer, who in turn will submit them to the trust company prior to 1:00 p.m. New York City time. Also, prospective holders may submit their bids through broker-dealers at that time. At this point,

- Any bid by an existing holder with a rate higher than the maximum rate allowed will be treated as a sell order, and any similar bid by a potential holder will not be accepted.
- All bids with rates above that determined by the auction and all sell orders by existing holders constitute irrevocable offers to sell. A bid by a potential holder is an irrevocable offer to purchase shares. The number of shares purchased or sold may be subject to proration procedures.
- If an existing holder does not submit any order, the trust company will deem that a hold order has been entered on behalf of the holder.

The trust company will assemble all orders and determine whether enough clearing bids have been made (i.e., whether the number of AMP shares that are the subject of submitted bids by potential holders equals or exceeds the number of shares that are the subject of submitted sell orders). For example, if 75 shares are the subject of bids and 25 shares the subject of sell orders, clearing bids exist. If enough clearing bids have been made, the winning bid rate wil be determined and will become the applicable rate for the next dividend period. The winning bid is the lowest rate that would result in existing holders continuing to hold stock that, when added to shares to be purchased by potential holders, would equal the available auction market preferred (the number of shares of stock not subject to hold orders). Thus, with 100 shares outstanding, if hold orders amount to 25 shares, available shares will be 75.

Let us review an example (others may be found in the prospectuses):

100 Shares Outstanding; Maximum Rate, 8.75%

	Bidder	Number of Shares	Order
	1	25	Hold
	2	25	Continue to hold if new rate is at least 6.00%
Existing	3	25	Continue to hold if new rate is at least 6.20%
holders	4	15	Continue to hold if new rate is at least 6.35%
	5	10	Sell
	6	10	Buy if new rate is at least 6.00%
Potential	7	25	Buy if new rate is at least 6.10%
holders	8	30	Buy if new rate is at least 6.25%
	9	25	Buy if new rate is at least 6.35%
	10	20	Buy if new rate is at least 6.40%

100 shares outstanding less 25 shares subject to hold orders equals 75 available shares. There are bids for 110 shares, which exceeds the 10 shares subject to a sell order; thus, there are enough clearing bids. The winning bid is 6.20 percent (and the dividend rate for the next dividend period) because at the next lowest bid, 6.10 percent, only 60 shares would continue to be held or purchased, which is less than the available AMP of 75 shares. Bidder 4 sells his 15 shares, as his bid of 6.35 percent was greater than the winning bid; Bidder 5 sells its 10 shares, as it was a seller at any rate. Of those whose bids were below the winning bid of 6.20 percent,

> Bidder 1 continues to hold 25 shares
> 2 continues to hold 25 shares
> 6 buys 10 shares
> 7 buys 25 shares

At this point, only 15 shares are available (75 shares initially available less the 60 shares purchased). Therefore, Bidder 3 continues to hold 15 shares and must sell 10 shares, as the winning bid rate was equal to his bid of 6.20 percent.

At settlement on the day after the auction, the following transactions take place:

Bidder 3 sells 10 shares	Bidder 6 buys 10 shares
4 sells 15 shares	7 buys 25 shares
5 sells 10 shares	
Total: 35 shares sold	Total: 35 shares purchased

After settlement, the ownership of the shares will be as follows:

Bidder 1 holds 25 shares
2 holds 25 shares
3 holds 15 shares
4 holds 0 shares
5 holds 0 shares
6 holds 10 shares
7 holds 25 shares

Total: 100 shares held

1. If enough clearing bids exist (as in the above example), the applicable rate for the next dividend period will be equal to the winning bid.
2. If there are not enough clearing bids (for other reasons than all outstanding shares being subject to hold orders), the applicable rate will be equal to the maximum rate.
3. If all of the shares are the subject of hold orders, the applicable rate for the next dividend period will be the minimum rate.

Case 2 is a "failed" auction. There has never yet been a failed auction to the best of the author's knowledge although one nearly did occur in 1985. In May of that year, Goldome Florida Funding had its first auction, and the dividend of 7.76 percent amounted to 109.94 percent of the 60-day corporate commercial paper rate. According to press reports at the time, the dividend rate should have been 125 or more basis points lower. Apparently, potential buyers were not lined up before the auction, and the underwriter bought much of the stock at the high dividend bid. Subsequent Goldome auctions were more in line with the results on similar collateralized auction rate preferred deals.

Under the auction procedures, there are instances in which holders wanting to sell stock might not be able to sell any or all of their shares. This could occur when there are no bids for a sufficient number of shares. The remarketing process is designed to help eliminate this potential problem, as the dividend rates should be at levels designed to bring buyers and sellers together.

NOTES

1. In 1978, AMAX Inc. privately placed an issue based on LIBOR. In 1980, Citibank and Chemical New York Corporation issued adjustable-rate preferred shares with the dividend rate adjusted every three years to 90 percent of the interest rate on certain adjustable-rate notes. The *Wall Street Journal* (November 17, 1980) reported the purchaser stating that the securities "are designed to make long-term investments feasible in today's uncertain economic environment by providing a measure of protection against wide upward fluctuations in interest rates." As is often the case with financial innovations, the private placement market is the first to test new ideas.

2. At the time of this writing, both the Senate and the House of Representatives were engaged in the revision of the tax laws. The dividends received deduction would be changed under both versions. The Senate's change would be negligible, while the House's would be somewhat more pronounced. Of course, what might eventually emerge in the final tax bill and signed into law by the President could be quite different from the proposals.

3. On September 12, 1980, Landmark Bancshares Corporation made a rights offering to its common shareholders inviting them to subscribe for 36,364 shares of Series I Variable Rate Cumulative Convertible Preferred Stock, $1 par value at $55 per share. The dividend was based on the prime rate of the Chase Manhattan Bank and subject to a minimum of 9 percent and a maximum of 13.25 percent on the $55 stated value ($4.95/$7.29 per share). Each share was convertible into 2.25 shares of common stock.

4. For a complete text of the letter, see Standard & Poor's *CreditWeek*, April 2, 1984, 1928.

5. The complete text may be found in *CreditWeek*, April 21, 1986, 1, 2.

6. The adjustable-rate preferred stock agreements have provisions for determining the base rate in case the Treasury bill rate, 10-year constant maturity, and 20-year constant maturity rates are not available.

7. "Dutch Auction Rate Transferable Securities Preferred Stock" and "DARTS" are trademarks of Salomon Brothers, Inc. "Money Market Preferred Shares" and "MMP" are trademarks of Shearson/Lehman Brothers, Inc. Acronyms for various financial instruments appear to be a marketing fad of the Eighties devised by Wall Street "yuppies."

8. The dividend rates for AMCAP Corporation's Adjustable Tender Preferred Stock and MidFed Capital Corporation's Remarketable Preferred Stock are set by remarketing agents. They are designed to enable the agents to remarket the shares at the liquidation prices of $250,000 and $5,000, respectively.

9. For a discussion of preferred stock refunding, see Chapter 7.

10. The author considers this is an interesting provision, and wonders why something similar has not been tried as a regular feature of corporate bonds—that is, if the issue got downgraded the coupon could be increased by a certain amount, and if it got upgraded the coupon could be similarly decreased. Certainly bondholders would get some benefit if the fortunes of the company declined and the company would benefit if it showed improvement.

CHAPTER 7

PREFERRED STOCK REDEMPTIONS

It is important to know the redemption features of preferred stocks that you own or are considering for purchase. Corporations will redeem senior securities when it is to their advantage, i.e., when it adds to common shareholder wealth. A high current yield ought to be a sign that something can go amiss, not only from a credit quality standpoint but from a premature redemption. This chapter reviews the redemption features of straight and adjustable-rate nonconvertible preferred stocks.

INTRODUCTION

The redemption of preferred stock is not as complex a subject as corporate bond redemptions, but it is, of course, important to participants in the preferred market. Preferred stock calls, like debt redemptions, are common; yet they trouble investors, who often are not fully aware of the terms of the issues they hold. It is important to read the prospectuses of issues owned or being considered for purchase, especially those with the higher dividend rates and yields. Because provisions vary from issue to issue—even those of the same company—to rely on blanket statements about redemption features may prove costly. How often do you hear someone say, "I don't have time to read a prospectus"? Well, investors must make time if they want to keep their portfolios healthy. Investigate *before* you invest!

After a company issues a preferred stock, circumstances may change. A time may come when the issuer finds it desirable to eliminate the shares from its capitalization; for example, voting rights might impair control of a preferred stock issuer by the common shareowners. Or circumstances might change in such a manner that it becomes advantageous to refund a preferred stock with bonds to increase earnings for the common stock. Such a refunding would change a nondeductible expense (preferred dividends) to a tax-deductible expense (bond interest). From the end of 1985 through the spring of 1986, Occidental Petroleum Corporation redeemed seven preferred issues, creating annual savings of nearly $152 million. With some 110 million common shares outstanding, net earnings per share would be boosted by about $1.38. Funds for these redemptions (over $1.1 billion) came from cash on hand and the sale of the company's marketable securities, the proceeds from the earlier sale of an overseas oil and gas operation, and the sale of senior notes and common stock. There are also a few stocks that give the issuer the right to exchange the preferred for debt, thus changing the nondeductible dividend payment to a dedubtible interest charge. The holder, of course, improves his or her position in the capitalization structure but, if a corporate investor, loses the benefit of the dividends received deduction.

Another reason for redemption could be the issuer's desire to restructure its capitalization. In 1985, PacifiCorp and Atlantic Richfield Company redeemed preferreds for this reason. PacifiCorp's recapitalization was a step toward increasing the common equity while reducing the cost of high-dividend preferred. The Atlantic Richfield call was unexpected, as the stock was trading around $40 per share on the New York Stock Exchange when the redemption was announced on August 19. The redemption price for this 3.75 percent Series B issue was $101.50. The shares resumed trading the next day at 101.

The most important reason for redeeming a senior security is a decline in financing costs, which makes it possible for the issuing company to save money by replacing high-cost issues with lower-cost ones. Virtually all issuers of preferred stock provide for periodic redemption of the shares through a sinking fund arrangement, redemption of the stock in whole or in part by call, or conversion into common stock.

REDEMPTION PROVISIONS

Of the publicly issued preferreds that were outstanding as of December 31, 1985, only 13 issues had no call or redemption provisions (see Table 7-1). These are probably truly perpetual issues, as there is no way other than through liquidation or reorganization that an issuer can retire the stock against the owner's will. It could make open market purchases or ask for tenders of the shares, but the stock cannot be involuntarily given up by the investor. Of course, reorganization does not necessarily mean going through the bankruptcy courts. Both Bethlehem Steel Corporation and United States Steel Corporation had had issues of 7 percent noncallable cumulative preferred

Table 7-1
Noncallable Preferred Stocks:
Selected Details
as of December 31, 1985

Issue	Dividend Rate	Par or Stated Value	Approximate Number of Shares Outstanding
Bangor Hydro-Electric	7.00%	$100.00	25,000
Celanese Corporation	7.00	100.00	25,638
Central Maine Power	6.00	100.00	5,713
New England Power	6.00	100.00	80,140
Pacific Gas & Electric	5.00	25.00	400,000
Pacific Gas & Electric	5.50	25.00	1,173,163
Pacific Gas & Electric	6.00	25.00	4,211,662
PacifiCorp	6.00	100.00	5,932
PacifiCorp	7.00	100.00	18,060
Southern Calif. Edison	5.00	8.33	480,000
Southern Calif. Gas	6.00	25.00	79,011
Southern Calif. Gas "A"	6.00	25.00	783,032
Wisconsin Electric	6.00	100.00	44,508

stock outstanding for years before they disappeared from the balance sheets in the mid-1960s. Bethlehem Steel merged with Bethlehem Limestone Company, resulting in the exchange of preferred shares for cash and 4½ percent subordinated debentures due 1990. United States Steel, then a New Jersey corporation, merged with a subsidiary organized under Delaware law with the Delaware corporation being the survivor. This merger provided for the exchange of the noncallable preferred for a new issue of 4⅝ percent subordinated debentures due 1996.

There are a few other issues that appear to be noncallable at first glance but contain sinking fund features that provide for the periodic retirement of the shares. A careful reading of the data in preferred stock guides is most important, and if any doubt remains, additional sources should be consulted. Reynolds Industries had an issue of $4.10 preferred that was noncallable but had a sinking fund with an option to double the payments. More than 7 million shares were outstanding at the end of 1983, but through repurchases and the use of a sinking fund, the issue was retired in early 1986. (Use of the minimum sinking fund alone would have retired the shares by early 1991.) An interesting example is Uniroyal, Inc.'s 8% Noncallable, Cumulative-to-the-Extent-Earned First Preferred. The company was acquired in a leveraged buyout in 1985. The common stockholders received a premium over the market for their shares, but the preferred holders were not offered one sou—they were not bought out, since management wanted the stock to remain outstanding. The shares dropped from about 68 to 50. The preferred holders sued Uniroyal and some members of the management team, claiming that the stock should be redeemed and not allowed to remain outstanding as the buyout was really a liquidation. A settlement was reached that would allow the preferred holders to vote on two proposals after the consummation of the acquisition in 1985. One proposal would make the stock redeemable so as to permit the retirement of one-sixth of the shares annually starting in 1995; the other would make the shares cumulative whether or not earned. Thus, these shares left the exclusive class of truly perpetual stocks.

The remaining issues have redemption features of one type or another. Most currently are callable at any time, in whole or in part, at the option of the issuer at preset prices plus accrued and unpaid dividends up to the call date. Generally, the call price is initially at par or the offering price plus the annual dividend rate; it is then reduced periodically to par or the initial offering price at some future date. In many cases, the call price is reduced at five-year intervals; in others, it is decreased by a set amount annually.[1]

The aforementioned call schedules are found in most issues, but there are exceptions. BankAmerica Corporation has a preferred with an interesting "wrinkle." Its Special Series C Preferred is callable beginning September 1, 1990, at the "adjusted" stated value. The shares, issued when BankAmerica acquired Seafirst Corporation in July 1983, have a stated value of $25 each. The acquisition was structured so that if certain of Seafirst's loans resulted in net losses greater than $350 million, the stated value would be reduced to as low as $2. The reduction would occur on September 1, 1988, based on the evaluation of the actual and estimated future loan losses, recoveries, and certain legal expenses. At March 31, 1986, loan charge-offs were such that the stated value, if adjusted at that date, would be reduced to $4.60 a share. The company stated that "it appears highly probable that the stated value of the Special Preferred Stock will be reduced to $2.00 per share in 1988."[2]

The dividend on the preferred is $2.875 per annum, but it could be adjusted in September 1988 to as low as $2.25. Thus, if the stated value is reduced to $2, the shares will almost certainly be called at the first opportunity—after all, at that price the annual dividend cost to the company would be greatly in excess of the redemption price. The current yield would be 112.5 percent based on the $2.25 dividend; and any investor thinking that shares yielding that much would remain outstanding had better think again. At the beginning of April 1986, the shares were trading around $14, providing a current yield of more than 20.54 percent. However, all dividend and redemption payments from May 31, 1986, through the redemption date of September 1, 1990, will amount to only $13.6875. This is an example of an investment (or a speculation) with a high current return but an expected low total return.

Most new issues have some type of deferred redemption provision. Some might not be callable under any circumstance for the first five to ten years; others might be currently callable but protected against lower-cost refunding for a certain period. This is similar to provisions found in corporate debt issues. A noncallable provision is far more absolute than a nonrefundable clause. Yet many investors are confused about this, treating refunding protection like call protection; this misconception has cost many investors considerable sums over the years.

Many issues are currently callable but cannot be redeemed for a certain period if the company sells debt or equity ranking equal or superior to the preferred if the interest or dividend cost is less on the new issue than on the outstanding preferred. This is refunding protection, and it prevents the issuer from taking advantage of lower money costs for a certain number of years after the sale of the stock. However, if the issuer sells junior preferred or common equity prior to the expiration of the refunding protected period, the proceeds may be used to retire or refund the higher-cost preferred.

A well-known example of redemption through the use of common stock is Commonwealth Edison's call of its 9.44% Cumulative Prior Preferred Stock. The company issued 1 million shares of the preferred stock in June 1970 at $100 each; less than two years later, it redeemed the stock at $110. Just prior to the redemption announcement, the stock was trading at about $119 to $120 a share. The funds for the redemption came from the sale of common stock and common stock purchase warrants, clearly junior securities. The preferred prospectus stated:

> Prior to August 1, 1980, none of the shares . . . may be redeemed through refunding, directly or indirectly, by or in anticipation of the incurring of any debt or the issuance of any shares of the Prior Preferred Stock or of any other stock ranking prior to or on a parity with the Prior Preferred Stock, if such debt has an interest cost . . . or such shares have a dividend cost . . . less than the dividend cost . . . of the 9.44% . . . Stock. Subject to the foregoing, the 9.44% Prior Preferred Stock will be redeemable at the option of the Company as a whole at any time or in part from time to time at the following per share redemption prices: $110 if redeemed before August 1, 1980; . . . [3]

The company was sued in a class action case by some institutional holders under claims of alleged violations of the Federal securities laws and those based on breach of contract. The major institutional plaintiffs had analyzed the original prospectus prior to purchasing the shares and apparently come to the conclusion that they had protection against early call up to 1980. They did—but it was refunding protection and not call protection. The company prevailed, as the judge decided that the redemption provision did not prohibit redemption directly out of an issue of junior securities, to wit, common shares.[4]

Another example of a refunding redemption during the refunding protected period is Rochester Gas and Electric Corporation's 11.00% Preferred Stock, Series O, refunded with 7.60% Cumulative Preference Stock on January 20, 1978. The 11.00% Series O was not redeemable prior to October 1, 1985, through certain refunding operations. However, the shares were called at $111 plus accrued dividends of $1.5278 with the proceeds of the lower-cost junior stock. The redemption announcement was made December 20, 1977, the same day that the company sold the preference stock. In September 1977, the shares traded on the New York Stock Exchange at between $117 and $119 (the high of $121 had been set one month earlier). Those buyers had a loss of six to ten points in less than five months.

While a great many preferred issues restrict redemption of shares for five or ten years through certain refunding operations, including the sale of lower-cost preferred and debt, some are protected against refunding only if the lower-cost funds come from the sale of preferred stock; the companies could sell debt to retire the higher-cost preferred shares. In the September 1985 acquisition of Nabisco Brands, Inc. by R. J. Reynolds Industries, Inc., Reynolds issued 9,750,000 shares of $12.96 Series C Cumulative Preferred Stock. The initial offer to purchase Nabisco's common stock, dated June 4, 1985, stated that the preferred stock to be issued in the transaction would " . . . be nonrefundable prior to the fifth anniversary date of its issuance, and otherwise will be redeemable at the option of the Purchaser at redemption prices of 109% of the stated value in the first year declining evenly to the stated value on the eleventh anniversary of the date of issuance; . . . "

Six months later, in March 1986, Reynolds announced that it would redeem half of the outstanding issue with the proceeds from new debt. This caught some preferred holders by surprise, as they had assumed that the company could not sell lower-cost debt to refund the preferred. However, they were wrong. In the Special Meeting Proxy issued by Nabisco and dated August 5, 1985, a more complete description of the preferred's call features was given. Page 1 of the prospectus proxy had a brief description that stated: "During the first five years, no optional redemption may be effected as part of a refunding from the proceeds of issuance of preferred stock having an aggregate annual dividend cost of less than the dividend rate on the Reynolds Series C Preferred Stock." Page 22 also discussed this redemption feature. Finally, Appendix E of the prospectus/proxy was a Certificate of Designation, Rights and Preferences of the Series C Cumulative Preferred Stock; this stated the conditions of optional redemption in section 3. While there was plenty of information available giving the correct details under which an optional redemption could be made, some investors had looked in the wrong place.

In the decision concerning Florida Power & Light Company's debt retirement through the maintenance and replacement fund in 1978, the judge stated:

> The terms "redemption" and "refunding" are not synonymous. A "redemption" is simply a call of bonds. A "refunding" occurs when the issuer sells bonds in order to use the proceeds to redeem an earlier issue of bonds. . . . The refunding bond issue being sold is closely linked to the one being redeemed by contractual language and proximity in time so that the proceeds will be available to pay for the redemption. Otherwise, the issuer would be taking an inordinate risk that market conditions would change between the redemption of the earlier issue and the sale of the later issue.[5]

These sentiments can also be applied to preferred stock redemptions.

SINKING FUNDS

Sinking fund provisions for preferred stocks are similar to those for bonds. They provide for the periodic retirement of stock, usually on an annual basis. They often commence on or after the call or refunding protected period has expired, but there are some that operate prior to that time. A fixed number of shares or a certain percentage of the original issue is specified for retirement. Often this will amount to about 2 to 8 percent of the original number of shares, 5 percent being the most common. Commonwealth Edison's issue of $10.875 Preference Stock requires that all of the outstanding 350,000 shares be retired at par through the sinking fund on November 1, 1989, the date on which the call protected period terminates. Thus, this issue has another feature common to most bonds—a form of maturity.

Most sinking funds allow the issuer the noncumulative option to increase payments (usually to double the amount at any one time). Due to lower interest and dividend rates during the mid-1980s, many companies have utilized this option. Sinking fund payments may be made in shares of stock purchased in the open market or by calling the required number of shares at the sinking fund call price, usually par value. There have been instances in which a company wishing to retire an entire issue of sinking fund preferred called the maximum number of shares allowed for the sinking fund at the lower sinking fund redemption price and redeemed the balance at the normal call price. Wisconsin Power & Light Company utilized the doubling option by calling 15,000 shares of its 12% Preferred Stock at $100 a share on or about August 31, 1985. Immediately following that redemption, it announced that it would again double the sinking fund and retire another 15,000 shares at $100 each on September 30, 1985. This second redemption was on a pro rata basis with 25.36 percent of each holder's shares redeemed at the stated value, which satisfied the sinking fund requirement for the period ending August 31, 1986. Further, the company called the remaining 44,147 shares at $105. Gulf States Utilities redeemed 460,000 out of 500,000 shares of its $13.64 Dividend Preferred Stock on March 18, 1986, at $105 per share by lot rather than pro rata. The refunding protected period had expired on October 2, 1985. The remaining 40,000 shares were to be left outstanding until the doubled sinking fund would retire them at $100 each on November 15, 1986.

Many preferred stock market participants refer to issues without sinking funds as perpetual preferreds but, as mentioned above, this is probably a misuse of that term. Non-sinking fund issues need not be perpetual; yet they have no date at which they definitely would be retired. Sinking fund operations can provide some measure of market support if the issuer must come into the open market and purchase stock at less than the redemption price. However, in periods of lower interest and dividend rates and higher preferred prices, a call below market prices can result in capital losses.

Some preferred issues have purchase funds. Generally these are, to some extent, optional on the issuer's part, as it will have to use its best efforts to retire a portion of the shares periodically if they can be purchased in the open market, or through tender, at less than the redemption or liquidation price. If the stock is selling above the applicable price, the purchase fund cannot be put into operation. Again, the purchase fund may provide some market support to the issue in a higher dividend rate environment, but when rates are lower it is inoperative. In the case of Occidental Petroleum's $15.50 Cumulative Preferred Stock issued in connection with the acquisition of Cities Service Company in 1982, Occidental was required to use its best efforts to purchase shares in the open market at or below the liquidation value ($100 per share), with the proceeds derived from certain asset sales in excess of $100 million. Any shares so purchased would then be credited against any sinking fund payments when the sinking fund became operational.

Redemption through the Sale of Assets

It is important to read prospectuses carefully. While preferreds are not bonded securities as is mortgage debt, with its release and substitution of property clauses, there have been instances of preferred stock retirement prior to the end of the refunding protected period because of asset sales. Crown Zellerbach Corporation's $3.05 Cumulative Preferred Stock, Series B, issued May 19, 1982, at $20 per share, is one such example. It was protected against refunding prior to April 15, 1987, and had the normal stepped-down call schedule starting immediately at $23.05 and declining to $20 a share in 1997. However, it also had a special provision for its retirement prior to April 15, 1997, if the company sold certain assets aggregating at least $100 million in any 12-month period. The redemption premium under these circumstances was one-half the regular redemption premium. It started at $21.52 per share and declined to $20 in 1997. On May 20, 1983, the company redeemed this stock at the special redemption price of $21.42 a share (the regular call price at that time was $22.85). The proceeds came from the sale of its interests in Crown Zellerbach Canada Ltd. and a small steamship company. In late October 1982, it announced that it had a preliminary agreement for the sale of these assets, and the use of the proceeds should have come as no surprise to preferred holders. The shares sold at 21⅞ at the end of December and rose as high as 23⅞ in 1983 prior to the retirement of the stock.

FIGURING THE VULNERABILITY TO CALL FIXED-DIVIDEND PREFERREDS

Numerous issues become eligible for refunding every year as the refunding protected period expires. This means not that they will be called through the refunding process but only tht they are vulnerable to refunding, especially if rates are at levels below the yield based on call price plus estimated expenses associated with the call or refunding. Of course, they often can be retired prior to the expiration of the refunding prohibition period with other funds, as previously mentioned.

The yield based on call price, or the breakeven yield, is a relatively simple calculation: The dividend is divided by the call price (as opposed to the market price). The yield based on the call price plus call expenses means that we simply add the estimated expenses of the call on a per share basis to the call price and divide that into the dividend (numerator of the fraction). The higher the breakeven yields over current dividend rates for similar new-issue financing, the more vulnerable the shares are to redemption. The difference between the breakeven yield and the yield on new financings indicates the issuer's potential savings.

In early November 1985, Alabama Power's 15.68% Preferred ($3.92 annual dividend) was selling around 31 ¼ per share, providing a current yield of 12.54 percent. At that time other Alabama issues were providing yields to investors of between 10.5 and 11.2 percent. The 15.68 percent issue was nonrefundable but currently callable at $28.92; when the refunding protected period expired on February 2, 1986, the redemption price dropped to $27.94. At this lower call price, the breakeven yield was 14.03 percent; when expenses were included, it was reduced to 13.78 percent. The higher current yield on this issue relative to the market for comparable issues was a clue that the high return could not last—and didn't, as the stock was called for redemption on February 3, 1986, at $27.94. The stock had traded as high as 33⅜ at the end of the previous May, meaning that some investors may have lost 5.435 points or 16.28 percent of their investment in just eight months.

Investors wishing to avoid redemption of their shares have little choice but to sell the vulnerable issues and go into those having either greater call and refunding protected periods or lower dividend rates. In the latter case, the lower dividend rates mean lower breakeven yields. Alabama Power's 9.00% Preferred with a call price of 104.50 on September 2, 1987, when the refunding period expires, has a yield based on the call price of 8.61 percent. This is distinctly better in a lower interest rate environment than the 14.03 percent breakeven yield on the 15.68 percent stock. Of course, better call and/or refunding protection comes at the price of a lower current return. However, this is one of the prices investors must pay for improved protection against the impact of adverse redemptions.

Sinking funds raise the threshold level at which refundings can take place. For example, the yield based on the call price of $27.82 for Preferred Appalachian Power's $3.75 is 13.48 percent. However, if the company were to exercise the option doubling the sinking fund payment from 80,000 to 160,000 shares at $25 on April 1, 1986, and call the remaining 1,440,000 shares at $27.82, the weighted average call price would decline to $27.54, producing an adjusted yield based on a call of 13.62 percent. The use of the sinking fund and the option would save Appalachian Power $451,200 compared with calling the 160,000 shares at the regular call price.

Let us look at refunding from an issuer's viewpoint using Pacific Gas & Electric's 16.24% Preferred as the issue to be refunded (see Table 7–2). There are 5 million shares outstanding and the call price, when it first became refundable on April 1, 1986, was $30.25 a share. Further, let us assume that the new preferred can be sold at a dividend cost of 10 percent. What would be the savings to the company?

The annual dividend savings for this refunding amount to $7,800,000. As the issues have no sinking fund, the dividend savings will accrue over an infinite period; we will use 25 years for the purpose of our calculations. The present value of those savings over a

Table 7-2
Pacific Gas & Electric Company:
a Refunding Comparison

	Old 16.25% Preferred	New 10% Preferred
Issue size	$125,000,000	$125,000,000
Annual dividend	$ 20,300,000	$ 12,500,000
Annual dividend savings	$ 7,800,000	
Present value of savings (10%, 25 years)	$71,397,505	
Call premium	$26,250,000	
2% expenses	2,500,000	
Total	$28,750,000	
Net advantage of refunding	$42,647,505	

25-year period amounts to over $71 million. There are immediate expenses relating to the call and the issuance of the new preferred plus the call premium that total $28,750,000, thus providing a net advantage to the refunding of $42,647,505. It should be noted that the call premium and the expenses related to preferred redemptions (and to costs of repurchasing the company's other stock from shareholders) are not deductible for income tax purposes.

Adjustable-Rate Preferreds

In 1986 and 1987, adjustable-rate preferred stocks (ARP) started to lose their call and/or refunding protection. The advent of lower-cost Dutch auction market preferred (DAMPS), or auction rate preferred stock, probably further increased the vulnerability of many ARP issues to refunding.

Table 7-3 presents data on three companies that in early 1986 had outstanding adjustable-rate preferreds callable by the end of 1987. In addition, they had auction rate preferred shares with the investing public. This will give us some idea of the differences in the dividend costs between the two types of issues. We also show the approximate amount of the dollar savings that could accrue to the common shareholders if refundings were to take place. It should be

Table 7-3
Net Advantage of Refunding Adjustable-Rate Preferred Stocks
with Dutch Auction Market Preferred Shares

Example 1:   Citicorp Price Adjusted Rate Preferred Stock

Issue size		$100,000,000
Call premium		$ 0
Estimated refunding expenses @ 2%		$ 2,000,000
Average dividend rate—1985:	Average dividend amount:	
PAR	7.718%	$7,718,375
DAMP	5.769	$5,768,780
Difference	1.949%	$1,949,595
Present value of annual dividend Savings for 25 years @ 5.75%		$25,525,554
Less: Call premium and expenses		2,000,000
Net advantage of refunding		$23,525,554

Example 2:   Manufacturers Hanover Trust Company
Series B Adjustable Rate Preferred Stock

Issue size		$200,000,000
Call premium		$ 6,000,000
Estimated refunding expenses @ 2%		$ 4,000,000
Average dividend rate—1985:	Average dividend amount:	
ARP	10.813%	$21,626,000
DAMP	6.312	12,624,667
Differences	4.301%	$ 9,001,333
Present value of annual dividend Savings for 25 years @ 6.40%		$110,820,437
Less: Call premium and expenses		10,000,000
Net advantage of refunding		$100,820,437

Example 3a: United States Steel Corporation
Adjustable Rate Preferred Stock
(refunded with uninsured DAMP)

Issue size		$200,000,000
Call premium		$ 6,000,000
Estimated refunding expenses @ 2%		$ 4,000,000
Average dividend rate—1985:	Average dividend amount:	
ARP	11.625%	$23,250,000
DAMP (uninsured)	8.323	16,646,000
Difference	3.302%	$ 6,604,000

Table (continued)

Example 3a:	United States Steel Corporation Adjustable Rate Preferred Stock (refunded with uninsured DAMP)

Present value of annual dividend Savings for 25 years @ 8.40%	$68,152,686
Less: Call premium and expenses	10,000,000
Net advantage of refunding	$58,152,686

Example 3b:	United States Steel Corporation Adjustable Rate Preferred Stock (refunded with insured MMP)

Issue size		$200,000,000
Call premium		$ 6,000,000
Estimated refunding expenses @ 2%		$ 4,000,000
Average dividend rate—1985:		Average dividend amount:
ARP	11.625%	$ 23,250,000
DAMP (insured)	5.808	11,616,143
Difference	5.817%	$ 11,633,857
Present value of annual dividend Savings for 25 years @ 5.76%		$151,588,485
Less: Call premium and expenses		10,000,000
Net advantage of refunding		$141,588,485

noted that these are estimated savings; due to the variability of the dividend rate, it would be difficult to lock in fixed savings. While non-sinking fund shares have an indefinite life, we will use a 25-year horizon for this analysis. If we used a longer time span, the savings would be somewhat greater. Also, our interest rate assumption is based on the average auction dividend rate; a different rate would obviously change the figures.

The average dividend rates for 1985 for the two types of issues indicate that fairly substantial savings can accrue to the companies if the outstanding ARP are refunded with Dutch auction preferreds. In the case of Citicorp's Price Adjusted Rate Preferred Stock (PAR), Fourth Series, the difference in the average dividend rates is 195 basis points. In the case of Manufacturers Hanover Trust Series B, it is 450 basis points. For United States Steel Corporation, the difference is 330 basis points in the case of the uninsured market auction shares and 582 basis points for the insured shares. Given the yield differentials and the appeal of auction rate preferred shares for corporate investors, it is likely that many adjustable-rate preferreds (especially those issued by banks and financial institutions) may be prime candidates for refunding. Issues selling close to or above their call prices are the most vulnerable ones. Lower-quality issues or those perceived by the market to possess more investment risk might not be able to refund with auction rate preferred stock unless some type of third-party guarantee or collateralization is provided.

Of course, there may be outright redemptions. On February 3, 1986, Allied-Signal Inc. called for redemption all of its outstanding adjustable-rate preferred stock. The shares, issued in early 1983, were called at $100 each plus accrued dividends. Another outright redemption example is the call by Crocker National Corporation of its adjustable-rate preferred on May 29, 1986, at $52.50 per share plus accrued dividends; the shares had been issued just one year earlier, when Crocker was acquired by Midland Bank. The call was due to the acquisition of Crocker by Wells Fargo & Company in mid-1986.

NOTES

1. For example, Gulf States Utilities Company sold some $11.50 Dividend Preferred Stock on January 29, 1986, at $100 per share. The call price schedule is $111.50 per share through January 31, 1991, $105 from February 1, 1991, through January 31, 1996, $103 from February 1, 1996, through January 31, 2001, and $101 thereafter. West Texas Utilities 7.25 percent preferred, issued at $100 per share in March 1986, also has a call price at the initial offering price plus the annual dividend rate. However, the redemption price drops from $107.48 to $102.72 a share for the year beginning April 1, 1991, $101.82 for the next year, $100.91 for another year, and $100 on and after April 1, 1994.

2. Letter from BankAmerica Corporation to shareholders of Cumulative Preferred Stock, Special Series, April 25, 1986. Each quarter shareholders receive a letter analyzing the status of the loan pool. The loan pool charge-offs are mentioned several times, as is the probability that the stated value will be reduced in 1988 by $23 per share.

3. Prospectus of Commonwealth Edison Company, 9.44% Cumulative Prior Preferred Stock, June 24, 1970.

4. The May 19, 1978, decision of *The Franklin Life Insurance Company v. Commonwealth Edison Company*, U.S. District Court, Southern District of Illinois, presents a quite thorough review of the facts and events of this redemption. The concluding paragraph of the decision is of particular interest, it states:

> Although I believe Edison could have avoided this entire matter by making its right express, I cannot say that Edison's drafting, which stated expressly the methods by which redemption was prohibited and impliedly reserved to itself all other methods, violated the Federal Securities Laws or violated plaintiffs' vested contract rights. The decision here has not been quick nor easy. Drafting could have alleviated not only the time and effort spent here but the expectations of plaintiffs.

5. *Samuel Lucas, et al., v. Florida Power & Light Company*, U.S. District Court, Southern District of Florida, final opinion dated October 31, 1983.

CHAPTER 8

CONVERTIBLE SENIOR SECURITIES

In this chapter, we discuss those convertible bonds and preferred stocks that are viewed as common equity substitutes—i.e., whose prices may increase with underlying common stock. Other types of convertibles that merely maintain principal value, such as convertible adjustable-rate preferrd stocks, are covered in other chapters.

WHAT IS A CONVERTIBLE SECURITY?

A convertible bond or preferred stock is one that can usually be exchanged or converted at the holder's option into a fixed number of shares of common stock (or sometimes other securities) of a corporation.[1] Unlike with some adjustable-rate preferreds that are convertible into a fixed dollar amount of shares, any appreciation in the underlying common stock will be reflected in the market price or value of the "regular" type of convertible security. Referred to as hybrid securities, convertible securities combine elements of senior securities with those of junior equity. While they appeal primarily to common stock buyers, they sometimes attract traditional fixed-income investors. Being equity substitutes, they are affected more often by individual company events than by interest rate and economic factors.

Convertibles are not new to the twentieth century. Dewing notes that convertibles of one type or another have been around since at least the seventeenth century.[2] In our corporate history, they were used by such infamous characters as James Fisk, Jr., Daniel Drew, and Jay Gould in their battles for the Erie Railway with Commodore Cornelius Vanderbilt in the 1860s.[3] Mostly, however, convertible bonds and preferreds have been used for legitimate corporate purposes by economically sound companies. Many well-known corporations have utilized this form of financing, including American Telephone and Telegraph, Eastman Kodak, International Business Machines, Greyhound Corporation, and Union Pacific Corporation.

The size of the outstanding publicly issued convertible market can only be estimated. For example, *Moody's Bond Record* carried details about 767 convertible bonds in its January 1986 issue. The outstanding par value of these issues amounts to $30.5 billion, but many have par values of less than $10 million each. Eliminating all of the issues with outstanding amounts under $10 million leaves 486 issues that might be considered candidates for purchase by investors. The par amount of these bonds is $29.7 billion. Of course, included in these listings are issues that were once convertible into common stock but are now convertible into cash or other securities and a few foreign issues. The Merrill Lynch Capital Markets convertible database of the Fixed Income Research Department tracks more than 350 convertible bonds and over 150 convertible preferred stocks.

Convertible bond financing has had its ups and downs, as shown in Table 8–1. These data, from the Securities and Exchange Commission, show 1985 as a record year for the issuance of convertible debt. Yet as recently as 1978, volume as at the low point, with only $407 million issued. Manufacturing companies have been the largest utilizers of convertible debt financing, followed by financial concerns; electric and gas utilities have not been much of a factor. For convertible preferred stock financing, 1983 was the busiest year. Again, new-issue activity has fluctuated considerably over the past decade, as can be seen from the 1979 to 1985 period in Table 8–2.

Table 8-1

Gross Proceeds from Primary Public Convertible Bond Offerings by Industry, 1965–1985 ($ Millions)

	Total Business	Manufacturing	Extractive	Electric Gas, and Water	Transportation	Communication	Sales and Consumer Finance	Financial and Real Estate	Commercial and Other
1985	$8,018	$2,678	$ 25	$291	$540	$130	0	$2,396	$1,958
1984	3,408	1,247	5	280	110	70	1	433	1,262
1983	5,871	1,958	217	256	425	400	0	811	1,804
1982	2,915	905	4	0	300	549	0	489	668
1981	4,271	2,309	211	77	0	226	0	411	1,037
1980	4,665	2,558	490	140	344	135	0	607	392
1979	2,229	325	85	0	200	0	200	1,384	35
1978	407	271	12	0	0	10	0	69	45

Note: A breakdown of the convertible financing volume by industry type is not available for years prior to 1978.

Figures may not add due to rounding.

Source: U.S. Securities and Exchange Commission, SEC Monthly Statistical Review, various issues.

Table 8-2
Gross Proceeds from Convertible Preferred
Stock Financing, 1974–1985
($Millions)

1985	$2,317	1979	$512
1984	789	1978	310
1983	3,042	1977	394
1982	454	1976	251
1981	417	1975	399
1980	1,266	1974	25

PROVISIONS OF CONVERTIBLE SECURITIES

As with any senior security, it is important for investors to review the terms of the convertible securities in which they are interested, especially *before* making the investment. There are always exceptions to general statements, and recognizing them may mean the difference between profit and loss. While the indentures and certificates of incorporation are the best sources of information on the terms of securities, they may not be readily available. Therefore, investors must make do with the prospectus, which usually acknowledge that the descriptions of the security are brief summaries of certain indenture provisions and are not professed to be complete. The statements are qualified in their entirety by reference to the indentures or the incorporation certificates.

The first part of the description of the issue generally gives the maturity, if applicable, the interest or dividend record and payment dates, the size of the issue, denominations, and similar information. The next section discusses the status or ranking of the security. Convertible debentures of U.S. corporations are mostly subordinated in right of payment to the senior debt and will be so designated in their titles. Seldom will the most senior level of debt in the capitalization structure be convertible (one exception is Dana Corporation's 5⅞% Convertible Debentures due in 2006). Some companies might have issued convertible debentures or notes that, upon closer inspection, will have been found to be junior to other issues that may be secured or, by express definition in the legal documents, of senior standing. Convertible preferreds, however, are mostly (but not always) senior equity ranking equally with other outstanding preferreds. Sometimes you will come across preference or other junior preferreds. Many recent convertible preferreds have the word "exchangeable" in their titles, meaning that the issuer has the right to force holders to turn in their preferred shares for convertible debentures having similar terms. This improves the investor's ranking in the capital structure from an equity to a creditor's position. But if the investor is a corporation that can take advantage of the dividends received deduction, it will lose the deduction with the new debt instrument. The issuing company moves the payment from dividends paid out of after-tax dollars to interest paid with pre-tax dollars, thereby benefiting the earnings available for common shareholders. Legal opinions found in prospectuses generally consider the forced exchange a taxable event. Issue holders should refer to the relevant sections of the prospectuses and their tax advisors for up-to-date information on the issues' tax status.

The next section of the prospectus usually covers conversion rights. It states the price and number of shares into which the security is convertible. The conversion price for a majority of new issues is usually set at 20 to 25 percent above the common's closing price on the day the offering was priced. Some issuers have the right to lower the conversion price in order to induce the holder to convert. There are issues whose conversion price increases during the life of the conversion privilege. This is designed to foster early conversion if the stock's price increases. If the security is convertible into an odd number of shares, the issuer normally will pay cash rather than issue fractional shares.

In most cases the holder receives common shares of the issuing company, but some convertible debentures are exchangeable into common shares of another company (not to be confused with the exchangeable preferred just discussed). They may be converted into the shares of the parent, such as Ford Motor Credit into the shares of Ford Motor Company, or into the shares that constitute an investment for the issuer, such as General Cinema's debentures into the stock (and some cash) of R. J. Reynolds. National Distillers and Chemical Corporation's 6% Subordinated Exchangeable Debentures of May 15, 2011, are exchangeable into 20.4082 shares of Cetus Corporation. International Business Machines Corporation has an issue convertible into shares of Intel Corporation.

Thus, an investor is now concerned with two companies: (1) the issuing company, which is responsible for servicing the debt, and (2) the company into whose stock the security is exchangeable. The investor wants both to remain healthy and to prosper so that there will be little chance of the interest or dividend not being paid on a timely basis and that the market value of the underlying equity increases so as to make the exchangeable senior security more valuable. If the issuing corporation is unhealthy and fails to meet its obligations, default and bankruptcy will follow, and the exchangeable security holder will be left as a subordinated general unsecured creditor or in a senior equity status even if the underlying stock is that of a very sound company. The exchangeable holder does *not* have the right to the shares. They may be impaired, as the underlying shares are likely to be deemed assets of the bankrupt's estate and, along with its other assets, must be used to satisfy the claims of the general creditors. Also, when some convertibles are exchanged or turned in for the underlying stock of a different company, a taxable event may have occurred. It is best to consult the prospectus of the exchangeable issue in order to see if the counsel states that taxes will have to be paid. Because changes in regulations may have occurred from time to time, advice from one's tax advisor is also recommended.

The conversion section of the prospectus also gives information about the adjustment of the number of shares that will be issued upon conversion or exchange in cases of stock splits, dividends, reverse splits, recapitalizations, and issuance of warrants, assets, and other securities. Without these antidilution provisions it would be foolish to buy convertibles, as a company may split its stock, entitling the convertible holder to only the old number of shares upon conversion.

If a security is converted after the interest or dividend payment date and prior to the record date, adjustments are not made for the accrued dividend or interest. Because of this, the conversion price of the underlying stock may be greater than is first apparent. Convertible bonds trade like other bonds, namely at a certain price *plus* accrued interest to the settlement date. If investors sell the bonds in the open market they get the accrued interest, but if they convert they lose the accrued. However, when investors convert during the period from the record date for the payment of the interest or dividend through the end of the day prior to the payment date, they may or may not have the right to the interest or dividend payment due on that date. It all depends on the terms of the particular issue. In many cases, securities surrendered for conversion during this period must be accompanied with a check for the full amount of the interest or dividend to be received on the payment date. In others, the interest or dividend will be paid to all holders of record even if they had converted prior to the payment date.

Most issues allow conversion to begin immediately after issuance, but from time to time you will run across a preferred or a bond with a delayed conversion feature. One example is AmBrit Inc.'s 12⅛% Cumulative Convertible Exchangeable Preferred Stock. Issued in March 1986, the conversion privilege does not begin until March 1, 1987.

Most conversion rights expire at or just prior to the maturity or redemption date. A few issues lose the conversion privilege a number of years prior to maturity. Dana Corporation's 5⅞% debentures of June 15, 2006, lose their conversion feature on December 15, 1993. After that date, the bonds will be just straight securities. United Air Lines and Trans World Airlines have outstanding debt issues that once were convertibles but are now just ordinary straight subordinated debt. Failure to convert when the issue has been called may mean a substantial loss—yet time and again, investors fail to convert when it is in their best interests to do so. Bond investment is not a passive activity; it requires investors to remain alert to daily business and market events that may have an impact on their portfolios.

A few issues allow investors to have the company redeem the securities for cash upon request at certain times; in other words, investors may "put" the bond or preferred back to the issuer. Some issues provide that in lieu of paying cash for the put, the company may issue other securities. The above-mentioned AmBrit shares have a put feature operative on March 1, 1991. The company may pay for the put of the old preferred in shares of a new preferred, in cash, or in subordinated five-year notes. In a number of issues, the put may become effective only on certain dates or due to certain events, such as a decrease in the issuer's tangible net worth for several quarters or a change in the control of the company. These terms are spelled out in the issuing documents, as a change of control that is considered friendly and approved by the board of directors may not constitute a change of control for purposes of the put. The put may be a valuable feature, allowing the holder to get out whole in case the conversion privilege doesn't turn out to be as profitable as expected when the bonds were first purchased. The put, especially one exercisable only for cash, will act as a floor for the security's market price.

Most convertibles used to be callable at the issuer's option immediately upon issuance: they provided little or no call protection to the investor. In the early 1980s, a number of companies called their convertibles less than a year after they had been issued; in some cases, they were called before the first interest payment date came around. One financial writer called this a "scam" in that the companies paid out little interest and, through forced conversion, effectively sold common shares 15 to 25 percent above the market when the convertibles were first sold. Yet many would say this was not a scam. While the corporations benefited from the good markets, so did investors. They had a higher-yielding substitute for the equity that provided some downside protection in case it was needed. The convertible security ranked higher in the capitalization structure in the event of financial distress of the issuer. Also, the bonds were called with substantial profits for the investors. While they did not make as much profit as the common shareholders, they made substantial gains at less risk than a straight investment in the underlying shares would have entailed. Further, the gains probably came much sooner than they had expected when they originally purchased the convertibles, which increased their per annum rates of return. Certainly investors would like to have such profitable "scams" day in and day out!

Because many investors now demand some type of protection against early call, issuers have begun to add delayed redemption features to the new convertible bonds and preferreds. Some issues have absolute redemption bars for a certain number of years. But many come with conditional redemption protection. For example, the issuer may agree not to call the issue for at least two or three years unless the common stock trades at 130 to 150 percent, as the case may be, of the conversion price for a certain period of time (often 20 trading days) prior to the date of redemption. Thus an early call, if it came, would not hurt the investor, as it would occur when the securities were trading at good premiums over the redemption price. If the convertibles were not called, it would normally mean that the underlying stock had not performed as well as anticipated, but at least the investor would receive the income advantage for several years.

While corporations generally call their converts to force the conversion and not to redeem the securities for cash, there are times, such as the low interest rate period of 1985 to 1986, when cash calls occur. In these cases, companies want to pay off their more costly securities. Investors usually have at least 30 days in which to exercise their options after a call has been announced. If a forced conversion, investors can convert into common stock, but they will normally lose the accrued interest or dividend. Investors can also sell the converts, in which case the accrued interest theoretically will be paid. The bid will be higher than the call price or the conversion value less the accrued interest. Here the buyers (usually convertible arbitrageurs) make an adjustment. They lower their bids as they will not be getting the accrued interest even though they must pay it when purchasing bonds. They are in the market to buy and convert the bond while simultaneously selling the resulting shares, thus locking in a small but sure profit. The third course is to take the cash redemption price. This is done only if the call price plus the accrued dividend or interest is more than what investors would receive upon conversion or market sale.

Finally, convertibles may be called to satisfy sinking fund requirements. A sinking fund can be a valuable feature when the issue is selling at a discount, but when it is trading above the call price it is a negative. In most cases, the sinking fund may be satisfied with bonds previously redeemed or converted but not yet credited for sinking fund requirements. If these credits are not available, the company must purchase the requirements in the open market or call the securities.

JARGON OF CONVERTIBLES

It used to be said that one should never buy a common stock without checking to see whether a convertible security was available. The convertible might be found to be a better alternative to an investment in the common shares—after all, convertibles are substitutes for direct participation in common equities. While they often will not provide as much appreciation potential as the underlying common stock, they generally will provide a greater current return. There is also less business risk to a convertible security, which is a senior to common shares. Some institutional investors are barred from investing in common stock and purchase of convertible debentures offer a way around this prohibition. At times, convertible debentures may be viewed as near substitutes for straight corporate debt; the bonds are selling near the theoretical investment value, and the long-term option to convert them into common stock is available at little or no cost to the purchaser.

Let us look at some of the jargon used in the world of convertibles, along with details about a few specific issues for illustrative purposes. We will use United States Steel Corporation's convertible debentures and convertible preference stock and the price data as of April 30, 1986, for the main example. The price and yield details are shown in Table 8–3 and the terms of the issues in Table 8–4. Figures 8–1 and 8–2 show the historical price and conversion relationships from mid-1983 to May 1986. In Table 8–3, the dividend for the common stock is the amount paid during the preceding 12 months for the years ended December 31, 1983, 1984, and 1985. The dividend at 4/30/86 is the indicated amount based on the current quarterly payment of $0.30 per share.

Table 8–3
United States Steel Corporation:
Price Data and Dividend History

	Common Stock			5¾% C.S.D. 7/1/2001			$2.25 Preference Stock	
	Price	Dividend	C.Y.	Price	Y.T.M.	C.Y.	Price	C.Y.
12/31/83	30⅜	$1.00	3.29%	63¾	10.25%	9.02%	29⅜	7.66%
12/31/84	26⅛	1.00	3.82	57¼	11.63	10.04	26⅞	8.37
12/31/85	26⅝	1.10	4.13	68⅞	9.64	8.35	28	8.04
4/30/86	20⅛	1.20	5.96	71½	9.29	8.04	26¾	8.41

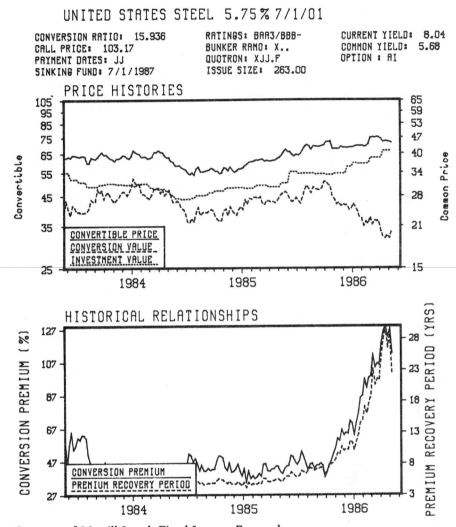

Courtesy of Merrill Lynch Fixed Income Research.

Figure 8-1

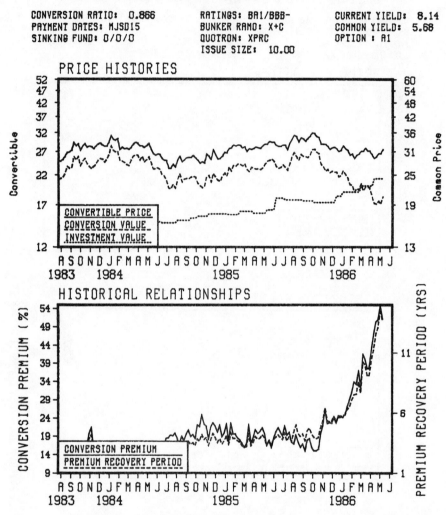

UNITED STATES STEEL $2.25

CONVERSION RATIO: 0.866	RATINGS: BA1/BBB-	CURRENT YIELD: 8.14
PAYMENT DATES: MJSD15	BUNKER RAMO: X+C	COMMON YIELD: 5.68
SINKING FUND: 0/0/0	QUOTRON: XPRC	OPTION : A1
	ISSUE SIZE: 10.00	

PRICE HISTORIES

CONVERTIBLE PRICE
CONVERSION VALUE
INVESTMENT VALUE

HISTORICAL RELATIONSHIPS

CONVERSION PREMIUM
PREMIUM RECOVERY PERIOD

Courtesy of Merrill Lynch Fixed Income Research.

Figure 8-2

Conversion price: The price of the common stock at which the bond or preferred is convertible.

> Debenture: $62.75 per share
> Preference stock: $28.875 per share

Conversion ratio: The number of shares into which the bond or preferred is convertible. This is obtained by dividing the conversion price into the par value of the bond or preferred.

> Debenture: $1,000.00/62.75 = 15.936 shares
> Preference stock: $25.00/28.875 = 0.8658 shares

Conversion parity: The market value of the convertible security divided by the number of shares into which it is convertible. This is the price at which the common stock must trade in order for the conversion value to equal the market price of the convertible.

Debenture: Price $715.00/15.936 = $44.87. The common stock must trade at $44.87 in order for the total value of the underlying shares to be worth the present market price of the convertible debenture. Dividing the par value ($1,000) of the debenture by the number of shares gives the original conversion price of original conversion parity of the debenture.

Preference stock: Price $26.75/0.8658 = $30.90. The conversion parity of the preference stock is $30.90, i.e., the common must rise to that price in order for the conversion value to equal the present market price.

Table 8-4
United States Steel Corporation: Terms of Issues
5¾% Convertible Subordinated Debentures Due July 1, 2001

Issue date: June 22, 1976   *Ratings:* Baa3 (Moody's); BBB– (S & P)

Interest payment dates: January 1 and July 1

Amount issued: $400,000,000   *Amount outstanding:* (12/31/85): $254,000,000

(Table 8-4 continued)

Table 8-4 (*continued*)

Redemption: Currently callable at 102.88 through June 30, 1987, at 102.59 through June 30, 1988, and at prices declining by about 0.29 annually to 100.00 on or after July 1, 1996.

Sinking fund: $20 million each July 1, 1987, through July 1, 2000, will retire 70 percent of the issue prior to maturity. Credit may be taken against the sinking fund obligation for debentures previously acquired, converted, or redeemed other than through the sinking fund, and the company has the noncumulative option to double payments.

Conversion: Convertible at $62.75 into 15.936 shares of common stock.

$2.25 Convertible Exchangeable Cumulative Preference Stock
(Stated Value $25 per Share)

Issue date: June 9, 1983   *Ratings:* ba1 (Moody's); BBB— (S & P)

Dividend payment dates: March 15, June 15, September 15, and December 15

Number of shares issued: 10,000,000

Number of shares outstanding (12/31/85): 9,994,800

Redemption: Redeemable on or after June 15, 1986, at $26.575 through June 14, 1987, at $26.35 through June 14, 1988, and at prices declining by $0.225 each year to $25.00 a share on and after June 15, 1993.

Sinking fund: None

Exchange: The preference stock is exchangeable in whole at the option of the company on any dividend payment date on and after June 15, 1986, for its 9% Convertible Subordinated Debentures due 2013.

Conversion: Convertible at $28.875 into 0.8658 shares of common per preference share.

Following are the data pertinent to Table 8–4.

Conversion value: The number of shares into which the security is convertible multiplied by the market price of the common stock.

		Debenture	Preference Stock
	Number of shares upon conversion	15.936	0.8658
Times:	Common market price	$20.125	$20.125
Equals:	Conversion value	$320.71	$17.424

If you were to convert these securities, you would obtain common stock worth $320.71 per bond or $17.42 per preference share.

Conversion premium: The market price of the convertible minus the conversion value. This may also be expressed in percentage terms with (a) the conversion premium divided by the conversion value or (b) the market price divided by the conversion value.

		Debenture	Preference Stock
	Market price	$715.00	$26.75
Less:	Conversion value	320.71	17.42
Equals:	Premium (dollar)	$394.29	$ 9.33
Premium			
(a)		$394.29/320.71 =	$9.33/17.42 =
		122.94%	53.56%
(b)		$715.00/320.71 =	$26.75/17.42 =
		222.94%	153.56%

Thus, the investor is paying a premium of $394.29 over the conversion worth of the debenture for the right or option to convert it into common shares at the earlier of the call or the maturity. This is equal to a premium of 122.94 percent—in other words, the bond is selling at 222.94 percent of its underlying conversion value. The convertible preference shares have a smaller conversion premium of $9.33, which amounts to only 53.56 percent of the conversion value.

Premium recovery period: The length of time over which the dollar conversion premium is recovered through the difference between the higher income generated by the convertible security and the dividend income on the underlying shares that could be purchased for the same cost. This is one of the most important calculations used in determining the relative attractiveness of a convertible issue compared with the common stock. Generally, the higher the premium recovery period, the less attractive the convertible. Many investors view a recovery period of three years or less as most desirable, buying the convertible when the premium recovery period is under three years and buying the stock when it is over three years. However, there could be other relatively attractive convertibles with premium recovery periods of between three and six years. Each issue must be carefully analyzed within the context of the goals, objectives, and risk parameters of the individual investment portfolio.

The market price can purchase one debenture or preference share or 35.528 shares of common per bond or 1.329 shares of common per preference share:

	Debenture	Preference Stock
Market price of convertible	$715.00	$26.75
Divided by: Market price of common	20.125	20.125
Equals: Number of shares that could be purchased for the cost of one convertible security	35.528	1.329
Annual income from convertible	$ 57.50	$ 2.25
Annual income from investment in common stock (dividend $1.20 per share)	$1.20 × 35.528 = $42.63	$1.20 × 1.329 = $1.59
Difference in income	$14.87 $394.29/14.87 =	$0.66 $9.33/0.66 =
Premium recovery period	26.52 years	14.14 years

Another calculation uses the percentage of premiums and yields. Thus, for the convertible debenture the formula is:

Percentage premium

$$\frac{\overline{\text{Premium} + 100.00}}{\text{Yield differential}} \times 100 = \text{Premium recovery period}$$

$$\frac{\overline{(122.94\%)}}{(8.04\% - 5.96\%)} \times 100 = \frac{0.551449}{2.08} \times 100$$

$$= 26.52 \text{ years}$$

These premium recovery periods are considered high, and the issues would not appeal to most convertible market participants. If investors thought that the common stock of United States Steel was an attractive speculation, they would more than likely invest directly in the common, as it would give them much greater upside potential. If the stock were to double from 20⅛ per share to 40¼, the conversion worth of the bond would still be only $641.42. The bond would probably rise somewhat, but not to the same extent as the common. If the convertible debenture rose to a price of 80 ($800 per bond), the premium over conversion value would be 24.73 percent. Assuming that the dividend remained unchanged, the premium recovery period would decline to 4.72 years. If the bond increased to a price of 90, the conversion premium would be 40.31 percent and the premium recovery period would be 7.33 years. At these levels, the convertible debenture might have appeal. However, if the common shares doubled in price, it is very possible that the common dividend would have been increased. If the dividend rose to $1.80 per share, the premium recovery period, at a bond price, of 80 would be 7.31 years and, at a price of 90, 15.04 years.

Investment value: The theoretical value at which the convertible issue would trade if it were a nonconvertible security, taking into account the rating, redemption features, sinking fund provisions, and so on.

If the high premium recovery period makes the issues unattractive for the normal convertible buyer, who might buy them, and why? Straight bond investors might be interested in the U.S. Steel convertible debenture if they feel that it is selling close to or at the maturity yield level at which a regular nonconvertible subordinated issue of similar standing and features might trade. Convertibles selling at or near these theoretical investment values are called "busted converts." At the end of April 1986, the yield to maturity was 9.29 percent for the 5¾ percent convertibles.

Figure 8–1 shows the investment value estimated by Merrill Lynch, which was about equal to a yield to maturity of 10.74 percent at an approximate price of 63. Others might give it a slightly higher investment value, such as 66, which is a 10.2 percent yield. Thus, the downside risk, assuming the rating and interest rate conditions remain the same, is about 5.5 to 8.5 points, or 91 to 145 basis points. This investment value provides some degree of price protection in case the stock does not rise but instead drifts lower. Figure 8–1 also shows that while the common declined from the low 30s toward the end of 1985 to around 20 at the end of April 1986, the bond's price actually rose slightly; this was aided by the declining level of interest rates. Also note the tremendous rise in the premium recovery period and the conversion premium during that time.

However, while the theoretical investment value may impose some limit on the possible price decline under certain market conditions, convertible prices may go through these so-called support levels "like a hot knife through soft butter" during other times. The late winter to early spring of 1966 was one of these periods when investment support levels meant little. At that time, interest rates were rising and stock prices plummeting. Commercial banks were under pressure from the Federal Reserve System to reduce their lending for speculative activities. Many banks either withdrew their lines of credit to speculators in convertible bonds or asked for substantially more collateral value to support the loans. At that time, one could borrow 90 percent or more against the market value of convertible bonds. Thus, there were declining investment values due to rising interest rates; declining conversion values due to lower stock prices; decreased speculative interest due to both factors plus a drying up of the source of funds for fueling purchases; and increased selling pressure as banks called in many of their loans and speculators sold to satisfy the calls. It was an unpleasant time to be in the convertible bond market, especially for brokers, traders, and speculators.

Price risk

There are several types of price risk associated with convertibles. We mentioned one just above: the risk to the investor if the underlying common stock price suffered a severe drop so that the bond would sell more on the merits of a straight bond investment without much of a premium for the conversion factor. In this case, the risk— the difference between the investment value of the bond and its market price—amounts to 7.7 to 11.9 percent of the market price. Of course, investment values change along with markets.

Another type of price risk is due to the risk of call and the consequent forced conversion. The U.S. Steel debenture example has little risk of call at the present time; the bond is selling considerably below par, and the conversion value is far beneath the market price. However, let us look at the convertible preference stock and change a few facts. The common is now selling at 30 per share, giving the preference stock a conversion worth of $30.30. Further assume that it is currently redeemable at $26.575 a share and selling at 32 a share. This is a 20.4 percent premium over the redemption value and a 5.6 percent premium over conversion worth. At these levels, the conversion premium will decline to close to zero upon any further rise in the stock; it is now becoming vulnerable to call. Usually, as the conversion value rises through par, the conversion premium starts to decrease so that there is little or no premium around the 120 percent of par level. The investor's risk at these levels in the event the company calls the convertible is the amount of the conversion premium. If this happens, the investor certainly will prefer to convert and get the conversion value of the stock over redeeming the shares at $26.575. Figure 8–3 shows the narrowing of the GTE Corporation conversion premium as the common shares rose in late 1985 until being called on May 19, 1986, at 106.65.

Still another type of price risk is not due to a drop in the common stock or forced conversion but involves the redemption of the convertible at the company's option. The conversion value might be under the redemption price. The driving force behind this type of call is the same as that for straight senior securities, i.e., the desire to remove higher-cost securities from the balance sheet. Conversion is not forced, as investors would gain more by taking the redemption

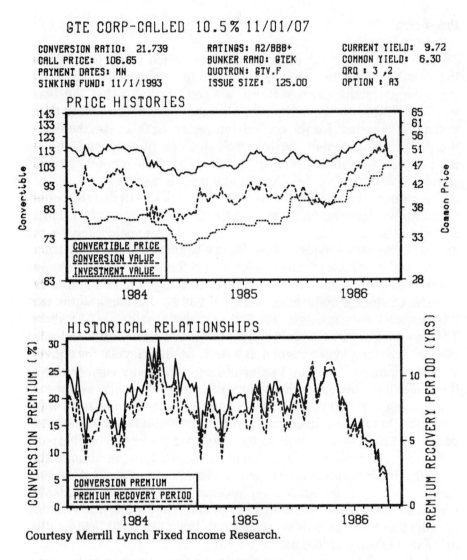

GTE CORP-CALLED 10.5% 11/01/07

CONVERSION RATIO: 21.739   RATINGS: A2/BBB+   CURRENT YIELD: 9.72
CALL PRICE: 106.65   BUNKER RAMO: GTEK   COMMON YIELD: 6.30
PAYMENT DATES: MN   QUOTRON: GTV.F   QRQ : 3 ,2
SINKING FUND: 11/1/1993   ISSUE SIZE: 125.00   OPTION : A3

Courtesy Merrill Lynch Fixed Income Research.

Figure 8-3

price than by exchanging the convertible for common shares. Admittedly, such redemptions are not too common and thus have caught many investors unawares. They just cannot imagine a call of a convertible whose conversion value is under the par value. A call would not force conversion, and many investors know (or think they do!) that converts are almost never called unless the company can be practically 100 percent certain that most, if not all, of the securities will be converted. Such redemptions are exceptions that can cost investors dearly.

The spring of 1986 saw several redemptions of this type. National Medical Enterprises had an issue of $124 million of 12⅝% Convertible Subordinated Debentures due November 15, 2001. Convertible into 27.72 shares at $36.06, the bonds were trading on the New York Stock Exchange on April 8 at 114, and the common was selling at 24½ per share. The conversion value was $679.14 and the conversion premium $460.86, or 67.86 percent. Currently callable at 100, the convertibles were at a 14 percent premium over the redemption price. Prior to the opening of the next day's trading, the company announced the call of the bonds at 100 plus accrued interest on May 15. The stock closed on April 9 at 24⅝. It did not decline in price, as there was little chance of the bonds being converted and thus resulting in more shares in the market. However, the premium disappeared. The converts traded that day between 100 and 101 and closed at 100, down 14 points overnight. At $140 per bond, investors lost a grand total on the issue of $17,360,000.

Another, similar redemption was Champion International Corporation's $4.60 Convertible Preference Stock. On April 25, 1986, the Company officially announced the call of the preferred at $52.30 a share plus $0.72 of accrued dividends for a total amount of $53.02. The redemption date was May 25. As Table 8-5 shows, just one month earlier the shares trading at 58⅝ were at a 10.695-point premium over conversion value. Although, this was 6.325 points above the call price, few people, if any, paid attention to this price risk. In the week ended April 18, the price of the convertible dropped 3.5 points to $52.50. During that week, the company announced in the prospectus for a new offering of $150 million of 6½% Convertible Subordinated Debentures due April 15, 2011, that it would redeem the preferred. It stated:

> Promptly after the sale of the Debentures, the Company intends to call all of its Preference Stock, $4.60 Cumulative Convertible Series, $1 par value . . . for redemption. If there is no material change in the current market price of the Common Stock through the date on which the $4.60 Preference Stock conversion rights will expire, it is anticipated that substantially all of the $4.60 Preference Stock will be redeemed at the redemption price per share of $52.30 plus accrued dividends.[4]

Table 8–5
Champion International Corporation
Preference Stock, $4.60 Cumulative Convertible Series
(Selected Details)

Convertible into 1.667 shares.
Callable at $52.30 plus accrued dividends through September 30, 1986

Week Ended	Price of Common	Price of Preferred	Conversion Value	Conversion Premium	Premium over Call Price
4/25/86	$26.750	$52.625	$44.592	$ 8.033	$0.325
4/18/86	26.875	52.500	44.801	7.699	0.200
4/11/86	27.625	56.000	46.051	9.949	3.700
4/4/86	26.250	56.250	43.759	12.491	3.950
3/28/86	28.750	58.625	47.926	10.699	6.325

Yields

Current—the interest rate or the preferred dividend divided by the market price of the security.

Differential—the difference between the current yield of the convertible and the current yield of the underlying common stock.

Table 8–6
Selected Details Liquid Option Notes (LYONS)

Issue Date	Issue and Maturity Date		Principal Amount ($ Millions)	Initial Offering Price	Initial Yield to Maturity
11/06/85	Beverly Enterprises[b]	7/16/03	$500	25%	8.00%
7/25/85	G. Heileman Brewing	4/3/03	345	25	8.00
11/26/85	Lomas & Nettleton Financial	9/3/01	575	25	9.00
8/2/85	Merrill Lynch & Co.	2/21/06	1,000	20	8.00
1/31/86	Natl. Medical Enterprises	12/1/04	920	25	7.50
8/23/85	Joseph E. Seagram & Sons[c]	3/5/06	575	20	8.00
5/8/85	Staley Continental, Inc.[b]	2/14/01	402.5	25	9.00
2/14/86	Trinity Industries, Inc.	11/23/01	275	25	9.00
4/12/85	Waste Management, Inc.	1/21/01	840	25	9.00

[a]Callable prior to date shown if common stock trades at 50 percent or more than conversion price per terms of issue.
[b]Issue is senior debt.
[c]Convertible into common shares of and guaranteed on a subordinated basis by The Seagram Company Ltd.
[d]Adjusted for two-for-one stock split in December 1985.

To maturity—the conventional yield to maturity for bonds (preferred stocks have no yields to maturity).

LIQUID YIELD OPTION NOTES

In 1985, Wall Street investment bankers added another "animal" to the menagerie of investment products. Liquid Yield Option Notes, known as LYONs (registered trademark of Merrill Lynch & Company, Inc.), joined their fellow CATs, TIGRs and other feline zero coupon investments. LYONs are zero coupon convertible securities. Between April 1985 and February 1986, Merrill Lynch was the sole underwriter for all nine issues, selling $5,432.5 million par value and raising $1,279.375 million before underwriting discounts and commissions. The securities met with favorable investor response as the underwriter exercised its "greenshoe" option, allowing it to increase the offerings for eight of the nine issues. Without this extra financing, the par value would have totaled $4,790 million and the amount netted by the issuers $1,128.75 million. Buyers of this new security have included foreign investors, pension funds, and individual retirement accounts. Table 8–6 gives selected details on these convertible issues.

Table 8-6 (*continued*)

Common Price at Issue	Conversion Price	Number of Shares per LYON	Initial Call Date[a]	Call Price	First Put at Holder's Option	Price	Yield to Maturity
33.500	37.537	6.66	9/30/87	305.67	9/30/88	296.36	6.00%
19.875	21.872	11.43	6/30/87	306.50	6/30/88	297.00	6.00
36.625	40.323	6.20	2/01/88	318.06	2/01/89	301.32	6.00
33.625	37.665	5.31	8/15/87	246.77	8/15/88	238.81	6.00
20.125	22.543	11.09	12/31/87	302.54	12/31/88	296.75	6.00
38.750	43.384	4.61	9/15/87	247.59	9/15/88	239.44	6.00
18.750	20.627	12.12	4/01/87	312.94	4/01/88	296.36	6.00
16.000	17.606	14.20	12/31/87	312.22	12/31/88	295.88	6.00
26.063[d]	28.670[d]	8.72[d]	6/30/87	321.13	6/30/88	301.87	6.00

From the issuers' viewpoint, the sale of LYONs provides a favorable long-term rate, making it a less expensive source of funds than regular convertible and zero coupon debt. There is no cash outlay for interest charges, but the companies can take a tax deduction for the original issue discount, thus aiding cash flow. Interest is computed on a semiannual, bond-equivalent basis.

Underwriting discounts charged on these issues (before deducting expenses paid by the issuer) range from 0.7 to 0.875 percent of the principal amount due at maturity (also, of course, payable at the time the initial payment is received from the buyers). But based on the discounted price to the public, the underwriting discounts are at a higher rate of 3.5 percent. However, had the issuers viewed the underwriting fee as excessive, the debt probably would not have been sold.

None of the issues has a sinking fund, but all have deferred call protection for approximately the first two years after issuance. However, if the market price of the common exceeds 50 percent of the initial conversion price for a specified period prior to the start of the regular redemption feature, the securities may be called. The call schedule is the original offering price plus the redemption premium (initially at the offering yield, then scaled down annually to zero 10 years after issuance) plus the accrued original issue discount.

Because Waste Management, Inc. was the first company to publicly offer zero coupon convertibles, we will use its LYON issue as an example.[5] The call schedule is shown in Table 8–7. If the bond is called between the dates shown, the redemption price will include an additional sum due to the continual accretion of the original issue discount. The notes cannot be called prior to June 30, 1987, unless the closing price of the stock on the New York Stock Exchange equals or exceeds $43.01 for at least 20 trading days within a period of 30 consecutive trading days ending within 5 days prior to the date of the redemption notice. The other issues have similar call features except that all but Heileman and Staley have the trading period ending within 15 days of the redemption date.

In addition, the holders may require the issuer to redeem the LYONs at the holders' option once a year starting about three years after issuance. This annual put requires several months' prior notification to the issuer. The initial yield to the holders' put is

Table 8-7
Waste Management, Inc.
Redemption Schedule for Liquid Yield Option Notes Due 2001

Redemption Date	(1) LYONs Issue Price	(2) Redemption Premium (%)	(3) Redemption Premium ($) (1) × (2)	(4) Accrued Original Issue Discount at 9%	(5) Redemption Price (1) + (3) + (4)
At issuance	$250.00	9.00%	$22.50	$ 0.00	$272.50
June 30, 1986	250.00	8.10	20.25	27.58	297.83
June 30, 1987	250.00	7.20	18.00	53.13	321.13
June 30, 1988	250.00	6.30	15.75	81.02	346.77
June 30, 1989	250.00	5.40	13.50	111.49	374.99
June 30, 1990	250.00	4.50	11.25	144.75	406.00
June 30, 1991	250.00	3.60	9.00	181.08	440.08
June 30, 1992	250.00	2.70	6.75	220.75	477.50
June 30, 1993	250.00	1.80	4.50	264.07	518.57
June 30, 1994	250.00	0.90	2.25	311.38	563.63
June 30, 1995	250.00	0.00	0.00	363.04	613.04
June 30, 1996	250.00	0.00	0.00	419.45	669.45
June 30, 1997	250.00	0.00	0.00	481.06	731.06
June 30, 1998	250.00	0.00	0.00	548.34	798.34
June 30, 1999	250.00	0.00	0.00	621.60	871.80
June 30, 2000	250.00	0.00	0.00	702.03	952.03
At maturity	250.00	0.00	0.00	750.00	1,000.00

several percentage points lower than the purchase yield, but it increases each year by one percentage point until it gets to the original purchase yield. This is similar in concept to the redemption provisions of United States Series EE Savings Bonds.

Table 8-8 shows the optional put schedule for Waste Management, Inc. This put feature offers the bondholder some protection in the event of a rise in interest rates (lower bond values) or a sharp decline in the stock's value. Zero coupon bond prices are much more volatile than the prices of coupon debt instruments, and the put can provide a floor for the investor. However, the put can come at a time when the issuer would rather not pay out the cash because it is either in poor financial condition or would rather retain the monies for

Table 8-8
Waste Management, Inc.
Schedule of Redemption Prices for Put at Holders' Option

Purchase Date	Purchase Price	Yield to Holder	Conversion Parity of LYON	Percentage Increase in Parity over Prior Year
June 30, 1988	$301.87	6.00%	$ 34.618	—
June 30, 1989	333.51	7.00	38.247	10.48%
June 30, 1990	375.58	8.00	43.071	12.61
June 30, 1991	431.08	9.00	49.436	14.78
June 30, 1992	470.75	9.00	53.985	9.20
June 30, 1993	514.07	9.00	58.953	9.20
June 30, 1994	561.38	9.00	64.378	9.20
June 30, 1995	613.04	9.00	70.303	9.20
June 30, 1996	669.45	9.00	76.772	9.20
June 30, 1997	731.06	9.00	83.837	9.20
June 30, 1998	798.34	9.00	91.553	9.20
June 30, 1999	871.80	9.00	99.978	9.20
June 30, 2000	952.03	9.00	109.178	9.20

other corporate purposes. Failure to make payment on a put is an event of default and, if not cured, may eventually lead to bankruptcy proceedings. However, under the put provisions, the issuer can make no payments if an event of default has occurred and has not been cured.

The conversion rate is subject to the normal adjustments in cases of stock dividends, combinations, subdivisions, and reclassifications. However, upon conversion no adjustment is made for the accrued interest or original issue discount, as it is deemed paid by the common stock received by the investor upon conversion. In effect, it is lost. Therefore, while the number of shares into which the LYON may be converted is fixed, the conversion price slowly and steadily increases. Waste Management's LYON is convertible into 8.72 shares of common (adjusted for the two-for-one split of December 1985) which, based on the $250 original issue price, gives a conversion price of $28.67. However, this bond accretes interest; it doesn't pay it out. Being issued at a 9 percent yield to maturity, it will be worth $273.01 a year after issuance, $298.13 two years after issuance, and so on to $1,000 at maturity. The conversion price thus rises to $31.308 at the end of the first year, $34.189 at the end of the second year, and $34.618 on June 30, 1988, when the investor can ask the company to redeem the LYON for $301.87. Table 8-8 above shows the increasing conversion parity for the stock.

Table 8-9 shows LYON market data for May 30, 1986. The conversion price at the initial offerings range from 10 to 12 percent above the market price of the common at the time of pricing. At the 1986 valuation, the conversion premiums for eight of the issues were lower, while only one—that of Merrill Lynch—rose from 12 to 17.6 percent. Also, all of the market prices were above the theoretical accreted values for that date (based on the initial yield to maturity). This is attributed to the strong stock and bond markets during the 1985 to 1986 period.

In analyzing LYONs for possible purchase, the conventional premium recovery period method is useless since the bonds pay no interest. One has to look at the conversion premiums in order to decide whether or not to purchase it. But keep in mind that if the stock does not move, the conversion premium is steadily increasing. Some convertible market analysts therefore feel that potential dilution is limited, because as time passes there is increasingly less incentive for holders to convert. The common must rise by 9.2 percent a year (more in earlier years) if the conversion premium is to be kept level; if it rises by less than that percentage, the conversion premium will increase.

SILVER INDEXED BONDS

One bond that may be viewed as a type of convertible security is the silver indexed bond. While it is not convertible into the commodity in the same way that regular convertible issues are exchangeable for common stock, the redemption prices are payable at the greater of $1,000 per bond or the indexed principal amount. The indexed principal amount is the specified market price of silver multiplied by the number of ounces of silver to which the bond is linked. For example, in mid-1986 Sunshine Mining Company had four issues outstanding of which three were indexed to 50 ounces of silver and one to 58

Table 8-9
Liquid Yield Option Notes (LYONS)
Market Data (as of May 30, 1986)

Issue	Maturity Date	Market Price	Yield to Maturity	Accreted Price at Purchase Yield
Beverly Enterprises	7/16/03	29.250	7.31%	26.092
G. Heileman Brewing	4/3/03	32.250	6.83	26.685
Lomas & Nettleton Financial	9/3/01	29.000	8.28	26.100
Merrill Lynch & Co.	2/21/06	22.875	7.62	21.283
Natl. Medical Enterprises	12/1/04	28.750	6.85	25.607
Joseph E. Seagram & Sons	3/5/06	29.500	6.27	21.218
Staley Continental, Inc.	2/14/01	31.875	7.93	27.401
Trinity Industries, Inc.	11/23/01	28.000	8.39	25.594
Waste Management, Inc.	1/21/01	40.750	6.23	27.556

Note: All of the issues are listed on the New York Stock Exchange.

ounces (see Table 8–10).[6] Thus, had silver been trading at $40 per ounce during the period immediately preceding the determination date for the redemption payment, the indexed principal amount would have been $2,000 and $2,320, respectively.

The first issue came to market in April 1980, just a little after the great silver bubble had burst when the commodity peaked at $48.70 an ounce on the New York Commodity Exchange, Inc. A year earlier, silver had been trading under $6 an ounce. The bonds did not appeal to the typical institutional buyer of convertible securities. Rather, they attracted foreign buyers and speculators who liked the concept of having a fixed-income security linked to a commodity that would increase in value as inflation went up. Also, they could get income while effectively holding a position in a non-income-producing commodity. However, for much of the lives of the bonds the premium over the indexed value and the premium recovery

Table 8-9 (*continued*)

Price of Common	Current Yield (%)	Conversion Value	Premium over Conversion Value		Conversion Parity	
			($)	(%)	Current	At Initial Put Date
41.125	0.97	273.89	$18.61	6.80%	$43.919	$44.048
28.125	1.85	321.47	1.03	0.03	28.215	25.984
45.250	3.09	280.55	9.45	3.37	46.774	48.600
36.625	2.18	194.48	34.27	17.62	43.079	44.974
24.000	2.33	266.16	21.34	8.02	25.924	26.758
63.750	1.57	293.89	1.11	0.04	63.991	51.939
26.250	3.05	318.15	0.60	0.02	26.300	24.450
19.250	2.60	273.35	6.65	2.43	19.718	20.837
45.500	1.23	396.76	10.74	2.71	46.732	34.618

periods were thought to be excessive by many convertible market participants. But while silver fell in price, the bonds held up remarkably well as the premiums increased. For example, at the end of September 1980 the 8½s of April 15, 1995, were trading at $1,390 per bond and the indexed value of silver was $1,055 ($21.10 per ounce). The conversion premium was $335, or 31.75 percent, and the premium recovery period was 3.94 years. By the end of April 1986, the indexed principal amount had fallen to $255 ($5.10 an ounce), a decline of 75.8 percent, while the bond's price dropped by only 34 percent to $917.50. The premium was $662.50, or 259.8 percent of the indexed principal amount; the recovery period was 7.79 years.

In May 1986, the prices of these silver indexed issues came under pressure as investors recognized that the company had some problems. Large losses were reported for fiscal 1985 and the first quarter of 1986 due to the drop in silver prices and the effect of lower

Table 8-10
Sunshine Mining Company:
Selected Details of Silver Indexed Bonds

Issue Date	Coupon	Date Maturity	Issue Price	Ounces of Silver	Price of Silver at Issue	Indexed Principal Amount	Premium over Index Value ($)	Premium over Index Value (%)	Premium Recovery Period (Years)
4/10/80	8.50%	4/15/95	100.00	50	$16.000	$800.00	$200.00	25.0	2.35
12/11/80	8.50	12/15/95	100.00	50	14.810	740.50	259.50	35.0	3.05
2/11/83	8.00	2/15/95	97.50	50	14.125	706.25	268.75	38.1	3.36
4/11/85	9.75	4/15/04	90.00*	58	6.608	383.26	516.74	134.8	5.30

*From the List of Original Issue Discount Instruments, Publication 1212, U.S. Department of Treasury, December 1985.

oil and natural gas prices on its oil subsidiary. It closed two mines in an effort to trim costs. Under these conditions, company officials thought that it would be best to make an exchange offer of new bonds for old.

Commodity indexed bonds such as the Sunshine issues have had their day. If and when inflation threatens again, bonds of this type will be sought by speculators and others wishing a hedge against the possibility of further debasement of the currency.[7] While much of the analysis done for regular convertible issues may be applied to these bonds, it should be remembered that these are indexed to, not convertible into, the price of silver and that the indexed principal amount is payable by the company upon redemption. Bondholders cannot put the bonds to the issuer and get the indexed principal amount or the actual silver as they can with most regular convertible bonds, but they can trade them in the public market.

USABLE SECURITIES

Usable bonds and preferred stocks are not convertible securities in the sense discussed in the preceding sections. Instead, when combined with certain warrants, they become what are known as "synthetic convertibles."

A warrant is a longer-term option giving the holder the right to buy shares of stock at a fixed price (subject to adjustment under certain conditions) for a certain period of time. The time period is what differentiates a warrant from a common stock option. An option usually has a life of under one year that is typically measured in months. A warrant's life, on the other hand, is longer and is measured in years. Some warrants may be without any terminal date; these are called perpetual warrants. Atlas Corporation has perpetual warrants listed on the American Stock Exchange that give the holder the right to purchase common stock at $31.25 a share.

Warrants have been created out of corporate bankruptcy and reorganization, being given as part of the new company's securities in a recapitalization. Some have been issued with straight bonds (and a couple with preferred stock) as a "sweetener" to reduce the issues' cost of capital. When issued with these senior securities, the package is called a unit. After issuance, the warrants may be detached from the other part of the unit and both traded separately. A bond or preferred stock that can be used in lieu of cash upon the exercise of the warrant is known as a *usable security*.

The conventional convertible security combines a straight fixed-income obligation and a long-term option to buy stock into one instrument or piece of paper. A synthetic convertible allows the two parts to be separated and freely traded, each on its own merits. Just as with a convertible, a warrant allows a delay in the issuance of the common shares from the time it or the convertible is initially issued to the time of exercise or conversion. But the exercise of a warrant does not necessarily mean that debt is reduced. If the exercise price is paid in cash, the associated debt remains outstanding.

A usable security trading below par effectively reduces the exercise price of the warrant. For example, if a warrant has an exercise price of $10 per share, the exercise of 100 warrants to purchase 100 shares of common stock will require $1,000 in cash. If the terms of the warrant specify the exercise price to be paid in the form of a usable debt or preferred instrument in lieu of cash, an investor will use the usable security as long as it is selling below par value (taking into account any accrued interest on the bond). A usable bond trading at 80 would reduce the exercise price from $10 to $8; in effect, the investor would be paying for the stock with a security worth $0.80 on the dollar.

Because of this usable feature, a lower coupon discount issue might trade at a lower yield to maturity and higher price than it would if it were an ordinary straight issue. The amount of the premium over the normal pricing or valuation or the demand for the usable bond depends on several factors, including the likelihood of the warrants being exercised and the time to their expiration. The more likely the exercise of the warrants and the closer to their expiration date, the greater may be the demand for the bond. Such demand normally increases as the time to the warrants' expiration date approaches, assuming that the warrants likely will have value and thus be exercised.

Another important factor is called availability. This is the relative amount of bonds outstanding compared with the amount of bonds needed to exercise all of the warrants. Early in 1986 American

Airlines, Inc. issued $200 million of 6¼% Subordinated Debentures due March 1, 1996, with 200,000 warrants to purchase 16.19 shares of AMR Corportion at $61.766 a share. Thus, if all warrants are exercised before the expiration date of March 1, 1996, AMR Corporation will issue 3,238,000 shares of common stock. The cost of these shares is $199,998,310. The warrant exercise terms allow the payment to be made in cash, by check, or "by the tender of the Debentures or by any combination thereof. For purposes of paying the exercise price of Warrants. Debentures will be valued at their principal amount, without credit for accrued interest, and applied only in integral multiples of $1,000 up to an amount not exceeding such exercise price."[8] Thus, $100,000 principal amount of debentures will pay the cost of 1,619 shares of common upon the exercise of the warrants. If the common price rises, the warrants will more than likely be exercised. As long as the bonds trade below par, a wise speculator will use them in lieu of cash. At a bond price of 80, the exercise price of the warrants is effectively reduced from $61.766 to $49.4128 a share.

This potential demand for the bond may also be viewed as an opportunity for the bondholder to redeem it early and thus to increase the yield. Assume that these bonds have nine years remaining to maturity and are trading at 85 for a yield to maturity of 8.39 percent. Further suppose that the stock turns out to be a big winner and that the warrants get exercised by 1992 so that the bonds will then be worth par (assuming that all of the bonds are used to pay the exercise price). Therefore, the effective yield from 85 to the 1992 redemption price of par will be 10.37 percent, nearly 200 basis points more than to the 1996 maturity. The warrants are subject to redemption on and after March 1, 1988, if the stock price equals or exceeds 115 percent of the effective exercise price for a certain period prior to the date of the redemption notice. This would further add to the near-term demand for the bonds.

In 1983, Pan American World Airways, Inc. issued $100 million of 13½% Senior Debentures due May 1, 2003, with warrants to purchase 10 million shares of common at $8 per share. The warrants expire on May 1, 1993, and are subject to early redemption on May 1, 1986. To exercise all of the warrants would require only $80 million face amount of the debentures, or 80 percent of the issue. Thus, the amount of the bonds outstanding exceeds by 25 percent the amount needed for the exercise of all the warrants. Because the amount of bonds needed to exercise the warrants in full is less than the amount of bonds outstanding, the potential demand from warrant holders will not be as great, making it less likely that this issue will get overvalued based solely on the demand factor.

There have been cases where there were not enough bonds outstanding to satisfy potential demand from warrant holders. In 1983, Western Air Lines, Inc. sold 90,000 units consisting of $90 million 10¾% Senior Secured Trust Notes due 1998 with 3,240,000 shares of common stock and warrants to purchase 9 million shares of common. The warrants, exercisable at $9.50 (and the notes may be used in lieu of cash), expire June 15, 1993, but are callable as early as June 15, 1986. Therefore, at issuance the availability factor was 95 percent. The principal amount of notes outstanding exceeded the exercise price of the warrants by $4.5 million. In 1985, the company repurchased $13.9 million face amount of the notes, reducing the outstanding amount to $76.1 million. Now the availability factor changes for the better to 112.4 percent. There are not enough bonds outstanding to satisfy all the potential demand if the warrants are exercised. Thus, warrant holders wishing to exercise their rights should gladly pay any price up to a fraction below par (omitting consideration of accrued interest) for the bonds.

The world of usable securities is limited. In mid-June 1986, the Value Line Convertible Survey's statistical section had only 48 warrants with which senior securities could be used in lieu of cash. Of these, 3 had preferred stock as the usable security and 45 debt instruments. Synthetic converts are not widely used by market participants. Equity-oriented investors/speculators are more than likely to buy the warrants alone for an undiluted stock market play. Fixed-income investors normally would purchase the debt instrument without the warrant if it were selling at a sufficiently attractive price as a bond without considering the usable feature.

CONVERTIBLE STRATEGIES

The Hedge

Convertibles typically are purchased by investors as alternatives to common stock when they have a positive outlook on the market and the shares. However, there are times when they may be bearish on the market in general and certain stocks in particular; in which case short positions may then be justified. A short sale involves the sale of stock that is not owned in the hope of buying it back (or covering) at some future date at lower prices. When stock is sold short, the shares must be borrowed from an investor who owns them in order to make delivery to the purchaser. To cover one's position and close out the short sale, one must either purchase the stock in the open market or obtain it through the conversion of a convertible. Just as one should not buy a common stock without first looking to see if there is a potential convertible substitute, so should one not short a common stock without first seeking out a convertible for it. If the subject of the short sale has a convertible, one may investigate the convertible hedge as a means of reducing the risk of the market moving against the short position.

A convertible hedge involves a long position in the convertible security and a short position in the shares into which it is convertible. The purpose of the hedge is to reduce or eliminate the loss in the event the common stock price goes up instead of down. To be a candidate for the long side of a hedge, a convertible should be trading close to or at its conversion value, ideally just at that point in the 115 to 130 price range where the conversion premium all but disappears. It should provide a greater yield than the underlying common so that the interest income may be used to pay any dividend payments due on the shorted shares. Also, the greater the volatility of the shorted shares, the greater the chance for profit.

If the price of the underlying stock declines, the profit from the hedge will come primarily from a widening of the conversion premium. If the price of the underlying stock rises, the loss on the short position will be offset by the gain or the narrowing of the conversion premium on the long position in the convertible. There are various names given to convertible hedges depending on the balance or imbalance between the common share equivalent of the long position and the common shares on the short side. A full hedge is one in which the long and short sides are equally matched and that, if the common stock price moves up, will be evenly offset by the expected increase in value of the convertible. Table 8–11 gives selected details about a hypothetical convertible that we will use for illustrative purposes.

Table 8-11
XYZ Company
8.00% Convertible Subordinated Debentures Due June 1, 2005
(Convertible at $50 into 20 Shares of Common Stock)

Price of common	$62.50
Price of convertible	$1,250
Conversion value	$1,250
Conversion premium	0
Dividend per common share	$2 per annum

In a full hedge, we would have the long and short side in balance. Thus, we would

Buy: 100 par value 8% Convertibles   Cost: $125,000
        at 125

Short: 2,000 common shares at 62½   Proceeds: $125,000

If the stock rose to 90 (an increase of 44 percent), in six months' time we would get a loss on the short position of 27½ points a share for a total amount of $55,000. The bonds must be worth a minimum of 180 (20 shares times $90) to produce a profit of $55,000 with which to offset the loss. In addition, we would have had to pay two quarterly dividends of $0.50 each, or a total of $2,000, to the lenders of the stock that we shorted. However, we would have also received six months' interest, or $4,000, on the bonds, thereby producing an overall profit of $2,000 on the hedge. Had the hedge been entered into when there was still some slight conversion premium to the bonds, the gain on the bonds would have been reduced to the extent of that premium.

But what if the hedge went the way we wanted, namely the common stock declined? Again, assume the stock dropped to 35, a decline of 27½ points over a six-month period. Here we would have a gain on the short position of $55,000. The bond would also drop in price, but most likely not as much as the common. The conversion premium would start to reappear as the common price declined. Let us assume that the bond dropped to 90. At this level the premium over conversion worth would be $200 ($900 − $700), or nearly 29 percent. In addition, suppose the premium recovery period is seven years. At 90 we would have a loss of 35 points in the bond for a total of $35,000. Thus, the hedge would have produced a net gain of $20,000 (without much risk) before commissions, interest received, and dividends paid out. A speculator engaging in these hedges need only put up funds equal to the long position. Common stock can be shorted without any additional margin required as long as the portfolio holds securities convertible into at least an equal amount of the stock.

Our full hedge produced profits on the downside with little risk. But there are also partial hedges in which the two sides are not in balance. A half-hedge with the hypothetical company in Table 8-11 would have involved the shorting of 1,000 shares and a quarter-hedge the shorting of 500 shares, at the same time being long 100 bonds. The partial hedge may also produce profits on the downside, depending on where the long position starts to develop a premium over conversion value, and may produce profits on the upside with reduced risk. Let us run through the numbers with a half-hedge assuming that we are not as bearish as the fully hedged investor. A rise in the stock to 90 would produce a loss on 1,000 shares of 27½ points, or $27,500. On the long side, our 100 bonds at a cost of 125 would produce a $55,000 profit for a net gain of $27,500. On the downside, the short position of 1,000 shares would show a profit of $27,500. With a loss of $35,000 on the bonds, a net loss of $7,500 would result.

Actually, many speculators might start out with a half-hedge and adjust the long and short sides depending on market conditions and movement. For example, as the stock declines, the short position might be gradually increased or the long position decreased, resulting in a more fully hedged and profitable situation. There are many variations that can be produced with a convertible hedge. Investors should be alert to the opportunities for profitable trading with reduced risks as they arise.

The convertible hedge is nothing new. It was used in the 1940s and 1950s by an investment company managed by the gurus of security analysis, Benjamin Graham and David L. Dodd. The annual reports of the Graham-Newman Corporation for the fiscal years ended January 31, 1950, to January 31, 1957, the year the company was liquidated, reveal a number of convertible hedges, both full and partial, throughout this period. We don't know how profitable they were or what activity occurred between the reports, but it is interesting that sophisticated investors such as Graham and Dodd used the technique. Hedges included companies such as Avco Manufacturing, Fedders-Quigan Corporation, Gar Wood Industries, Tung-Sol Electric, Inc., Crucible Steel Company of America, Allegheny Corporation, American Airlines, American Cyanamid, Dow Chemical, National Container, Olin Mathieson Chemical, Pfizer & Company, Inc., and Granite City Steel. Some positions appeared on the financial statements for only one year, while others were carried for more than five years. It is likely that all the short positions involved hedges to some degree.

On a more modern note, the prospectus dated June 20, 1986, for the Ellsworth Convertible Growth and Income Fund, Inc. mentions that the fund is allowed to make short sales of securities which it owns or which it has the right to acquire through conversion or exchange of other securities." It goes on to say that it "may make a short sale in order to hedge against market risks when it believes that the price of a security may decline causing a decline in the value of a security . . . convertible into or exchangeable for such security. . . . The extent to which . . . gains or losses are reduced will depend upon the amount of the security sold short relative to the amount the Company owns, either directly or indirectly, and, in the case where the Company owns convertible securities, changes with the convertible premiums."

Thus, convertible hedging is an appropriate technique for equity speculators who wish to engage in short selling. It can reduce the risk of loss in the event the stock goes up rather than down. It is important that they act unemotionally and map out the upside and downside projections for both the long and short positions. A good chart of the historical prices and relationships of the convertible and the underlying stock is a valuable aid for convertible hedgers. It allows them to see where the securities have been so that they can project where they might go in the future. It can also assist more active speculators as they vary the degree of the hedge.

Writing Covered Calls

Another convertible strategy is to use convertibles in writing covered call options. A call option is a right to buy common stock at a predetermined price for a certain period of time, usually under one year. The issuer or writer of the call option is obliged to sell the underlying shares at the exercise price during the option period. This obligation terminates when the option expires or when the call is covered, i.e., repurchased. Few calls are exercised, as call owners more often than not sell profitable calls in the market. For writing the call option, the buyer pays the seller (writer) a premium that is determined in part by the remaining life of the option, the exercise price in relation to the common's price, and the volatility of the underlying stock. A covered option means that the option writer has the shares or securities convertible into the shares held in his or her account or portfolio. The options are written on the underlying common shares and not on the convertible securities. We will examine covered call writing with convertibles only briefly; there are many investment books on this topic for those wanting to learn more about it.

Writing covered call options is done in order to enhance the returns on one's total portfolio. The best results are obtained in stable or rising markets. In order to determine the number of convertible bonds or convertible preferred shares needed to write calls, we divide the number of shares to be received upon conversion of one bond or preferred share into the number of shares for which the call option is being written. In our hypothetical company example in Table 8–11, each bond is convertible into 20 shares. Thus, to write one covered call option for 100 shares, we will need 5 bonds, and for 2,000 shares we will need 100 bonds. As the bonds are selling right on the conversion value of 125, any rise in the stock should be fully reflected in their price. On the downside we expect the conversion premium to reappear, thus reducing our loss. The bonds normally would decline at a slower rate than the underlying common. In addition, they offer a greater return than the stock—another advantage of many convertibles.

Therefore, for our 100-bond long position we can write 20 covered call options. A six-month option exercisable at 65 with the stock at 62½ is worth about $350 to $400 per 100 shares; we will use the midpoint of $375 as the premium received. Let us look at the possible results of writing covered call options against both the convertible and the underlying shares of our hypothetical company. Table 8–12 shows that using convertibles instead of the underlying common stock in a program of writing covered call options may lead to

Table 8-12
XYZ Company
Covered Call Option Data at Expiration Date
(Option Is Exercisable at 65)

Common price ($):	35	50	62 ½	75	90
Convertible price ($):	900	1,100	1,250	1,500	1,800
Option value ($):	0	0	0	10	25

Cost of 100 convertibles		$125,000
Less: Option premium received		7,500
Net cost of convertible position		$117,500

Profit (loss) on:					
Convertible	($35,000)	($15,000)	0	$25,000	$55,000
Option	7,500	7,500	$7,500	(12,500)	(42,500)
Profit (loss)	(27,500)	(7,500)	7,500	12,500	12,500
Interest income	4,000	4,000	4,000	4,000	4,000
Net profit (loss)	($23,500)	($3,500)	$11,500	$16,500	$16,500
Rate of return					
on investment	(20.0%)	(3.0%)	9.8%	14.0%	14.0%

Cost of 2,000 shares of stock		$125,000
Less: Option premium received		7,500
Net cost of stock position		$117,500

Profit (loss) on:					
Stock	($50,000)	($25,000)	0	$25,000	$55,000
Option	7,500	7,500	$7,500	(12,500)	(42,500)
Profit (loss)	(47,500)	(17,500)	7,500	12,500	12,500
Dividend income	2,000	2,000	2,000	2,000	2,000
Net profit (loss)	($45,500)	($15,500)	$9,500	$14,500	$14,500
Rate of return					
on investment	(38.7%)	(13.2%)	5.5%	12.3%	12.3%

better investment results. In this case, there were less losses on the downside and greater returns when the stock rose.

Of course, the final results of covered call writing strategies depend on a number of factors, including the income differential between the convertible and the common, the premium received for writing the call, the conversion premium, if any, of the convertible, and the price action of the securities. The above is a very passive example. In actual practice, some investors might wish to limit their losses or take their gains at certain predetermined price levels by closing out or repurchasing the calls they have written.

Before attempting any covered call writing program, investors should go through exercises similar to the above in order to see what the results might look like. Again, they should look at price history charts to get some idea of the past (and maybe the future) relationships among the common, the convertible, and the option. There are several investment services and brokers that aid investors in their call writing activities.

Convertibles are wonderful securities for investors who lack perfect foresight. If our crystal ball worked, we would go only with those investments that would be tremendously profitable; we would not need securities that provide some degree of downside protection. But then, few of us are perfect investors—and thus the need for convertible securities.

NOTES

1. While most convertible securities may be exchanged for common stock, some are convertible into straight debt, cash, and/or preferred stock. Most of these have been created out of mergers and acquisitions. For example, Avco Corporation has an issue of 5.50% Convertible Subordinated Debentures due November 30, 1993, that are convertible into $926 of cash per $1,000 debenture. The debentures were originally convertible into 18.52 shares of Avco's common. In 1985, Textron acquired Avco for $50 per share; bonds may now receive the cash value of the underlying security, namely $50 times 18.52 shares, or $926. The cash value provides a floor to the market price of the issue. LTV Corporation's Series C $5.25 Convertible Preferred Stock is convertible into 3.92 shares of common and 0.78 shares of Series D $1.25 Convertible Preferred Stock.

2. Arthur Stone Dewing, *The Financial Policy of Corporations,* vol. 1, 5th ed. (New York: Ronald Press, 1953). He states: "Conversion from one type of security into another has existed in England for a long period of time. Scott mentions the case of an early London Water Company in which King Charles I was allowed to convert his stock into bonds."

3. George Wheeler, *Pierpont Morgan and Friends: The Anatomy of a Myth* (Englewood Cliffs, N.J.: Prentice-Hall, 1973). In discussing Daniel Drew's three methods of twisted finance, Wheeler describes the first method, which consisted of violations of the New York State railway act, as follows:

That law permitted the roads to issue bonds to raise money "to complete, equip and operate" the line. To help sustain the value of the bonds, a "sweetener" was allowed in which the buyer could convert the bond into a share of common stock. The theory was that the buyer would pay a better price for the bond and thus maintain its value if he knew that later, when the stock rose above par, he would have an additional profit through the conversion feature. But Drew had his own theories. He had the company issue the bonds in violation of the legislative provisions that they were only to be brought out for the specific purposes cited, and he immediately used the convertible feature despite the fact that the stock was far below par value.

For an interesting discussion of the troubled Erie of the period, see Charles Francis Adams, Jr., and Henry Adams, *Chapters of Erie* (Ithaca, N.Y.: Great Seal Books, 1956). The original articles were published in 1869 and 1871.

4. Prospectus for $150 million Champion International Corporation 6½% Convertible Subordinated Debentures due April 15, 2011, April 17, 1986, p. 4.

5. Prospectus for $750 million (later increased to $840 million) Waste Management, Inc. Liquid Yield Option Notes Due 2001 (Zero Coupon–Subordinated), April 12, 1985, various pages.

6. In June 1986, the company offered to exchange a portion of the four issues for new bonds that would be indexed to a greater number of ounces of silver but would lack the benefit of sinking funds. Also, the interest on the new bonds would be payable in cash or additional shares of common stock at Sunshine's option.

7. Bonds whose principal amounts are indexed to commodities are not new. American financial history provides us with a nice example. The State of Massachusetts Bay had a 6% Treasury Certificate dated January 1, 1780, and payable March 1, 1782, stating that it was

> to be paid in the then current Money of said State, in a greater or less Sum, according as Five Bushels of CORN, Sixty-eight Pounds and four-sevenths Parts of a Pound of BEEF, Ten Pounds of SHEEPSWOOL, and Sixteen Pounds of SOLE LEATHER, shall then cost, more or less than One Hundred and Thirty Pounds current Money, at the then current Prices of said ARTICLES—This Sum being Thirty-Two Times and an Half what the same quantities of the same Articles would cost at the prices affixed to them in a Law of this State made in the Year of our Lord One Thousand Seven Hundred and Seventy-seven, intitled, "An Act to prevent Monopoly and Oppression." The current Prices of said Articles, and the consequent Value of every Pound of the Sum herein promised, to be determined agreeable to a LAW of this State, intitled, "An ACT to provide for the Security and Payment of the Balances that may appear to be due by Virtue of a Resolution of the General Assembly of the Sixth of February One Thousand Seven Hundred and Seventy-nine, to this State's Quota of the CONTINENTAL ARMY, agreeable to the Recommendation of CONGRESS and for Supplying the Treasury with a Sum of Money for that Purpose.

This and other debt issues of the American Revolution are described in William G. Anderson, *The Price of Liberty* (Charlottesville, Va.: University Press of Virginia, 1983).

8. Prospectus for 200,000 Units of American Airlines, March 7, 1986, p. 15–16.

CHAPTER 9

RATINGS AND RESEARCH

A bond or preferred stock rating is an assessment of the issuer's ability to meet the terms of the issue in a timely manner. This chapter reviews corporate bond and preferred stock ratings, their uses, and their limitations.

BACKGROUND OF THE RATING AGENCIES

Bond research is done by three parties—the rating agencies, Wall Street broker/dealer firms, and the investor. In this chapter we will focu on the activities of the first two. Up until the late sixties there were three recognized, full-service rating organizations, i.e., agencies whose ratings were accepted by the vast majority of professionals in the markets and by regulatory authorities. They are capable of rating the full range of debt securities from commercial paper to term bonds, corporate and governmental, domestic and international. Moody's Investors Service, Inc. (Moody's) and Standard & Poor's Corporation (S&P) have been the two most widely accepted services because of their broad coverage and widespread publication activities. Fitch Investors Service, Inc. (Fitch) is considerably smaller in terms of its professional staff and range of publications and thus is not as widely accepted among professional investors.

Figure 9-1 traces some of the history of Moody's and Standard & Poor's. S&P goes back to 1860, when Henry V. Poor published *History of Railroads and Canals of the United States*.[1] Over the next 50 years it expanded its activities, publishing *Poor's Manual of Railroads of the United States* (1868), *Poor's Manual of Industrials* (1910), and *Poor's Manual of Public Utilities* (1913). As part of its railroad manual activities, Poor's Bureau of Information and Investigation engaged in customized research on railroads (existing, new, and projected), their mortgages, bonds, leases, and other contracts, and on old securities and defunct companies. The 1905 *Manual* contained an advertisement of H. W. Poor & Co., Bankers of 18 Wall Street. It said: "Railway Investment A Specialty. We are in correspondence with nearly every Railroad Company in the country through our connection with . . . 'Poor's Manual of Railroads.'"

John Moody & Company, founded in 1900, published *Moody's Manual of Industrial and Corporation Securities*. The second edition, which appeared in 1901, included railroad and public utility securities. In 1905, the company started *Moody's Investors Magazine*, but it fared poorly, as costs exceeded revenues, and was sold in 1908. Several books were published, but the panic of 1907 took its toll. The company expanded into the printing business in 1904 to 1905, a business about which Moody admittedly knew "practically nothing." He overextended the firm, and it went deeply into debt. Costs and payroll rose, and the company still had to use expensive outside printers. The panic resulted in reduced business and lower revenues. The manual business suffered, and John Moody lost control of the company. He left the firm in 1908, and Roy W. Porter became editor of Moody's manuals. He bought control of the company in 1914 and merged it five years later with Poor's Railroad Manual Company to form Poor's Publishing Company.

Meanwhile, in 1906, James L. L. Blake founded the Standard Statistics Bureau. In 1907, Blake engaged John Moody to be the editorial supervisor of the Standard Bond Descriptions service. Each sheet or "card" contained descriptions of the various outstanding bonds and analyses of the investment position of each. (Today's S&P sheets on listed and over-the-counter equity securities are referred to as "cards" in the trade. Until the early 1970s there had been a bond service that utilized the card format.) Blake expanded his activities

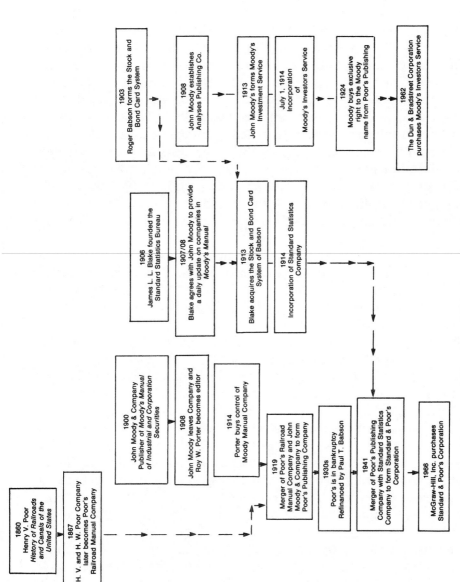

Figure 9-1 The Interrelationship of Moody's and Standard & Poor's

in 1913, when he acquired the Stock and Bond Card System started
by Roger Babson in 1903. In 1914 Standard Statistics Company was
incorporated and in 1923 began to rate corporate debt securities.

While the financial publishing industry as a whole survived the
Roaring Twenties, Poor's Publishing Company ran into trouble during the Great Depression and found itself bankrupt. One of the
reasons may be that it had spent considerable sums on fixed investment in a Massachusetts printing plant. Paul T. Babson (Roger's
cousin) provided the needed financing, gained control of Poor's, and
removed it from bankruptcy. In 1940, the company sold its manual
subscription list to Moody's Investors Service. However, Babson
could not make the company profitable and, in 1941, arranged a
merger with Standard Statistics Company. The name of the new
company was Standard & Poor's Corporation. In 1966, McGraw-
Hill, Inc., purchased S&P.

John Moody did not retire from the business in 1908 after losing
control of his first venture. He set out and organized Analyses
Publishing Company at 35 Nassau Street in New York City. In 1909
it published the first edition of *Moody's Analyses of Railroad Investments Containing in Detailed Form an Expert Comparative
Analysis of Each of the Railroad Systems of the United States, with
Careful Deductions, Enabling the Banker and Investor to Ascertain
the True Values of Securities by a Method Based on Scientific Principles.* This book introduced the now familiar system for rating
fixed-income securities. The ratings, adopted from the mercantile
and credit rating system in use since the late 1800s by credit reporting firms, ran on a scale from "Aaa" (highest class) to "E" (very
weak or defaulted). The preface to the 1910 edition refers to the first
as "comparatively incomplete," although it was widely accepted. Its
purpose was to analyze the railroads; thus, it was not a statistical
record or a replacement for the manuals. On July 1, 1909, the first
issue of *Moody's Weekly Review of Financial Conditions* appeared
(this was published by Moody as an individual owner rather than by
Analyses). In 1910, Analyses published *Moody's Analyses of Investments,* which covered public utility and industrial issues. At the
Nassau Street address Moody also published *Moody's Magazine,*
"The International Investor's Monthly—A High-Class Monthly
Publication Devoted Exclusively to the Interest of the Investor."

This seems to have been an early effort to catch the "global investor." It appears from the advertisement in the 1910 railroad book that Moody also conducted an investment advisory service for conservative individual investors and savings banks, trustees of estates, and financial institutions.

Over the next few years, Moody formed Moody's Investment Service, a sole proprietorship, to supplement the annual *Analyses* and provide weekly and monthly investment reviews and advice. On July 1, 1914, just prior to the start of World War I and the closing of the NYSE and other stock exchanges, Moody's Investors Service was incorporated. The manual and other activities were brought under the umbrella of one company. The motto on the title page of the 1916 edition of the *Analyses* stated that the publications were "Founded to Endure and Investors Make Secure." The preface says:

> The success of *Moody's Analyses of Investments* during recent years as a business enterprise has been little short of remarkable. Each year its circulation and popularity have grown until today [1916] it is used and recognized as the great authority on investment values. Thousands of banking institutions and individual investors rely on its ratings in all their investment purchases and bond sellers and dealers find it of ever increasing value. It is the only publication in existence which furnishes investment ratings and analyses of an authoritative character. A few crude imitators have attempted to appropriate Mr. Moody's ideas, but such attempts have failed as they are bound to do so. The ultimate disaster of the pirate is his well deserved punishment.

In 1918, Moody's issued its manual of foreign and American government securities. In 1924, Moody's bought back from Poor's Publishing the right to the Moody's name.[2] Moody's continued to grow through the years and in 1962 was acquired by the Dun & Bradstreet Corporation.

Fitch Publishing Company was organized in 1913 by Francis Emory Fitch (its origins go back to the 1880s). The initial publication, *The Fitch Bond Book,* was a compendium of information on the outstanding bonds of that time. It expanded its publication activities and first rated corporate debt in 1922. The ratings were first published in the 1923 issue of *The Fitch Bond Rating Book.* During the 1930s, Fitch worked with federal government regulatory officials on guidelines for investment by commercial banks in corporate debt securities. In 1960, Fitch sold most of its publications and printing plant to Standard & Poor's so that it could concentrate on its debt rating activities. Included in the sale were the rights to use its rating symbols. (Previously, Poor's rating symbols had ranged from A** to D and Standard Statistics' from A1+ to D). In the late sixties, new management took over Fitch and revitalized the moribund agency.

In 1971, Fitch verbally refined its rating categories just as bond market participants had been doing, describing issues in conversations, over the telephone, and in speeches, as being in the upper half of the rating category, or mid-range, or lower third. Two years later it began to utilize the plus (+) and minus (−) signs in the rating symbols (well before Standard & Poor's took a similar step in 1977 and Moody's in 1982). The modifications were greatly welcomed in the bond world. All bonds in a rating category are not of the same quality or possess the same default risk, and the modifiers emphasized that point. More recently, Fitch helped establish the London-based Euroratings Limited, a full-service firm for Euromarket and international debt issuers and investors.[3]

The other two investment services are Duff & Phelps, Inc. (D&P) and McCarthy, Crisanti & Maffei, Inc. (MCM). D&P was founded as a partnership in 1932 to evaluate the utility industry for professional investors and investment firms. Since its founding it has given opinions on the creditworthiness of corporate debt instruments and, in the early seventies, developed its own rating system. In 1980 it became a public, or recognized, rating agency covering long-term debt, preferred stocks, and commercial paper. MCM was formed by several analysts from Wall Street who saw a need for an additional debt-oriented research "boutique" to provide rating information for their subscribers. By not accepting fees for rating debt issuers, MCM felt that it could better serve its investor-clients without any possible conflicts with the issuers. Established in 1975, it has gained wide acceptance among knowledgeable fixed-income investors. MCM was acquired by Xerox Financial Services in 1985.

Of the five agncies, Moody's and S&P employ the largest numbers of professionals on their corporate rating staffs. In 1976, *Fortune* reported that each of these two agencies had about 30 corporate analysts. Today, Moody's probably has 125 or so professionals and

S&P about 225 on their corporate rating staffs, including those in the structured transactions area (structured transactions are mortgage-backed securities and other asset-based financings). This is a far cry from the mid-sixties, when S&P had three full-time analysts, one old-timer who worked on a part-time basis, a statistical assistant, and a secretary in the corporate bond rating department.

The rating agencies are much better today than they used to be, in the opinion of many bond professionals. Since they now charge issuers for ratings, they can afford larger and better-trained staffs (previously, their main source of income had been from the sale of bond-related publications and some fee income for rating private placements). Competition between them and the new entrants in the business have forced the old-line agencies to develop new products and to expand and upgrade their staffs and publications in order to serve the needs of investors. They are now much more responsive to developments in the market and corporate finance. They act more promptly to changes—and also anticipate more changes. Ratings used to be assigned and revised only when a company came to market with a new issue or if there was a drastic change in the protection afforded investors. Often, gradual deterioration went unnoticed or ignored by the agencies for a considerable period of time. The improvement in the quality of the rating services over the past several years has greatly benefited the investment community.

FIXED-INCOME RESEARCH ACTIVITIES
OF BROKERAGE FIRMS

On the sell side of Wall Street, fixed-income research can be divided into three types. The first is interest rate forecasting (also known as crystal ball gazing)—trying to determine in which direction interest rates, and thus bond prices, may go. The second is technical or market analysis. Technical analysts are concerned with yield spread analysis, determining whether issues and/or sectors of the market are rich or cheap based on historical price and yield relationships. They analyze market risk and the structure of debt portfolios as well as engage in market strategy. The third area involves the fundamentals of the issuer and the issue. This includes the quality of the corporation and the trend of that quality, as well as the terms of the issue. These factors go into rating debt and preferred stocks. Many fixed-income analysts are generalists as far as financial analysis is concerned but specialists as far as *securities* are concerned. Many of the more seasoned bond analysts have probably covered a wide range of industries from electric utilities to industrial, bank, and finance issuers. Some of the work is of a more general nature, such as redemption and industry studies; other work is, to use a cliché, "transaction oriented."

Fixed-income research activities of a fundamental nature—i.e., research into credit quality and terms of issues for sales, trading, and client purposes—did not get started in earnest until the late 1960s. Prior to that time, some firms employed bond statisticians, but these generally were little more than number crunchers. Of course, at Salomon Brothers & Hutzler, there was the reknowned Sidney Homer, a pioneer in the analytical studies of bond market history, bond market values, and the economic forces that create bond market trends. Homer was the author of such books as *The Bond Buyer's Primer*, *A History of Interest Rates*, *The Great American Bond Market*, and *Inside the Yield Book*. However, he was concerned about the market itself. Ratings and issue terms apparently were of less interest until some individuals came to Wall Street in sales and trading capacities. These analysts tied market activities together with corporate fundamentals for the main purpose of selling more bonds to their clients. At that time deterioration started to appear in the fundamentals of many utilities. Companies whose financial measurements had once qualified them for the top ratings started to show weakening in their income statements and balance sheets. Every once in a while, a downgrade would occur.

This was the start of corporate bond research activity as we now know it. Being a corporate bond analyst on Wall Street during the late sixties and early to mid-seventies was an exciting job. Despite the decline in the fundamentals of many companies (particularly utilities), many issues would trade within five or ten basis points (or less) of one another, with little notice being given to the differences in call and refunding protection and the apparent trend in debt quality ratings. One could tell salespeople, traders, and investors to buy XYZ bond and sell ABC for little or no sacrifice in yield even if the purchased issue was far superior to the other based on the fundamental factors. Sell-side analysts were trying to determine fundamental values and having their clients sell what they thought were overvalued issues and buy those that were fairly valued or even undervalued. Many portfolio managers, lacking their own analytical staffs, often were very receptive to these analysts' ideas. (Although we call them analysts, the few firms having fundamental bond analysis capability as part of their sales and trading operations had only one or two on their staffs.) Swapping, or portfolio improvement, was easy to do although, compared to present-day techniques, was quite primitive.

As an increasing number of rating changes occurred, as solid companies such as Penn Central and Consolidated Edison developed problems ranging from financial distress to actual bankruptcy, as inflation got worse and interest rates rose, as markets became more volatile, and as the bond business became more competitive and capital intensive, more and more investment banking and brokerage firms saw the need for corporate bond research staffs. They started to appreciate the importance of fundamental corporate bond and preferred stock research to their sales, trading, and investment banking activities. While each was set up differently, all provided services that they felt were needed. Some firms now employ 15 or more professional bond analysts. Some analysts are part of the sales/trading areas, others are part of their firms' general securities research departments.

What are the functions of a corporate debt research unit? Fixed-income analysts direct their efforts toward satisfying the needs of bond salespeople, traders, and portfolio managers. Their job is to help their firms make money by providing information that will permit trading and buying and selling of securities to be carried out with reduced risk. Of course, analysts cannot work miracles. If the idea is good but the bid or offering inadequate, the trade likely will not be done. Likewise, if the bid or offering is good but the idea poorly presented, the trade might fall through. Traders, salespeople, and analysts are all part of the same team, although their time horizons may differ. Salespeople and traders tend to be concerned with what is happening right at the moment; analysts may take a longer-term view, one that is less affected by near-term supply and demand considerations. However, well-rounded professionals should be able to take into account both the near and long-term pictures for the benefit of all parties using their services.

DEBT AND PREFERRED STOCK RATINGS

The following quotes are from the introduction to *Standard & Poor's Ratings Guide:*[4]

> In determining a rating, history, and a myriad of statistics and ratios that reflect that history is of importance only insofar as it may help us to anticipate the future.

> In determining a rating, both quantitative and qualitative analyses are employed. Ultimately, the judgement is qualitative in nature and the role of the quantitative analyses is to help make the best possible overall qualitative judgment because, ultimately, a rating is an opinion.

> A critical factor in the rating process is that each rating entity, whether a municipality or a corporation, is a coalescence of various types of resources which are controlled or influenced by individuals. This coalescence does not function automatically. It requires an overall controlling mechanism known as management. Even situations deemed to be "unmanageable" (some people considered Penn Central to be unmanageable in 1970; New York City to be unmanageable in 1978) are nonetheless reflections on the managements which had previously permitted conditions to become "unmanageable."

Ratings are assigned to the particular issue, not the issuer. This is why a company may have a few different ratings on its debt. For example, S&P assigns to the senior debt of General Motors Acceptance Corporation an "AA+" rating and to the subordinated debt an "AA" rating. Moody's assigns four different ratings to the various debt securities of the Public Service Company of New Hampshire. The first mortgage bonds are rated "B1," the general and refunding mortgage bonds "B2," the deferred interest third mortgage bonds "B3," and the debentures "Caa." Standard & Poor's rates the first mortgage bonds "B−" and the other three types "CCC." Fitch assigns three ratings ("B," "CCC," and "CCC−") to the issues. McCarthy, Crisanti & Maffei gives the issues a "B" rating, while Duff & Phelps gives them 16 and 17.

A thorough analysis is made of the issuer's (and guarantors, if applicable) operations and need for past, present, and future funds. The industry and the issuer's position within it are also assessed in terms of the past, present, and future. Finally, the caliber of the issuer's management is reviewed (even though this is to a great extent reflected in the company's financial statements). The financials are, to some degree, a report card on management. The analyst considers the three Cs of credit—the character of the management, the collateral, if any, behind the repayment of the debt, and the capacity of the issuer to service its debt. While the analyst relies on numbers and ratios to get a picture of the company's debt-servicing ability, a rating is a judgment of an issuer's ability to meet all of its obligations when due, whether during prosperity or during times of stress. The purpose of bond or preferred ratings is to rank issues in terms of the probability of default.

Ratings are based not on where we are in an economic or business cycle but on the fundamentals of the company and the issue. A corporation may have had a poor year, but this does not necessarily mean that a downgrading is imminent. If the raters feel, based on their experience and analysis, that the downturn is only temporary, the rating will likely remain untouched. However, if the rating review reveals that the deterioration may be more permanent, the rating can be lowered. In many cases, the reason for a lower rating is that the issuer has increased its debt load to such an extent that a return to the former levels is not anticipated for quite a while, if at all. Such was the case when Colt industries announced its proposed restructuring plan on July 21, 1986. The rating agencies immediately placed the company's bonds on their watchlists for possible downgrading. S&P said at that time: "If the transaction is completed as planned, long-term ratings will fall well below investment grade." The restructuring would increase total long-term debt from some $340 million to about $1.74 billion while reducing common equity.

Another consideration in assigning a rating to an issue is a review of the indenture (or certificates of incorporation in the case of a preferred stock), or the contact between the lender and the borrower. It states whether the debt is secured, senior unsecured, or subordinated. It might have covenants designed for the protection of the bondholder, such as a negative pledge clause in the case of unsecured debt. It outlines the sinking fund and other redemption features.

In June 1986, Calton Inc. came to market with an issue that had an interesting provision. The offering was $50 million of 12¼% Senior Notes due June 15, 1996, rated B2 by Moody's and B— by Standard & Poor's. The following is from the prospectus dated June 13, 1986:

> Initially, the indebtedness evidenced by the Senior Notes will rank parri passu with the Company's other Senior Debt. In the event that the Company's Fixed Charge Coverage Ratio for any 12 month period at the end of any fiscal quarter is equal to or less than 120%, the holders of a majority of the Company's Senior Funded Debt may at their option modify the ranking of the Senior Notes (all and not in part) such that the Senior Notes shall become subordinate to the prior payment when due of the principal of and interest on all Senior Debt. If the Senior Notes are so subordinated, they shall thereafter be known as the "Subordinated Notes due 1996," shall bear interest at a rate of 125 basis points (1.25%) per annum in excess of the rate borne by the Senior Notes and shall be the same as the Senior Notes in other respects. In the event that the Company's Fixed Charge Coverage Ratio for any 12 month period at the end of any fiscal quarter is equal to or greater than 360%, the Company may at its option modify the ranking of the Senior Notes (all and not in part) such as the Senior Notes shall become Subordinated Notes due in 1996, which shall bear interest at a rate of 37.5 basis points (.375%) per annum in excess of the rate borne by the Senior Notes. The Subordinated Notes due 1996 will be subordinated to the Company's Senior Subordinated Notes.

In its *Bond Survey* of June 2, 1986, Moody's stated that "The rating is also based on the risk that the note could be converted into subordinated debt, depending on the company's performance." Standard & Poor's said in its May 26, 1986, issue of *CreditWeek* that because of this feature, "the issue is being rated on a subordinated basis." This was a highly unusual feature in a corporate bond. It appears that had this provision not been in the indenture, the issue would have been rated on a senior basis and the ratings undoubtedly would have been somewhat higher.

Ratings are of a longer-term nature. While investment banking firms are often short-term oriented, especially on the sales and trading sides, rating agencies must take the long-term view to determine whether the trends they are watching will continue. Sell-side bond analysts don't often have that long term luxury. They must react on the spot to rumors, headlines, and short items on the news ticker, occasionally shooting from the hip with "quick and dirty" responses to inquiries. They often have no time to do in-depth analysis, as the demands of the markets will not allow it. If they cannot give traders a quick (and, hopefully, correct) answer, the latter might be unable to sell a bond position before the bids drop lower or might not be in the market with the correct bid. Salespeople might find that they are the second call to the client, and that the trade has already been done because some other firm got there first.

Following are just a few of the rating changes and their causes from one week in July 1986.

Moody's Investors Service (*Moody's Bond Survey*, July 14, 1986)
Upgrade
Connecticut Light & Power Company:

First and Refunding Mortgage Bonds	Baa2 to Baa1
Preferred Stock	baa2 to baa1

"The upgrade was a result of the approval of a rate settlement agreement on July 1 by the Connecticut Department of Public Utility Control (CDPUC), and the financial benefits of Connecticut L & P's greatly reduced construction and the benefits of the company's reduced financing and construction requirements over the next several years."

Downgrade
Pioneer Corporation:

Senior Notes due 1990	A2 to Baa2

"The rating change is the result of the acquisition of Pioneer by Mesa Limited Partnership, which assumed Pioneer's debt."

"The merger of Mesa and Pioneer creates an entity with long-lived, high-quality gas reserves. Although financial leverage is now moderate, Moody's believes it could increase because of the partnership's policy of distributing substantially all available net cash flow to its unit holders. The partnership's fixed charge is expected to be satisfactory for the intermediate term."

Mack Trucks Inc.:

Senior Debt	Baa3 to Ba1

"The rating action recognizes our expectations of continued weakness in Mack's operating returns and cash flows over the next several years because of excess capacity industrywide and persistent price discounting. The rating also considers the heightened financial risks associated with instituting critical capital investment programs during a period of industry stress."

Standard & Poor's Corporation (*CreditWeek*, July 14, 1986)

Upgrade
Philadelphia Electric Company:
    Preferred Stock   BB to BB+

"Financial stress associated with construction of the two-unit Limerick nuclear facility is expected to moderate somewhat, reflecting the early 1986 commercial operation of Limerick 1 and related rate relief awarded last month. Nonetheless, further improvement in credit quality will be constrained by the extensive capital needs that remain for funding the continued construction of Limerick 2, scheduled for 1990. Significant infusions of common equity will be needed, especially in view of the company's leverage capital structure."

Dyco Petroleum Corporation:
    Senior Subordinated Notes   B− to BB+

"The upgrade primarily reflects the improved financing flexibility available to Dyco since it was acquired by Diversified Energies Inc. in late 1985. Moreover, the parent's capital structure will be strengthened significantly by a planned 1.5 million share common stock offering. Underlying the credit quality of Diversified Energies is the healthy and sizable dividend stream of its principal subsidiary, Minnegasco Inc., an 'AA' rated natural gas distributor."

Downgrade
Coca-Cola Company:
    Senior Debt Ratings   AAA to AA+

"The downgrade reflects the company's more aggressive financial and strategic policies adopted over the past few years. The company's plan to acquire JLT Corp. and the Coca-Cola bottling operations of Beatrice Cos. Inc., which follows a series of smaller acquisitions and share repurchases, will require $2.4 billion of additional debt. Because these assets, along with Coke's existing bottling operations, are expected to be spun off into a free-standing bottler, the direct financial impact of these acquisitions will be temporary. It is anticipated that Coke will retain a sizable equity interest in the new venture and that debt and equity issued by the new unit will provide funds for repaying the acquisition-related debt. While it is expected that any debt of the new bottling company will be without recourse to Coca-Cola, it is S&P's judgment that Coca-Cola would have a strong business incentive to insure the financial viability of the new company. Although creditor protection remains excellent, the rating reduction reflects the impact of strategic decisions, including the anticipated new bottling venture, to use financial resources more aggressively to meet business objectives."

Canadian National Railway Company
    Long-Term Obligations   AAA to AA

"CN is 100%-owned by the government of Canada, but its obligtions are not guaranteed. Key factors in the rating decision are a strong but diminished level of government support, deteriorating earnings performance contributing to higher debt levels, and proposed deregulation of the transport sector."

Ratings used to be assigned for the life of the issue. That still applies today; however, rating changes do seem to occur more often than was the case two decades ago. While there are now more issues that carry ratings, continual economic change and the resulting impact on individual companies and industries are the major influence on rating revisions today. In 1985 Moody's made 277 corporate debt rating changes, of which 153 were downgrades. Of the downgrades 102, or 67 percent, were caused by negative changes in the company's fundamentals. However, the remaining downgrades—51, or 33 percent—were caused by what Moody's calls "decapitalizations," which were up from 24 percent in 1984.[5]

McCarthy, Crisanti, & Maffei, Inc. issued a comparison of bond ratings on companies rated in common by it, Moody's, and S&P (see Figures 9-2a thorugh 9-2d). The study covered the period from the end of 1979 to the end of 1985. It is interesting to note that MCM's ratings are, in general, lower than those of the other two services and that the ratings of Moody's and S&P are very close to each other. The figures also show the downtrend in credit quality for American industry as a whole. Of course, individual industry sectors may be somewhat different. The electric utility industry appears to be in what some stock market technical analysts might call a saucer formation. The downgradings are being outnumbered by the upgradings, resulting in a slightly better-quality rating for the whole electric utility industry. The ratings of finance companies also have shown some recent improvement. The figures show that rating activity is not static but continually changing.[6]

It was also said that Moody's relied more on the analysis of the balance sheet, while Standard & Poor's and Fitch were more earnings oriented. That might have been true at one time, but it is probably not so today. It is likely that today's ratings are more balanced, taking into account earnings, cash flows, balance sheets, and economic and political considerations, among other things. The rating changes given earlier probably occurred for many different reasons.

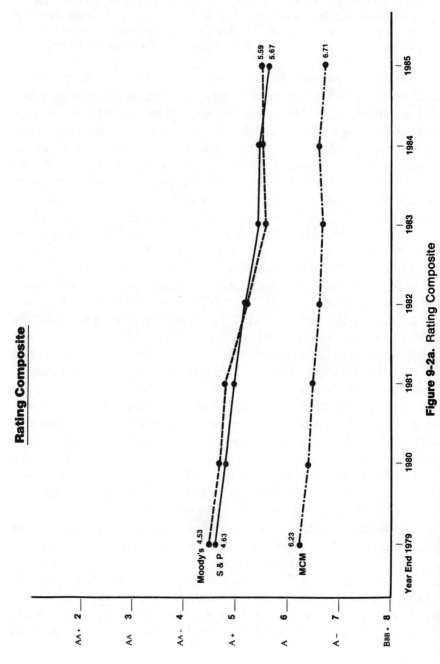

Figure 9-2a. Rating Composite

Courtesy of McCarthy, Crisanti & Maffei, Inc.

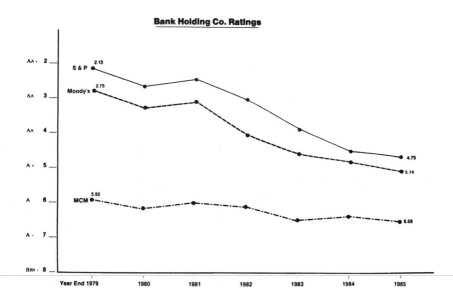

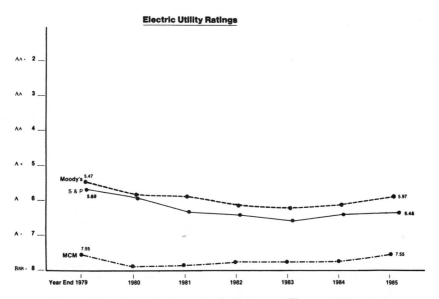

Figure 9-2b. Bank Holding Co. Ratings and Electric Utility Ratings
Courtesy of McCarthy, Crisanti & Maffei, Inc.

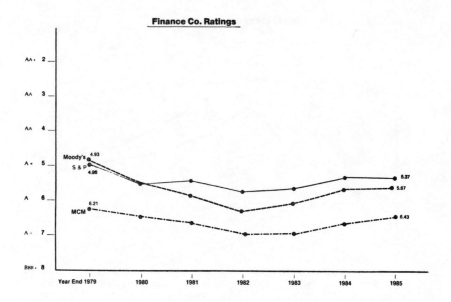

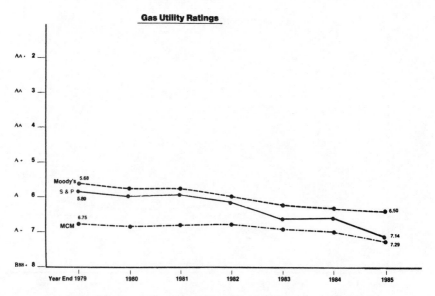

Figure 9-2c. Finance Co. Ratings & Gas Utility Ratings

Courtesy of McCarthy, Crisanti & Maffei, Inc.

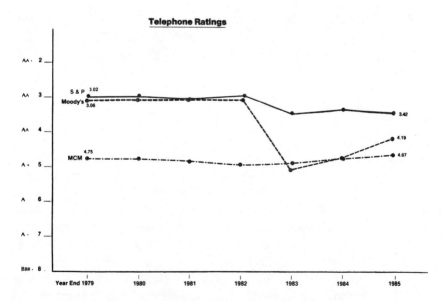

Figure 9-2d. Industrial Ratings & Telephone Ratings

Courtesy of McCarthy, Crisanti & Maffei, Inc.

The ratings of preferred stock involves much of the same type of analysis as that for rating debt except, of course, the issue is whether *dividends* rather than interest will be paid in a timely fashion. Actually, the debt and preferred ratings were closely linked, and the rating designations use the same or similar characters. Modest use of preferred stock by an issuer will probably result in a rating that is the same as the senior debt's (although the definitions are different), while a greater amount of preferred in the capitalization will result in lower ratings. Analysts look at the protective measurements for dividends, such as coverage, the company's return on assets and capital, leverage, and the seniority of the issue vis-à-vis other issues, as well as the other factors that make up a debt rating. But remember that preferred stock is equity and not debt. It ranks behind even junior debt in the pecking order for a claim on the company's assets in the event of bankruptcy, reorganization, or liquidation.

On July 16, 1986, Standard & Poor's and Moody's downgraded the ratings of BankAmerica Corporation, the holding company of Bank of America N.T. & S.A. The senior debt was lowered from Baa1/A− to Baa3/BBB, the subordinated from Baa2/BBB+ to Ba1/BBB−, and the preferred from baa2/BBB− to ba3/B. According to the Dow Jones News Wire Service, S&P stated that "the downgrade on preferred stock reflects the absence of operating earnings to cover the dividend requirement, leaving future payments vulnerable to omission."

What is Wrong Here?

Table 9-1 shows the rating symbols used by all five of the recognized rating agencies; more complete definitions may be found in the appendix to this chapter. Moody's and Duff & Phelps' symbols are different from the others. D&P uses Arabic numerals, while Moody's uses upper- and lower-case letters and all lowercase letters for its preferred ratings. MCM uses two different sizes of capital letters in some of its reports, the first larger than the others in the symbol. However, many printers do not have two sizes of capital letters, and thus the symbols often look like the S&P and Fitch symbols. The following statements contain some frequently seen errors. For example, *The Wall Street Journal* reported the following on July 18, 1986:

> Moody's Investors Service Inc. yesterday also lowered its ratings on about $2 billion of LTV and its units' debt to single-Ca and double-Ca from ratings ranging from B1 to B3.[7]

Single-Ca is written "Ca," while double-Ca is written "Cca." Moody's does have a single-Ca rating, as shown in Table 9-1, but it has no double-Ca rating; rather, it has a single-C double-a rating written as "Caa."

From another well-respected journal, we see:

> Of the 252 issues, 29% were rated by Moody's as high grade (AAA or AA), 66% were rated medium grade (A or BAA) and 5% were rated low grade (less than BAA).[8]

What is wrong here? A couple of things. To repeat, Moody's symbols for bonds have the first letter capitalized. Thus, the "AAA" and "AA" symbols should have been written as 'Aaa" and "Aa." The symbols used were Standard & Poor's or Fitch's! The single-A symbol is correct, as it is used by four out of the five agencies. The last symbol, "BAA," is incorrect—in fact, it does not even exist, at least for the official rating authorities. The correct symbol is "Baa." Some analysts, however, might use symbols like "BAA" for their own ratings; they are often found on computer printouts or runs that do not have lower case letters.

All of this is important because the proper writing of ratings indicates to other professionals that you know what the business is about and understand its finer points. If you make an error in something as basic as writing a rating symbol, people might (understandably) believe that you also make errors in much of your other work. Admittedly, many people accept shoddy workmanship, but such errors will reflect poorly on you, your work, and your firm.

Table 9-1 shows that Moody's goes down only to the rating of "C." However, when the rating designations were first used in 1909, Moody's had even lower ratings. Issues in the "C" to "Caa" classes were speculative, with moderate to little security of principal. Issues rated "Daa," "Da," and "D" were described as "of doubtful nature

Table 9-1

Moody's	S&P	Fitch	D&P	MCM	Meaning
Investment Grade—High Creditworthiness					
Aaa	AAA	AAA	1	AAA	Gilt edge, prime, maximum safety
Aa1	AA+	AA+	2	AA+	
Aa2	AA	AA	3	AA	Very high grade, high quality
Aa3	AA−	AA−	4	AA−	
A1	A+	A+	5	A+	
A2	A	A	6	A	Upper medium grade
A3	A−	A−	7	A−	
Baa1	BBB+	BBB+	8	BBB+	
Baa2	BBB	BBB	9	BBB	Lower medium grade
Baa3	BBB−	BBB−	10	BBB−	
Distinctly Speculative—Low Creditworthiness					
Ba1	BB−	BB−	11	BB+	
Ba2	BB	BB	12	BB	Low grade, speculative
Ba3	BB−	BB−	13	BB−	
B1	B+	B+	14		
B2	B	B	15	B	Highly speculative
B3	B−	B−	16		
Predominantly Speculative—Lower Grade or Default Situations					
	CCC+				
Caa	CCC	CCC	17		Substantial risk,
	CCC−				in poor standing
Ca	CC	CC			May be in default, highly speculative
C	C	C			Extremely speculative;
	CI				CI = Income bonds—no interest is being paid
		DDD			Default
		DD		DD	
	D	D			

Note: Preferred stock rating symbols are the same, except that Moody's symbols are all lowercase letters: "aaa," "aa," and so forth.

and of almost purely speculative value . . . and the differences between them are more of those of degree than of character." There was even a rating of "E," which was given to very weak or defaulted issues, many of the latter awaiting reorganization. Stock ratings at that time used the same symbols as bonds and covered all types of equity, from guaranteed issues that might be in a stronger position than some bond issues to preferreds and junior equity. Preferred ratings went as low as "F." Issues rated "Daa," "Da," and "D" were "usually of very doubtful value, in danger in many cases of the vicissitudes of reorganization, assessment paying, or scaling down in principal." Issues rated "E" or "F" were those "which, through reorganization, litigation or otherwise, are in a hopeless position with little or no value or which are already subject to some assessment which practically eliminates whatever value they may have previously enjoyed."[9]

Limitations on the Uses of Ratings

Ratings are only a guide to the so-called "credit quality" of an issue. They are not "buy," "hold," or "sell" indicators. They will not in themselves tell if a bond issue is rich, cheap, or fairly priced. They will not indicate if the bond's price is going to go up or down. The "1," "3," "+," and "−" modifiers are not signals pointing the way to an upgrade or downgrade. Many issues at the upper end of a rating category might be on their way down and others at the lower end in an uptrend. The issue's ranking in the capital structure (subordinated or senior, secured or unsecured) is taken into account for rating purposes, as are certain other terms and covenants affecting the protection of the lender. But other indenture features, such as call/refunding protection and sinking fund terms, generally are not factors in a rating decision and thus cannot help investors determine the issue's vulnerability to early redemption. Moody's has several paragraphs on rating limitations in its monthly *Bond Guide,* and S&P has devoted many pages to the use of ratings in its publications. The following is from Moody's *Bond Guide* for July 1986:

Bonds carrying the same rating are not claimed to be of absolutely equal quality. In a broad sense they are alike in position, but since there are only nine rating classes used in grading thousands of bonds, the symbols cannot reflect the fine shadings of risks which actually exist. Therefore, it should be evident to the user of ratings that two bonds identically rated are unlikely to be precisely the same in investment quality.

As ratings are designed exclusively for the purpose of grading bonds according to their investment qualities, they should not be used alone as a basis for investment operations. For example, they have no value in forecasting the direction of future trends of market price. Market price movements in bonds are influenced not only by the quality of individual issues but also by changes in money rates, and general economic trends, as well as by the length of maturity, etc. During its life even the best quality bond may have wide price movements, while its high investment status remains unchanged.

The matter of market price has no bearing whatsoever on the determination of ratings which are not to be construed as recommendations with respect to "attractiveness." The attractiveness of a given bond may depend on its yield, its maturity date or other factors for which the investor may search, as well as on its investment quality, the only characteristic to which the rating refers.

Since ratings involve judgments about the future, on the one hand, and since they are used by investors as a means of protection, on the other, the effort is made in assigning ratings to look at "worst" potentialities in the "visible" future, rather than solely at the past record and the status of the present. Therefore, investors using the ratings should not expect to find in them a reflection of statistical factors alone, since they are an appraisal of long term risks, including the recognition of non-statistical factors.

Why Ratings Are Important to Market Participants

Sound investment management requires that definite standards be applied in the selection of securities. This is true for equities as well as bonds and for institutions as well as individuals. As Charles D. Ellis states:

In investment management, the real opportunity to achieve superior results is not in scrambling to outperform the market, but in establishing and adhering to appropriate investment policies over the long term—policies that position the portfolio to benefit from riding with the main long-term forces in the market. Investment policy, wisely formulated by realistic and well-informed clients with a long-term perspective and clearly defined objectives, is the foundation upon which portfolios should be constructed and managed over time and through market cycles.[10]

Despite their limitations, ratings are important to market participants for several reasons. Many institutions and governmental bodies have established investment parameters that allow them to invest in corporate bonds of only certain quality levels, namely in the investment-grade range (the four highest rankings). Of course, there may be additional criteria as part of the overall portfolio or investment policies. Some institutions look upon Baa/BBB issues as semi–investment grade and thus are restricted to the top three grades. In a number of cases, the investment guidelines may allow a small portion of the investment portfolio to be in non-investment-grade issues, but most of the bonds must be of respectable quality. This allowance for non-investment-grade issues is often called a "basket clause."

S&P has determined that qualified investments for "AAA"-rated structured financings can include, among many others, obligations rated "AAA."[11] The commercial paper rates in the *Statistical Release H.15 (519)* of the Board of Governors of the Federal Reserve System are those placed by companies whose bond ratings are "AA" or the equivalent. Many mutual funds and investment companies have limitations on their investments that are based on debt ratings of Moody's and/or S&P, for both short-term defensive purposes and longer-term investment. A number of years ago, the Comptroller of the Currency issued regulations governing the bond investments of banks under its control. Bonds thus eligible for investment were those in the top four investment grades.

A lower rating on a bond or preferred stock means that it will cost the issuer more to raise funds than if the security were rated higher because of the increased risk of default as one moves down the quality ladder, all other things being equal. It only makes sense that investors want to get paid more for taking on additional risk, and ratings are an indication of that risk. Ratings are also important to issuers, as a lower rating may mean that the security may not even come to market. In May 1970, Standard & Poor's Corporation rated "BB" the proposed $100 million debt offering of Pennsylvania Company, a real estate company in the Penn Central System. The deal never made it to the market and was another event leading up to the subsequent bankruptcy filing of Penn Central.

Ratings are also important in determining the value of an investment-grade, fixed-income instrument. The value of a bond is determined by a number of factors. One is the yield curve, i.e., the maturity of the issue, its coupon, and the level of interest rates using U.S. Treasury issues as the benchmark. Another is the bond's redemption features, including call and/or refunding protection, or lack thereof, and the sinking fund. This affects the length of time the investment may be in one's portfolio and one's expectations of the flow of income from the bond. Finally, the actual or perceived quality of the bond issue must be reflected in its valuation. As mentioned earlier, increased default risk means that investors will want a higher yield. If analysis reveals that the issue may be upgraded, people might value the bond at a higher price. If it appears vulnerable to downgrading, investors will want the bonds at a lower price (higher yield). Other factors include the amount outstanding, how much of a sinking fund issue is controlled by a few investors, whether or not it is listed on a major stock exchange, whether it is a public or privately placed issue, and whether it is a foreign or domestic issue. These factors affect the liquidity and marketability of the bond and thus what investors and traders are willing to pay for it.

After the issue's quality and expected trends in the rating, its vulnerability to premature redemption, and its place on the yield curve have been determined, a value will be given to the bond. Depending on the issue, it might be assigned a valuation of 275 basis points above the level of the Treasury yield curve at a similar maturity date. Another issue with only slightly different terms might be valued at 265 basis points above the yield curve. Thus, at that time the two issues should trade at a spread of 10 basis points. If the actual spread is different, a trade might be accomplished by selling the richer bond and buying the cheaper one. Investors constantly compare one bond with another since bond investment is, to a great extent, based on relative valuation.

Finally, what about split ratings—ratings that differ between the two major rating agencies? As we saw in Figures 9–2a through 9–2d, the Moody and S&P ratings are often the same, which accounts for the narrowness of the spread between the two. But differences of opinion do occur. As Ederington says,

> We find that in general split ratings represent random differences of opinion on issues whose credit worthiness is close to the borderline between ratings. The respective positions of the two agencies could easily have been reversed; i.e., on another day or with a slightly different set of analysts, either agency might assign a different rating. In only a decided minority of cases do splits appear to represent a more fundamental difference of opinion, and in those cases the differences appear to be with respect to aspects of the issue other than public accounting information.
>
> ... therefore, split ratings evince the complexity and subjectivity of bond creditworthiness evaluations and it is this subjectivity that leads most users to demand a second rating.[12]

Split ratings do affect what investors are willing to pay for bonds. A study on split ratings and reoffering yields on new debt issues appeared in *Financial Management* in the summer of 1985. It concluded:

> The paper's empirical analysis reveals that the reoffering yields on split-rated bonds are not significantly different from the yields on the lower rating involved in the split while they are significantly different from the yields on the higher rating involved in that same split. It thus appears that investors' perceptions of the true default risk of a split-rated issue are more accurately represented by the lower of the two ratings ... "[13]

Therefore, in doing bond value analysis, split ratings must be taken into consideration.

APPENDIX

Debt and Preferred Stock Rating Definitions

Standard & Poor's Bond Guide bases its bond ratings primarily on the following factors:

I. Likelihood of default-capacity and willingness of the obligor as to the timely payment of interest and repayment of principal in accordance with the terms of the obligation;

II. Nature and provisions of the obligation;

III. Protection afforded by, and relative position of, the obligation in the event of bankruptcy, reorganization or other arrangement under the laws of bankruptcy and other laws affecting creditors' rights.

Moody's Bond Record states:

Limitations to Uses of Ratings: Bonds carrying the same rating are not claimed to be of absolutely equal quality. In a broad sense they are alike in position, but since there are only nine rating classes used in grading thousands of bonds, the symbols cannot reflect the fine shadings of risks which actually exist. Therefore, it should be evident to the user of ratings that two bonds identically rated are unlikely to be precisely the same in investment quality.

In order to use ratings properly, it is important to know the precise definitions of the rating categories—what they are and what they are not. Here we will focus on the Moody's and Standard & Poor's definitions.

DEFINTIONS OF BOND RATINGS

Moody's Investors Service

Aaa: Bonds which are rated *Aaa* are judged to be of the best quality. They carry the smallest degree of investment risk and are generally referred to as "gilt edge." Interest payments are protected by a large or by an exceptionally stable margin and principal is secure. While the various protective elements are likely to change, such changes as can be visualized are most unlikely to impair the fundamentally strong position of such issues.

Aa: Bonds which are rated *Aa* are judged to be of high quality by all standards. Together with the *Aaa* group they comprise what are generally known as high grade bonds. They are rated lower than the best bonds because margins of protection may not be as large as in *Aaa* securities or fluctuation of protective elements may be of greater amplitude or there may be other elements present which make the long term risks appear somewhat larger than in *Aaa* securities.

A: Bonds which are rated *A* possess many favorable investment attributes and are to be considered as upper medium grade obligations. Factors giving security to principal and interest are considered adequate but elements may be present which suggest a susceptibility to impairment in the future.

Baa: Bonds which are rated *Baa* are considered as medium grade obligations, i.e., they are neither highly protected nor poorly secured. Interest payments and principal security appear adequate for the present but certain protective elements may be lacking or may be characteristically unreliable over any great length of time. Such bonds lack outstanding investment characteristics and in fact have speculative characteristics as well.

Ba: Bonds which are rated *Ba* are judged to have speculative elements; their future cannot be considered as well assured. Often the protection of interest and principal payments may be very moderate and thereby not well safeguarded during both good and bad times over the future. Uncertainty of position characterizes bonds in this class.

B: Bonds which are rated *B* generally lack characteristics of the desirable investment. Assurance of interest and principal payments or of maintenance of other terms of the contract over any long period of time may be small.

Caa: Bonds which are rated Caa are of poor standing. Such issues may be in default or there may be present elements of danger with respect to principal or interest.

Ca: Bonds which are rated Ca represent obligations which are speculative in a high degree. Such issues are often in default or have other marked shortcomings.

C: Bonds which are rated C are the lowest rated class of bonds and issues so rated can be regarded as having extremely poor prospects of ever attaining any real investment standing.

In April 1982, Moody's added numerical modifiers, "1," "2," and "3," to each rating category from "Aa" through "B." The modifier "1" indicates that the security ranks in the higher end of its generic rating category; the modifier "2" indicates a mid-range ranking; and the modifier "3" indicates that the issue ranks in the lower end of its generic rating category.

Standard & Poor's Corporation

AAA: Debt rated AAA has the highest rating assigned by Standard & Poor's. Capacity to pay interest and repay principal is extremely strong.

AA: Debt rated AA has a very strong capacity to pay interest and repay principal and differs from the higher rated issues only in small degree.

A: Debt rated A has a strong capacity to pay interest and repay principal although it is somewhat more susceptible to the adverse effects of changes in circumstances and economic conditions than debt in higher rated categories.

BBB: Debt rated BBB is regarded as having an adequate capacity to pay interest and repay principal. Whereas it normally exhibits adequate protection parameters, adverse economic conditions or changing circumstances are more likely to lead to a weakened capacity to pay interest and repay principal for debt in this category than in higher rated categories.

BB: Debt rated BB has less near-term vulnerability to default than other speculative issues. However, it faces major ongoing uncertainties or exposure to adverse business, financial or economic conditions which could lead to inadequate capacity to meet timely interest and principal payments.

The BB rating category is also used for debt subordinated to senior debt that is assigned an actual or implied "BBB−" rating.

B: Debt rated B has a greater vulnerability to default but currently has the capacity to meet interest payments and principal repayments. Adverse business, financial or economic conditions will likely impair capacity or willingness to pay interest or repay principal.

The B rating category is also used for debt subordinated to senior debt that is assigned an actual or implied BB or BB− rating.

CCC: Debt rated CCC has a currently identificable vulnerability to default, and is dependent upon favorable business, financial and economic conditions to meet timely payment of interest and repayment of principal. In the event of adverse business, financial and economic conditions, it is not likely to have the capacity to pay interest and repay principal.

The CCC rating category is also used for debt subordinated to senior debt that is assigned an actual or implied B or B− rating.

CC: The rating CC is typically applied to debt subordinated to senior debt that is assigned an actual or implied CCC rating.

C: The rating C is typically applied to debt subordinated to senior debt that is assigned an actual or implied CCC− rating.

CI: The rating C is reserved for income bonds on which no interest is being paid.

D: Debt rated D is in default.

The "D" category is also used when interest payments or principal repayments are expected to be in default at the payment date and payment of interest and/or repayment of principal is in arrears.

The concept of an implied senior debt rating is critical to the interpretation of S&P's rating. This is particularly so in the junk bond sector, which is largely a subordinated debt universe. S&P rates specific debt securities rather than overall creditworthiness and generally assigns different ratings to debt securities of a single issuer based on their relative ranking in liquidation or bankruptcy. The likelihood of default, however, is virtually the same for all debt securities of a single issuer and is indicated by the senior debt rating. Likewise, the senior debt of one issuer may be rated the same as the subordinated debt of another, although the risk of default for the first is higher. For instance, senior debt rated "B+" has a higher risk of default than subordinated debt rated "B+".

If senior debt is not rated, an implied senior rating is determined. If the actual or implied senior debt rating is speculative, namely "BB+" or lower, subordinated debt, with few exceptions, will be rated two designations below the senior rating.

Plus (+) or Minus (−): The ratings from "AA" to "B" may be modified by the addition of a plus or minus sign to show relative standing within the major rating categories.

DEFINITIONS OF PREFERRED STOCK RATINGS

Moody's Investors Service

Moody's Rating Policy Review Board extended its rating services to include quality designations on preferred stock on October 1, 1973. The decision to rate preferred stock, which Moody's had done prior to 1935, was prompted by evidence of investor interest. Moody's believes that its rating of preferred stock is especially appropriate in view of the ever increasing amount of these securities outstanding and the fact that continuing inflation and its ramifications generally have resulted in the dilution of some of the protection afforded them as well as other fixed-income securities.

Because of the fundamental differences between preferred stocks and bonds, a variation of our familiar bond rating symbols is being used in the quality ranking of preferred stock. The following symbols are designed to avoid comparison with bond quality in absolute terms. It should always be borne in mind that preferred stock occupies a junior position to bonds within a particular capital structure and that these securities are rated within the universe of preferred stocks.

Moody's applies numerical modifiers "1," "2," and "3" in each rating classification. The modifier "1" indicates that the security ranks in the higher end of its generic rating category; the modifier "2" indicates a mid-range ranking; and the modifier "3" indicates that the issue ranks in the lower end of its generic rating category.

aaa: An issue which is rated "aaa" is considered to be a top-quality preferred stock. This rating indicates good asset protection and the least risk of dividend impairment within the universe of preferred stocks.

aa: An issue which is rated "aa" is considered a high-grade preferred stock. This rating indicates that there is a reasonable assurance that earnings and asset protection will remain relatively well maintained in the foreseeable future.

a: An issue which is rated "a" is considered to be an upper medium-grade preferred stock. While risks are judged to be somewhat greater than in the "aaa" and "aa" classification, earnings and asset protection are, nevertheless, expected to be maintained at adequate levels.

baa: An issue which is rated *"baa"* is considered to be a medium-grade preferred stock, neither highly protected no poorly secured. Earnings and asset protection appear adequate at present but may be questionable over any great length of time.

ba: An issue which is rated "ba" is considered to have speculative elements and its future cannot be considered well assured. Earnings and asset protection may be very moderate and not well safeguarded during adverse periods. Uncertainty of position characterizes preferred stocks in this class.

b: An issue which is rated "b" generally lacks the characteristics of a desirable investment. Assurance of dividend payments and maintenance of other terms of the issue over any long period of time may be small.

caa: An issue which is rated "caa" is likely to be in arrears on dividend payments. This rating description does not purport to indicate the future status of payments.

ca: An issue which is rated "ca" is speculative in a high degree and is likely to be in arrears on dividends with little likelihood of eventual payments.

c: This is the lowest-rated class of preferred or preference stock. Issues so rated can be regarded as having extremely poor prospects of ever attaining any real investment standing.

Standard & Poor's Corporation

A Standard & Poor's preferred stock rating assesses the capacity and willingness of the issuer to pay preferred stock dividends and any applicable sinking fund obligations. A preferred stock rating differs from a bond rating insofar as it is assigned to an equity issue, which is intrinsically different from, and subordinate to, a debt issue. Therefore, to reflect this difference the preferred stock rating symbol normally will be no higher than the rating symbol assigned to, or that would be assigned to, the senior debt of the same issuer.

AAA: This is the highest rating that may be assigned by Standard & Poor's to a preferred stock issue and indicates an extremely strong capacity to pay the preferred stock obligations.

AA: A preferred stock issue rated "AA" also qualifies as a high-quality fixed income security. The capacity to pay preferred stock obligations is very strong, although not as overwhelming as for issues rated "AAA."

A: An issue rated "A" is backed by a sound capacity to pay the preferred stock obligations, although it is somewhat more susceptible to the adverse effects of changes in circumstances and economic conditions.

BBB: An issue rated "BBB" is regarded as backed by an adequate capacity to pay the preferred stock obligations. Whereas it normally exhibits adequate protection parameters, adverse economic conditions or changing circumstances are more likely to lead to a weakened capacity to make payments for a preferred stock in this category than for issues in the "A" category.

BB, B, CCC: Preferred stock rated "BB," "B," and "CCC" are regarded, on balance, as predominantly speculative with respect to the issuer's capacity to pay preferred stock obligations. "BB" indicates the lowest degree of speculation and "CCC" the highest degree of speculation. While such issues will likely have some quality and protective characteristics, these are outweighed by large uncertainties or major risk exposures to adverse conditions.

CC: The rating "CC" is reserved for a preferred stock issue in arrears on dividends or sinking fund payments but that is currently paying.

C: A preferred stock rated "C" is a non-paying issue.

D: A preferred stock rated "D" is a non-paying issue with the issuer in default on debt instruments.

NR indicates that no rating has been requested, that there is insufficient information on which to base a rating, or that S&P does not rate a particular type of obligation as a matter of policy.

Plus (+) or Minus (−): To provide more detailed indications of preferred stock quality, the ratings from "AA" to "B" may be modified by the addition of a plus or minus sign to show relative standing within the major rating categories.

NOTES

1. For further information on the background of Moody's and Standard & Poor's, see *120 Years of Preserving the "Right to Know"*, published around 1984 by S&P, and *Credit Analysis for the Global Capital Markets*, printed in 1986 by Moody's. Also quite helpful is a speech, "Fifty Year Review of Moody's Investors Service," given by John Moody, chairman, in early 1950. I appreciate the assistance of Mr. Harold H. Goldberg of Moody's in obtaining a copy of this speech for me. Some of the other background information for this part of the chapter was obtained from early issues of the various manuals, including the sections with advertisements of banks, brokers, and financial publishers.

2. Poor's had acquired that right and combined it with the old John Moody & Company in 1919, but the Moody name could be used only in a limited way—namely as a partial label on the title page in Poor's manuals. The manuals were titled *Moody's Manual of Railroads and Corporation Securities*. For instance, the 1914 edition was published by Moody Manual Company and the 1923 edition by Poor's Publishing Company.

3. See the 1985 promotional brochure describing Fitch Investors Service for additional details about its organization. I am grateful to Richard D. Cacchione, Presi-

dent of Fitch, for a copy of his paper "Rating Agencies in Developing Capital Markets," presented in July 1986 at the XI Annual Conference of the International Association of Securities Commissions.

4. Kiril Sokoloff and Joan Matthews, *Standard & Poor's Ratings Guide* (New York: McGraw-Hill, 1979).

5. Harold H. Goldberg, "Corporate Bond Market Outlook 1986," *Moody's Bond Survey*, February 10, 1986; 7677–7683. The term "decapitalization" is defined here as "those management actions which result in a leveraging of company financials following treasury stock purchases, leveraged buyouts, or acquisitions financed through borrowings. It is not intended to include events such as asset write-offs or operating losses."

6. McCarthy, Crisanti & Maffei, Inc., *Recent Trends in Corporate Bond Ratings*, January 1986.

7. Robert L. Simison and Karen Blumenthal, "LTV Corp. Files for Protection from Creditors under Chapter 11," *The Wall Street Journal*, July 18, 1986, 3.

8. Ileen Malitz, "On Financial Contracting: The Determinants of Bond Covenants," *Financial Management*, vol. 15, no. 2, Summer 1986, 21.

9. John Moody, *Moody's Analyses of Railroad Investments Containing in Detailed Form an Expert Comparative Analysis of Each of the Railroad Systems of the United States, with Careful Deductions, Enabling the Banker and Investor to Ascertain the True Values of Securities by a Method Based on Scientific Principles* (New York: Analyses Publishing, 1910).

10. Charles D. Ellis, *Investment Policy: How to Win the Loser's Game* (Homewood, Ill.: Dow Jones-Irwin, 1985).

11. Standard & Poor's *CreditWeek*, July 14, 1986, 7.

12. Louis H. Ederington, "Why Split Ratings Occur," *Financial Management*, vol. 15, no. 1, Spring 1986, 46.

13. Randall S. Billingsley, Robert E. Lamy, M. Wayne Marr, and G. Rodney Thompson, "Split Ratings and Bond Reoffering Yields," *Financial Management*, vol. 14, no. 2, Spring 1985, 65.

CHAPTER 10

FINANCIAL STATEMENT
ANALYSIS

This chapter reviews some of the financial ratios used in debt and preferred stock analysis for two of the larger segments of corporate issuers, namely industrial and electric utility companies. The analysis of financial statements cannot be learned overnight, as it is part of a long process involving accounting, statistics, and securities analysis courses. This chapter gives an overview of some of the more important quantitative measurements.

INTRODUCTION

It should be apparent by now that a bond quality rating is not based entirely on financial ratios or statistics; the quality of management, the economics of the industry, the company's near- to intermediate-term outlook, and the legal provisions of the debt instrument are also important considerations. In their classic work *Security Analysis,* Graham, Dodd, and Cottle devote several chapters to the selection of fixed-income securities. Bond investors and analysts would do well to review these pages every few years.[1]

Graham, Dodd, and Cottle point out that the bond form is basically less attractive than other issue categories since it offers a limited return (in most cases, that is, excluding equity and commodity indexed debt). *Selection must emphasize the avoidance of loss and is thus a negative art.* It is a process of exclusion and rejection rather than of search and acceptance. The authors give four principles that are applicable to the selection of bonds:

1. Safety is measured not by specific lien or other contractual rights but by the *ability* of the issuer to meet *all* of its obligations.
2. This ability should be measured under conditions of recession or depression rather than prosperity.
3. Deficient safety cannot be compensated for by an abnormally high coupon rate alone.
4. The selection of all *senior* securities for investment should be subject to the rules of exclusion and to specific quantitative tests.

All fixed-income investors should have criteria for investment purposes, not only for their overall portfolios but for individual issues as well. Many portfolio managers and bond investors have some guidelines, such as refusing to buy "sin bonds" (bonds of companies in the tobacco and alcoholic beverage industries), refusing to buy bonds of companies doing business with or in the Republic of South Africa or the Soviet Union and its captive states, or insisting that the issues of any one company not comprise more than 3 to 5 percent of the portfolio. But investors should also look into minimum standards for individual issues. While many use only ratings as guides for issue investment, this is probably insufficient. By relying solely on the ratings of an outside party, portfolio managers abrogate their own responsibility for making investment judgments on issuer quality. Many would feel that they had invested by the rules if they stayed within the rating guidelines even if the issue was downgraded soon after. Independent analysis might have revealed some deterioration in the credit that could have signaled prudent investors to avoid the issuer. Of course, portfolio managers can always pass the buck to the rating agency by claiming they satisfied the investment criteria. While this argument may satisfy some, portfolio trustees, beneficiaries, sponsors, and others may find it of little merit. Portfolio managers are responsible for running investments according to the rules established by the sponsors, and some of those rules should be issue and issuer specific.

Other criteria might include minimum company size and profitability, with the latter measured over a period of at least five years, and possibly more, to include one complete business cycle. Looking at the financial statements of many companies for a five- to ten-year period often can be quite revealing. Of course, many common stock analysts use only a two- or three-year historical review at best. Bond investors and analysts should not allow themselves to fall into that category of surface analysis. Certain specific tests might be required, such as coverage of interest charges being at least a specific ratio for four out of the last five years. Debt might be restricted to not more than a certain percentage of the capitalization, again over a period of several years. Satisfaction of minimal cash flow standards and asset tests should be required.

These minimum standards cannot be the same for all issuers, as industries differ in their measurements, standards, or averages. A minimum interest coverage ratio of 3 times might be satisfactory for certain industrial companies, but it would be much too stringent for debt of some good financial institutions. Oil companies will have different levels of financial parameters than retailers.[2] Allowance must be made for these differences, particularly for companies that are showing meaningful improvement in their financial measurements and operations. Investments in those issuers might be allowed up to a certain percentage of the portfolio, such as a 10 percent basket for companies that are improving but do not entirely satisfy the other requirements. Finally, one must not forget the terms of the issue. One may wish to prohibit investment in a company's junior debt if the issuer barely meets some of the established quantitative tests. The subordinated debt of a strong issuer may provide incremental return without any threat to the portfolio's safety. The higher return from the subordinated debt of a weak issuer may not be enough to offset any principal loss due to downgradings or financial distress.

To summarize, bonds are securities with limited returns, and fixed-income analysis is a negative art. Bond portfolio managers get paid for avoiding losses that are preventable; they don't get paid for being heroes with other peoples' funds that have been entrusted to them.

RATIO DEFINITIONS

We will first look at the financial ratios of industrial companies in general and then move into electric utilities.

The financial ratios described in the following sections are used by many analysts of senior securities. Although few analysts have exactly the same definition for each ratio, it is important that they be consistent when making comparisons among companies and use the same methodology in calculating the financial ratios. Using ratios as a comparative measurement when they have been calculated differently may be misleading and result in adverse investment consequences. Investment portfolio managers should be particularly careful when using certain financial ratios and data they have received in the process of a transaction, especially when time is short. The information may have come from different sources. The purpose may have been to speed up the trade, and no harm may be done; in some cases, however, the purpose may be to deceive the manager so as to close the trade quickly. Professional bond managers would do well to compare the ratio definitions used by their own analysts with those of the analysts at the investment banking firms serving them so that any discrepancies may be ironed out. *Caveat emptor.*

Leverage and Capitalization Ratios

Pretax Interest Coverage

$$\frac{\text{Net income before extraordinary items + Gross interest}}{\text{Gross interest expense + total income taxes + Minority interest −}}{\text{Gross interest expense}}$$

This formula can also be simply stated as *EBIT/I*, which means earnings before interest and taxes divided by interest.

We adjust net income so as to eliminate the effects of capitalized interest while we add back capitalized interest to interest charges to get gross interest charges. The use of capitalized interest reduces interest charges and increases net income. However, a corporation's liability is for gross interest charges, not for the lower figure of interest charges reduced by capitalized interest. Also, the financial statements will often show an interest charge figure from which interest income has been deducted; the analyst must adjust for this other income.

The following is from the Report of the Committee on Finance of the United States Senate concerning the Tax Reform Act of 1986:[3]

> Interest on debt must be capitalized if such debt is incurred or continued to finance the construction or production of (1) real property . . . , or (2) other property with a class life of 20 years or more . . . if the property is to be used by the taxpayer in its trade or business or an activity for profit.
>
> . . . any interest expense that would have been avoided if production or construction expenditures had been used to repay indebtedness of the taxpayer is treated as construction period interest subject to capitalization. Accordingly, under the bill, debt that can be specifically traced to production or construction expenditures first must be allocated to production or construction.

The report states that under Financial Accounting Standards Board Statement Number 34, "interest expense that could have been avoided includes interest costs incurred by reason of additional borrowings to finance construction, and interest costs incurred by reason of borrowings that could have been repaid with funds expended for construction." This is, in effect, the opportunity cost of funds.

Companies that have heavy rental payments for leased facilities, such as supermarket chains and many retailers, require another coverage measure, one that takes into account rental payments in addition to interest payments. Therefore, to both the numerator and denominator of the interest coverage ratio we add rental expense. The Securities and Exchange Commission adds one-third of rentals, but many companies prefer to use total rentals in order to get a more accurate measurement of the protection afforded the debtholder. To many, rents are a form of debt and fixed charges. After all, if you pay only one-third of your rental payments, you get to use only one-third of the rental property, and you may wind up in court as the defendant in a lawsuit by plaintiffs seeking to get the full rental payment that was originally agreed upon.

The coverage of preferred stock dividends will be taken up in the section on electric utility companies. Preferred stock is much less important in the industrial area and dividend requirements are small, especially when compared with utilities.

Total Capital

Short-term notes + Debt due within one year + Long-term debt + Minority interest + Preferred stock + Common equity + Surplus

Long-term debt is comprised of debt and related obligations due in more than one year, including long-term lease obligations (capitalized leases), bonds, mortgages, debentures, notes, and similar debt and all other obligations that require interest payments (or, in the case of zero coupons bond, the accretion of the interest factor). Short-term debt is debt and similar obligations due within one year, including current maturities of long-term debt, bank loans, and commercial paper borrowings. When looking at companies in bankruptcy, short-term debt will often appear to be quite large as an act of default frequently accelerates the maturity of all debt, making it due and payable immediately.

Net Tangible Assets/Long-Term Debt

$$\frac{\text{Total assets} - (\text{Intangibles} + \text{Current liabilities} + \text{Deferred taxes and investment tax credits} + \text{Other liabilities} + \text{Minority interest})}{\text{Long-term debt}}$$

This ratio is an indication of the asset protection afforded the debtholders of a company. It is expressed as a percentage; thus, "412.92 percent" means that for every dollar of long-term debt outstanding there is nearly $4.13 of tangible assets. Intangibles such as patents and copyrights are often excluded even though they may have some real value. This ratio is based on the book values of the assets. Often, by the time a corporation has arrived at the brink of financial distress or declared bankruptcy, the assets have been dissipated, and the ratio might be less meaningful. One example is the book value of the assets of many steel companies; it is doubtful that they are really worth what the accounting books say they are, especially when the assets cannot produce a profit. On the other hand, book values can be understated, especially in the case of some natural resource companies and others with significant real estate and tangible assets that might have been purchased many years ago at significantly lower prices. While many asset values increase during an inflationary period, they can also decrease at other times, as was the case in the petroleum industry in 1985 and early 1986. A number of companies had to revalue their properties downward due to the great decline in oil prices over the preceding few years.

Another ratio that is essentially similar is tangible shareholders' equity plus long-term debt divided by long-term debt. Here we subtract all intangible assets from net worth to get tangible net worth or tangible shareholders' equity.

Cash Flow/Long-Term Debt

$$\frac{\text{Total funds from operations}}{\text{Long-term debt}}$$

Cash flow is the lifeblood of a company; it is what pays the debt service, capital outlays, and dividends. It is simply net income plus noncash charges and is modified by some. We use total funds from operations, which is basically the sum of net income, extraordinary items, deferred taxes, and depreciation minus unremitted earnings of unconsolidated subsidiaries. Generally, the higher the figure, the better the protection for the debtholder. The ratio is an indication of the cash available from operations and that could be used to service the debt. In 1985, the 57 rated industrial companies used to calculate the ratios in Table 10–3 had a cash flow to long-term debt ratio (on a composite basis) of 109.51 percent, indicating that cash flow for the year was slightly more than 1 times the outstanding long-term debt; a year earlier, the ratio for the same group of companies had been

125.22 percent. Some analysts use the reciprocal of the ratio, that is, divide debt by cash flow. In this case, the figure would be 91.32 percent for 1985 and 79.86 percent for 1984. This implies that the long-term debt theoretically could be repaid in approximately 11 months (10 months in 1984) from cash flow. Obviously, the timing of the cash flow stream is not the same for each month of the year.

There are other definitions of cash flow that some analysts may wish to use. To the above traditional definition one may adjust for changes in working capital. Lower accounts receivable and higher accounts payable mean additional cash and cash flow. Increases in inventory and accounts receivable mean a reduction in a company's cash flow. Others would exclude capital expenditures from cash flow, thus getting a sort of discretionary cash flow figure (assuming that capital expenditures are not discretionary; some are and some are not).

Gentry, Newbold, and Whitford analyzed the various components of cash inflows and outflows in a study on predicting bankruptcy.[4] They pointed out that the components that are sources of funds include operations and financial or net financing flow component (change in capitalization from the sale or retirement of stocks and bonds). Components that are uses of funds include working capital, fixed coverage expenses (or interest and lease payments), capital expenditures, dividends, other asset and liability flows, and changes in cash and marketable securities. The sources and uses of funds may be positive or negative. The study found, among other things, that healthy firms invested more in capital equipment than firms in distress, that firms in distress suffered a "shortfall in inflows from operations, which forced a reduction in dividend payments," and weak firms were reducing the levels of receivables to create an inflow of cash.[5] As time goes on, corporate bond market analysts will pay increasing attention to the lifeblood of American industry. (Maybe some equity analysts will also jump on the bandwagon!)

Liquidity Ratios

Current Ratio

$$\frac{\text{Current assets}}{\text{Current liabilities}}$$

The ratio for the 57 "Aaa"/"AAA" companies composite in Table 10–3 is 1.41 times for 1985, indicating that for every dollar of current liabilities (those obligations such as loans, commercial paper, accounts payable, and taxes that are due within one year) there is $1.41 of current assets. Current assets are cash and similar liquid items, short-term investments such as commercial paper and certificates of deposit, accounts receivable, and inventory, namely those items that can very easily be turned into cash without any diminution in value. Traditionally, a ratio of 2:1 has been considered the norm for American industrial concerns, but in the last decade or so there have been few times that a rating category achieved this level. Also, because industries have varying working capital requirements, what is a satisfactory ratio for one industry or company may not be so for another.

The difference between current assets and current liabilities is called working capital. Going back 50 years to the first edition of Graham and Dodd, we see that they suggest that working capital be at least equal to the amount of long-term debt. In the 1976 through 1985 period, only the "Aaa"/"AAA" companies had an average working capital to long-term debt exceeding 100 percent; it was 147.52 percent. The "Aa2"/"AA" average was 92.14 percent, "A2"/"A" 84.99 percent, and "Baa2"/"BBB" figure 77.83 percent.

Quick Ratio

$$\frac{\text{Cash and equivalents} + \text{Receivables}}{\text{Current liabilities}}$$

The quick ratio is also known as the *acid test ratio*. Basically cash and equivalents plus current receivables—generally highly liquid items or "near" cash—the ratio indicates the borrower's ability to meet its current obligations.

Profitability Ratios

Pre-tax Margin

$$\frac{\text{Pre-tax net income before minority interest}}{\text{Net sales}}$$

The pre-tax margin, also known as the *margin of safety,* was widely used years ago in analyzing railroad securities. Representing the percentage of revenues (sales) remaining after all expenses, including fixed charges, have been paid, it indicates how far sales or revenues could decline (assuming expenses remained the same) before coverage of fixed charges became jeopardized. The higher the margin of safety, the greater the bondholder's protection against the effects of a decline in revenues. This assumes that all other expenses remain the same but, when revenues fall off, some other expenses may also decline. Nevertheless, this is an interesting ratio that analysts are advised to use more often, especially in the speculative-grade area. The pre-tax margin for the 57 companies on a composite basis is 10.8 percent for 1985, down from 14.44 percent for the same group in 1984. The preliminary prospectus dated February 19, 1986, for Macy Merger Corporation shows a margin of safety based on the summary consolidated forecast data for 1987 of *only* −0.67 percent. Amazingly, it is predicted to improve each year through 1996, from 0.34 percent in 1988 to 7.17 percent in 1996. These are still slim numbers indicating the risks that debtholders of the company might face, especially in view of the observation made earlier that the business cycle has not been repealed or replaced by permanent prosperity. There was talk about the repeal of the business cycle in the early sixties, but even the politicians of that time could not hold back the tides of nature.

Available Income as a Percentage of Sales (or of Total Assets)

$$\frac{\text{Income available for interest charges}}{\text{Sales or total assets}}$$

This ratio measures the profitability of a corporation, indicating the income available for the payment of gross interest charges derived from sales or earned on assets.

The following two ratios show what the company is earning on the investment of the common shareholders and on the invested capital of all investors (equity and debt).

After-tax Rate of Return on Average Common Equity

$$\frac{\text{Net income} - \text{Preferred dividends}}{\text{Average common equity}}$$

Pre-tax Rate of Return on Average Total Capital

$$\frac{\text{Interest expense} + \text{Income taxes} + \text{Income before extraordinary}}{\text{items} + \text{minority interest}}$$
$$\frac{}{\text{Average total capital}}$$

Miscellaneous Ratios

Cash Flow/Capital Expenditures

$$\frac{\text{Total funds from operations}}{\text{Capital expenditures}}$$

Capital expenditures are those outlays used for additions to a corporation's plant and property but excluding amounts for the acquisition of other companies. This ratio indicates a company's ability to finance its plant and equipment expenditures from current operations. Cash flow (funds from operations) is before any dividend payments. Retained cash flow is obtained by subtracting dividend payments (both common and preferred) from the funds from operations.

The following seven ratios are probably the more important ones used in corporate bond quality analysis:

1. Pre-tax interest coverage
2. Debt as a percentage of total capital
3. Working capital as a percentage of long-term debt
4. Long-term debt as a percentage of net plant
5. Net tangible assets as a percentage of long-term debt
6. Cash flow as a percentage of long-term debt
7. Pre-tax rate of return on average total capital

Other analysts may have their own favorite ratios that are not in-cluded in the above listing. However, it cannot be overemphasized that financial ratios are not the last word when it comes to rating bonds and determining their suitability as investments; there are many other factors to consider.

FINANCIAL RATIOS OF INDUSTRIAL COMPANIES, 1976–1985.

The industrial companies used in Tables 10-1, 10-2, and 10-3 are those whose senior public debt was rated straight "Aaa"/"AAA," "Aa2"/"AA," "A2/A," and "Baa2"/"BBB" at the end of each of the last 10 years. Excluded are those companies that carried a rating modifier ("1" or "3," "+" or "−"). Not all the companies that carried a particular rating have been included, chiefly because of the un-availability of data and the fact that the data were presented in a manner not consistent with the author's computer program.[6] How-ever, in the author's opinion, the ratios presented are representative for the rating categories.

The above-mentioned rating categories have been used so that the data will be based on those credits for which there was some un-animity of opinion between the two most widely recognized rating services. A split rating can occur for any number of reasons, includ-ing the timing of the rating change. Thus, a company rated "Aa2"/"AA" on November 30 could be "A2"/"AA" on December 31 and "A2"/"A" two weeks later. This split rating reflects not a basic dif-ference of opinion on the credit standing of the company but only a small timing difference. However, there are cases where the split rating is based on a major difference of opinion between the raters. But it must be remembered that there are numerous instances in which qualified individuals look at the same data, interview the same management, and have similar in-depth professional knowl-edge of the topic yet still arrive at different conclusions.

The number of companies used in the ratio analysis for 1985 declined to 57, down from 60 in 1984, 72 in 1983, and a peak of 167 in 1980. The rating modifiers allow for fewer issuers to be within the mid-range rating criteria. The 57 companies had combined revenues of $435.4 billion and net income of $27.5 billion for fiscal 1985. Total assets were $367.8 billion and total capitalization of $224.2 billion. Capital was comprised of $68.4 billion of debt, $2.3 billion of minority interest, $1.8 billion of preferred stock, and $171.6 billion of common equity.[7]

The annual ratios for each category shown in Table 10-3 are based on a composite income statement and balance sheet, in effect making one giant company out of many smaller ones. Thus, the composite ratios are not averages of ratios but a picture of how, for example, the nine "Aaa"/"AAA" companies for 1985 look as a whole. It should come as no surprise that the average "Aaa"/"AAA" company is considerably larger than the average "Aa2"/"AA" concern. Table 10-1b shows that the average triple-A company has 3.65 times the revenues of the average double-A industrial issuer, that net income is 5.49 times greater, and total assets 4.08 times as much. As one descends the quality scale, the company size generally gets smaller and the firm less strong financially. In the summary of *Corporate Bond Quality and Investor Experience*, W. Braddock Hickman states:

> Market values generally reflect a preference for the power and financial stength of large corporations as distinguished from smaller ones of similar quality standards, and for the liquidity which is provided by larger issues of bonds. Default rates and loss rates were lower for larger issues than for smaller ones.[8]

Table 10-1 shows some selected income statement and balance sheet figures for an average company in each category and their relationship to lower-rated issuers for fiscal 1985. The "Baa2"/ "BBB" category has been distorted slightly in the past couple of years by the inclusion of the giant USX Corporation (formerly known as the United States Steel Corporation). The category may continue to average greater than "A2"/"A"-rated companies for a while as more large firms are downgraded.

Table 10-2 summarizes the rating categories that posted year-to-year improvement in fourteen selected financial ratios since 1976. Thus, in 1985, most of the rating categories showed worse results than in 1984.

Table 10-3 shows the 33 groupings of financial ratios and statis-

Table 10-1 Selected Data on Industrial Corporations, 1985
($ Millions)

| | Issuer Category | | | |
	Aaa/AAA	Aa2/AA	A2/A	Baa2/BBB
Revenues	$25,529	$6,986	$3,049	$3,956
Net income	2,047	373	134	79
Cash flow	3,975	543	302	287
Total assets	22,528	5,526	2,452	3,270
Total debt	2,585	1,347	685	1,096
Common equity	11,406	2,492	1,068	980
Total capital	14,163	3,880	1,774	2,239

Table 10–1b
Relative Size Comparison
(Rating Category to Rating Category)

	Aaa/AAA to Aa2/AA	Aa2/AA to A2/A	A2/A to Baa2/BBB
Revenues	3.65 ×	2.29 ×	0.77 ×
Net income	5.49	2.78	1.70
Cash flow	7.32	1.80	1.05
Total assets	4.08	2.25	0.75
Total debt	1.92	1.97	0.63
Common equity	4.58	2.33	1.09
Total capital	3.65	2.19	0.79

Table 10–2
Rating categories posting year-to-year
Improvement in Selected Financial Ratios

Ratio	1985/1984	1984/1983	1983/1982
Fixed charge coverage	A	Aaa, Aa, Baa	All
Total debt to capital	None	Aaa, Aa	Aaa, Aa, A
Short-term debt to total debt	A	Aa	Aaa
Working capital to long-term debt	A	Aaa, Aa, A	Aaa, Aa, Baa
Long-term debt to plant	Aaa	Aaa, Aa, Baa	Aaa, Aa, A
Net tangible assets to long-term debt	None	Aaa, Aa, A	Aaa, Aa, A

Table 10-2 (*continued*)

Ratio	1985/1984	1984/1983	1983/1982
Cash flow to long-term			
debt	Baa	All	Aaa, Aa, A
Current ratio	A	Aaa, Aa, A	Aaa, Aa, Baa
Pre-tax margin	None	All	All
Available income as			
percent of:			
Sales	None	All	All
Assets	None	All	All
Rate of return on:			
Common	A	Aaa, Aa, Baa	All
Total capital	A	All	All
Retained cash flow to			
capital expenditures	Aa	A, Baa	All

Ratio	1982/1981	1981/1980	1980/1979
Fixed charge coverage	None	Baa	None
Total debt to capital	Aaa	Aa, Baa	Aaa, A
Short-term debt to			
total debt	All	Baa	All
Working capital to			
long-term debt	None	Aa, Baa	None
Long-term debt to plant	Aaa, Aa, Baa	Aaa, A, Baa	Aaa, A
Net tangible assets to			
long-term debt	None	Aa, A, Baa	Aaa, A
Cash flow to long-term			
debt	None	A, Baa	Aaa
Current ratio	A	Aa, Baa	A
Pre-tax margin	None	Aaa, Baa	None
Available income as			
percent of:			
Sales	A	Aaa, Baa	None
Assets	None	Aaa, Baa	None
Rate of return on:			
Common	None	Aaa, Baa	None
Total capital	None	Aaa, Baa	Aaa
Retained cash flow to			
capital expenditures	Aaa	Baa	None

(*continued*)

Table 10-2 (*continued*)

Ratio	1979/1978	1978/1977	1977/1976
Fixed charge coverage	Aaa, Aa	Aa, A, Baa	Aaa
Total debt to capital	Aaa, Aa, Baa	Aaa, Aa	Aaa, Aa
Short-term debt to total debt	Aaa	Aa, A	A
Working capital to long-term debt	Baa	Aaa, Aa	Aaa
Long-term debt to plant	All	Aaa, Aa	Aaa, Aa, Baa
Net tangible assets to long-term debt	All	Aaa, Aa	Aaa, A
Cash flow to long-term debt	All	All	Aaa, Aa
Current ratio	None	Baa	Aaa, Baa
Pre-tax margin	Aaa, Aa	Aa, A, Baa	Aaa
Available income as percent of:			
Sales	Aaa, Aa	Aa, A, Baa	Aaa
Assets	Aaa, Aa, Baa	Aa, A, Baa	Aaa, Aa
Rate of return on:			
Common	All	All	Aaa, Aa, Baa
Total capital	All	Aa, A, Baa	Aaa, Aa
Retained cash flow to capital expenditures	Baa	Aaa, Aa, A	Aa

Note: The Moody modifier of "2" has been left out due to space considerations.

tics for the composite rankings from 1976 through 1985. Where applicable the 10-year average, the standard deviation, and the high and low for each ratio are shown. The last column (standard of deviation divided by the average) is a measure of relative dispersion, or coefficient of dispersion, and relates the standard deviation to the mean, or average. For example, in the "Aaa"/"AAA" category, the average coverage was 13.07 times for the 10-year period and the standard deviation was 1.34. In a normal distribution, approximately 68.3 percent of items would fall within a range of +1 or −1 standard deviation from the mean, or between 14.44 and 11.73 times. In the "Aa2"/"AA" category, the average coverage is 7.26 times with a standard deviation of 1.80 (the range of +1 or −1 standard deviation

Table 10-3
Financial Ratios of American Industrial Companies, 1976-1985

ALLRATIO.SSF	1985	1984	1983	1982	1981	1980	1979	1978	1977	1976	TEN-YEAR AVERAGE	STANDARD DEVIATION	RANGE HIGH	RANGE LOW	STD.DEV./ AVERAGE
LEVERAGE & CAPITALIZATION															
Pretax Coverage of Interest Charges (x)															
Aaa/AAA	11.84	15.06	11.62	10.86	12.15	13.71	14.74	13.21	14.31	13.15	13.07	1.34	15.06	10.86	10.29%
Aa2/AA	4.16	7.50	5.99	4.85	6.11	8.76	10.20	8.80	7.57	8.09	7.20	1.80	10.20	4.16	25.00%
A2/A	4.08	3.09	3.18	2.63	3.55	4.12	5.11	5.59	4.69	5.12	4.12	0.95	5.59	2.63	22.99%
Baa2/BBB	1.93	2.18	1.03	-1.02	3.42	2.91	4.35	4.39	3.62	4.04	2.69	1.62	4.39	-1.02	60.37%
Short-Term Debt as % of Total Capitalization															
Aaa/AAA	6.29	4.68	3.66	4.99	5.67	4.75	6.72	7.14	7.08	6.57	5.76	1.13	7.14	3.66	19.58%
Aa2/AA	15.96	4.89	5.51	5.70	6.34	5.74	5.86	3.90	4.49	4.27	6.27	3.32	15.96	3.90	52.92%
A2/A	5.52	5.59	5.52	4.53	5.82	5.78	6.24	4.97	4.95	5.94	5.49	0.50	6.24	4.53	9.03%
Baa2/BBB	5.91	4.72	3.78	2.69	6.03	7.55	7.74	6.75	5.67	5.06	5.59	1.51	7.74	2.69	27.03%
Long-Term Debt as % of Total Capitalization															
Aaa/AAA	11.96	12.27	13.42	14.35	13.97	13.41	14.52	14.64	15.14	15.99	13.97	1.18	15.99	11.96	8.44%
Aa2/AA	18.75	21.51	23.70	24.71	23.55	24.28	23.34	25.91	26.44	26.43	23.86	2.24	26.44	18.75	9.41%
A2/A	33.10	30.51	30.49	34.82	30.57	30.61	30.68	31.35	30.42	29.98	31.25	1.44	34.82	29.98	4.61%
Baa2/BBB	43.04	44.22	37.00	37.26	30.72	32.77	32.47	36.72	35.14	33.70	36.30	4.20	44.22	30.72	11.56%
Total Debt as % of Total Capitalization															
Aaa/AAA	18.25	16.95	17.08	19.34	19.64	18.16	21.24	21.78	22.22	22.56	19.72	2.01	22.56	16.95	10.17%
Aa2/AA	34.71	26.40	29.21	30.41	29.89	30.02	29.20	29.81	30.93	30.70	30.13	1.94	34.71	26.40	6.45%
A2/A	38.63	36.10	36.01	39.35	36.39	36.39	36.92	36.32	35.37	35.92	36.74	1.20	39.35	35.37	3.26%
Baa2/BBB	48.94	48.94	40.78	39.95	36.76	40.32	40.21	43.47	40.81	38.76	41.89	3.87	48.94	36.76	9.23%

(continued)

Table 10-3 *(continued)*

ALLRATIO.SSF	1985	1984	1983	1982	1981	1980	1979	1978	1977	1976	TEN-YEAR AVERAGE	STANDARD DEVIATION	RANGE HIGH	RANGE LOW	STD.DEV./ AVERAGE
Preferred Stock as % of Total Capitalization															
Aaa/AAA	0.01	0.00	0.00	0.01	0.18	0.19	0.48	0.44	0.55	0.40	0.27	0.20	0.55	0.00	75.87%
Aa2/AA	0.79	0.88	0.35	0.31	1.38	1.61	1.46	0.94	0.20	0.21	0.81	0.51	1.61	0.20	62.76%
A2/A	0.33	2.28	2.86	1.89	2.24	2.60	1.68	2.41	2.07	1.97	2.03	0.66	2.86	0.33	32.28%
Baa2/BBB	6.30	6.67	0.53	2.39	0.30	0.91	1.00	0.98	0.60	0.63	2.11	2.25	6.67	0.30	106.97%
Minority Interest as % of Total Capitalization															
Aaa/AAA	1.20	1.42	0.98	0.98	1.47	1.71	1.54	1.14	1.28	1.29	1.33	0.20	1.71	1.26	14.88%
Aa2/AA	0.27	0.44	0.51	0.76	1.02	1.29	1.36	1.08	0.57	0.15	0.75	0.40	1.36	0.15	54.06%
A2/A	0.85	1.37	1.42	1.33	1.24	1.20	0.96	0.91	0.84	1.02	1.11	0.21	1.42	0.84	19.00%
Baa2/BBB	0.98	0.53	0.07	0.07	0.18	1.05	0.89	0.57	1.26	0.75	0.75	0.39	1.26	0.07	52.23%
Common Equity as % of Total Capitalization															
Aaa/AAA	80.54	81.63	81.93	79.01	78.46	79.82	77.18	76.39	76.09	75.70	78.68	2.17	81.93	75.70	2.76%
Aa2/AA	64.23	72.28	69.93	68.52	67.71	67.08	67.98	68.17	68.31	68.94	68.32	1.94	72.28	64.23	2.83%
A2/A	60.19	60.25	59.71	54.43	60.13	59.81	60.44	60.36	61.73	61.09	59.81	1.88	61.73	54.43	3.15%
Baa2/BBB	43.78	43.86	56.76	59.27	61.28	57.79	58.24	55.18	57.29	58.69	55.21	5.89	61.28	43.78	10.68%
Short-Term Debt as % of Total Debt															
Aaa/AAA	34.38	27.59	21.41	25.81	28.85	26.13	31.63	32.78	30.53	29.10	28.82	3.61	34.38	21.41	12.52%
Aa2/AA	45.99	18.54	18.87	18.74	21.20	19.12	20.07	14.48	13.26	14.50	20.40	8.92	45.99	13.08	43.74%
A2/A	14.30	15.49	15.32	11.52	16.00	15.89	16.91	13.70	14.00	16.54	14.97	1.53	16.91	11.52	10.23%
Baa2/BBB	12.07	9.63	9.25	6.72	16.39	18.73	19.25	15.54	13.91	13.06	13.46	3.93	19.25	6.72	29.20%
Short-Term Debt as % of Current Liabilities															
Aaa/AAA	15.00	11.77	9.06	12.31	12.78	10.09	14.26	15.34	15.26	14.93	13.08	2.14	15.34	9.06	16.37%
Aa2/AA	31.76	12.23	12.92	13.55	15.65	13.51	14.48	13.26	17.27	15.82	16.05	5.44	31.76	12.23	33.90%
A2/A	14.55	17.43	16.53	14.69	15.59	15.96	15.44	13.69	14.10	18.09	15.61	1.36	18.09	13.69	8.69%
Baa2/BBB	17.00	16.42	10.30	8.17	18.03	21.44	20.92	20.31	14.27	12.47	15.93	4.32	21.44	8.17	27.13%

Short-Term Debt as % of Current Assets

Aaa/AAA	10.63	7.97	6.41	9.09	9.46	6.92	9.50	9.84	9.46	9.36	8.86	1.27	10.63	6.41	14.31%
Aa2/AA	24.34	7.73	8.83	9.34	9.87	9.01	9.35	6.97	8.96	8.20	10.26	4.76	24.34	6.97	46.42%
A2/A	8.39	10.71	10.44	8.42	9.56	9.15	9.03	7.35	7.46	9.09	8.96	1.05	10.71	7.35	11.77%
Baa2/BBB	12.85	11.44	5.90	4.73	9.51	11.39	10.64	9.99	7.78	6.95	9.12	2.53	12.85	4.73	27.70%

Total Liabilities as % of Total Equity

Aaa/AAA	97.47	89.52	89.94	92.28	94.85	93.45	95.17	95.34	92.01	91.89	93.19	2.40	97.47	89.52	2.58%
Aa2/AA	119.04	103.40	116.21	117.90	103.38	113.58	109.83	96.22	92.02	90.23	106.18	10.20	119.04	90.23	9.61%
A2/A	138.85	122.23	122.98	130.18	126.01	124.09	133.26	124.75	118.49	115.00	125.58	6.63	138.85	115.00	5.28%
Baa2/BBB	193.54	184.81	153.58	145.05	115.68	129.00	131.33	141.70	146.97	139.67	148.13	22.94	193.54	115.68	15.49%

Working Capital as % of Long-Term Debt

Aaa/AAA	144.11	154.28	124.06	100.05	111.46	160.49	162.85	177.52	176.62	163.79	147.52	25.64	177.52	100.05	17.38%
Aa2/AA	81.71	108.24	83.39	76.57	100.54	87.57	95.17	102.49	91.13	95.02	92.18	9.51	108.24	76.57	10.31%
A2/A	84.19	65.99	63.77	65.99	77.13	88.16	93.43	100.12	102.65	108.44	84.99	15.51	108.44	63.77	18.25%
Baa2/BBB	26.08	28.21	73.95	64.25	97.38	94.82	110.00	93.56	94.36	95.65	77.83	28.08	110.00	26.08	36.08%

Long-Term Debt as % of Net Plant

Aaa/AAA	14.32	14.83	15.64	16.71	16.81	17.67	21.20	22.69	24.82	25.51	19.02	3.96	25.51	14.32	20.84%
Aa2/AA	40.01	29.01	30.50	31.18	34.70	33.53	32.20	37.56	37.59	38.92	34.52	3.64	40.01	29.01	10.53%
A2/A	58.89	45.37	45.30	52.12	46.51	50.79	51.77	53.54	52.61	54.93	51.18	4.16	58.89	45.30	8.12%
Baa2/BBB	50.82	49.71	51.36	48.54	55.76	67.27	65.40	69.69	69.60	67.96	59.61	8.63	69.69	48.54	14.47%

Net Tangible Assets as % of Long-Term Debt

Aaa/AAA	756.50	765.10	703.16	649.14	656.16	691.15	628.18	618.98	591.25	572.67	663.23	61.86	765.10	572.67	9.33%
Aa2/AA	412.92	422.02	387.61	372.27	386.64	378.24	400.85	362.13	356.47	359.59	383.87	21.42	422.02	356.47	5.58%
A2/A	271.16	298.98	296.80	267.92	317.31	299.88	299.86	289.26	301.27	301.19	294.36	14.04	317.31	267.92	4.77%
Baa2/BBB	208.41	211.43	255.28	257.52	297.27	272.57	274.46	246.98	260.63	271.26	255.58	26.28	297.27	208.41	10.28%

Cash Flow as % of Long-Term Debt

Aaa/AAA	234.74	248.08	206.77	185.23	188.95	198.59	163.30	145.88	131.62	121.97	182.51	39.86	248.08	121.97	21.84%
Aa2/AA	74.62	103.56	83.25	75.57	84.21	91.11	95.50	77.56	66.91	65.76	81.81	11.59	103.56	65.76	14.17%
A2/A	51.41	53.11	45.62	40.01	49.25	49.03	53.92	51.44	45.56	48.95	48.83	3.96	53.92	40.01	8.11%
Baa2/BBB	29.75	29.34	21.47	29.24	50.41	34.09	45.07	37.55	33.92	43.13	35.40	8.29	50.41	21.47	23.43%

(continued)

Table 10-3 (continued)

ALLRATIO.SSF	1985	1984	1983	1982	1981	1980	1979	1978	1977	1976	TEN-YEAR AVERAGE	STANDARD DEVIATION	RANGE HIGH	RANGE LOW	STD.DEV./ AVERAGE
LIQUIDITY															
Current Ratio (x)															
Aaa/AAA	1.41	1.48	1.41	1.35	1.35	1.46	1.50	1.56	1.61	1.60	1.47	0.09	1.61	1.35	6.13%
Aa2/AA	1.30	1.58	1.45	1.46	1.45	1.58	1.50	1.90	1.93	1.93	1.62	0.21	1.93	1.30	13.11%
A2/A	1.73	1.63	1.58	1.58	1.74	1.63	1.74	1.86	1.89	1.99	1.75	0.12	1.99	1.58	6.98%
Baa2/BBB	1.32	1.43	1.75	1.73	1.90	1.88	1.97	2.03	1.83	1.79	1.76	0.21	2.03	1.32	12.17%
Quick Ratio (x)															
Aaa/AAA	0.86	0.92	0.94	0.86	0.84	0.91	0.94	0.97	0.99	1.00	0.92	0.05	1.00	0.84	5.75%
Aa2/AA	0.75	0.88	0.83	0.80	0.79	0.77	0.87	1.07	1.07	1.17	0.90	0.14	1.17	0.75	15.65%
A2/A	0.92	0.78	0.79	0.79	0.79	0.84	0.80	0.96	0.91	0.91	0.85	0.07	0.96	0.78	7.66%
Baa2/BBB	0.58	0.65	0.67	0.78	0.95	0.96	1.03	1.09	0.80	0.82	0.82	0.16	1.09	0.58	19.46%
Cash and Equivalents as % of Current Assets															
Aaa/AAA	19.10	21.00	25.11	20.71	17.27	20.57	20.00	22.15	21.83	22.96	21.07	2.04	25.11	17.27	9.67%
Aa2/AA	9.23	15.09	16.27	15.27	10.87	11.20	15.27	15.84	16.06	20.73	14.58	3.15	20.73	9.23	21.63%
A2/A	8.33	8.76	9.47	7.91	12.99	10.16	10.13	12.21	12.42	11.97	10.44	1.75	12.99	7.91	16.79%
Baa2/BBB	6.34	8.45	7.53	12.11	11.40	10.58	11.38	13.15	10.06	13.35	10.44	2.23	13.35	6.34	21.39%
Current Liabilities as % of Total Liabilities															
Aaa/AAA	53.43	54.37	54.77	55.48	59.42	62.71	63.74	63.47	63.12	62.83	59.33	4.12	63.74	53.43	6.94%
Aa2/AA	64.94	52.90	52.21	51.83	54.06	54.44	53.07	44.20	41.20	43.29	51.21	6.53	64.94	41.20	12.76%
A2/A	45.18	41.96	43.39	39.95	46.62	46.79	49.42	46.44	46.45	45.28	45.15	2.58	49.42	39.95	5.72%
Baa2/BBB	35.84	30.75	40.32	38.05	46.45	46.44	47.56	42.07	46.74	48.45	42.27	5.63	48.45	30.75	13.31%
Accounts Receivable as % of Current Assets															
Aaa/AAA	42.20	41.53	41.69	42.45	44.53	41.57	40.41	42.26	39.73	39.55	41.59	1.39	44.53	39.55	3.33%
Aa2/AA	48.19	40.81	40.24	39.77	38.76	40.14	40.60	40.62	39.65	39.66	40.84	2.52	48.19	38.76	6.16%
A2/A	44.63	39.24	40.24	37.42	35.61	37.87	39.05	36.90	35.86	33.69	38.05	2.86	44.63	33.69	7.53%
Baa2/BBB	37.63	37.18	30.82	33.00	38.83	40.69	40.67	41.08	33.47	32.16	36.55	3.68	41.08	30.82	10.07%

Inventory as % of Current Assets

Aaa/AAA	31.49	30.79	28.11	30.36	32.09	32.94	34.11	34.36	35.52	35.25	32.50	2.26	35.52	28.11	6.94%
Aa2/AA	34.16	39.69	40.00	41.36	46.45	45.15	40.94	40.12	41.93	37.76	40.76	3.29	46.45	34.16	8.07%
A2/A	40.90	47.48	46.74	50.15	47.48	47.97	49.30	45.62	49.21	51.76	47.66	2.81	51.76	40.90	5.90%
Baa2/BBB	50.78	49.63	53.94	50.92	46.91	43.79	43.92	43.50	53.39	51.76	48.85	3.82	53.94	43.50	7.82%

PROFITABILITY

Pretax Margin (%)

Aaa/AAA	14.44	15.21	13.19	10.96	11.30	10.66	11.53	10.97	11.56	11.22	12.10	1.52	15.21	10.66	12.53%
Aa2/AA	7.60	9.83	8.79	7.40	9.15	11.08	12.82	12.33	10.72	11.21	10.09	1.77	12.82	7.40	17.49%
A2/A	7.00	7.51	7.24	5.76	5.89	6.44	7.38	7.62	6.29	7.27	6.84	0.65	7.62	5.76	9.53%
Baa2/BBB	3.93	5.22	0.04	-5.58	7.11	5.83	6.94	7.62	4.82	5.38	4.13	3.82	7.62	-5.58	92.54%

Available Income as % of Sales

Aaa/AAA	15.28	16.20	14.38	12.11	12.30	11.74	12.57	11.70	12.21	11.95	13.04	1.54	16.20	11.70	11.83%
Aa2/AA	8.97	11.37	10.44	9.35	10.75	12.61	14.13	13.86	12.30	12.71	11.65	1.68	14.13	8.97	14.45%
A2/A	8.92	10.90	10.16	8.99	7.94	8.27	8.92	9.00	7.77	8.82	8.97	0.90	10.90	7.77	10.07%
Baa2/BBB	7.44	9.88	2.24	-0.03	9.72	7.86	8.27	9.24	6.30	8.86	6.98	3.15	9.88	-0.03	45.15%

Available Income as % of Assets

Aaa/AAA	17.31	19.97	18.25	16.51	18.26	18.09	18.65	17.60	18.34	17.30	18.03	0.89	19.97	16.51	4.93%
Aa2/AA	11.34	16.65	15.28	13.61	15.52	18.85	19.36	16.93	14.09	14.00	15.56	2.34	19.36	11.34	15.02%
A2/A	11.09	11.34	11.03	10.71	10.94	11.88	13.14	12.31	10.59	11.92	11.50	0.76	13.14	10.59	6.65%
Baa2/BBB	9.00	10.63	3.17	-0.03	12.34	10.08	12.82	12.56	9.70	10.54	9.08	4.01	12.82	-0.03	44.13%

Rate of Return on Average Common Equity--after tax (%)

Aaa/AAA	18.59	20.91	17.31	16.01	18.87	17.12	17.83	16.42	16.40	15.43	17.49	1.54	20.91	15.43	8.83%
Aa2/AA	15.36	15.65	13.07	11.94	18.86	18.93	19.35	16.61	13.87	13.79	15.54	2.32	19.35	11.94	14.93%
A2/A	12.99	10.43	10.96	10.86	11.47	13.97	15.83	14.02	10.93	12.62	12.41	1.69	15.83	10.43	13.63%
Baa2/BBB	6.79	7.10	-2.80	-16.30	12.26	11.08	16.81	15.15	10.26	12.45	7.28	9.41	16.81	-16.30	129.26%

Rate of Return on Total Capital--pretax (%)

Aaa/AAA	29.59	32.27	29.23	25.86	30.09	29.19	26.68	27.94	28.65	26.75	28.63	1.80	32.27	25.86	6.29%
Aa2/AA	18.10	25.40	23.63	20.91	24.95	29.70	30.85	24.43	19.62	19.58	23.72	4.06	30.85	18.10	17.12%
A2/A	17.01	16.27	16.18	15.19	16.80	18.08	20.23	18.81	15.64	16.95	17.12	1.45	20.23	15.19	8.49%
Baa2/BBB	14.09	14.91	4.63	-4.81	17.87	15.60	20.03	16.81	15.13	15.86	13.01	7.07	20.03	-4.81	54.30%

(continued)

Table 10-3 *(continued)*

ALLRATIO.SSF	1985	1984	1983	1982	1981	1980	1979	1978	1977	1976	TEN-YEAR AVERAGE	STANDARD DEVIATION	RANGE HIGH	RANGE LOW	STD.DEV./ AVERAGE
MISCELLANEOUS															
Cash Flow as % of Capital Expenditures															
Aaa/AAA	144.43	160.72	164.97	127.87	113.03	118.11	128.95	143.19	144.93	153.64	139.98	16.64	164.97	113.03	11.89%
Aa2/AA	151.26	131.96	138.02	108.25	123.83	121.39	127.52	140.17	116.93	108.38	126.77	13.22	151.26	108.25	10.43%
A2/A	147.56	145.82	144.99	106.68	107.11	110.76	122.42	132.41	117.11	132.30	126.72	15.32	147.56	106.68	12.09%
Baa2/BBB	125.90	177.73	107.09	76.52	124.80	97.48	134.40	119.63	133.52	192.07	128.91	32.78	192.07	76.52	25.43%
Retained Cash Flow as % of Capital Expenditures															
Aaa/AAA	109.07	122.50	126.06	97.17	85.63	90.77	99.30	107.71	106.25	114.52	105.90	12.37	126.06	85.63	11.68%
Aa2/AA	111.42	106.83	109.21	85.41	99.44	100.07	106.06	114.69	95.73	86.60	101.55	9.49	114.69	85.41	9.35%
A2/A	121.93	122.27	108.10	81.57	85.91	87.56	99.52	108.40	92.11	106.86	101.42	13.77	122.27	81.57	13.57%
Baa2/BBB	105.07	149.90	75.15	59.39	106.20	81.37	114.26	101.00	110.36	168.85	107.16	31.16	168.85	59.39	29.08%
Tax Rate (%)															
Aaa/AAA	43.69	43.15	47.61	46.24	42.82	49.09	49.64	50.88	52.59	52.18	47.79	3.50	52.59	42.82	7.32%
Aa2/AA	40.70	48.76	54.01	50.80	44.26	51.00	51.95	46.06	42.89	43.05	47.35	4.32	54.01	40.70	9.12%
A2/A	36.98	41.18	40.02	33.27	41.12	37.34	40.21	42.58	42.32	41.93	39.70	2.81	42.58	33.27	7.08%
Baa2/BBB	48.50	53.74	N.M.	-6.86	40.15	37.62	37.00	41.05	44.34	39.76	37.26	16.89	53.74	-6.86	45.33%
Number of Companies															
Aaa/AAA	9	10	14	17	17	21	22	20	20	19					
Aa2/AA	13	15	18	22	40	40	38	37	26	23					
A2/A	26	28	29	30	68	83	74	60	47	44					
Baa2/BBB	9	7	11	11	17	23	26	29	22	20					
Total Companies	57	60	72	80	142	167	160	146	115	106					

Moody's Average Yields
of Industrial Bonds (%)

Aaa	11.06	12.61	11.56	13.35	13.70	11.57	9.39	8.58	7.86	8.23
Aa	11.57	12.95	12.00	14.03	14.19	11.99	9.65	8.74	8.04	8.59
A	12.09	13.43	12.53	15.00	14.62	12.44	9.91	8.94	8.36	8.88
Baa	12.46	13.84	12.90	15.77	15.48	13.39	10.42	9.35	8.87	9.67

Spreads in Basis Points
Between

Aaa & Aa	51	34	44	68	49	42	26	16	18	36
Aa & A	52	48	53	97	43	45	26	20	32	29
A & Baa	37	41	37	77	86	95	51	41	51	79

% Difference Between

Aaa & Aa	104.61%	102.70%	103.81%	105.09%	103.58%	103.63%	102.77%	101.86%	102.29%	104.37%
Aa & A	104.49%	103.71%	104.42%	106.91%	103.03%	103.75%	102.69%	102.29%	103.98%	103.38%
A & Baa	103.06%	103.05%	102.95%	105.13%	105.88%	107.64%	105.15%	104.59%	106.10%	108.90%

Source: "U.S. Industrial Corporations, Financial Ratios 1973-1985," Merrill Lynch Capital Markets, June 1986.

is 9.06 to 5.46 times). The standard deviation is relatively greater for the "Aaa"/"AAA" category than for the "Aa2"/"AA" category—10.29 versus 25.00 percent.

ANALYSIS OF ELECTRIC UTILITY SENIOR SECURITIES

In this section we will briefly review some of the factors that go into the analysis of electric utility bonds and preferred stocks.

Pre-tax Coverage of Interest Charges

Many analysts feel that pre-tax coverage of interest charges is probably the most important indicator of credit quality for an electric utility company. Yet there are different ways to calculate this ratio, the one eliminating the allowance for funds used during construction from net income the preferred method, in the author's opinion. Capitalization of interest in the general industrial company does not amount to much. In 1985 it was slightly less than 2.5 percent of net income for the composite of 57 industrial companies referred to earlier. However, capitalized interest and allowance for other funds used during construction (AFC or AFUDC) are much more important for electric utility companies. Based on data for 1985 from the Edison Electric Institute, AFC amounted to 39 percent of the combined net income of investor-owned electric utilities, down from 41.7 percent in 1984 (see Tables 10–4a and 10–4b). In 1984, the allowance for funds used during construction accounted for 110 percent of the net income of Kansas Gas & Electric Company. Yet companies with very modest construction programs may report little or no AFUDC. The allowance does not represent cash earnings—that is only a bookkeeping matter—but the greater the amount of AFUDC, the lower the quality of earnings. Generally, the greater the AFC, the lower the rating, all other things being equal. Therefore, the better interest coverage figure is obtained through the same formula as that found in the industrial section above, again with the net income adjusted to reflect the elimination of AFC.

Table 10-4a

Combined Income Statements of Investor-Owned Electric Utilities

(All Departments, Years Ended December 31)

($ Millions)

	1985	1984	1983	1982	1981	1980	1979
OPERATING REVENUES	$144,642	$139,499	$129,785	$121,062	$111,506	$95,326	$80,021
Operating expenses:							
Operation	75,931	74,787	71,947	69,962	66,553	56,720	46,050
Maintenance	9,666	8,932	8,012	7,556	6,728	6,003	5,137
Depreciation/depletion	10,447	9,476	8,609	7,856	7,221	6,552	6,043
Amortization and property losses	677	567	467	308	221	131	80
Taxes other than income taxes	9,880	9,477	8,746	8,044	7,451	6,580	5,897
Federal income taxes	5,000	4,363	2,973	3,035	1,854	1,328	821
State income taxes	796	806	621	755	405	331	267
Deferred income taxes	6,719	6,914	6,659	4,155	3,695	3,054	3,009
Total income taxes	12,515	12,083	10,253	7,945	5,954	4,713	4,097
Total operating expenses	119,115	115,325	108,036	101,691	94,127	80,699	67,304
Operating income	25,530	24,174	21,749	19,371	17,378	14,627	12,717
Other income (non-operating, net)	2,347	2,135	1,736	1,831	1,733	1,232	918
Allowance for other funds used during construction	5,098	5,155	4,980	3,889	2,939	2,533	2,189
Income before interest charges (gross)	32,976	31,465	28,466	25,091	22,050	18,392	15,824

(continued)

Table 10-4a (*continued*)

	1985*	1984	1983	1982	1981	1980	1979
Interest charges:							
Interest on long-term debt	14,470	13,540	12,430	11,483	10,213	8,488	7,198
Interest on short-term debt	504	595	536	813	1,261	1,142	597
Amortization of debt discount expense and premium	131	98	106	72	59	44	35
Other interest expense	465	600	587	615	438	285	218
Allowance for borrowed funds used during construction—credit	(2,777)	(3,061)	(3,009)	(2,917)	(2,550)	(2,094)	(1,538)
Total interest charges	12,794	11,771	10,649	10,066	9,421	7,865	6,510
Income before extra-ordinary items	20,183	19,694	17,816	15,025	12,628	10,527	9,314
Extraordinary items	(1,659)	(22)	(228)	121	28	2	(12)
Net income	18,525	19,672	17,589	15,146	12,656	10,529	9,302
Preferred dividend charges	2,877	2,828	2,715	2,502	2,251	2,042	1,750
Available for common stock	15,647	16,844	14,874	12,643	10,405	8,487	7,552
Common dividends	11,817	11,077	10,306	8,968	7,587	6,429	5,587
Net income after dividends	$3,830	$5,767	$4,568	$3,676	$2,818	$2,058	$1,965

Selected Income Statement Ratios

Fixed charge coverage— Pre-tax	3.56	3.70	3.64	3.28	2.97	2.94	3.06
Fixed charge coverage— Pre-tax; excluding AFUDC	2.59	2.59	2.47	2.25	2.09	2.07	2.20
Preferred dividend coverage:							
After-tax: including AFUDC	2.10	2.16	2.13	2.00	1.89	1.86	1.92
After-tax: excluding AFUDC	1.51	1.49	1.43	1.37	1.34	1.32	1.39
Pre-tax: including AFUDC	2.58	2.67	2.59	2.38	2.20	2.14	2.21
Pre-tax: excluding AFUDC	1.98	1.98	1.88	1.74	1.64	1.59	1.68
Income tax rate	40.32%	38.05%	36.83%	34.41%	31.99%	30.92%	30.58%
AFUDC as % net income	39.02%	41.72%	44.84%	45.30%	43.47%	43.95%	40.02%
Rate of return on average common	12.44%	14.41%	14.13%	13.63%	12.63%	11.41%	n.a.

Note: Total may not equal sum of components due to independent rounding.
Source: Edison Electric Institute, *Statistical Year Book of the Electric Utility Industry*, various years.

Table 10-4b
Combined Balance Sheet of Investor-Owned Electric Utilities
(All Departments, Years Ended December 31)

	1985	1984	1983	1982	1981	1980	1979
ASSETS: Utility plant							
Electric	$420,437	$372,516	$343,600	$319,723	$290,723	$265,233	$241,401
Depreciation and amortization	92,567	77,938	70,527	64,552	58,783	53,324	49,161
Net electric plant	327,870	294,578	273,073	255,171	231,940	211,909	192,240
Nuclear fuel	13,979	11,587	9,421	8,056	7,449	6,704	5,788
Amortization	5,461	4,219	3,755	3,591	3,324	2,754	2,029
Net nuclear fuel	8,518	7,368	5,665	4,465	4,125	3,950	3,759
Net total electric utility plant	336,388	301,946	278,738	259,636	236,065	215,859	195,999
Other	n.a.	18,567	20,058	17,084	16,241	14,673	13,775
Amortization	n.a.	6,368	6,546	5,462	4,959	4,502	4,130
Net other utility plant	n.a.	12,199	13,513	11,622	11,282	10,171	9,645
Total utility plant	434,416	402,670	373,078	344,862	314,413	286,610	260,964
Accumulated Depreciation and Amortization	98,028	88,525	80,828	73,605	67,066	60,580	55,320
Net total utility plant	336,388	314,145	292,250	271,258	247,347	226,030	205,644
Other Property and investment	9,557	9,359	8,367	6,656	5,737	4,593	4,006
Total current and accrued assets	40,427	37,823	33,196	31,799	28,100	25,928	21,644
Total deferred debits	16,194	18,065	12,011	7,486	6,532	5,064	4,465
TOTAL ASSETS	$402,567	$379,392	$345,814	$317,198	$287,716	$261,615	$235,759

LIABILITIES
Capitalization:

Common capital stock	$29,179	$32,616	$35,406	$40,491	$44,642	$47,842
Other paid-in capital	18,538	20,509	23,838	27,305	31,580	33,886
Retained earnings	23,035	24,865	27,511	30,984	35,369	40,423
Total common stock equity	70,752	77,990	86,755	98,779	111,691	122,151
Preferred stock	23,881	25,755	26,817	28,616	29,479	29,882
Long-term debt						
Mortgage bonds:	82,014	88,579	93,783	98,998	104,244	108,997
Other long-term debt	14,244	16,978	20,780	24,694	28,034	32,696
Total long-term debt	96,258	105,557	114,563	123,692	132,278	141,693
Total capitalization	190,891	209,302	228,136	251,088	273,448	293,727
Current and accrued liabilities	25,990	29,564	32,395	33,356	33,898	36,851
Deferred income taxes	10,449	13,341	15,931	18,310	21,075	26,438
Deferred investment tax credits	6,343	7,133	8,271	10,408	12,059	14,136
Other credits, reserves etc.	2,086	2,275	2,984	3,936	5,334	8,241
TOTAL LIABILITIES	$235,759	$261,615	$287,716	$317,198	$345,814	$379,392
Selected Balance Sheet Ratios						
Capitalization						
% Mortgage bonds	42.96%	42.32%	41.11%	39.43%	38.12%	37.11%
% Other long-term debt	7.46%	8.11%	9.11%	9.83%	10.25%	11.13%
% Total long-term debt	50.43%	50.43%	50.22%	49.26%	48.37%	48.24%
% Preferred stock	12.51%	12.31%	11.75%	11.40%	10.78%	10.17%
% Common equity	37.06%	37.26%	38.03%	39.34%	40.85%	41.59%
Net plant as % total assets	87.23%	86.40%	85.97%	85.52%	84.51%	82.80%
Net plant as % mortgage bonds	39.88%	39.19%	37.92%	36.50%	35.67%	34.70%
Net plant as % total LT debt	46.81%	46.70%	46.32%	45.60%	45.26%	44.28%

n.a.: not available
Note: Total may not equal sum of components due to independent rounding. Data comprising "Net Electric Plant" for 1985 includes "other."
Source: Edison Electric Institute, *Statistical Year Book of the Electric Utility Industry*, various years.

Tables 10-4a and 10-4b also show that in the past few years, the coverage of interest charges for the American electric utility industry has gradually improved, both including and excluding AFC from the coverage calculations. Table 10-5 which summarizes selected financial ratios of over 100 electric utilities, confirms this. Note that Tables 10-4a and 10-4b are based on a composite income statement and balance sheet and Table 10-5 on the average ratios of individual companies.

Coverage of Interest Charges and Preferred Dividends

As preferred stock is much more important to utility companies than to industrial corporations, preferred stock dividend coverage is reviewed in this section. There are several methods for calculating the coverage of interest charges and preferred stock dividends (combined), including on an after-tax and pre-tax basis and with and without AFC. The author prefers the methods that exclude the fictitious income of AFC. Many analysts also prefer the pre-tax method even though preferred dividends are paid out of after-tax dollars. The latter method now is probably used more by "old-timers" than by newer entrants into preferred stock investing.

The after-tax formula is:

$$\frac{\text{Net income before extraordinary items and dividends} + \text{Interest charges}}{\text{Interest charges} + \text{Preferred dividends}}$$

Of course, the more conservative method would be to adjust net income and interest charges for AFC. The after-tax method has been used by the New York State Banking Department in its list of securities that are considered legal investments for savings banks. Subdivision 26(a) of Section 35 of the banking law states:

Preferred stock of any corporation . . . provided (1) the net earnings of such corporation available for its fixed charges for a period of five fiscal years next preceding the date of investment by such savings bank shall have averaged per year not less than one and one-half times the sum of the following, computed as of the date of such investment: its annual fixed charges, if any, its annual maximum contingent interest, if any, and its annual preferred dividend requirements . . . the term, "dividend requirements" shall be construed to mean cumulative or non-cumulative dividends whether or not paid."[9]

In the pre-tax method, preferred dividends must be adjusted to a pre-tax equivalent basis—in effect, to an amount that would have to be earned before income taxes to take care of the preferred dividends. To convert the preferred dividend requirement to a pre-tax basis requires that the dividends be multiplied by [1/(1 − tax rate)]. Thus, if the dividends total $500,000 dollars and the tax rate is 40 percent, the pre-tax equivalent will be $500,000 · (1/1 − .4) or $500,000 · (1/.6) or $500,000 · 1.6667, which equals $833,333. If we apply a 40 percent tax rate to the $833,333, we end up with $500,000 after taxes. Therefore, the formula for the coverage of interest charges and preferred dividends on a pre-tax basis (excluding AFC) is:

$$\frac{\text{Available income (pre-tax)}}{\text{Interest charges} + [\text{Preferred dividends} \cdot (1/1 - \text{Tax rate})]}$$

Capitalization

As with any corporation, the amount of debt and preferred stock in the capitalization structure is important for assessing the quality of the senior security. Utility companies are no exception. Table 10–4a shows the Edison Electric Institute's combined income statements and Table 10–104b its combined balance sheets for American investor-owned electric utilities. Again, over the past few years the industry has shown improvement and greater protection for debtholders, with the common equity inching up to 41.9 percent in 1985 from 37 percent in 1979. Preferred stock was 9.9 percent of 1985's average capital structure against 12.5 percent in 1979 and debt 48.2 versus 50.4 percent.

Tax Rate

The income tax rate is another important consideration when assessing the credit quality of an electric utility issuer. Generally speaking,

Table 10-5
Selected Ratios of Electric Utility Companies, 1979–1985

	1985	1984	1983	1982	1981	1980	1979	Seven-Year Average	Standard Deviation	Range High	Range Low	S.D. Average
Interest Charge Coverage (ex-AFC)												
Aaa/AAA	n.a.	n.a.	3.44	3.44	4.03	3.69	3.20	3.54	0.29	4.03	3.20	0.08
Aa/AA	4.00	3.98	3.77	3.20	2.88	2.83	2.96	3.37	0.49	4.00	2.83	0.14
A/A	2.95	3.05	2.88	2.69	2.46	2.33	2.33	2.67	0.28	3.05	2.33	0.10
Baa/BBB	1.71	2.18	2.10	1.97	1.92	1.79	1.81	1.93	0.16	2.18	1.71	0.08
Not Investment Grade	1.33	1.94	1.90	1.62	1.39	1.34	n.a.	1.59	0.25	1.94	1.33	0.16
All	2.82	2.97	2.79	2.52	2.39	2.31	2.42	2.60	0.24	2.97	2.31	0.09
Debt as Percent of Total Capital												
Aaa/AAA	n.a.	n.a.	42.00	44.67	43.33	44.67	46.67	44.27	1.56	46.67	42.00	0.04
Aa/AA	46.17	45.87	46.52	48.28	49.45	50.56	50.20	48.15	1.83	50.56	45.87	0.04
A/A	49.27	49.94	49.97	50.70	51.93	52.52	52.43	50.97	1.22	52.52	49.27	0.02
Baa/BBB	52.73	52.64	52.33	52.93	54.26	54.57	55.35	53.54	1.08	55.35	52.33	0.02
Not Investment Grade	56.00	50.18	49.00	51.50	52.67	53.33	n.a.	52.11	2.26	56.00	49.00	0.04
All	49.69	49.48	49.58	50.83	51.94	52.40	52.27	50.88	1.22	52.40	49.48	0.02

Allowance for Funds Used During Construction as a Percentage of Net Income

Aaa/AAA	n.a.	n.a.	30.00	27.67	21.33	21.00	25.67	25.13	3.52	30.00	21.00	0.14
Aa/AA	13.60	17.23	18.90	22.08	27.59	29.52	27.80	22.39	5.65	29.52	13.60	0.25
A/A	24.59	23.30	28.20	30.09	32.00	34.60	36.61	29.91	4.57	36.61	23.30	0.15
Baa/BBB	66.00	52.82	52.52	53.73	48.26	47.37	44.17	52.12	6.51	66.00	44.17	0.12
Not Investment Grade	54.80	49.64	57.70	79.25	21.50	28.50	n.a.	48.57	19.15	79.25	21.50	0.39
All	34.62	32.31	36.25	38.99	35.88	36.45	35.44	35.71	1.87	38.99	32.31	0.05

Effective Income Tax Rate

Aaa/AAA	n.a.	n.a.	31.00	32.67	37.33	37.33	37.00	35.07	2.69	37.33	31.00	0.08
Aa/AA	42.97	42.84	42.31	39.60	37.00	34.96	36.07	39.39	3.15	42.97	34.96	0.08
A/A	37.98	39.76	38.43	36.82	33.43	32.88	28.24	35.36	3.75	39.76	28.24	0.11
Baa/BBB	29.13	32.93	32.36	30.73	27.79	22.23	23.39	28.37	3.89	32.93	22.23	0.14
Not Investment Grade	13.40	31.09	33.50	44.00	49.37	25.50	n.a.	32.81	11.78	49.37	13.40	0.36
All	35.73	37.90	37.03	35.31	32.92	30.34	29.67	34.13	2.98	37.90	29.67	0.09

(continued)

Table 10-5 *(continued)*

	1985	1984	1983	1982	1981	1980	1979	Seven-Year Average	Standard Deviation	Range High	Range Low	S.D. Average
Rate of Return on Common												
Aaa/AAA	14.78	15.46	16.50	17.17	16.70	15.83	12.60	15.76	1.64	17.17	12.60	0.10
Aa/AA	14.25	14.68	15.49	14.00	13.70	12.48	12.33	14.03	1.20	15.49	12.33	0.09
A/A	14.25	14.68	14.13	13.02	12.93	11.39	11.38	13.11	1.24	14.68	11.38	0.09
Baa/BBB	11.29	15.24	13.77	13.26	12.80	11.20	10.28	12.55	1.60	15.24	10.28	0.13
Not Investment Grade	6.40	9.25	11.94	5.55	2.20	2.27	n.a.	6.27	3.51	11.94	2.20	0.56
All	13.19	14.49	14.21	13.18	12.85	11.48	11.45	12.98	1.10	14.49	11.45	0.08
Regulatory Quality (5 = highest; 1 = lowest)												
Aaa/AAA	n.a.	n.a.	4.00	5.00	5.00	5.00	5.00	4.80	0.40	5.00	4.00	0.08
Aa/AA	2.91	3.16	3.62	3.29	3.51	3.50	3.49	3.35	0.23	3.62	2.91	0.07
A/A	2.57	2.89	3.17	2.94	3.26	3.10	3.01	2.99	0.21	3.26	2.57	0.07
Baa/BBB	2.15	2.83	3.08	2.65	3.00	3.13	2.84	2.81	0.31	3.13	2.15	0.11
Not Investment Grade	2.20	2.66	3.12	2.25	3.00	3.00	n.a.	2.71	0.37	3.12	2.20	0.14
All	2.53	2.93	3.27	2.94	3.27	3.26	3.17	3.05	0.25	3.27	2.53	0.08

Number of Companies						
Aaa/AAA	0	0	1	3	3	3	3
Aa/AA	30	31	29	25	22	27	30
A/A	41	33	30	33	43	42	49
Baa/BBB	30	28	33	40	34	30	23
Not Investment Grade	5	11	10	4	3	3	0
Total Companies	106	103	103	105	105	105	105
Moody's Public Utility Averages (%)						
Aaa/AAA	11.68	12.72	12.52	14.22	14.64	12.30	9.86
Aa/AA	12.06	13.66	12.83	14.79	15.30	13.00	10.22
A/A	12.47	14.03	13.66	15.86	15.95	13.34	10.49
Baa/BBB	12.96	14.53	14.20	16.45	16.00	13.95	10.96
Group	12.29	14.03	13.31	15.33	15.62	13.15	10.39
Spreads in Basis Points Between						
Aaa & Aa	-38	-94	-31	-57	-66	-70	-36
Aa & A	-41	-37	-83	-107	-65	-34	-27
A & Baa	-49	-50	-54	-59	-65	-61	-47
% Difference Between						
Aaa & Aa	103.25	107.39	102.48	104.01	104.51	105.69	103.65
Aa & A	103.40	102.71	106.47	107.23	104.25	102.62	102.64
A & Baa	103.93	103.56	103.95	103.72	104.08	104.57	104.48

[The Aaa public utility average was suspended from January 17 through October 11, 1984.]

n.a. not applicable

Adapted from the annual Electric Utility Industry Financial Summary, various years, published by the Fixed Income Research Department of Merrill Lynch Capital Markets the higher the tax rate, the better the quality of the earnings. Income tax rates for electrics have increased in recent years as a greater number of companies have sought to "normalize" taxes because of accelerated depreciation rather than "flow through" the tax savings to their customers. Of course, higher taxes result in greater pre-tax coverage of interest charges (and preferred dividends).

Rate of Return on Common Equity

This is calculated as previously described. Electric utilities are allowed by their regulatory commissions to earn a certain amount on their capital, including common equity. However, what is allowed is not always what is earned. Many factors may affect actual returns compared with what a commission may allow, including management effectiveness, cost controls, and the timing of rate relief. Obviously, the higher the returns and the closer they are to allowed returns, the better it is for the investor. The higher the rating of a company's debt, the higher the rate of return on common equity.

Regulatory Quality

The quality of regulation is a very important consideration for fixed-income analysts. A number of points must be considered, including the accounting practices allowed by the particular commission, permissible rates of return, the timing of rate relief, the structure of the rate base, and the responsiveness (or lack thereof) of the regulators to company requests and needs. Commissions are not consistent from year to year and come under considerable political and consumer pressure, which can—and—does affect their decisions and investors' view of their quality. Jurisdictions in which utility companies must resort to the courts for fair and equitable relief year after year because the public service commission has not approved adequate rate relief are viewed as having poor regulation. Many utility analysts, both debt and equity, as well as some financial information firms such as Duff & Phelps, issue reports analyzing the quality of regulation among the various jurisdictions. These can be useful guides for the fixed-income investor. Table 10-5 includes a summary of the regulatory quality for more than 100 companies by rating category on a scale of 5 (highest) to 1 (lowest). The seven-year average shows that the higher the regulatory quality, the higher the rating of the company's debt.

Finally, there are still other considerations in assessing debt and preferred stock quality. These include the characteristics of the service territory and the markets served by the company, plant reliability and efficiency, the effect of deregulation, and possible expansion of the company's horizons into new and uncharted waters through mergers, acquisitions, combinations and split-ups, power and fuel supply, (nuclear energy scares many investors), and environmental considerations.

NOTES

1. Benjamin Graham, David L. Dodd, and Sidney Cottle, *Security Analysis: Principles and Techniques,* 4th ed. (New York; McGraw-Hill, 1962). The first three editions of this classic book were written by Graham and Dodd. Even though Cottle was added as a contributor, the book is still referred to as "Graham and Dodd."

2. *Standard & Poor's Credit Overview, Corporate and International Ratings* (New York; Standard & Poor's Corporation, 1983). This booklet gives brief summaries of the criteria for rating many debt issuers, ranging from the food, retailing, and technology industries to utilities, banks, railroads, and insurance companies. It includes both financial and nonfinancial rating criteria.

3. *Tax Reform Act of 1986, Report of the Committee on Finance of the United States Senate* (Washington, D.C.: U.S. Government Printing Office, 1986), 143–144.

4. James A. Gentry, Paul Newbold, and David T. Whitford, "Predicting Bankruptcy: If Cash Flow's Not the Bottom Line, What Is?" *Financial Analysts Journal,* September/October 1985.

5. A reduction in dividend payments is an outright signal to senior security holders that something is wrong with the issuer. Preferred holders might be concerned that the omission of their dividends will be next. While a dividend reduction or omission may at times be somewhat beneficial for debtholders if the company is conserving cash that might be needed to service the debt sometime in the future and thereby avoid a default, it should send bond investors (as opposed to speculators) scurrying for the exits. It means that earnings are unsatisfactory for one reason or another, and while it may be only a temporary dip that stock investors may be willing to overlook, bond investors should be cautious and immediately review the situation if they have time. It would be better for the bondholders to sell their

holdings before the banks came in and decided to limit, reduce, or cancel their lines of credit or loans.

6. The computer is a great aid for security analysts, but it should not substitute for thinking. Analysts who input their own data directly from the annual report or Form 10-K will get much more out of it than those who simply read a computer printout of the balance sheet, income statement, and related ratios and statistics. The footnotes to the financial statements are most important, and the neophyte bond investor must scrutinize them carefully.

7. The *Value Line Investment Survey* publishes an annual review called *The Value Line Industrial Composite* that presents the pooled results of over 900 major industrial companies followed by the service. Data are presented on a per share as well as composite basis.

8. See *Long Term Corporate Bond Experience* (New York: American Bankers Association, 1958). This is a "review of the findings from the 'Corporate Bond Quality and Investor Experience,' report of the National Bureau of Economic Research." The book, authored by W. Braddock Hickman, was published by Princeton University Press in 1958. It is must reading for corporate bond investors.

9. *List of Securities Considered Legal Investments for New York Savings Banks* (Albany, N.Y.: New York State Banking Department, July 1, 1980), 123.

CHAPTER 11

CHAPTER 12

SPECULATIVE-GRADE SENIOR SECURITIES

It is appropriate that the final chapter of this book—Chapter 11—concerns an area of bond investing that, while quite rewarding to some, is fraught with risks—namely speculative-grade securities. Many issuers with speculative-grade debt and preferreds in the marketplace may well end up in bankruptcy during the next economic downturn (recession or depression) seeking the protection of the courts under the Bankruptcy Reform Act of 1978. Under Chapter 11 of the act they will try to reorganize their operations and capital structures, reducing their fixed obligations and giving the old-debt holders greater ownership interest in what they hope will be a revitalized entity. Failing that, they will liquidate under Chapter 7. In this chapter, we will review the merits and pitfalls of speculative-grade securities. Here we will normally use "bonds" or "debt" to include preferreds unless we are specifically referring to senior equities.

WHAT ARE SPECULATIVE-GRADE SECURITIES?

Speculative-grade securities are those instruments rated below investment grade, i.e., "Ba1" ("ba1") and lower by Moody's Investors Service and "BB+" and lower by Standard & Poor's Corporation (and comparable ratings by the other rating agencies). They are also known as junk bonds, high-interest bonds (HIB), high-opportunity debt, and high-yield securities.[1] These other terms can be somewhat misleading. Speculative-grade securities may not be high yielders at all, as they may be paying no dividend or interest and there may be little hope for the resumption of such payments. Even the return expected from a reorganization or liquidation may be low. Also, some high-yield instruments may not be speculative-grade at all but carry investment-grade ratings. The higher yields may be due to fears of premature redemption in the case of high coupon or dividend-paying issues or by sharp sell-off in the securities markets, which have driven down the prices of issues with investment merit. Using the term "high-yield securities" for those with speculative elements may be an attempt to conceal the risks associated with them.

Although the term "junk" tarnishes the whole spectrum of less-than-investment-grade securities, it will be used here occasionally. Junk bonds are not useless stuff, as the term implies; everything has a price or value. Many investors do overpay for their speculative-grade securities at times, and thus feel they have purchased worthless garbage. However, this is also the case when they have overpaid for high-grade securities. At other times relatively handsome profits may be made from buying junks, in which case these securities may even be quite attractive. Also, not all securities in this low-grade sector of the market are on the verge of default or bankruptcy; many issuers might be on the fringes of the investment-grade sector. Participants in this area of the market should be somewhat more discriminating in their use of terms.

The securities that fall into this less than investment-grade-classification have been issued by the following types of companies:

1. Youthful and growing concerns that may be lacking the stronger balance sheet profile of many established corporations but often have attractive income statements, adequate financial measurements, and lots of future promise.
2. Companies that have fallen on hard times, whose balance sheet and income statement financial parameters have deteriorated significantly, and that may be in default or near bankruptcy. In these cases, investors are interested in the workout value of the

securities in a reorganization (liquidations are not that common), whether within or outside of the bankruptcy courts. Some refer to these issues as "special situations." Those issuers that have not defaulted, appear likely to survive and continue to meet their debt service requirements in a timely fashion, and were once rated investment grade have been referred to as "fallen angels" by some market participants.

3. Established firms whose financial ratios neither measure up to the strengths of investment-grade corporations nor possess the weaknesses of companies on the verge of bankruptcy. Subordinated debt of investment-grade issuers may be included here. Debt securities in this category are often called "businessmen's risk" issues. Many of these companies formerly had their financial needs satisfied by commercial banks and finance companies.

4. Some also include a few electric utilities rated at the lower end of the investment-grade category. Because of the problems these companies had over the past decade with the construction of nuclear plants, their bonds declined in price as many investment-grade portfolio managers bailed out of them. They didn't want the problems associated with holding the bonds and possibly having to explain to their superiors or plan sponsors how or why they continued to hold the issues. The portfolio managers might have felt it was better to sell the bonds while still investment grade than to wait until the other shoe dropped and the bonds fell into the speculative-grade category. But at these lower prices and higher yields, the bonds represented value to many other speculators. The market perception of the risk of default contradicted that of the credit rating agencies and some other analysts. The higher yields may have led to discounting the possibility of additional downgrading. Also, a few non-electric utilities at the lower end of the "Baa"/"BBB" category might be classified by some as "speculative" due to the declining fortunes of these firms; most might agree that the next stop on the rating trail will be "Ba"/"BB" or lower.

SIZE OF THE MARKET

The market of publicly traded lower-rated bonds is growing larger every day. The size of the junk market varies depending on one's source of data, but the following is an indication. The Merrill Lynch High Yield Bond Group's Composite Index of speculative-grade debt was comprised of 909 issues at June 30, 1986, with a principal amount of $64.3 billion. This included $9.6 billion of nuclear utility bonds, $6.5 billion from the broadcasting industry, $5.9 billion issued by miscellaneous financial institutions, $4.6 billion of troubled oil and gas industry participants, and $4.6 billion of conglomerate company debt. In early 1986, one popular business publication estimated the market at $82 billion of straight issues and another $16 billion of convertibles. A major investment banking firm estimated the market of junk senior securities at more than $100 billion, including preferred stock, municipal bonds, busted convertibles, and private placements with registration rights, all rated lower grade. No matter how you slice it, this is a sizable market.

What about new-issue activity? Again, the volume of new-issue financing will vary depending on one's definition. Table 11–1a shows that new-issue volume for 1983, 1984, and 1985 amounted to 80.3 percent of the total new-issue junk bond financing over the 1977

Table 11–1a
Speculative-Grade New-Issue Activity, 1977–1985
($ Millions)

	Total	Baa/BB, Ba/BBB	Ba/BB, Ba/NR, NR/BB, Ba/B, B/BB	B/B, NR/B, B/NR	NR/NR	Caa/CCC, Caa/NR, NR/CCC, B/CCC, Caa/B, Caa/D, NR/CC
1977	$ 952.5	$ 70.0	$ 371.5	$ 498.0	$ —	$ 13.0
1978	1,463.8	40.0	427.8	984.0	—	12.0
1979	1,240.5	—	323.0	903.5	—	14.0
1980	1,351.1	165.2	250.0	827.5	83.4	25.0
1981	1,523.6	100.0	290.0	939.6	194.0	—
1982	2,548.0	50.0	1,205.0	1,058.0	195.0	40.0
1093	7,614.0	1,060.0	2,737.5	2,574.0	747.5	495.0
1984	14,687.8	3,540.0	4,072.0	5,183.7	1,137.0	755.1
1985	14,567.6	510.0	4,260.0	6,251.4	1,259.9	2,286.3
Total	$45,948.9	$5,535.2	$13,936.8	$19,219.7	$3,616.8	$3,640.4

Source: Derived from data in *High Yield Handbook*, February 1986, published by The First Boston Corporation.

to 1985 period. This table includes split-rated issues, those that have been given an investment-grade rating by one rating service and a speculative-grade rating by the other. To these figures must be added debt issued in exchanges and bonds created from bankruptcy and other reorganizations. All of this means that there are plenty of senior securities in the marketplace that may or may not prove to be rewarding investments.

Some observers place the start of the present era of speculative-grade bond investigating in the late winter and early spring of 1977. It is true that new issues of corporate debt rated below investment grade were sold or underwritten by investment bankers from time to time prior to 1977. However, in that year, some prestigious investment banking firms began to get into the act. Lehman Brothers underwrote three "single-B"-rated issues in March, raising $178 million. In early April, Drexel Burnham Lambert underwrote $30 million of subordinated debentures for Texas International Company. In 1977, slightly less than $1 billion of new speculative-grade issues was underwritten. For the next several years, volume ranged between $1.2 billion and $1.5 billion. It jumped 67 percent for 1982 over 1981, nearly tripled in 1983, and rose another 93 percent in 1984 to nearly $14.7 billion. In 1985, there was a very modest decline to about $14.6 billion.

The quality makeup of this new-issue volume is interesting (see Table 11-1b). Nonrated issues and those carrying "single-B" and lower designations accounted for 53.7 percent of 1977's volume. This steadily rose to 69.3 percent in 1980 and then declined to 48.2 percent for 1984's financing. In 1985 there was a sharp decline at the quality end of the category ("Baa"/"BB" and "BBB"/"Ba"), while the volume of the other sectors increased. The low end of the lower-grade speculations (which are the lowest of the low) accounted for 67.3 percent of the total junk financing. In the nine-year period, slightly less than 58 percent of this financing was at the lower end of the spectrum. Also note the increase of financing in the "triple-C" category. In 1985 it was 15.7 percent and $2,286.3 million of the year's activity, up from 5.15 percent and $755.1 million in 1984.

This large increase in speculative debt financing, especially at the lowest-quality levels, has led some to wonder if junk bond market participants perhaps have lost track of their senses. It is true that

Table 11-1b
Speculative-Grade New-Issue Activity, 1977-1985
(% Distribution)

	Total	Baa/BB, Ba/BBB	Ba/BB, Ba/NR, NR/BB, Ba/B, B/BB	B/B, NR/B, B/NR	NR/NR	Caa/CCC, Caa/NR, NR/CCC, B/CCC, Caa/B, Caa/D, NR/CC
1977	100.00%	7.35%	39.00%	52.28%	—	1.37%
1978	100.00	2.73	29.23	67.22	—	0.82
1979	100.00	—	26.04	72.83	—	1.13
1980	100.00	12.23	18.50	61.25	6.17	1.85
1981	100.00	6.56	19.03	61.67	12.74	—
1982	100.00	1.96	47.29	41.52	7.65	1.58
1983	100.00	13.92	35.95	33.81	9.82	6.50
1984	100.00	24.10	27.72	35.29	7.74	5.15
1985	100.00	3.50	29.24	42.91	8.65	15.70
Total	100.00%	12.05%	30.33%	41.83%	7.87%	7.92%

Source: Derived from data in *High Yield Handbook,* February 1986, published by The First Boston Corporation.

creditors become less wary as the business cycle expands—in fact, they become more optimistic just when they should start to be more careful. Banks become less selective as to whom they lend, and the terms of loans become less restrictive. Investment banking firms become less selective about their underwritings—after all, they want to maintain or even increase their market share, and one way to do it is to finance everyone who wants it. The good, solid long-term investment banking and customer relationships that have been the mainstay of the investment banking industry for years can get shunted aside for shorter-term accommodations. Investor customers will often buy what they have to offer with an undiscerning eye.

It has even been suggested that some investment banks have certain clients "in their hip pocket." These clients have a very close relationship with their investment bankers and participate in one another's new issues. The sales credits offered to salespeople to move the merchandise is often somewhat higher than those on investment-grade offerings. Also, due to the sharp decline in interest rates over the 1984 to 1986 period, investors wanting high yields must go to lower-rated securities. They are not satisfied with the 7 to 10 percent yields of government bonds and investment-grade corporates but want the 11 to 15 percent or higher yields offered by speculative-grade bonds. While above-average yields denote above-average risks, many investors apparently do not care. Yet there is no such thing as a "free lunch." High yield to maturity or high current return may become no yield or return at all. Maybe the more appropriate measurement should be "yield to default" or "yield to reorganization." In the 1984 to 1986 period, the market for speculative-grade securities was such that investors were willing to acquire issues that probably would have never reached the marketplace a decade earlier. Hickman says:

> ... the trends in default rates are roughly comparable with trends in net and gross new financing, default rates tending to be high on securities issued during years of high financial volume and vice versa. ... This would seem to suggest that some issues, perhaps those of marginal quality, can find a ready market only when the market is buoyant, and that in periods of market pessimism only the top grade issues can be placed ... "[2]

It is the author's view that the business cycle is not dead and investors should keep up their guard.

PERFORMANCE OF HIGH-YIELD BONDS

Let's now briefly review recent performance of the high-yield market in general. Obviously there have been some individual disasters; some issuers have gone bankrupt or dropped substantially in price as they tried to remain out of court. But, as we shall see later, all is not lost. Certainly the investor holding Republic Steel, McLean Industries, Western Union, and Zapata Corporation debentures in mid-July 1986 would have felt as though all *was* lost. In the two-week period from the close on July 11 to the close on July 25, these bonds lost a large part of their value. Republic Steel (now J&L Steel) was carried down by the bankruptcy of the LTV group of companies. The declines in the other issues were due to the very marginal nature of their operations and investors' perceptions that they too might have to file for bankruptcy. The Republic Steel 12⅛s of 2003 dropped from 58⅝ to 18⅞, a decline of 68 percent, not including approximately $15 of accured and unpaid interest. The Western Union 16s of 1991 went from 100 to 49½ before closing at the end of the period at 67, a price erosion of 33 percent. The Zapata 10⅞s of 2001 fell only 18 points, from 50 to 32, while the McLean Industries 12s of 2003 went from 70⅞ to 40 in that two-week span. However, most proponents feel that looking at the grand picture instead of isolated cases gives a truer view of the returns available from speculative-grade bonds.

Table 11–2 shows the total returns for indices comprising all high-yield bonds, government bonds, and investment-grade corporate bonds for selected time spans ending December 31, 1984, December 31, 1985, and June 30, 1986. The Merrill Lynch Taxable Bond Indices, from which this table is derived, started tracking speculative-grade bonds only since the beginning of 1984. Note the variation in total return between the indices at various points in time. Calendar 1984 was a stellar year for low-grade bond performance, with a total return of 27.06 percent, nearly double that of the government master and considerably better than the 16.2 percent turned in by all investment-grade corporates. And 1985 wasn't too shabby with the speculative-bond index beating governments by a decent margin and lagging just a bit behind investment-grade corporates. The period ending June 30, 1986, presented various returns. Certainly the one-month June return for junks was disastrous, while the three-month return was quite good. The six- and 12-month returns were considered relatively respectable, although, given the greater risks involved, investors should have done better.

Of course, total returns do vary from period to period. At some times high-grade issues will outperform junk, while in others junk will be the star performer. Holding down returns from speculative-grade issues over the 1985 through 1986 period has been the poor performance of debt of oil-related companies and miscellaneous finance companies. For the year and a half ending June 30, 1986, the High Yield Bond Group of Merrill Lynch Capital Markets reported that its Industry Sector Index of Total Return was at 131.89; 100.00 was the base at the end of 1984. Of the 27 sectors in this index, 4 performed worse than the oil group: the miscellaneous finance sector

Table 11-2
Summary of Merrill Lynch Taxable Bond Indices:
All High Yield Bonds, Government Master, and Corporate Master

| | Total Return for Period Ending June 30, 1986 (Annualized Rates of Return) | | | |
Index	1-Month	3-Month	6-Month	12-Month
All High Yield Bonds	00.48%	16.03%	23.91%	22.18%
Government master	33.94	4.87	21.06	20.21
Corporate master	10.52	3.78	19.53	22.34

Note: All High Yield Bonds—par value, $54.4 billion; average coupon, 12.16 percent; average yield, 12.33 percent. Government master—par value, $950.1 billion; average coupon, 10.39 percent; average yield, 7.4 percent. Corporate Master—par value, $368 billion; average coupon, 9.9 percent; average yield, 9.49 percent.

| | Total Return for Period Ending December 31, 1985 (Annualized Rates of Return) | | | |
Index	1-Month	3-Month	6-Month	12-Month
All High Yield Bonds	41.30%	26.46%	20.48%	24.61%
Government Master	42.54	32.89	19.37	20.65
Corporate Master	55.19	43.61	25.22	25.36

Note: All High Yield Bonds—par value, $40.7 billion; average coupon, 11.93 percent; average yield, 13.52 percent. Government Master—par value, $897.7 billion; average coupon, 10.92 percent; average yield, 8.6 percent. Corporate Master—par value, $341.4 billion; average coupon, 10.08 percent; average yield, 10.29 percent.

| | Total Return for Period Ending December 31, 1984 (Annualized Rates of Return) | | | |
Index	1-Month	3-Month	6-Month	12-Month
All High-Yield Bonds	29.66%	32.32%	29.36%	27.06%
Government Master	17.44	30.15	33.10	14.82
Corporate Master	17.04	36.25	42.45	16.20

Note: All High Yield Bonds—par value, $30.5 billion; average coupon, 11.05 percent; average yield, 15.14 percent. Government Master—par value, $797.8 billion; average coupon, 11.55 percent; average yield, 10.79 percent. Corporate Master—par value, $326.8 billion; average coupon, 10.04 percent; average yield, 12.22 percent.

(124.82), the health care industry (111.01), shipping and container companies (122.61), and the steel industry (121.80). The oil and gas sector's value was 125.17. The finance sector was comprised of 64 issues for $5,926 million par value, or 9.2 percent of the total index. The health care index had 28 issues with a par value of $1,913 million (3 percent), and the shipping and container index had 11 issues amounting to $716 million and only 1.1 percent of the whole index. The steel sector was made up of 23 issues for $1,619 million (2.5 percent) and the oil and gas sector 62 issues for $4,639 million (7.2 percent). These five groups totaled $14,813 million, or 23 percent of the total par value of bonds in the index. The top five performing sectors and their index values at June 30, 1986, were airlines (138.24), machinery (139.96), textiles (139.54), nuclear electric utilities (139.68), and miscellaneous utilities (141.47).

Total returns are one thing in the evaluation of portfolio performance. They should be looked at not as a short-term measurement but as a longer-term one. Many investors use yield spreads as a current guide to relative valuation and to help them answer such questions as: Should we increase our participation in the speculative-grade market and reduce the number of higher-grade issues? Is the market paying us enough to justify the additional risk of more speculative-grade issues? Table 11-3 shows the yields and spreads at the end of each month from December 31, 1984, to June 30, 1986, for the High Yield Composite and the Investment Grade Index. The range was a high of 378 basis points and the low 275 basis points, for an average of 315 basis points.

If one can consistently obtain a 300–basis point advantage in a diversified portfolio of lower-rated bonds over one of higher-grade issues, the additional dollars will add up over a period of time. On a $1 million portfolio, an extra 300 basis points is $30,000 annually. If we take $15,000 semiannually and compound it at only 10 percent (5 percent semiannually), the amount at the end of 15 years will be $996,583. If we obtain more modest returns and get only a 200–basis point advantage over a high-grade portfolio, we will still have an incremental increase in our wealth of $664,388. An incremental 100 basis points ($10,000 annually) will still amount to $332,194 in 15 years. These amounts are nothing to quibble about—this is money

Table 11-3
Yields and Spreads between Composite High-Yield Sector
and Investment Grade Corporate Bonds,
12/31/84–6/30/86

Date	High-Yield Sector	Investment-Grade Corporates	Spread
12/31/84	15.19%	12.22%	297 bp
1/31/85	14.72	11.92	280
2/28/85	15.26	12.51	275*
3/31/85	15.19	12.40	279
4/30/85	15.09	12.13	296
5/31/85	14.62	11.25	337
6/30/85	14.24	11.25	299
7/31/85	14.34	11.54	280
8/31/85	14.01	11.20	281
9/30/85	14.07	11.31	276
10/31/85	14.09	11.07	302
11/30/85	13.97	10.75	322
12/31/85	13.45	10.29	316
1/31/86	13.64	10.36	328
2/28/86	13.28	9.67	361
3/31/86	13.17	9.39	378*
4/30/86	13.13	9.43	370
5/31/86	13.10	9.65	345
6/30/86	13.10	9.49	361

*Range of spreads: high 378 basis points, low 275 basis points.

Source: Derived from data of the High Yield Bond Group of Merrill Lynch Capital Markets.

that a high-grade investor will not get. Even if the extra income is not reinvested, it will certainly buy a nice vacation, finance an education, or buy a few stamps for one's collection. It can also provide a cushion for the unexpected. The extra reward comes because of the extra risk involved. The less risk a portfolio incurs, the smaller the expected reward. Substantially increasing risk and expected near-term reward can, and often does, lead to underperformance. Just saying that one can obtain a steady 100-, 200- or 300-basis point advantage over higher—grade securities doesn't necessarily mean that one *will* actually achieve it.

Altman and Nammacher give various data on default rates.[3] The average default rate in the 1970 to 1984 period based on the par value of all straight and convertible public debt outstanding was 0.16 percent. For low-rated straight debt only (including utilities), the rate of default was 2.24 percent and 2.54 percent excluding utilities. Railroads have led the defaults in the 1970 to 1984 period, accounting for 24.4 percent of the defaulted paper, followed by retailers with 12.6 percent and financial service firms with 10.5 percent. In the summer of 1986, it looked as though oil-related firms might be included in this category of high defaults. It should be mentioned that the period under review was one in which there were some recessions but no depressions and relative prosperity despite high interest rates and inflation. Also, the issuance of deliberately speculative issues was not marked in the earlier part of that period as it has been in the mid-1980s. Therefore, in this case, the recent past might be an inaccurate guide for future default rates, especially if a very severe economic downturn hits the country. This is what concerns many observers. If a severe downturn in economic activity comes about, what will happen to many of the junk issues? Are investors prepared to face the consequences of their actions? Will speculators be there to snap up some of the bargains that might result if an economic crisis hits?

Default rates can be misleading when examining the impact on a portfolio's expected return. If there were a 5 percent default rate, the portfolio's total return would not necessarily take a 500–basis point loss. To cost a portfolio that much would mean that the bond was purchased at par and became completely worthless upon default or bankruptcy and that the portfolio manager could salvage nothing from it. But defaults don't mean that the bond's price goes to zero. The prices of the various LTV Corporation issues one week after it filed for bankruptcy in July 1986 ranged from 19½ to 63⅛ for the 21 issues tracked by the author, for a simple average of 38.33. The debt included well-secured first mortgage bonds on a good steel plant to unsecured subordinated debentures. The average price one month prior to bankruptcy was 71.85, with a range of 56 to 90. Thus, the loss on a portfolio depends on the actual loss incurred or reported. Not everyone buys their bonds at par. Of course, to this must be added the loss in accrued coupon income; one may assume slightly less than six months' interest on average, but that would vary depending on the last interest payment date and the coupon rate. Also, each portfolio would have different degrees of risk and thus possibly different default experience.

Hickman had several qualifications about the higher returns available from low-grade issues that bear repeating here. He stated:

> The major conclusion that investors obtained higher returns on low-grade issues than on high grades should not be accepted without proper qualification. For it cannot be emphasized too strongly that this finding emerges only when broad aggregates of corporate bonds are considered over long investment periods, and given the price and yield relationships that existed during these periods. In effect, the aggregate results reflect the experience of all investors over long periods, rather than that of any particular investor over any given short period.
>
> Another qualification is that realized yields and loss rates were not nearly so regularly related to quality as were promised yields and default rates. Because of the disparity in the performance of low-grade bonds, small investors (and many large investors that may have been inhibited from practicing the broadest type of diversification) would frequently have fared best by holding only the highest grade obligations. This conclusion follows both from the higher average default rate on low-grade securities and from the wider scatter of realized yields obtained on them over given periods.
>
> A third qualification is that realized yields were subject to extreme aberrations over time, since they reflected not only the risks of the business cycle but the state of the capital market as well. The average yields realized over selected periods of offering and extinguishment, or over selected chronological periods during which the issues were outstanding, indicate that the market usually overpriced low-grade issues (and underestimated default risks) at or near peaks of major investment cycles. As a general rule, low grades fared better than high grades when purchased near troughs and sold near peaks of the investment cycle; but by the same token, losses were heavy on low grades purchased near peaks and sold near troughs. The same is true of investments in declining as against growing industries. Low grade issues of a declining industry rarely worked out as well as high grade issues.[4]

WHO ARE THE JUNK BOND INVESTORS?

Buyers of speculative-grade bonds run the full range of the debt investor category. Of course, individuals are important, both through direct purchase of junk debt or indirectly through mutual funds, unit trusts, and the like. But individuals in general probably should not be in this market to any great extent in the view of some experts. Many have individual retirement accounts and other self-directed pension plans that can build up the interest income tax deferred until the plan is liquidated. But many advisers feel that these funds should not be used for speculation; they constitute retirement money, with which little credit risk should be taken. More appropriate investments would be higher-grade bonds. Further, although diversification is very important for reducing both market and credit risk, many individuals do not have portfolios large enough to permit proper diversification or, if they do, don't practice it. Also, many investors tend to be quite emotional, which may cloud their judgment at a critical time. Greed can make many things look much safer than they actually are. How often do we hear the excuse "I don't want to take the loss"? It really doesn't matter—the loss exists whether or not it is taken, and without the particular investment position the investor perhaps would be better able to think more clearly and rationally.

Further, many have neither the time nor the knowledge and experience to adequately analyze the market for speculative bonds. Besides reviewing the operations and credit status of the issuer, one must look at the terms of the issue. It is not enough to look at an equity analyst's bullish opinion on the outlook for the common stock of the company in question. If things work out, the common can be worth many times what it is currently selling for. Bonds, on the other hand, cannot trade to far above par and at maturity normally will not be worth more than par. Also, many equity analysts are unfamiliar with the nature of debt and therefore may not be properly qualified to aid fixed-income investors. This is not to say that they should be completely ignored; they often have important information about a company and an industry that could be very helpful for a fixed-income investor. But one must be careful not to get swept away in the analyst's euphoria.

As few individual investors can achieve proper diversification, many turn to the mutual fund industry instead. A mutual fund is an investment company that continually buys and sells its shares to investors. It pools the funds from many people to make a variety of investments. There are several different types of funds, each with different objectives. There are straight bond funds, both high grade and low grade, while other funds are more balanced, having investments spread throughout the quality ranges. Some funds invest a portion of their assets in bankrupt situations that appear to have profit potential. Their chief advantage is that they can achieve the diversification individuals must have and the portfolio is under constant professional management. While this does not guarantee profits, it can reduce investor's worries. Also, most funds provide for the automatic reinvestment of dividends, which is another aid for longer-term investors seeking to build their assets through the periodic compounding that this process offers.

Mutual fund assets have grown tremendously over the 1982 to 1986 period. Just looking at a select group of high-yield funds shows that the average size in terms of assets increased from under $166 million in July 1982 to over $761 million at the end of June 1986. The number of issues in these funds (not average per fund) rose from 82 to 139. In 1982, a third of the average portfolio was in issues rated "BBB" (or equivalent) and higher and 45 percent in issues rated "B" and lower (or nonrated). In 1986, less than 13 percent was invested in investment-grade issues, while two-thirds was allocated to the low end of the rankings.

There are also unit investment trusts for high-yield bonds. A unit investment trust is another type of financial vehicle that invests in a fixed portfolio of securities. The advantage here is also professional selection of the initial portfolio along with diversification (although often not as broad as with some mutual funds) and monthly payment of interest. However, management of the trust's holdings after the initial sale is usually less than with a continually managed mutual fund. The adverse financial condition of a portfolio holding may not necessarily require the sale of the security from the trust. The sponsor of the trust is usually empowered to direct the trustee to sell investments upon the occurrence of certain events, such as default or decline in price due to market or credit conditions, if their retention would be detrimental to the investors' interests. Hopefully, the sponsor can or will act before "the horse is out of the barn." The author believes, however, that mutual funds provide more comfort for most investors than unit investment trusts.

Of course, insurance companies buy and hold high-yield paper.

In some cases, the portfolio holdings were once high grade but have declined in quality due to economic and business conditions.

Insurance companies are big enough to achieve the broad diversification of credit and market risk. They have large staffs who can analyze and monitor the credits in the portfolio. Because of their investment in private placements, they often have close relationships with the issuers. Also, they can further diversify some of the credit risk by buying issues of privately held companies (issues not available to most public bond buyers).

Private and public pension funds are increasing their activity in the lower-grade sector. With interest rates in 1986 considerably lower than just a few years earlier, these funds have had to sacrifice quality for higher income. Some of the funds are so big that an investment considered large by most standards might be rather modest by comparison. These funds can also achieve the needed broad diversification, and they usually offer professional management. But care must be exercised in selecting the individual securities. After all, who will pay for the manager's mistakes? Ultimately it will be beneficiaries; widows, orphans, and retired people, who can least afford the possibility of reduced income.

Some critics have attacked pension plans and their relationship with junk bonds. An article in The New York Times[5] discussed the problems that might arise from corporations terminating their pension funds in order to recapture excess assets ("Whom do these assets belong to anyway?" is a question some have asked) and buying single-payment annuities from insurance companies. The article said that the annuity contracts were often purchased " . . . from those companies that offer the best price. Of course, the companies that offer the best prices are those that have invested heavily in high-yield bonds." It goes on to say that "these unsuspecting retirees and employees, who typically have no role in the bargaining and get none of the savings, are left to depend on an insurance company of uncertain worth." Obviously this does not apply to all pension plan terminations, but plan sponsors should be careful when terminating plans and make sure that the annuity contracts subsequently purchased are with reliable and substantial insurance companies.

Another type of junk bond investor has also raised the ire of some finanical critics: the savings and loan association. S&Ls are deposit-accepting financial institutions that typically invest in res-idential mortgage loans, commercial real estate mortgage loans, land loans, and consumer and other loans. More recently, however, their business activities seem to have expanded into the management of corporate debt and equity securities. In some cases these securities investments are not too substantial, but in others they are rather large. Columbia Savings and Loan Association, a state-chartered S&L with deposits insured by the Federal Savings and Loan In-surance Corporation (FSLIC), is among the 20 largest S&Ls in the country. Long a subject of the respected financial writer (and biographer of Bernard Baruch) James Grant, Columbia reported, as of June 30, 1986, total assets of $8,284 million, capital funds of $551 million (subordinated debt of $116 million and stockholder's equity of $435 million), and investment securities of $2,991 million. Invest-ment securities (36.1 percent of total assets) consisted of $930 million of unrated corporate debt, $1,400 million of corporate debt rated under investment grade, and the balance mostly in preferred and common stocks.[6]

Columbia invested in these securities for their yields or poten-tial rates of return, which are higher than those offered by mortgages and, of course contain more risk. As the offering circular states:

> Risk of loss on default of borrowers is generally greater with respect to cor-porate debt securities than with mortgage loans because in most instances cor-porate debt securities of the type in which the Association has invested are un-secured and generally subordinated to other creditors of the issuer. In addition, investments by the Association in debt or equity securities of an issuer are generally much larger than investments in any particular mortgage loan, thus resulting in greater impact on the Association in the event of default or decline in market value.

Columbia has also utilized margin borrowing for its securities trad-ing activities.

The big question, in some observers' minds, is whether or not it is appropriate for a thrift institution, especially one that is federally insured, to play in the speculative bond market. Grant has brought up the question of whether these investments fall within the suit-ability guidelines established by the California Savings and Loan Commissioner. He writes: "Yet the Commission's definition of corporate debt draws the line at speculation. . . . [The] Code states: 'Corporate debt means a marketable obligation evidencing the indebtedness of any corporation . . . which is commonly regarded as a debt security and is not predominantly speculative in nature.'"[7] By definition, debt rated below investment grade is predominantly speculative in nature. As the August 1986 offering circular states, "For at least a year the FHLBB [Federal Home Loan Bank Board] has been studying the appropriateness of investments by insured institutions in low-rated and unrated corporate debt securities." It is also reviewing the S&L's corporate debt investments for compliance with applicable laws and regulations.[8] Who pays if defaulted junk bonds are a contributing factor in a savings and loan association's demise? The Federal Savings and Loan Insurance Corporation does thus, the burden eventually falls on taxpayers and the more responsible thrifts in the form of increased deposit insurance premiums.

HOW TO REDUCE RISK IN A
SPECULATIVE-GRADE PORTFOLIO

Defaults are not a thing of the past, and more will occur; it is a fact of corporate life. In general, downgradings continue to outpace upgradings, and economic volatility is here to stay. Competition is tough, and many companies will suffer financial stress. Indeed there are risks in holding speculative bonds—they do default at times. Bond ratings are, after all, an indication of the risk of default.

However, investors can reduce the risk of default and still obtain incremental yields on their portfolios through careful selection of issues. First, the lower the portfolio is on the quality ladder, the greater is the amount of diversification required. On the other hand, minimal diversification is needed for a portfolio comprised entirely of Treasury bonds. If one goes into agency issues, one should include several issues of the various agencies. A 100 percent Federal Farm Credit Bank System or Federal National Mortgage Association portfolio is asking for trouble if farm problems worsen or the mortgage picture turns bleak due to increased foreclosures.

An investment-grade corporate bond portfolio requires even more diversification among issuers and issuer types. While ratings imply similar degrees of risk among bonds within the same category, it is better to err on the side of caution, especially if you have fiduciary responsibility for the portfolio. A portfolio comprised of only speculative-grade bonds (not recommended) needs maximum diversification. It should be based on selection and not on the random purchase of 30 or 40 bond issues. One guideline might be to have no more than 3 percent of one's investable funds or value of the portfolio in any one issue and no more than 4 to 5 percent in any one issuer. This means that the portfolio might contain upwards of 30 to 35 issues and 20 to 25 issuers. Of course, investors should not modify their guidelines if there aren't a sufficient number of qualified issues available for investment; they should just make do with those issue that fit rather than draining their cash reserves.

Investors might also limit the amount of subordinated debt in their portfolios. Subordinated debt of financially strong companies poses little concern, but as credit risk increases, some thought should be given to senior versus subordinated debt. Some investors may want to allow investment in subordinated debt rated no lower than "Ba"/"BB," implying that the senior debt is investment grade. Of course, this may reduce the universe of possible investment opportunities, but investors should not lose sight of the fact that they are seeking to minimize risk while still trying to achieve a better return; not seeking to maximize short-term income without regard for risk. Most senior issues have negative pledge clauses; most subordinated debt issues do not. If a company runs into financial difficulty and needs additional financing, banks may provide the funds only if the new loan (or the existing one, as the case may be) is secured by accounts receivable, inventory, or certain other assets. Senior debt that has a negative pledge clause would also fall under the security umbrella. The subordinated debt normally would be excluded.

In the fall of 1981, International Harvester Company and its finance subsidiary (now Navistar International Corporation and Navistar Financial Corporation) were in a bit of a fix due to a period of substantial operating losses. Their public debt securities were selling on the basis that the companies were about to file for bankruptcy (and many thought it was only a matter of time). They were locked out of the commercial paper and long-term debt markets and had to rely on more costly bank financing. The companies entered into negotiations with their banks in an attempt to restructure their bank debt. The negotiations were successful, and the parent's short-term debt was extended for two years. As part of the agreement, the parent had to pledge its fixed assets, including plants and certain other properties but excluding inventories and receivables. The finance subsidiary's bank loans became secured by self-liquidating finance paper. Both companies had senior debt outstanding with negative pledge clauses. Because of this, the senior debentures and notes of both companies became secured. The parent's subordinated debt lacked any negative pledge clause and remained unsecured. Of course, the successful bank loan negotiations benefited the companies by providing them with the time needed to work toward eventual recovery. But the benefits were not as comforting for the subordinated holders as for the senior (and secured) creditors.

If an issuer has both senior and subordinated debt outstanding, investors normally should choose the senior. The senior issue's priority ranking may mean less price risk in the event of bankruptcy. If there are several issues of senior debt outstanding, the one with the lowest dollar price is to be preferred (but keeping in mind the accrued interest to be paid at purchase). Again the idea is to reduce loss in the event something unexpected occurs, such as the unexpected bankruptcy of the LTV Corporation in July 1986. In the event of bankruptcy, the claim of all the senior debt against the bankrupt's estate would be approximately the same, namely principal plus accrued interest to the date of the filing of the bankruptcy petition. LTV (the parent company) had publicly held unsecured senior and subordinated debt; for example, the three senior issues (9¼s of 1997, 13⅞s of 2002, and 14s of 2004) traded on a yield-to-maturity basis prior to bankruptcy. Six weeks before the filing (June 6, 1986), the closing prices of the three issues were 70, 90⅛, and 92, respectively. The promised yields to maturity were 14.96, 15.55, and 15.30 percent, and the current returns were 13.21, 15.23, and 15.22 percent. Six weeks after bankruptcy (August 29, 1986), the issues were trading at 35⅜, 37⅛, and 35⅝, respectively, down 49.5, 58.8, and 61.3 percent. These prices were about 37 to 39 percent of the debtholders' claim taking into account the original issue discount. The subordinated debt on June 6 ranged in price from 58 for the 7⅞% Reset

Notes due April 1, 1998, to 86 for the 5% Subordinated Debentures due January 15, 1998, a difference of 48.3 percent. On August 29 the prices of these issues were 21½ and 26½, a differnce of 23.3 percent. Before bankruptcy, the issues had been selling at 97.5 and 91.5 percent of the claim value; after bankruptcy, they sold at 36.1 and 27.9 percent.

Some investors think that a short-maturity bond is safer than a long-dated instrument and thus are willing to buy it on a yield-to-maturity basis instead of on a more realistic one. It is true that if the company does not go under, the short bond may provide a very attractive return. But again, if the issuer defaults, there may be a big drop. In 1985 and 1986, up to the date of LTV's filing, many said that they liked the LTV 5s due January 15, 1988—after all, the bonds had only about two years to go until they matured, and maybe the company would make a good exchange offer for them. The speculators figured that nothing could happen in that short space of time. Bankruptcy wasn't too likely, as many expected industry conditions to improve over the next year or two and the company was reducing the operating loss from steel while its aerospace business was profitable. Were these speculators wrong! The bankruptcy filing struck like a bolt of lightning. The 5s of 1988 had a 15.12 percent yield to maturity on June 6, but investors didn't achieve it; the high yield caused by the short maturity, had lulled them into a quick loss.

If the issuer goes bankrupt and reorganizes (or liquidates), the chances of recovering a larger amount of the claim are greater for senior debtholders than for holders of junior paper. We will look at some examples of what bankrupt companies have paid to their debtholders later on.

Another good rule to follow is to limit, if not restrict completely, the use of bonds that do not pay interest in cash. These include zero coupon bonds, deferred coupon debt (also called zero/coupons), and coupon issues with the interest payable at the issuer's option in cash, common stock, or a combination. Briefly, a zero coupon bond is one that does not pay periodic interest and is sold at a discount from face value. The return comes from the difference paid for the issue and what one expects to get at redemption. There is no cash return prior to the final payment date. A deferred coupon bond is a combination of a regular coupon issue and a straight zero. For a certain period of time (typically four to five years) it will pay no interest, but at a specific future date interest payments at a predetermined rate will accrue and be paid semiannually. An example of this type of debt instrument is National Gypsum Company's Subordinated Redeemable Discount Debentures due June 30, 2004. The debentures will pay interest at an annual rate of 15½ percent, starting with the semiannual interest payment date of December 31, 1991. From the time of issuance in early 1986 to June 30, 1991, the debentures will not accrue or pay interest. In mid-September 1986, the issue traded on the New York Stock Exchange at 47⅛. Using June 30, 1991, as the "maturity date" (it starts to accrue interest at 15.5 percent the next day), we get a yield of 16.33 percent. If one uses 15.5 percent as the proper yield for this paper, the issue should have been priced at 48.90. The price of the bond on July 1, 1991, will depend on what investors will demand for it. If it is worth 15.5 percent to the 2004 maturity, it will trade at par. If the company is perceived as being less speculative, it will sell at a higher price.

A number of financially weak companies have issued, mostly through exchange offers, bonds (and also preferred stock) that permit them to pay the interest in shares of common stock if they so choose. The shares delivered in lieu of the cash payment are usually valued at between 75 and 90 percent, depending on the trading volume of the stock, of the average sale price of the stock for a specified period prior to the payment date. The purpose of this provision is to help the company conserve cash. The bonds have been issued or proposed by such firms as Petro-Lewis Corporation, LTV Corporation, Western Union Corporation, Sunshine Mining Company, and Mesa Capital Corporation, among others. They normally will trade with accrued interest if they have been paying cash interest; otherwise, they will trade flat, i.e., without accrued. Mesa Capital Corporation, for example, has an agreement with the New York Stock Exchange that its 12 percent Subordinated Notes due August 1, 1996, will trade with accrued interest. Mesa may make payment in common only if it has given public notice to that effect at least 10 days prior to the start of the applicable interest period. If it pays stock interest, the notes will trade flat until the Exchange has determined otherwise.

In lower-grade bond investments, cash flow should come from the portfolio, not bookkeeping accretions of invisible interest or blizzards of paper certificates. Investors should try to get some cash return out of the investment and to decide where and when to reinvest the interest payments—an option that non-interest-bearing securities don't offer. Also, if a company is so strapped for cash that it is unable to pay interest in dollars, it is foolish to stay with the investment and take the big risk that the situation may not get any better.

Careful analysis is essential for reducing the risk of default in a speculative bond portfolio. The prospectuses of new issues must be diligently reviewed for the terms and the nature of the issuer's business and industry to evaluate whether or not the issue makes sense for the portfolio. Many new-issue prospectuses, especially for lower-rated issues, have sections called "risk factors," "certain considerations," and "risk and special factors" that point out some of the possible risks to consider before making the investment. Sometimes these risks may be insignificant or just point normal business hazards, but these sections often mention risks that some investors might not have considered. They are in the prospectuses for a good reason and thus should not be ignored.

Based on a review of a small number of issues covering more than $1.5 billion of speculative-grade debt, these sections include some of the following risks:

1. The company might have a high debt to equity ratio. In many cases debt may be equal to eight, nine, or more times equity and, in a few, there might not be any equity.
2. Restrictions have been placed on the company by its senior creditors (such as banks) that may require the company to use proceeds from asset sales to repay them.
3. The company may have been experiencing operating losses. It may have a negative interest coverage ratio because earnings are inadequate to cover fixed charges. It is in a weak financial condition, and losses are expected to continue so long as depressed industry conditions persist. In addition to operating cash flow, the company may need additional funds in the future to pay the principal, interest, and preferred dividends on the securities being offered or outstanding. It may have to refinance its operations or sell some assets to meet these expected obligations.

4. The subject issue subordinated to other debt.
5. There may be no public market for the securities and a warning that none may develop.
6. The impact of interest rate fluctuations on the profitability of the issuer must be considered, as well as the fact that future performance is subject to prevailing economic conditions and business and financial factors, including those beyond the company's control.
7. The indenture does not restrict the payment of dividends in certain cases.
8. Nonrecurring income may have an adverse impact on the financial statement.
9. Operating restrictions may have been imposed on the company by regulatory authorities.
10. There may be income tax deficiencies due the Internal Revenue Service.
11. There may be contingencies due to the bankruptcy of a subsidiary and possible payments due the Pension Benefit Guaranty Corporation.

Many of the new issues are from companies that are privately held, that is, the common stock is owned by a limited number of people, and thus the shares are not traded on a national securities exchange or in the normal over-the-counter market. Some have been issued by firms engaged in leveraged buyouts. If the securities are held by 300 or more persons, the company is considered a reporting one for purposes of the Securities and Exchange Commission and must submit certain reports to the SEC. The prospectus for Dart Drug Stores, Inc. 12.70% Senior Debentures due 2001 states that as it expects to have fewer than 300 debenture holders it " . . . will not file reports with the Commission or furnish information to Debentureholders in accordance with the Exchange Act reporting requirements. . . . Pursuant to the Indentures, however, the Company must furnish annual and quarterly reports to Debentureholders containing financial statements and certain other information. . . . "

Investors should make sure the indenture requires that quarterly financial statements with income statements and balance sheets and audited annual reports sent to all debtholders of record. These

statements should contain management's discussion of the operations and any other developments affecting the debtholders. Also,
they should contain a discussion of any of the financial ratios or tests
(if any) that must be satisfied according to the indenture. These
might include information concerning redemption if net worth
declines or the use of maintenance and replacement funds or certain
coverage tests. In many cases, bond investors don't even get these
reports. Many publicly held companies have shareholder meetings,
talks with analysts, and public affairs meetings where fuller discussions of the firms' operations and outlook take place. But many
privately held companies (even if some of the debt is publicly held)
will release only the minimal amount of information necessary to
satisfy the SEC, indentures, and their lawyers; They don't have to respond to outside investor queries. Of coure, a large institutional
buyer is in a much stronger position to ask for information. The investment banker may arrange meetings between the issuer and its
bondholders, but individual investors do not get invited. This is
another reason why individuals should invest in speculative-grade
debt through professional money managers.

There are the traditional new issues (and currently outstanding
issues) of lower-rated publicly held companies—those not involved
in the front-page battles to avoid being taken over by financial
"wizards." These are the run-of-the-mill "businessmen's risks" that
were mentioned earlier. The proceeds from the issues might be used
for regular business purposes, such as financing plant and equipment and research and development expenses; rather than blind
pools, which some companies use to play the acquisition game. In
1985, some 50 to 55 percent of the new money raised from low-grade
bond financing went for normal corporate purposes. Traditional
credit analysis can be utilized in these cases. Of course, leverage
may be higher than with investment-grade issues (but probably
lower than with the debt of leveraged buyouts), coverage of fixed
charges may be lower, and many other financial measurements
might appear weak. But investors can analyze the business, get some
sense of the worth of the assets (real, not blue sky) even under a
worst-case basis, and come to a decision that it is or is not a viable
entity and the risk is worth the potential reward. Such investigation
should be not one shot at the time of issuance or proposed purchase

but ongoing. Investors should evaluate the fundamentals of the industry and the company, see where they are now, and estimate where they might be in the future. They should look at cash flow and the firm's debt-servicing ability. A review of the collateral is necessary if the issues are collateralized.

After doing their preliminary work, investors must relate the value of the issue to other securities. Is the yield sufficiently high to compensate for the additional risk? Is it in line with comparably rated securities? If not, investors must find out why there is a difference. It could be that the market views the bond as better or worse than similar issues.

Defaulted and Bankrupt Issues

An issue that is bankrupt may be more attractive than one that is not. Certainly there are issues of many marginal companies that appear overpriced for the risks invovled. But these should be analyzed and periodically reviewed on both an ongoing and liquidation or bankrupt basis. Much of the analysis may involve educated guesswork as to what the assets might be worth in liquidation or reorganization. By doing so, the investor will be prepared to step in or to avoid the issue when and if the company goes under. It is emphasized that this area of speculation is not for the faint of heart or the uninformed. To participate in distressed securities, one must become familiar with the law and process of bankruptcy and the rights of creditors. It is a complex area of the securities world.

At the time a company files a bankruptcy petition, many bondholders are forced to sell their positions. Yet this is often the wrong time to do so. The market often cannot absorb the large amount of selling that usually accompanies a bankruptcy filing, and the securities may fall to levels far below what they are worth. Of course, this creates opportunity for the knowledgeable speculator. Hickman says: "The conclusion appears unmistakable; on the average, investors who sold at default suffered unnecessarily large losses, and those who purchased obtained unusually large gains. It is unfortunate that many financial intermediaries were forced by their directors or by regulatory authorities to sell at that time."[9]

Of course, buying a bond in bankruptcy is buying a number of uncertainties. You know your cost. You might have some idea of what your claim against the bankrupt is. But you do not know how long it will be before you receive a distribution, Some companies come out of bankruptcy in less than two years, while others take considerably longer. Two years is not considered a long reorganization period. It all depends on such factors as the complexity of the case, the friction between the various classes of creditors and claimants, the status of the company's current operations, management decisions, and other lawsuits pending against the bankrupt. Time is money, and the longer you must wait for a distribution, the lower the rate of return on the funds invested. You also do not know the exact value of what eventually will be paid or the breakdown of the distribution between cash (if any) and new securities. Essentially, you have bought a non-income-producing bond with an unknown future value and an indeterminate payout date.

The amount of the claim for unsecured debt is the face value of the security (or accreted principal amount in the case of debt with an original issue discount) plus accrued and unpaid interest to the date of bankruptcy. Claims for unmatured interest are disallowed, and interest stops accruing on the date of filing. Thus, two issues of equal ranking may have different claims depending on the amount of accrued interest and accreted original issue discount.

A well-secured or oversecured claim (in which the value of the collateral exceeds the amount of the debt) is allowed to accrue interest after bankruptcy. This is supposed to give adequate protection for the interest of the secured creditor. Thus, the claims of mortgage bonds that are well secured continue to increase until a settlement is reached. There appears to be a question in some jurisdictions as to whether or not undersecured creditors can claim adequate protection—that is, whether interest continues to accrue up to the value of the collateral even though the value is less than the full claim.[10] In cases where the collateral is worth less than the claim, the difference between the claim and the value of the collateral becomes a general unsecured claim against the bankrupt estate.

Let us look at the results of some bankruptcies and what investors have received upon reorganization or liquidation. We will use five companies that had both senior and subordinated debt outstanding and see how some bondholders might have fared. Two dates were used for pricing: the end of the month prior to the bankruptcy filing and the end of the month after it. There were ten senior debt and six subordinated debt issues for these five companies. In many cases, the prices used were valuations or bid prices, not actual trades, and were those nearest the chosen dates. The senior debt had an average price of 50⅛ the month prior to bankruptcy and a price of 35 the month after, a decline of about 30 percent. The six subordinated issues declined, on average, from 31¾ prior to bankruptcy to 19⅛ a month later, representing a 40 percent drop in price. Cases where the debt rises in price when a company files for reorganization are rare, but it happens at times. This might occur when the issue's price has been pounded down to below what it may truly be worth by sellers who fear holding the bonds if a bankruptcy occurs. Braniff International 9⅛s of 1997 and White Motor 5¼s of 1993 are two examples in which the prices were higher a month after bankruptcy; however, the reasons for the price movements of these two issues are unknown.

Table 11–4 summarizes the annualized returns made (or not made) by speculators in these securities from the date of the theoretical purchase to the date of the emergence from bankruptcy or the liquidation of the company. Additional details for each company are in Exhibits 11-1a through 11-1e. In most cases, cash was only part of the total package distributed to debtholders, with the remaining portion a combination of debt and equity securities. Senior creditors normally will have a greater portion of their distributions in cash than do subordinated creditors. As W. T. Grant Company was liquidated, the total distribution was in cash. White Motor's distribution was valued entirely on the cash portion, since the equity securities had restrictions against transfer and thus could not be adequately valued. Braniff International paid part of the claim of its subordinated debtholders in discount travel scrip.

The data show, of course, that greater returns go to those who bought after rather than before the company filed for bankruptcy. The returns for prebankruptcy investment include as a cost accrued interest paid at the purchase date, except in those cases where there was an interest payment between the purchase and bankruptcy dates. Most of the prices of these securities reflected the companies'

Table 11-4
Summary of Distributions upon
Settlement of Bankruptcy

| Company and Issue | Annual Rate of Return to Distribution Date from | | Percentage of Distribution Paid in Cash |
	One Month prior to Bankruptcy	One Month after Bankruptcy	
Braniff International Corporation [B]			
10% Notes—7/1/86	33.76%	55.94%	22.16%
9⅛% Debs—1/1/97	47.99	54.59	20.78
5% Sub Debs—12/1/86	−57.38	24.64	No cash
Daylin Inc. [B]			
8.35% Debs—4/15/97	−18.44%	2.11%	31.53%
5% Sub Debs—3/21/89	−59.67	22.99 to −57.90*	No cash
W. T. Grant Company [L]			
4¾% Debs—1/1/87	24.49%	55.76%	100.00%
4¾% Sub Debs—4/15/96	−4.35	17.92	100.00
White Motor Corporation [B]			
7¼% Debs—3/1/93	−0.59%	6.36%	100.00%
12% Debs—12/1/99	−9.69	1.02	100.00
5¼% Sub Debs—3/1/93	−29.26	−23.06	100.00
Wickes Companies Inc. [B]			
8¼% Notes—7/1/84	10.02%	41.04%	16.70%
8⅞% Debs—8/1/97	22.12	55.02	16.70
7⅞% Debs—5/1/98	29.11	55.02	16.70
10¼% Debs—7/15/04	23.76	49.20	16.70
5⅛% Sub Debs—5/1/94	21.86	47.26	8.77
9% Sub Debs—5/1/99	5.98	44.66	8.77

*As shown in Exhibit 11-1b, there was a wide price difference toward the end of the month after bankruptcy, which accounts for the returns shown here.
[B] Company filed for bankruptcy and reorganized.
[L] Company filed for bankruptcy and liquidated.

Exhibit 11-1a
Braniff International Corporation

Filed bankruptcy petition: May 13, 1982
Reorganization confirmed: December 15, 1983
Distribution: February 16, 1984

Issue: Notes, 10% due 7/1/86   *Yield to maturity:* 37.22%
Price at 4/30/82: $438.75   *Price at 6/30/82:* $382.50

The distribution to the noteholders was as follows:
   10.4825 units BRNF Liquidating Trust, Series B
   2.4993 shares Dalfort Corp. Series BB Convertible Preferred
   2.29936 shares Dalfort Corp. Series EE Convertible Preferred
   5.25854 warrants of Braniff Inc.
   $178.959914 cash plus additional cash for interest earned since December 15, 1983

The value of this distribution was approximately $807.62 per note, or 184.1 percent of the pre-bankruptcy price and 211.1 percent of the post-bankruptcy price.

Issue: Debentures, 9⅛%   *Yield to maturity:* 26.31%
      due 1/1/97
Price at 4/30/82: $355.00   *Price at 6/30/82:* $382.50

The distribution to the debentureholders was as follows:
   10.509329 units BRNF Liquidating Trust, Series C
   2.505714 shares Dalfort Corp. Series BB Convertible Preferred
   2.305253 shares Dalfort Corp. Series EE Convertible Preferred
   5.272009 warrants of Braniff Inc.
   $165.314764 cash plus additional cash for interest earned since December 15, 1983.

The value of this distribution was approximately $795.58 per debenture, or 224.1 percent of the pre-bankruptcy price and 208 percent of the post-bankruptcy price.

Issue: Subordinated Debentures, 5% *Yield to maturity:* 40.27%
due 12/1/86
Price at 4/30/82: $290.00   *Price at 6/30/82:* $50.00

The distribution to the subordinated debentureholders was as follows:
   2.050876 shares Dalfort Corp. common stock
   Contingent right to an additional 1.039917 shares of Dalfort Corp.
   $30 limited travel discount scrip

Exhibit 11-1a (*continued*)

The value of this distribution was approximately $72.04 per debenture, or 24.8 percent of the pre-bankruptcy price and 144.8 percent of the post-bankruptcy price.

Value of securities in distribution:

Dalfort Corp.		Dalfort Corp. Series	
common	$20.50	BB Preferred	$ 8.00
BRNF Liquidating		Dalfort Corp Series	
Trust	52.00	EE Preferred	18.50
Braniff Inc.		Travel discount	
Warrants	4.00	scrip	30.00

Exhibit 11-1b
Daylin Inc.

Filed bankruptcy petition: February 26, 1975
Reorganization confirmed: October 20, 1976
Distribution: October 20, 1976

Issue: Debentures, 8.35% due   *Yield to Maturity:*   12.32%
     4/15/97
Price at 1/31/75: $700.00   *Price at 3/31/75:* $500.00

The distribution to the debentureholders was as follows:
   72.981692 shares of common stock
   $575.51892 Class A Debenture, 8s of 1999 (non-interest-bearing for five years)
   $124.8962 Class A Non-Interest-Bearing Note due 1979
   $162.86263 cash

The value of this distribution was approximately $516.56 per debenture, or 73.8 percent of the pre-bankruptcy price and 103.3 percent of the post-bankruptcy price.

Issue: Subordinated Debentures,   *Yield to maturity:*   25.77%
     5% due 3/31/89
Price at 1/31/75: $220.00   *Price:* $195.00 (3/21/75); $40.00
                              (bid 3/31/75)

(continued)

Exhibit 11-1b (*continued*)

The distribution to the subordinated debentureholders was as follows:
  40.13533 shares of common stock
  $3.287 Class B Debentures, 8s of 1999 (non-interest-bearing for five years)
  $8.697 class B non-interest-bearing note due 1979

The value of this distribution was approximately $55.52 per debenture, or 25.2 percent of the pre-bankruptcy price and 28.5 percent of the post-bankruptcy price based on the 3/21/75 reported price or 138.8 percent of the reported 3/31/75 bid of $40.00 as reported by the National Bond Quotation Bureau.

Value of securities in distribution:

Common stock	$ 1.25
Class A Debenture 8s due 1999	315.00
Class A Note due 1979	650.00
Class B Debenture 8s due 1999	200.00
Class B Note due 1979	540.00

Exhibit 11-1c
W. T. Grant Company

Filed bankruptcy petition: October 2, 1975
Liquidation order issued: February 12, 1976
Adjudged bankrupt: April 13, 1976

Issue: Debentures, 4¾% due 1/1/87   *Yield to maturity:* 24.49%
Price at 8/31/75: $360.00   *Price at 10/31/75:* $150.00

The distribution to the debentureholders was as follows:
  $967.90 cash (par less $32.10 of trustees' expenses)

The date of the payment is unclear, as the settlement offer was extended several times, but it was probably before January 1, 1980.

The distribution was equal to 268.9 percent of the pre-bankruptcy price and 645.3 percent of the post-bankruptcy price.

Issue: Convertible Subordinated   *Yield to Maturity:* 20.52%
Debentures, 4¾% due 4/15/96
Price at 8/31/75: $245.00   *Price at 10/31/75:* $55.00

Exhibit 11-1c (*continued*)

The distribution to the debentureholders was approximately as follows:
$190.00 cash ($210.00 less $20.00 trustees' expenses)

The date of the distribution was about April 29, 1983, after being extended several times.

The distribution was equal to 77.6 percent of the pre-bankruptcy price and 345.5 percent of the post-bankruptcy price.

Exhibit 11-1d
White Motor Corporation

Filed bankruptcy petition: September 4, 1980
Reorganization confirmed: November 18, 1983
Distribution: November 28, 1983

Issue	Price at 7/31/80	Yield to Maturity	Price at 10/31/80
Debentures, 7¼% due 3/1/93	$505.00	16.88%	$410.00
Debentures, 12% due 12/1/99	672.50	18.15	480.00

The distribution to the debentureholders was as follows:
21.732 shares Northeast Ohio Axle, Inc. common
1.452 shares of Northeast Ohio Axle, Inc. Class A Series A Preferred
1.452 shares of Northeast Ohio Axle, Inc. Class B Series A Preferred
1.452 shares of Northeast Ohio Axle, Inc. Class C Series A Preferred
$495.17 in cash (subject to reduction by trustees' fees and expenses)

The preferreds will not pay dividends. Transfer of the stock is restricted until November 18, 1986. Class A Preferred will be redeemed through a special sinking fund starting in 1987, to be followed by the redemption of the Class B stock. The Class C shares will be redeemed on or before March 31, 1999.

The cash value of this distribution (the stocks have not been valued at the distribution date) was 98.1 percent of the pre-bankruptcy price and 118 percent of the post-bankruptcy price for the 7¼ percent debentures. The cash value of this distribution (the stocks have not been valued at the distribution date) was 74 percent of the pre-bankruptcy price and 103.3 percent of the post-bankruptcy price for the 12 percent debentures.

(continued)

Exhibit 11-1d (continued)

Issue: Convertible Subordinated   *Yield to maturity:*   16.54%
       Debentures, 5¼%
       due 3/1/93
Price at 7/31/80: $410.00   *Price at 10/31/80:* $440.00

The distribution to the subordinated debentureholders was as follows:
    $139.34 in cash (subject to reduction by trustees' fees and expenses)

The value of this distribution was 22.6 percent of the pre-bankruptcy price and 36.7 percent of the post-bankruptcy price.

Exhibit 11-1e
Wickes Companies Inc.

Filed bankruptcy petition: April 24, 1982
Reorganization confirmed: January 26, 1985
Distribution: December 20, 1984 (cash); January 28, 1985 (securities)

Issue	Price at 3/31/82	Yield to Maturity	Price at 5/31/82
Notes, 8¼% due 7/1/84	$650.00	31.08%	$350.00
Debentures, 8⅞% due 8/1/97	480.00	19.74	270.00
Debentures, 7⅞% due 5/1/98	390.00	21.49	270.00
Debentures, 10¼% due 7/15/04	455.00	22.72	300.00

The approximate distribution to the note- and debentureholders was as follows:
    $132.00 Wickes Companies 12% Extendable Notes due 1/31/87
    $359.00 Wickes Companies 12% Debentures due 1/31/94
    85.7 shares of Wickes Companies common stock
    $148.00 in cash

The value of this distribution was approximately $886.51 per $1,000 note or debenture. This is equal to the following percentages of the pre-petition and post-petition prices:

	Pre-petition	Post-petition
Notes, 8¼% due 7/1/84	136.4%	253.3%
Debentures, 8⅞% due 8/1/97	184.7	328.3
Debentures, 7⅞% due 5/1/98	227.3	328.3
Debentures, 10¼% due 7/15/04	194.8	295.5

Exhibit 11-1e (continued)

Issue	Price at 3/31/82	Yield to Maturity	Price at 5/31/82
Convertible Subordinated Debentures			
5⅛% due 5/1/94	$300.00	21.68%	$200.00
9% due 5/1/99	440.00	31.32	210.00

The approximate distribution to the subordinated debentureholders was as follows:
147.3 shares of Wickes Companies common stock
$50.00 in cash

The value of this distribution was approximately $570.15, or 190.1 percent of the pre-petition price of the 5⅛s and 285.1 percent of the post-petition price. It was 129.6 percent of the pre-petition price of the 9s and 271.5 percent of the post-petition price.

Value of securities in distribution:

12% Extendable Note due 1/31/87	$970.00
12% Debenture due 1/31/87	857.50
Common stock	3.53125

rather weak financial health just prior to bankruptcy. They were in the "twilight zone" of pricing—not high enough to create confidence that the issuers could survive and not low enough to reflect the companies' possible rebirth. The very high yields to maturity (an indication of expected return) pointed to the risks that were involved, yet many assumed those risks just at the wrong time. Also, most investors who purchased the senior debt after bankruptcy received greater returns than the subordinated debt buyers, as they had a greater portion of their claim against the bankrupt satisfied.

SUMMARY

Investment in speculative-grade debt can provide a portfolio with incremental returns over those available from higher-grade issues despite the increased risk of default. Careful analysis is imperative. It must be remembered that in general, bonds are securities with limited upside potential. Bond selection and investment are a negative art. Diversification among issuers is very important in order to reduce the negative impact of default on the portfolio. Again, as quality declines, the risk of default naturally increases, and bond prices become more subject to equity-related events than to interest rate developments. Of course, investors should be most concerned with the company's survival and ability to meet its debt obligations on a timely basis. While one cannot predict what havoc the next business downturn may wreak on the ranks of speculative-grade companies, it seems that with the increasing numbers of very highly leveraged corporations, the default rate is likely to be higher than at any time during the postwar period. The investment company approach is strongly recommended for most individual and small institutional investors. Here one gets ample diversification and professional management—two features crucial for success in the high-yield world of bonds.

NOTES

1. High-interest bonds (HIB) is a term for speculative-grade bonds used by financial writer Ira U. Cobleigh in his special report on this class of securities in 1986. "Junk" is not a recent term for speculative-grade issues. The April 1, 1974, issue of *Forbes* had an article called "The Big Money in 'Junk' Bonds." It said in part:

> What makes an issue a junk bond? While there is no precise definition, they typically come out of mergers or exchange offers. Some traders extend this definition to include the bonds of highly leveraged companies whose bonds are of questionable quality.

In the July 28, 1986, issue of *Forbes*, columnist Ben Weberman added to the cache of names for speculative-grade issues. "Gyrojunk" bonds are those that once were supported by substantial assets that, due to reorganization, divestitures, and spinoffs, are no longer available. "Geriatric" issues are those of companies that once had some standing in industrial America but are now included in its Skid Row. Steel industry issues fall into this class, as do "borderline geriatrics . . . which are beyond middle age that have reconciled their aging to reality." "Juvenile junks" are from young and growing issuers.

2. W. Braddock Hickman, *Corporate Bond Quality and Investor Experience* (Princeton, N.J.: Princeton University Press, 1958), 109. Hickman also quotes from

Measuring Business Cycles, a 1946 publication by Arthur C. Burns and Wesley C. Mitchell:

> After a severe depression industrial activity rebounds sharply, but speculation does not. The following contraction in business is mild, which leads people to be less cautious. Consequently, in the next two or three cycles, while the cyclical advances become progressively smaller in industrial activity, they become progressively larger in speculative activity. Finally, the speculative boom collapses and a drastic liquidation follows, which ends this cycle of cycles and brings us back to the starting point.

3. Edward I. Altman and Scott A. Nammacher, "The Default Rate Experience on High-Yield Corporate Debt," *Financial Analysts Journal,* July/August 1985, 25–41. Hickman says that the default rate for all industries in his study of 1900 to 1943 was 17.3 percent. Railroads had a default rate of 28.1 percent, public utilities (many street railway companies) 10.6 percent, and industrial concerns 14.8 percent. He defines the default rate as the proportions of the par amount of bond offerings that went into default at any time between the original offering date and the debt's extinction. These rates include the Great Depression and might be high for some future depression—but then, only time will tell.

4. W. Braddock Hickman, "Corporate Bonds: Quality and Investment Performance," Occasional Paper 59 (New York: National Bureau of Economic Research, 1957), 16–17.

5. Louis Lowenstein, "Taking Issue with the S.E.C.: Three New Reasons to Fear Junk Bonds," *The New York Times,* August 24, 1986.

6. See the offering circular dated August 13, 1986, for $100 million of Convertible Subordinated Debentures of Columbia Savings and Loan Association to find more details about the S&L's activities.

7. James Grant, "Junk Thrift," *Grant's Interest Rate Observer,* September 24, 1984, 4. For other remarks, see the October 22, 1984, and May 5, 1986, issues.

8. Donald J. Puglisi, "Investing in Corporate Debt Securities: New Powers for Thrifts," *Federal Home Loan Bank Board Journal,* December 1980. 11–18, 39–40. The Federal Home Loan Bank Board issued final regulations in the fall of 1980 allowing federally chartered savings and loan associations and federal mutual savings banks to invest in corporate debt securities. The limitations placed on the thrifts include the following: (1) At the date of purchase, the corporate debt securities must be rated in one of the four highest rating grades by at least one nationally recognized rating agency, which limits a thrift's ability to incur default risk; (2) no more than 20 percent of assets may be invested in consumer loans, commercial paper, or corporate debt securities, and there is a 1 percent of assets limit on investment in corporate debt securities of any one issuer; (3) the average maturity of all of the corporate debt holdings cannot exceed six years; (4) the securities must be marketable, not direct or private placements; (5) convertible securities cannot be convertible at the option of the issuer, must be written down to investment value at the time of purchase, and must be traded on a national securities exchange, and the

thrift cannot exercise the conversion privilege; and (6) the thrifts' investment policies and practices must be guided by the "prudent man" rule.

9. Hickman, "Corporate Bonds," 26.

10. "Bankruptcy Ruling Could Set Precedent for Deciding Secured Creditors' Claims," *Investor's Daily*, September 3, 1986, 2.

INDEX